2/24

New
Testament
Christology

New
Testament
Christology

FRANK J. MATERA

Westminster John Knox Press
Louisville, Kentucky

Book design by Sharon Adams
Cover design by Brooke Griffiths
Cover art courtesy of Picture Network International Ltd.

First edition
Published by Westminster John Knox Press
Louisville, Kentucky

This book is printed on acid-free paper that meets the American National Standards Institute Z39.48 standard. ♾

PRINTED IN THE UNITED STATES OF AMERICA
99 00 01 02 03 04 05 06 07 08 — 10 9 8 7 6 5 4 3 2 1

Library of Congress Cataloging-in-Publication Data

Matera, Frank J.
    New Testament christology / Frank J. Matera. — 1st ed.
      p.   cm.
    Includes bibliographical references and index.
    ISBN 0-664-25694-5
    1. Jesus Christ—Person and offices.   2. Bible stories.   3. Bible. N.T.—
Criticism, interpretation, etc.   I. Title.
BT202.M3783   1999
232'.09'015—dc21   98–42257

Contents

Preface

*I*n recent years, the scholarly community has given much of its attention to a third quest for the historical Jesus. This is an admirable project which, I hope, will bear fruit for the study of Christology. But as theologians grapple with the new data that this quest brings to the systematic study of Christology, it is important to remember that there already are a number of Christologies in the New Testament written by authors closer to the earthly Jesus than we are. This book was written to organize and summarize the Christologies already present in the New Testament to assist theologians and students in making greater use of the biblical data in the study of Christology. It differs from other New Testament Christologies by its use of narrative to uncover the Christology of the New Testament and by its focus on the Christology *in* the New Testament.

Many of the ideas in this book were developed in classes at the Catholic University of America, as well as at the Lutheran Theological Seminary in Gettysburg, Pennsylvania, where I taught a course on New Testament Christology in the fall of 1997. I am grateful to the students who patiently listened to my lectures and made suggestions for improvement. I am especially grateful to Tarmo Toom and to my colleagues at the Catholic University of America, Dr. Christopher Begg, Dr. John P. Galvin and Dr. William P. Loewe, as well as to John P. Meier of the University of Notre Dame, who read portions of the manuscript and made suggestions for improvement.

This book has been written with
gratitude to and appreciation for
Paul J. Achtemeier and Jack Dean Kingsbury:
teachers, colleagues, and friends in Christ.

Introduction

One of the most profoundly christological writings of the New Testament, the letter to the Hebrews, confidently asserts, "Jesus Christ is the same yesterday and today and forever" (13:8). And yet, anyone familiar with the history of Christian theology knows that sincere and faithful believers have held diverse and conflicting views about the person and significance of Jesus Christ. From the great christological debates of the patristic era to the contemporary discussion about the historical Jesus, Christians have understood Jesus Christ in diverse ways.

Although this diversity can be disturbing, it does not come as a surprise to those acquainted with the writings of the New Testament. For, although the author of Hebrews proclaims that Jesus Christ is the same yesterday, today, and forever, his own writing presents one of the most distinctive Christologies of the New Testament. Indeed, he is the only New Testament writer who explicitly presents Jesus Christ, the Son of God, as the high priest of a new covenant, a high priest according to the order of Melchizedek. Other writings of the New Testament, however, choose to present Jesus and the significance of his work in different ways.

Such diversity in the New Testament does not necessarily mean that its writings contradict each other. For example, although the Gospel of Matthew does not portray Jesus as a high priest, it is in substantial agreement with Hebrews on other points. Thus, like Hebrews, it identifies Jesus as the Son of God whose death saves his people from their sins. Diversity in the New Testament, then, does not necessarily mean contradiction. The presence of such

1

diversity, however, helps to explain how and why latter generations could understand the person and significance of Jesus differently.

Consider this example. If a group of Christians possessed only the Gospel of Mark, they would have a different understanding of Jesus than another group that possessed only the Gospel of John. Both groups would undoubtedly identify Jesus as the Son of God and the Son of Man, but in doing so, they would interpret these terms in different ways. Believers nourished by the Gospel of John would view Jesus as the incarnation of the preexistent Son of God who dwelt in God's presence: the Son of Man who descended from heaven and then ascended to the Father. In contrast to these believers, those nourished by the Gospel of Mark would view Jesus as the obedient and faithful Son of God who proclaimed the kingdom of God and died a shameful death of crucifixion. Despite this death, they continue to believe that he will soon return as the glorious Son of Man who will inaugurate God's kingdom in power. Do these Christologies contradict each other, or do they complement each other?

In my opinion—with which not all will agree—although these views do not perfectly complement each other, they do not contradict each other. Rather, the Gospels of Mark and John stand in a creative tension to each other, as do most of the writings of the New Testament to a greater or lesser degree. If Jesus Christ is the same yesterday, today, and forever, it is within the context of diversity that we must seek what is constant.

This book is concerned with the Christology *in* the New Testament. I emphasize that it is concerned with the Christology *in* the New Testament because New Testament Christology has been done in a variety of ways. For example, until relatively recently, most works of New Testament Christology focused on either (1) the development of Christology in the early Christian community or (2) the christological titles applied to Jesus. Both endeavors are immensely important for comprehending how the writers of the New Testament arrived at their understanding of Jesus' person and work. But both approaches, in my view, are prolegomena to the study of New Testament Christology. Properly speaking, New Testament Christology is the Christology embedded in the text of the New Testament. To that extent, it is a literary as well as a historical project.

A New Testament Christology must describe and synthesize as accurately as possible the diverse ways in which the writings of the New Testament present the person and significance of Jesus. This means that New Testament Christology begins with the diverse Christologies in the New Testament. Only after these Christologies have been thoroughly examined should one broach the task of *the* Christology of the New Testament: the work of identifying the overarching concepts that hold the diverse Christologies of the New Testament in a creative tension.

But how shall we proceed? The New Testament does not explicitly discuss Christology in the way that we understand that discipline today. In fact, one could say that most of the writings of the New Testament are more concerned with soteriology and the moral life of believers than with Christology (Hebrews and John being exceptions). Thus, rather than present an explicit Christology, most writings of the New Testament *presuppose* a Christology that, in turn, undergirds its soteriology and moral teaching.

In the case of the Gospels, Christology unfolds through narrative. Each of the Evangelists tells a story of Jesus, and at the end of the narrative, the perceptive reader or listener will have learned something about Jesus and his work. Other New Testament writings function in a different way. In most instances, they were written in response to the specific needs of their listeners. And, though they do not tell a story of Jesus, they presuppose an underlying narrative. Paul's letters are a good example. They do not recount a story of Christ, but they clearly presuppose a narrative that is intimately related to the story of Israel.

The working hypothesis of this book is simple: we can learn how the writings of the New Testament understand the person and work of Jesus Christ by paying attention to the explicit and implicit stories of Christ in the New Testament. These stories provide a literary-historical framework within which readers can understand (1) Jesus' relationship to God and humanity; (2) the significance of his life, death, and resurrection; and (3) the titles attributed to him. Focusing upon these stories prevents us from isolating the person of Jesus from the work he performs and challenges us to understand his role within a broader literary-historical context.

But a word of caution. Just as there are diverse Christologies in the New Testament, so there are a multiplicity of stories about Jesus in the New Testament. The story is never quite the same, and it shifts from writing to writing. In other words, there are as many stories of Christ as there are Christologies; indeed, there are so many Christologies because there are so many stories. Perhaps the diversity of our stories about Jesus accounts for the diverse ways we understand him today.

Recent scholarship has focused on recovering the historical Jesus. The results of such historical investigation will undoubtedly have important consequences for the way in which systematic theology will do Christology. But

3

inasmuch as the New Testament already provides us with a profound and diverse Christology, it is imperative to study and appropriate its understanding of Jesus as well. It is my hope that this work will contribute to and enrich the systematic study of Christology by providing readers with a fair and accurate account of the Christologies in the New Testament.

1

Crucified Messiah
and Obedient Son of God

*A*lthough the Synoptic Gospels are the first three writings in the canon of the New Testament, they are not its earliest writings. Ten to fifteen years before the composition of these Gospels, the apostle Paul had already written most, if not all, of his letters.[1] Nevertheless, the Synoptic Gospels and the Gospel of John offer the most detailed narratives of Jesus' life and ministry. Since the Fourth Gospel tells its story from another perspective, however, it is preferable to begin with the Synoptic Gospels, in which Christology develops from below.[2] The Gospel of Mark is an appropriate starting point for our study since it is the earliest of the canonical Gospels. Matthew and Luke employed it, independently of each other, in the composition of their Gospels.[3] In doing so, they developed the Christology of Mark in new and different ways.

THE GOSPEL OF MARK

The Gospel of Mark presents a fast-paced narrative that begins with the appearance of John the Baptist, focuses on Jesus' proclamation of the kingdom of God, and climaxes in a dramatic confrontation between Jesus and the religious leaders of Jerusalem that results in Jesus' shameful crucifixion. The narrative concludes when a group of women find the tomb where Jesus was buried to be empty, and a mysterious young man tells them that Jesus of Nazareth, the crucified one, has been raised and has gone to Galilee where his disciples will meet him (16:6–7).[4] Thus, the resurrection overcomes the

5

apparent victory of Jesus' opponents and resolves one of the fundamental conflicts of this narrative: Who has the authority (*exousia*) to speak and act for God before the people of God? Jesus or the religious leaders?[5]

In terms of Christology the Gospel clearly presents Jesus as the Messiah, the Son of God, whose destiny is the fate of the Son of Man, who must suffer, die, and rise from the dead if he is to return as a glorious and powerful figure at the end of the ages. Despite the utter simplicity of this story, its Christology is elusive. In what sense is Jesus the Messiah, the Son of God? Why do the characters of the narrative—especially the disciples—consistently fail to comprehend Jesus' person and ministry? Why does Jesus rebuke demons when they reveal that he is the Son of God? Why is the Roman centurion the only person in the narrative to confess that Jesus was God's Son? And why does this occur *after* Jesus' death, so that the centurion must say, "Truly this man *was* God's Son!" (15:39)? These questions are part of a larger literary motif in Mark's narrative, often referred to as "the messianic secret,"[6] and only a careful reading of the entire narrative can answer them.

Although there is no outline of Mark's Gospel with which all commentators agree, most recognize that Peter's confession at Caesarea Philippi (8:27–30) is a turning point in the narrative. Previous to this episode, Jesus' initial proclamation that the kingdom of God is at hand (1:15) provides the narrative's leitmotif, which identifies Jesus as the powerful herald of God's kingdom who, unlike the scribes, has been endowed with authority to teach, preach, and heal. After Peter's confession, Jesus' declaration that the Son of Man must be rejected by the chief priests and scribes, killed, and then rise after three days provides the leitmotif for the rest of the Gospel. The key to unlocking Mark's Christology is a proper understanding of the relationship between these two parts of the narrative: Jesus the herald of the kingdom (1:15–8:26) and Jesus the Messiah whose destiny is the fate of the Son of Man (8:31–16:8).

Privileged Information (1:1–13)

Narrators necessarily withhold a certain amount of information when telling their stories since the very nature of language makes it impossible to recount everything at once. More important, if a narrator did not withhold information, there would be little point in telling the story. Withholding information allows a narrator to build suspense and drama, as well as to initiate readers into the mystery of the text. Thus narratives move from the truth to the whole truth.[7] That is, although narrators begin their stories by telling readers the truth, they reserve the whole truth for the end of the story, when all the complications of the plot will be resolved.[8]

The opening verses of Mark's Gospel (1:1–13), which could be compared to a prologue,[9] present readers with reliable and privileged information about Jesus that is crucial for understanding his identity. The information is *reliable* because the narrative voice of Mark's Gospel is the voice of a trustworthy narrator who tells the story of Jesus from God's point of view.[10] Consequently, the Markan narrator never deceives the reader of his Gospel, even though he does not tell the whole truth at the outset of the story. The information is also *privileged* because it is given to the reader rather than to the characters of the story. Thus readers of Mark's Gospel enjoy a christological understanding of Jesus that the characters of the story do not. This discrepancy between what the readers know and what the characters do not produces the narrative's dramatic irony. Thus readers observe the characters of the story struggling to discover what they, the readers, already know: that Jesus is the Messiah, the Son of God. But as the readers will soon learn, even they do not know the whole truth about Jesus' identity since they have not yet learned that the destiny of God's messianic Son is the fate of the Son of Man.

To participate in the dramatic irony of Mark's Gospel readers must be aware that the Markan narrator communicates privileged information to them whenever he intrudes into the narrative. For example, when the narrator notes that Jesus had compassion on the crowd because the people were like sheep without a shepherd (6:34), he prepares the reader to understand that Jesus will act as God's Shepherd-Messiah, a christological insight of which the characters in the narrative are not aware. It is in the opening verses of his story, however, that the Markan narrator communicates the most important information for comprehending Jesus' identity. These verses can be structured as follows:

1:1–3	The beginning of the Gospel
1:4–8	The appearance of John the Baptist
1:9–11	The theophany at Jesus' baptism
1:12–13	The testing of Jesus in the wilderness

The first of these sections (1:1–3) should be read as a single sentence: "The beginning of the gospel of Jesus Christ, the Son of God, *as it is written* in the prophet Isaiah . . . ."[11] In this opening sentence, Mark proclaims that he is beginning a narrative of the good news *about* Jesus Christ, the Son of God, *as* foretold by Isaiah.[12] The quotation that follows is a mixed quotation from Mal. 3:1 ("See, I am sending my messenger ahead of you, who will prepare your way") and Isa. 40:3 ("the voice of one crying in the wilderness: 'Prepare the way of the Lord, make his paths straight'"). For the Markan narrator, however, the whole quotation comes from Isaiah and establishes that the gospel *about* Jesus was foretold by the prophet.[13] Thus John, who will be introduced in the next section, is the voice crying in the wilderness, and "the Lord" is Jesus.

The good news that Isaiah prophesied is about "Jesus Christ, the Son of God." Although the Markan narrator will use *Christos* (Christ/Messiah) as a title in 8:29, 12:35, 14:61, and 15:32, here he employs it as part of Jesus' name, as Paul regularly does in his letters. Messiahship has become so identified with Jesus that his person now defines the content of the term for believers. To say "Jesus Christ" is to proclaim that Jesus is the Messiah. But Jesus Christ is further defined as the Son of God, a designation that occurs at significant points in the narrative (1:11; 9:7; 14:61; 15:39).[14] Here, if it is part of the original text, it stands in apposition to Jesus Christ so that Jesus who is the Christ is identified as God's Son. Thus the opening verse announces the christological titles that dominate Mark's narrative: Jesus is the Christ (8:29), the Son of God (15:39).

At the outset of the narrative, then, the Markan narrator has communicated privileged information to the reader that the human characters within the world of the story must struggle to attain: Jesus is the Messiah, the Son of God, and the good news about him is the fulfillment of prophecy.

But there is more. In the next section (1:4–8), John the Baptist appears, as foretold by the prophet Isaiah. Because he is clothed in garments reminiscent of those worn by the great prophet Elijah (1:6; see 2 Kings 1:8), biblically literate readers will surmise that there is a relationship between John and Elijah, a suspicion that the conversation after Jesus' transfiguration will confirm (9:9–13). Although Jesus has not yet made his appearance, John prepares the way of the Lord by preaching a baptism that demands repentance and promising that a more powerful one (*ho ischyroteros*) will come after him and baptize with holy spirit (1:7–8).

Because of this privileged information, readers of Mark's story should not confuse Jesus with Elijah as some of the characters of the story will do (6:15). Nor should they confuse him with John, as Herod does when he identifies Jesus as John the Baptist raised from the dead (6:14, 16). Readers should remember that John is only a voice that prepares the way for Jesus, and that he identified Jesus as more powerful than himself. In light of these verses, then, there should be no confusion about these two great figures.

The promise that Jesus will baptize with holy spirit leads to a third section in which the Spirit descends upon Jesus, and God proclaims that Jesus is his beloved Son in whom he is pleased (1:9–11). When first introduced, Jesus is identified as coming from Nazareth of Galilee. At the end of the Gospel, the mysterious figure at the empty tomb will refer to Jesus of Nazareth, the crucified one (16:6), thereby establishing a literary inclusion between the opening and closing of Mark's story.[15] The one who is God's Son is a human being who, even after the resurrection, is remembered as Jesus of Nazareth, the crucified one.

Jesus' baptism becomes the occasion for the first of two theophanies in Mark's Gospel, the second being the transfiguration (9:2–8). As Jesus rises from the water, he sees the Spirit descend like a dove upon/into (*eis*) him, and God declares: "You are my Son, the Beloved; with you I am well pleased" (1:11). Since there is no indication that anyone else sees the Spirit or hears the voice, this is a theophany of which only Jesus and the Gospel readers are aware. Once more, then, readers are granted privileged information that is withheld from the characters of the story. The reader knows that Jesus is the Spirit-anointed Son of God who is pleasing to God.

Biblically literate readers will recognize that God's words echo the following texts: Ps. 2:7, spoken to the king on the day of his enthronement ("You are my son; today I have begotten you"); Isa. 42:1, spoken to the Servant ("Here is my servant, whom I uphold, my chosen, in whom my soul delights"); and Gen. 22:2, spoken to Abraham ("Take your son, your only [*agapēton*] son Isaac"). Since God's words do not exactly reproduce any of these quotations, there is no need to insist that one or the other is the primary text to which the Markan narrator alludes. Instead, the narrator leaves room for a surplus of meaning. Jesus is God's anointed Son as was the Israelite king of old; therefore he is God's royal Messiah. But he is no ordinary Messiah King, for he is also the Servant in whom God delights. Moreover, Jesus is God's beloved (*agapētos*) Son in a manner analogous to Abraham's only (*agapētos*) son, Isaac. From the outset of the narrative, then, the informed reader knows what the centurion will discover and confess at the end of the narrative: Jesus is the Son of God. But, as we shall see, not even the reader fully comprehends what divine sonship entails in Mark's narrative universe.

The final section of the opening verses presents Jesus in the wilderness, apparently triumphant over Satan, who has tested him for forty days (1:12–13). The same Spirit that descended upon Jesus and anointed him as God's Messiah has thrust him into the wilderness to be tested. At the end of this trial, angels minister to God's Son, indicating that Jesus has been triumphant. The Spirit-anointed Son of God has won an important victory over Satan that prepares for his proclamation that the kingdom of God is at hand. Thus this episode foreshadows Jesus' proclamation of the kingdom, especially its proclamation through Jesus' exorcisms.

We have seen that the opening verses of Mark's Gospel provide readers with inside information, withheld from the human characters of the story, that is essentially christological. This information can be summarized as follows. Jesus is the Messiah who has been anointed by the Spirit. As the Messiah, he is the Son of God with whom the Father is pleased. His ministry is the fulfillment of prophecy. Since the Spirit has anointed and enabled him to baptize with holy spirit, he is more powerful than John the Baptist, who is only his forerunner. Finally, Jesus has overcome Satan. Consequently, when readers hear the crowds marvel at Jesus' authority (1:22, 27), they should not be surprised, for they know what the crowds do not: the one who acts is the Spirit-anointed Messiah, the Son of God. Readers know the truth about Jesus, even if they do not yet know the whole truth.

The Initial Stage of Understanding (1:14–8:30)

The Gospel of Mark develops its Christology in two stages: the period prior to Peter's confession that Jesus is the Messiah and the period following that confession, culminating in the centurion's confession that Jesus was truly God's Son. In the first period, the Markan narrator focuses upon Jesus as the powerful and authoritative herald of God's in-breaking rule; in the second, upon Jesus' destiny as the Son of Man who must suffer, die, and rise from the dead before returning as God's glorious agent at the end of the ages. As each stage unfolds, the Markan narrator builds up the character of Jesus, episode by episode, so that by the end of the narrative readers arrive at the whole truth about Jesus' identity.[16]

The Herald of the Kingdom (1:14–3:12)
The readers of Mark's Gospel are already aware that Jesus is the Spirit-anointed Messiah who is God's Son. Consequently, when he inaugurates his public ministry by proclaiming that the time is fulfilled and the kingdom of God is at hand (1:15), they know that the one who makes this proclamation is none other than God's messianic Son.

This initial proclamation of the kingdom establishes the dominant theme of the narrative so that everything Jesus does (preach, teach, heal, and expel demons) is in the service of the kingdom of God. Accordingly, the Markan narrator portrays Jesus as Messiah, the Son of God, the herald of God's kingdom. Jesus is God's eschatological agent who announces that God is establishing his rule over creation and history through his ministry.

Jesus proclaims "the gospel of God"—best construed as God's good news that his rule is at hand—*after* John the Baptist has been handed over (*paradidōmi;* 1:14). The narrator employs this verb throughout the story to describe the destiny of Jesus, the Son of Man who will also be handed over and put to death (9:31; 10:33–34; 14:21, 41). Thus the fate of Jesus is already foreshadowed in the fate of the Baptist; for just as John was handed over and put to death by Herod, so Jesus, the Son of Man, will be handed over and put to death by Pilate.

The calling of Jesus' first disciples (1:16–20) follows his initial proclamation of the kingdom and exemplifies his authority without ever employing the word. Passing by the sea of Galilee, he calls Simon, Andrew, James, and John to follow him, and they abandon everything to do so (see Peter's comment in 10:28). The juxtaposition of this episode with Jesus' initial proclamation of the kingdom (1:14–15) suggests that his proclamation has profoundly affected these fishermen. For reasons left unexplained, they believe that he is the herald of God's kingdom. The episodes that follow will persuade them that their initial understanding of Jesus was correct.

In 1:21–45, Jesus performs a number of healings and exorcisms that effect the presence of God's kingdom for the sick and demon-possessed of Galilee. In rapid succession, he expels an unclean spirit from a man in the synagogue of Capernaum (1:21–28), heals Simon's mother-in-law (1:29–31), cures the sick and demon-possessed of Capernaum (1:32–34), inaugurates a preaching tour of Galilee during which he expels demons (1:35–39), and cleanses a leper (1:40–45). Through Jesus' mighty deeds, then, the kingdom of God invades Galilee and displaces Satan's rule.

By recounting Jesus' powerful deeds, the Markan narrator enhances his initial christological portrait of Jesus. He portrays Jesus as someone who teaches with authority (*exousia;* 1:21–22, 27), for not only does Jesus proclaim that the kingdom of God is at hand but he effects its presence by casting out demons and healing the sick.

Although the human characters of the narrative do not know Jesus' true identity, the demons do. For example, when a demon-possessed man confronts Jesus in the synagogue of Capernaum, he correctly states that Jesus has come to destroy them (Satan's minions) and announces, "I know who you are, the Holy One of God" (1:24). Jesus, however, orders the demon to be silent and then expels him (1:25). Likewise, when Jesus heals the sick and demon-possessed of Capernaum, the Markan narrator comments that Jesus did not allow the demons to speak because they knew him (1:34). Then, in a summary statement of Jesus' Galilean ministry, the narrator notes that whenever the unclean spirits saw Jesus, they cried out, "You are the Son of God!" (3:11).

The reader, who has been given privileged information, knows that what the demons proclaim is formally correct: Jesus is God's Holy One, the Son of God. But it is not yet apparent why he forbids them to publicize this.[17] While one might surmise that it is unseemly for unclean spirits to disclose the secret of Jesus' identity, the narrative will show that Mark's Christology is more profound: Jesus' sonship cannot be understood apart from his death and resurrection. His mighty deeds correctly identify him as the herald of God's kingdom, and, because of them, Jesus will be put to death. By themselves, however, they do not reveal the full extent of Jesus' identity.

In 2:1–3:6, Jesus' mighty deeds lead to a series of confrontations with the Pharisees and scribes, and the Pharisees and Herodians plot to destroy him (3:6). This cycle of controversies begins when Jesus heals a paralytic and forgives his sins. The scribes inwardly accuse him of blaspheming (2:7), foreshadowing the charge that will lead to Jesus' condemnation by the Sanhedrin (14:64). Next, when Jesus eats with Levi and his companions, the scribes of the Pharisees accuse him of eating with sinners and tax collectors (2:16). Then, when his disciples do not fast, people ask why the disciples of John and the Pharisees fast, but his do not (2:18). Soon after, when Jesus' disciples pluck grain on the Sabbath, the Pharisees reprimand him (2:24). Finally, when Jesus enters a synagogue on the Sabbath, the religious leaders watch to see if he heals on the Sabbath so that they can accuse him of violating the Sabbath (3:2).

Jesus shows himself superior to his opponents in every instance. Referring to himself as the Son of Man,[18] he claims authority (*exousia*) to forgive sins on earth (2:10). Defending his public behavior, he says that he has come to call sinners, not those who are righteous (2:17). Defending the behavior of his disciples, he compares them to wedding guests who cannot fast because the bridegroom (Jesus, the herald of the kingdom) is in their midst (2:19). Nor have the disciples violated the Sabbath since it exists for human beings, and the Son of Man is lord of the Sabbath (2:28). Finally, Jesus heals on the Sabbath since it is lawful to do good and save life on the Sabbath (3:4).

These episodes inaugurate a conflict that runs through the narrative. Who speaks and acts with God's authority? Jesus or the religious leaders? Does Jesus have a God-given authority to forgive sins, to associate with sinners, to dispense his disciples from fasting, and to act with supreme freedom on the Sabbath? Or is he blaspheming and violating God's commandments? While the readers of Mark's Gospel know the answer to these questions, the characters of the narrative do not. The beginning of Jesus' ministry, then, develops its christological portrait in several ways. Jesus Christ, the Son of God, is the powerful herald of the kingdom whose word is effective in deeds. Endowed with a teaching authority superior to that of the scribes, he forgives sins, associates with sinners, and acts as one who is lord of the Sabbath. Despite this portrait, the characters of the story are ignorant of Jesus' identity, even though demons continually cry out that he is the Son of God (3:11).

Disclosing the Mystery (3:13–6:13)

The call of the Twelve (3:13–19) marks a new phase in Jesus' ministry, for the Twelve will be the nucleus of his true family consisting of those who do God's will (3:35). It is to the members of this new family that Jesus reveals the mystery of the kingdom of God (4:11). They will also witness his authority (*exousia*) in word (4:1–34) and deed (4:35–5:43). But only after Jesus has revealed the mystery of the kingdom to the Twelve and performed a series of mighty deeds will he send them on mission with authority (*exousia*) over unclean spirits to preach repentance, cast out demons, and heal the sick (6:7–13). Thus the entire section begins with the call of the Twelve and concludes with Jesus sending them on mission.

The narrator focuses on the person of Jesus to provide readers with a more profound christological portrait of him. As the story unfolds, however, it becomes apparent that the human characters of the narrative are unable to penetrate the secret of Jesus' identity. Thus, even though Jesus reveals the mystery of the kingdom of God to them, his disciples do not understand who he is, and they ask, "Who then is this, that even the wind and the sea obey him?" (4:41). Likewise, although Jesus performs four mighty deeds that manifest his authority over the powerful and debilitating forces of nature, Satan, sickness, and death (4:35–5:43), the people of his hometown take offense at him (6:1–6). Thus readers are led through a somewhat puzzling narrative in which the human characters of the story are unable to comprehend the person of Jesus despite his authoritative teaching and mighty deeds.

The section we are considering begins with Jesus ascending a mountain, calling whom he wishes, and "making them twelve" (*kai epoiēsen dōdeka*), so that he can send them to preach and have authority (*exousia*) to cast out demons (3:13–14). From the outset, the narrator portrays Jesus as an authoritative figure who grants authority as well as exercises it. The number "twelve" recalls the twelve tribes of Israel and suggests that the newly constituted twelve will be the nucleus of a renewed Israel that responds to the good news of the kingdom. But even though this episode presents Jesus as

13

a powerful figure, the shadow of the Passion lies close at hand as the narrator identifies Judas, one of the Twelve, as the one who handed Jesus over (*paredōken auton;* 3:19).

This remark prepares the way for two other episodes in which Jesus is misunderstood by the members of his own family (3:20–21) and then by the scribes who have come down from Jerusalem (3:22–30). Jesus' family wants to take him home because of reports that he is beside himself, while the scribes claim that he is possessed and casts out demons by the prince of demons. The reader of the prologue, however, knows that both accusations are false since Jesus is "the mightier one" who overcame Satan in the wilderness. Thus these episodes highlight the inability of those who do not believe in Jesus' proclamation of the kingdom to understand who he is. The scribes attribute Jesus' exorcisms to Satan, and his family questions his mental stability.

For those who believe in his proclamation of the in-breaking rule of God, Jesus is the one who discloses the mystery of the kingdom (4:11). In a series of parables that the crowd cannot understand, he reveals, to those who are the nucleus of his new family, that the hidden kingdom will be revealed in power (4:1–34). Thus the narrator presents Jesus as one who knows the mystery of God's rule. Furthermore, his parables are allegories that provide important christological information since they disclose that the sower is Jesus, and the seed is the proclamation of the kingdom. Thus the parables teach that despite the insignificant beginnings of his ministry, the seed that Jesus sows will bear fruit when the kingdom of God appears in power.

Having disclosed the mystery of the kingdom to his disciples, Jesus crosses to the other side of the Sea of Galilee. This crossing will be the first of several boat trips to Gentile territory on the eastern shore of the lake,[19] and it results in a further display of Jesus' power, as he calms a storm that threatens the lives of his disciples (4:35–41). The healing of a demon-possessed man in the Gentile territory of the Gerasenes (5:1–20) follows this display of power over the chaotic forces of nature. When Jesus finally returns to Jewish territory on the western side of the lake, he heals a woman suffering from a hemorrhage and raises the daughter of Jairus (5:21–43). Thus the one who teaches with authority and reveals the mysteries of the kingdom shows that he is powerful over the chaotic forces of nature, Satan, sickness, and even death. Powerful in word, he is powerful in deed.

Although Jesus' powerful deeds contribute to the reader's understanding of his person, they do not reveal the secret of his identity to the characters of the narrative. The disciples to whom Jesus has granted the

14

mystery of the kingdom ask who is this man that wind and sea obey him (4:41). The Gerasenes beg Jesus to leave their territory (5:17), and the people of Jesus' hometown continue to identify him as the carpenter, the son of Mary, the brother of James and Joses, Judas, and Simon (6:3). Other characters are more receptive, however, even if they do not comprehend Jesus' full identity. When Jesus instructs the man from whom he expelled the demons to tell others how much the Lord (God) has done for him, the man tells them how much *Jesus* has done for him, thereby equating the work of Jesus with the work of God. Likewise, Jairus and the woman with the hemorrhage believe in Jesus' power to heal them and their loved ones.

The reader of Mark's Gospel understands the deeper meaning of the story and the irony of what is occurring. For example, when the possessed man addresses Jesus as "the Son of the Most High God" (5:7), the reader knows that this title is formally correct and a response to the disciples' query, "Who then is this?" (4:41). And when Jesus' compatriots identify him as the carpenter, the son of Mary (6:3), the reader knows that he is the Son of God. Thus the narrator delights in irony as he develops his Christology.[20]

To summarize, the authoritative herald of the kingdom of God is the one who grants authority to the Twelve to do what he does. The preacher of the kingdom is the teacher par excellence because he reveals the mystery of the kingdom of God. Powerful in word, he is powerful in deed.

Herod's Opinion and Peter's Confession (6:14–8:30)

In light of Jesus' powerful deeds, there is intense speculation about his identity (6:14–16). While many think that he is John the Baptist raised from the dead, others identify him with Elijah, and still others with one of the prophets of old. But when Herod Antipas hears of Jesus' activity, he resolutely declares that Jesus is John the Baptist (whom he beheaded) raised from the dead. Two chapters later, when Jesus asks his disciples at Caesarea Philippi who people say he is, the disciples repeat this list of opinions (8:27–29). The readers of Mark's narrative know that these opinions are erroneous since they have been privy to the Christology of the Markan prologue (1:1–13). They know that John was an Elijah-like figure (see 1:6) who identified Jesus as the mightier one (see 1:7–8). Consequently, the reader realizes that Jesus cannot be John the Baptist raised from the dead, Elijah, or one of the prophets.[21] Rather, he is the Messiah, as Peter will correctly confess at Caesarea Philippi (8:29). In this section, then, the narrative moves from these erroneous opinions about Jesus (6:14–16) to Peter's confession (8:27–30).

Between these two scenes that contrast Herod's opinion and Peter's confession, Jesus performs mighty deeds that identify him as Israel's Shepherd-Messiah. Moreover, when Pharisees and scribes from Jerusalem criticize his disciples for ignoring the traditions of the elders, he proves to be the authentic interpreter of God's commandment who declares all foods clean (7:17–19), thereby annulling the ritual boundary that separated Gentiles and Jews. But throughout this section, Jesus' disciples are unable to comprehend the christological meaning of these events, even when he appears to them in a Christophany walking on the Sea of Galilee (6:45–52). Consequently, Peter's confession is somewhat surprising and leads the inquisitive reader to inquire how the narrative moves from Herod's opinion to Peter's confession.

After the Markan narrator relates Herod's opinion, he presents the first of two stories in which Jesus feeds a great crowd. Once more, readers are granted privileged information, for Mark discloses that when Jesus saw the people, "he had compassion for them, because they were like sheep without a shepherd; and he began to teach them many things" (6:34). This comment to the reader is an unmistakable allusion to Ezekiel 34, where God promises to seek out the scattered sheep (Ezek. 34:12) and feed them on the mountain heights (Ezek. 34:13–16). In Ezekiel 34 God promises, "I will set up over them one shepherd, my servant David, and he shall feed them: he shall feed them and be their shepherd" (Ezek. 34:23). Although Davidic messiahship does not play a significant role in Mark's Gospel, the image of Jesus the Shepherd does (see Mark 14:27–28; 16:7). In this initial feeding scene, then, the Markan narrator presents Jesus as the Shepherd-Messiah who feeds Israel by teaching as well as by multiplying the loaves.

The disciples, who have not been privy to the narrator's comment, have not understood the full significance of Jesus' action in the wilderness. Consequently, when he manifests himself to them by walking on the sea and proclaiming, "Take heart, it is I; do not be afraid" (6:50), they are utterly astounded, and the narrator notes, "for they did not understand about the loaves, but their hearts were hardened" (6:52). That is, they did not comprehend that Jesus acted as Israel's Shepherd-Messiah when he fed the five thousand, because their hardened hearts could not comprehend the significance of this miracle.[22]

Between the feeding of the five thousand and the feeding of the four thousand, Jesus heals great crowds of people at Gennesaret (6:53–56), criticizes the Pharisees and scribes for making the tradition of the elders more important than the commandment of God (7:1–23), travels to the Gentile district of Tyre and exorcises a demon from the daughter of a Greek woman

(7:24–30), and heals a deaf man in the district of the Decapolis (7:31–37). Markan Christology unfolds in several ways in this section. First, Mark notes that at Gennesaret great numbers of people were healed by simply touching the tassel on Jesus' cloak (6:56).[23] Second, the power of Jesus is so great that he can exorcise a demon at a distance without coming into contact with it. Third, Jesus shows himself to be the authentic interpreter of God's will who obeys God's commandments. Finally, having declared that food does not defile a person, Jesus extends his healing ministry to Gentiles in the lands of Tyre, Sidon, and the Decapolis. With an allusion to the messianic text of Isa. 35:5–6, people declare, "He has done everything well; he even makes the deaf to hear and the mute to speak" (7:37).

When Jesus feeds a crowd of four thousand (8:1–9), he is still in Gentile territory. Thus the Shepherd-Messiah of Israel extends his ministry to those who are not Jewish. But the disciples do not comprehend the significance of his activity, for when he warns them about the yeast of the Pharisees and Herod (8:15), they completely misunderstand him. Consequently, Jesus reminds them of the feeding of the five thousand and the four thousand and asks, "Do you not yet understand?" (8:21). What the disciples do not understand is the significance of these events. In feeding the Jewish and Gentile crowds in the wilderness, Jesus acted in his capacity as God's Shepherd-Messiah who shepherds both Israel and the nations.

When Jesus and his disciples arrive at Bethsaida, he heals a blind man. But unlike the other miracles that Jesus has performed, this healing takes place in stages. In the first stage, the man sees, but he does not see clearly. Therefore, in the second stage Jesus places his hands upon the man's eyes a second time, and then the man sees everything clearly. The two stages in which this miracle occurs and its placement in the narrative (immediately before Peter's confession) suggest that it has a symbolic value. The situation of the disciples is analogous to the first stage of the healing: they see but do not see clearly. But in a second stage, when Jesus asks them who they say he is, Peter responds, "You are the Messiah" (8:29). For a *brief* moment, Peter and the disciples see everything clearly, for their eyes have been opened.[24] They finally understand what the reader already knows: that Jesus is the Shepherd-Messiah. But it will soon become apparent that even though Peter's confession is formally correct, it is inadequate. Jesus is the Shepherd-Messiah who heals, feeds, and teaches his people, the one who brings Jew and Gentile together. But he is also the Messiah who must suffer, die, and rise from the dead before he returns as God's glorious eschatological agent. To speak of Jesus' messiahship apart from his destiny as the Son of Man, therefore, is inadequate.

The Messiah's Destiny (8:31–10:52)

Peter's confession is a significant turning point in Mark's narrative, but having confessed that Jesus is the Messiah, Peter must learn that it is the Messiah's destiny to suffer, die, and rise from the dead, before returning in glory and power. Therefore, referring to himself as the Son of Man, Jesus teaches his disciples what it means to call him the Messiah. In effect, the Gospel of Mark redefines messiahship in terms of suffering, death, and resurrection. It replaces the royal Davidic Messiah who defeats Israel's enemies in this age with a Messiah who must fulfill his destiny as the Son of Man.[25] Only after he has passed through suffering and death will this Messiah return in power with God's holy angels at the end of the ages (8:38). Prior to Jesus' death and resurrection, however, his disciples are unable to comprehend this mystery of the Son of Man.

In the period before his royal entry into Jerusalem (8:31–10:52), Jesus teaches his disciples what it means for him to be the Messiah. Immediately after Peter's confession, he instructs them that the Son of Man must (*dei*) suffer many things and be rejected by the chief priests and the scribes, be killed, and rise after three days (8:31). Descending from the mountain where he has been transfigured in the presence of Peter, James, and John, he asks them why scripture says that the Son of Man must suffer many things and be treated with contempt (9:12).[26] Then, as he makes his way through Galilee, Jesus teaches his disciples that the Son of Man must be handed over to those who will kill him, but he will rise after three days (9:31). Finally, shortly before arriving at Jerusalem, Jesus provides his disciples with a detailed prediction of his passion, death, and resurrection that finds its fulfillment in the passion narrative (10:33–34). His disciples, however, are unable and unwilling to accept that the destiny of the Messiah is the fate of the Son of Man. After the first prediction, therefore, Peter takes Jesus aside and rebukes him (8:32). All the disciples fail to understand Jesus' second prediction and are afraid to ask what it means (9:32).[27] Finally, after Jesus' third and most detailed prediction, James and John request the seats of honor at his right and left when he enters into his glory, and the other ten become jealous (10:35–44). Consequently, Jesus must teach his disciples that he did not come to be served but to serve and give his life as a ransom for many (10:45). Although Jesus repeatedly teaches the disciples and plainly describes his destiny, they are unwilling and unable to accept his teaching.[28]

Lest there be any misunderstanding about Jesus' identity and destiny, the Markan narrator relates the story of Jesus' transfiguration. The scene purposely recalls the theophany at Jesus' baptism, when God declared that

Jesus is his beloved Son in whom he is well pleased (1:11). However, now the Father speaks to the three disciples (Peter, James, John) and adds a new phrase: "This is my Son, the Beloved; *listen to him!*" (9:7). These words clearly refer to what Jesus has just said about his destiny as the Son of Man. Thus God himself confirms that Jesus is his beloved Son who must suffer, die, and rise, and he commands the three disciples to listen to what his beloved Son has just said about the destiny of the Son of Man and the nature of discipleship (8:31, 34–38).

As Jesus and the disciples descend from the mountain, he instructs them to say nothing of what has happened until the Son of Man has risen from the dead (9:9).[29] But despite their experience on the mountain, the disciples do not understand why Jesus speaks of resurrection (9:10), even though God has revealed that Jesus is his beloved Son. The disciples do not comprehend that Jesus' destiny is the destiny of the Son of Man.

Although Jesus' teaching about his destiny as the Son of Man dominates this section, the narrative provides other christological information through a series of sayings and episodes that focuses on the importance of Jesus' person in relationship to his disciples. For example, when instructing the crowd and his disciples about the demands of discipleship, Jesus says that those who lose their life *for his sake* and the sake of the gospel of the kingdom will save it (8:35), thereby equating his person with the gospel. Likewise, he says that whoever receives a child in his name receives him, and whoever receives him receives the one who sent him (9:37). Then, a short while later, he promises that whoever gives his disciples a cup of water because they belong to Christ will not go unrewarded (9:41).[30] In every instance, the Markan Jesus presupposes the importance of his person. Although he will suffer and be rejected, those who act on his behalf, or in his name, will be rewarded.

While on his way to Jerusalem, Jesus also shows that he is the authentic interpreter of God's will. The Pharisees ask him if a man is allowed to divorce his wife, and Jesus reminds them of God's original will for man and woman, which did not provide for divorce (10:1–12). A rich man asks what he must do to inherit eternal life, and Jesus summons him to go beyond the commandments of the law (10:17–22). Jesus is not simply a teacher like others, he is the authentic interpreter of God's will. Thus it is significant that his disciples call him teacher.[31]

At the end of his journey to Jerusalem, Jesus enters the city, where blind Bartimaeus addresses him as "Son of David" (10:47–48). The address is clearly messianic, for Jesus is about to enter Jerusalem as its royal Messiah (11:1–11). The readers of Mark's narrative, however, know that Jesus does not fit traditional messianic expectations. He is the Messiah because he is the Son of God who must suffer, die, rise from the dead, and return as the glorious Son of Man, not because he is David's royal descendant.[32] Consequently, while Peter's confession and the cry of Bartimaeus are formally correct, they do not reveal the whole truth of Jesus' identity.

Messiah and Temple (11:1–13:37)

This section of the narrative begins when Jesus enters the royal city of Jerusalem and surveys its Temple (11:1–11), and it concludes when he predicts the destruction of Jerusalem's Temple and his glorious return as the Son of Man (13:1–37). The narrative revolves around the issue of Jesus' authority to teach and act in the Temple. As a result of this conflict, the religious leaders finally hand over (*paradidōmi*) Jesus to Pilate who, in turn, hands him over to be crucified as a messianic pretender, the king of the Jews.

Although the readers of Mark's story now know that Jesus will suffer and die in Jerusalem, the characters of the narrative do not. Consequently, when Jesus enters Jerusalem, they identify his arrival with the restoration of David's kingdom, crying, "Blessed is the coming kingdom of our ancestor David!" (11:10). But upon entering the city, Jesus goes directly to the Temple, looks at everything, and then leaves the city![33]

When Jesus returns to Jerusalem the next day, he goes to the Temple once more. This time he expels the merchants from its precincts and teaches in the presence of the crowds and the religious leaders and asks, "Is it not written, 'My house shall be called a house of prayer for all the nations'? But you have made it a den of robbers" (11:17).[34] Jesus' final miracle, the cursing of the fig tree (11:12–14, 21), encases the cleansing of the Temple and functions as a prophetic sign of the Temple's demise. Just as the fig tree withered and died because it did not bear fruit, so the Temple of Jerusalem will wither and die because it has not become a house of prayer for all the nations, Gentiles as well as Jews.

Aware that Jesus has acted and taught with authority, the chief priests, scribes, and elders (those who compose the Sanhedrin) ask him by what authority (*exousia*) he does these things (11:28). Jesus refuses to answer their question, however, since they will not say if the baptism of John was of divine or human origin (11:29–33). Instead, Jesus tells the parable of the vineyard, an allegory of his own ministry (12:1–11). He is the beloved son (12:6) whom the tenant farmers will kill in order to steal his inheritance. Aware that the allegory is directed at them, the religious leaders look for a way to arrest Jesus (12:12).

In terms of Christology, these episodes present Jesus as the beloved Son of God who has authority to act and teach in his Father's house, the Temple of Jerusalem. God sends his beloved Son to gather the harvest of Jerusalem's Temple. But there is no harvest to collect since the Temple has not become a house of prayer for Gentiles as well as Jews. Instead, Jerusalem's tenants (its religious leaders) will destroy the beloved Son, and his death will bring an end to their Temple.

Jesus' climactic parable, a story within a story, leads to further conflicts between him and the religious leaders, but in every instance he proves superior to them. Because he is God's beloved Son, Jesus knows what belongs to God and what belongs to Caesar (12:13–17). He understands that there will be a resurrection of the dead because God is the God of the living (12:18–27). Finally, he is able to discern the greatest commandment of the law (12:28–34).

Having answered the questions of his opponents, Jesus poses a messianic question (12:35–37): How can the scribes say that the Messiah is the son of David since, in Ps. 110:1, David calls the Messiah his Lord.[35] While the crowds are amazed by this exegesis, the reader understands its deeper significance for Mark's Christology. The Messiah is God's Son rather than David's. It is divine sonship rather than Davidic lineage that makes Jesus the Messiah. Although the Markan narrator allows Bartimaeus to address Jesus as "son of David," there is no claim in Mark's Gospel that Jesus is of Davidic descent. Jesus is son of David because he is God's messianic Son. He is not God's messianic Son on the basis of Davidic lineage.

At the conclusion of Jesus' Jerusalem ministry, one of his disciples praises the beauty of the Temple, causing Jesus to predict that the entire structure will be destroyed (13:1–2). Then, on the Mount of Olives, Peter, James, John, and Andrew ask Jesus when this will take place and what sign will precede it (13:3–4). Although Jesus responds to their question in the ensuing discourse (13:5–37), the climax of the discourse is the description of the Son of Man's parousia (13:24–27). Thus Jesus answers a question his disciples did not ask, and he relegates the destruction of the Temple to one of several signs that will precede his return.

From a narrative point of view, this discourse extends the time of the Markan narrative beyond the events of Jesus' death and resurrection. The reader learns that the story of Jesus will not be completed until the suffering Son of Man returns as the glorious Son of Man, something to which Jesus alluded after his first prediction but did not develop (see 8:38). Thus the narrative presents a new aspect of Jesus' messianic destiny. At a time known only to God, Jesus will return with great power and glory to gather the elect (13:26–27). In explaining his destiny, Jesus refers to himself as the Son of Man who will come "in clouds" with great power and glory, an allusion to the figure in the book of Daniel described as being one like a son of man (Dan. 7:13–14). Then, in one of the most remarkable christological statements of the New Testament, Jesus says that neither the angels in heaven nor the Son knows when these things will take place (13:32).[36]

Jesus' ministry in Jerusalem offers several christological insights. First, he is God's beloved Son who teaches and acts with authority in Jerusalem's Temple. Second, he has come for a harvest that includes Gentiles as well as Jews, but those charged with the harvest have not been faithful. Third, Jesus the Messiah is God's Son rather than the son of David. Fourth, at a future time, the Son will return as the glorious Son of Man to gather his elect, but before this can occur, Jesus must tread the path of the suffering Son of Man.

The One Who Was God's Son (14:1–16:8)

Mark's story finds its christological climax in the centurion's confession that Jesus was truly God's Son (15:39)[37] and the mysterious young man's announcement to the women at the tomb that Jesus of Nazareth, the crucified, has been raised and he is going ahead of his disciples to Galilee (16:6–7). Whereas the centurion's confession marks the first time that a human character within the narrative recognizes that Jesus was God's Son, the young man's announcement resolves the central conflict of the narrative's plot by assuring readers that Jesus was truly approved by God.

The passion story begins with a series of contrasting scenes. While the religious leaders plot to destroy Jesus (14:1–2) and Judas assists them by betraying him (14:10–11), an unnamed woman anoints Jesus' head, and Jesus interprets the gesture as an anointing for burial (14:3–9). Thus the conflict between Jesus and the religious leaders reaches a point of no return.

At a final supper with his disciples, Jesus interprets his impending death as a death on behalf of (*hyper*) many that will establish a covenant with God (14:22–24).[38] Quoting from the prophet Zechariah (see Zech. 13:7), he tells his disciples that the Shepherd will be struck down and they will be scattered (14:27), a remark that recalls the earlier imagery of Jesus the Shepherd-Messiah who fed crowds of five thousand and four thousand. Then, foreshadowing what the young man will say to the women at the tomb, he promises that after he has been raised up, he will go before them to Galilee (compare 14:28 and 16:7). Thus the Shepherd-Messiah will restore his scattered flock after his resurrection.

In the Garden of Gethsemane, Jesus struggles with his destiny as the Son of Man (14:32–42). Deeply distressed, he calls upon his Father to take away the cup of suffering that is his destiny, if possible. After a period of intense prayer, however, Jesus embraces the suffering that lies before him.

Jesus is arrested and led to the chief priest and the whole Sanhedrin, where false witnesses accuse Jesus of saying that he would destroy the Temple made by human hands and after three days construct another Temple not made by human hands (14:58). Although readers know that the accusation is false, they soon learn its ironic truth: Jesus' sacrificial death upon the cross will make the temple cult irrelevant, and the community of his disciples will form a new temple not made by human hands.[39]

Seemingly aware that this temple charge has messianic implications, the high priest asks Jesus if he is the Messiah, the Son of the Blessed One, and Jesus unequivocally answers, "I am" (14:62). Jesus then prophesies that his accusers will see him, the Son of Man, seated at the right hand of the Power, and coming with the clouds of heaven. This prophetic statement, a combination of quotations from Ps. 110:1 and Dan. 7:13, leads the high priest to accuse Jesus of blasphemy (14:64), the charge leveled against him during his Galilean ministry (2:7). Thus the major christological terms of Mark's story (Messiah, Son of God, Son of Man) converge for the first time.

Since the charge of blasphemy would mean little to the Romans, the Jewish leaders hand Jesus over to Pilate as someone who claims to be the king of the Jews. As a result of this, the Romans crucify Jesus as "the King of the Jews" (15:26); that is, someone who threatens their authority to rule.

Jesus' persecutors mock him as a would-be Temple destroyer who cannot save himself (15:29–32). Addressing him with derision as the Messiah, the King of Israel, they challenge him to descend from the cross so that they can see and believe. While the characters of Mark's narrative view Jesus' inability to save himself as a sign that he is a messianic pretender, the perceptive reader of Mark's narrative appreciates the irony of the situation. If Jesus tries to save himself, he will contradict his own teaching (see 8:35). Therefore, he must trust in the power of God to save him if he is to act as God's Son.

At the moment of his death, Jesus even experiences the absence of God's presence, crying out the opening words of Psalm 22, "My God, my God, why have you forsaken me?" (15:34). Bystanders mistake these words as a desperate call for Elijah, but the reader knows better, for Elijah has already come in the person of John the Baptist.

Jesus dies with a great cry and the temple curtain is torn from top to bottom. Witnessing the manner in which Jesus dies, the centurion proclaims that Jesus was truly God's Son (15:39), the first acknowledgment by a human character within the narrative that Jesus is God's Son. However, the centurion comes to this knowledge on the basis of Jesus' death. The manner in which Jesus dies convinces him that he was truly God's Son. While the centurion is not aware that the temple curtain has been torn, the readers of Mark's narrative are, and they know its significance: the death of God's Son has made the temple cult obsolete.

Although there are no resurrection appearances in Mark's narrative,[40] there is no doubt that the crucified one lives. Echoing Jesus' words, the young man tells the women that Jesus of Nazareth, the crucified one, has been raised and has gone before his disciples to Galilee, where they will see him (16:6–7). There, the Shepherd-Messiah will reconstitute his scattered flock.

Christology in Mark's Gospel

The Christology of Mark's Gospel is in the story it tells.[41] That story identifies Jesus as the Messiah, the Son of God, whose destiny is to suffer, die, rise from the dead, and return as the glorious Son of Man to gather the elect. Having completed a reading of Mark's narrative, we are in a better position to say something about each of these titles.

Jesus the Christ

Although *Christos* (Christ/Messiah) occurs only seven times in Mark's Gospel,[42] it plays a central role in his Christology. The Gospel begins by identifying Jesus as Christ (1:1); Peter confesses that Jesus is the Messiah (8:29); and when the high priest asks Jesus if he is the Messiah (14:61), he unequivocally responds, "I am." But it is also apparent that the Gospel of Mark does not apply this title to Jesus in the traditional sense of royal messianism. Thus Jesus asks the crowds of Jerusalem, How can the scribes say that the Messiah is David's son (12:35)? Jesus is not the Messiah because he fulfills the messianic expectations of a Davidic royal messianism. He is the Messiah because he is God's Son who fulfills his destiny as the Son of Man.

Mark's narrative, then, defines messiahship in light of Jesus' ministry, death, and resurrection. If we could ask the Evangelist what he understands by the Messiah, he might respond in this way:

> The Messiah is the Spirit-anointed Son of God who proclaims the arrival of God's kingdom in word and deed. He heals the sick, expels demons, and even extends his ministry to Gentiles. Most important, he gives his life as a

ransom for the many. Having suffered, died, and risen from the dead, he will return as the glorious Son of Man.

In other words, Mark would define messiahship in terms of Jesus, rather than define Jesus in terms of messiahship. Although Jesus does not fulfill traditional messianic expectations, his life and ministry are the norm for defining what it means to be God's anointed one.

Jesus Christ the Son of God

Jesus is the Messiah because he is the Son of God *(huios tou theou)*. While it does not appear that Jesus' contemporaries employed "Son of God" as a messianic title, it is clearly employed as such in Mark's Gospel. At the beginning of the Gospel, the Gospel identifies Jesus as the Son of God (1:1). When he asks Jesus if he is the Messiah, the high priest clarifies what he means by adding, "the Son of the Blessed One," a circumlocution for Son of God (14:61). At several points in the narrative, demons identify Jesus as God's Son (3:11; 5:7). Although their cries are not a confession of faith, what they say is formally correct since God himself identifies Jesus as his beloved Son (1:11; 9:7). Moreover, in the parable of the vineyard, Jesus allegorically refers to himself as the beloved Son (12:6), clearly echoing the Father's words at his baptism and transfiguration.

But what does it mean to confess Jesus as the Son of God? Israel (Hos. 11:1), the angels of Yahweh's council (Job 1:6), the king of Israel (Ps. 2:7), and even the righteous one could be called God's son (Wisd. Sol. 2:16, 18; 5:5).[43] Mark, however, intends more than this traditional usage since Jesus enjoys a unique sonship that none of those listed above could claim. First and foremost, he is the beloved *(agapētos)* Son in whom God is well pleased. Beloved of God, he calls God "Abba" (14:36) and exercises an authority that clearly comes from God. Jesus is God's Spirit-anointed Son (1:10) who casts out demons and heals the sick. Although Mark never explicitly calls him divine, Jesus is no ordinary man, and his disciples ask, "Who then is this, that even the wind and the sea obey him?" (4:41).

Mark develops the unique nature of Jesus' sonship by employing a secrecy motif often referred to as "the messianic secret." The real secret, however, concerns Jesus' sonship rather than his messiahship. None of the human characters of the narrative recognize Jesus as the Son of God until he has died. Only when Jesus has died does the centurion proclaim that this man was truly God's Son (15:39). Jesus' death, then, paradoxically reveals his divine sonship. Because of Jesus' death, disciples begin to understand that divine sonship exercises its power in weakness. The true Son of God does not save himself but waits for, and trusts in, God to save him.

Jesus Christ the Son of God, the Son of Man

Son of Man (*ho huios tou anthrōpou*) is the most enigmatic term of the Gospel, and yet it is central to Mark's Christology.[44] It is not a confessional title in the manner that Messiah and Son of God are since no one addresses or confesses Jesus as the Son of Man. The term is only found on Jesus' lips, and it is never employed to identify him. Thus, when Jesus refers to himself as the Son of Man for the first time (2:10), there is no reaction from any of the characters of the narrative. Son of Man is akin to a circumlocution rather than a title of honor.[45]

Jesus uses the term in several ways within the Gospel: to highlight his authority (2:10, 28); to refer to his suffering, death, and resurrection (8:31; 9:9, 13, 31; 10:33; 14:21, 41); to explain the significance of his death (10:45); and to point to his glorious return at the end of the ages (8:38; 13:26; 14:62). Instead of identifying who Jesus is, then, Son of Man defines Jesus' destiny. During his earthly ministry Jesus exercises authority to forgive sins and heal on the Sabbath. When this ministry is completed, he must suffer, die, and rise so that he can return at the end of the ages to gather God's elect.

Son of Man is the necessary complement to Messiah and Son of God, ensuring that neither title will be interpreted apart from Jesus' death and resurrection. For Mark, Jesus is the Messiah, the Son of God, because he fulfills the destiny of the Son of Man. Were Jesus not to fulfill this destiny, he would not be God's messianic Son. Markan Christology, then, can be summarized in the terms "Messiah," "Son of God," "the Son of Man." And yet, none of these can be understood adequately apart from Mark's narrative; for the Christology is in the story, and through the story we learn to interpret the titles.

THE GOSPEL OF MATTHEW

Whenever a narrator recounts an old story, there are changes. In some instances they are minor, but in others they alter the narrative to such an extent that it becomes a new story. Thus stories generate stories when narrators tell them anew.

The Gospel of Matthew is an example of a story that has been generated by retelling an old story: the story of Jesus as recounted by Mark. On the one hand, Matthew follows the story of his predecessor: Jesus' ministry begins in Galilee where he proclaims the kingdom of heaven[46] and concludes in Jerusalem where the religious leaders hand him over to Pilate, who has him crucified as the king of the Jews. But, on the other hand, in retelling

26

this story of Jesus, Matthew makes a number of changes. For example, he begins his narrative with an account of Jesus' genealogy and the wondrous events that accompanied his birth. Then, at significant moments in the story, he portrays Jesus as delivering extended discourses on righteousness, mission, the kingdom of heaven, community life, the hypocrisy of the religious leaders, and the events of the end time.[47] As a result, there is a slower pace to Matthew's Gospel, which affords readers an opportunity to reflect upon the character of Jesus and his teaching. Finally, Matthew provides a more complete and satisfying ending than Mark, which includes an appearance of the risen Lord to his disciples.

In retelling this story, Matthew is faithful to the major themes of Mark's narrative Christology, for he presents Jesus as the Messiah, the Son of God, whose fate is the destiny of the Son of Man.[48] But even though Matthew remains faithful to these central themes, the changes in his narrative profoundly affect his Christology. For example, the genealogy of Jesus and the events surrounding his birth enrich Matthew's understanding of what it means to call Jesus the Messiah, the Son of God. The Sermon on the Mount presents Jesus as the authoritative interpreter of the Mosaic law, the teacher of righteousness par excellence. The net result is a christological narrative that focuses on the abiding presence of Jesus, the obedient Son of God, for a community of disciples that awaits his return as the glorious Son of Man. Although Matthew emphasizes that Jesus is the crucified Messiah, he shows the church that the crucified one is its exalted Lord.[49]

In narrating his story of Jesus, Matthew employs a plot of conflict.[50] While the surface conflict is between Jesus and Israel's leadership, the deeper conflict is between God and Satan.[51] The plot can be stated in this way.

God sends Jesus to save his people from their sins by inaugurating the kingdom of heaven. Jesus will accomplish this through his ministry of teaching, preaching, and healing, and by shedding his blood for the forgiveness of sins. Aware that the kingdom of heaven will destroy his rule, Satan tries to prevent Jesus from accomplishing this mission.

In the course of this conflict, the characters of Matthew's narrative show themselves to be either "children of the kingdom" or "children of the evil one" (13:38) by the manner in which they respond to Jesus' mission. For example, even though the religious leaders view themselves as the legitimate representatives of Moses, they unwittingly aid Satan's cause when they accuse Jesus of casting out demons by the prince of demons (12:24). Even Peter acts in Satan's interest when he tries to keep Jesus from his

God-appointed destiny to suffer and die on the cross (16:22).[52] Despite these attempts by others to frustrate his mission, Jesus saves his people from their sins by dying on the cross. Raised from the dead and given full authority, he commissions his disciples to teach all nations what he has taught them. Thus the kingdom of heaven will be preached to all the nations if Jesus' disciples fulfill their commission. Matthew's story of Jesus unfolds in the following way.

1:1–4:16	The appearance of Israel's Messiah, the son of David, the Son of God
4:17–11:1	The Messiah's ministry of teaching, preaching, and healing to the lost sheep of the house of Israel
11:2–16:20	Israel's opposition to the Messiah's ministry and the establishment of a new community
16:21–20:34	The destiny of the Messiah to suffer, die, and rise from the dead in order to complete his mission
21:1–28:20	The final rejection, death, and vindication of the Messiah, and the Messiah's commission to his disciples to teach all nations

The Appearance of Israel's Messiah (1:1–4:16)

The beginning of Matthew's Gospel (1:1–4:16) can be viewed as an extended introduction to Jesus' ministry. Focusing on Jesus' ancestry, birth, baptism, and testing in the wilderness, the material of this section identifies Jesus in a number of ways. Thus Matthew presents readers with a clear portrait of Jesus' identity before describing his ministry to Israel. Jesus is the Davidic Messiah, the Son of God, who embodies the hopes and aspirations of his people Israel.

Matthew begins his story with a genealogy that firmly roots Jesus in the history of Israel and establishes his messianic credentials.[53] Jesus Messiah is son of David, son of Abraham (1:1–17). The genealogy includes the whole sweep of Israel's history: fourteen generations from Abraham to David, fourteen generations from David to the Babylonian exile, and fourteen generations from the exile to the Messiah. But when Matthew comes to Joseph, the supposed father of Jesus, he subverts his own genealogy. Instead of writing "Jacob begot Joseph, and Joseph begot Jesus," as one would expect, Matthew writes, "and Jacob begot Joseph the husband of Mary, from whom Jesus was born, the one called Messiah" (1:16, my translation). Thus Matthew suggests that there is no biological line of descent from Joseph to Jesus.

Matthew's reason for doing this becomes apparent when the angel of the Lord appears to Joseph in a dream and explains that Mary's child has been conceived from the Holy Spirit. The angel then instructs Joseph to call the child "Jesus" because he will save his people from their sins (1:21). Commenting on this scene, the narrator notes that this took place to fulfill what the Lord had spoken through the prophet: that a virgin would conceive a son, and his name would be called Emmanuel, "God is with us" (1:23).

The reader has learned a great deal about Jesus in this opening chapter. Jesus is the son of David by virtue of Joseph his adoptive father, but he was conceived from the Holy Spirit. Therefore, he has a unique relationship to God, different from any other human being.[54] His birth was the fulfillment of prophecy, and his mission (as made clear by the name given to him) is to save his people from their sins. Called Emmanuel, Jesus is the presence of God to his people (also see 18:20; 28:20).

In the second part of his infancy narrative, Matthew foreshadows the coming conflict between Jesus and the leaders of Israel, establishes that Jesus is the legitimate king of the Jews, shows his readers that the birth of Jesus the Messiah fulfills the prophetic scriptures, and presents Jesus as the messianic Son of God who relives the history of his people Israel.

The reaction of Herod and all Jerusalem to the question of the Magi ("Where is the child who has been born king of the Jews?") foreshadows the approaching conflict between Israel and its Messiah. Whereas the Gentile Magi come to worship the one born to be the king of the Jews, Herod and the whole of Jerusalem are deeply disturbed. Although the chief priests and scribes of the people know the prophetic text that the Messiah will be born in Bethlehem (2:6, see Micah 5:2), neither they nor Herod worship the newborn king of the Jews.[55] At the outset of the narrative, therefore, Matthew forebodes the response of Israel's leaders to Jesus: rather than accept him as the Messiah, the king of Israel, they will hand him over to Pilate to be crucified as a messianic pretender, the king of the Jews (27:37).

The Magi stand in sharp contrast to Herod and the religious leaders. They come to worship the king of the Jews (2:3), and, when they finally see the child with his mother,[56] they fall to their knees and worship him (2:11). Their behavior portends the response of other Gentiles in Matthew's narrative (see 8:5–13; 15:21–28) and prepares for the great commission of the risen Lord, who instructs his disciples to make disciples of all the nations (28:19). Thus, the Messiah of Israel will bring salvation to the nations, even though his primary mission is to the lost sheep of the house of Israel (15:24).

The reaction of Herod, the king, to the birth of Jesus, the king of the

Jews, invites readers to compare two kinds of kingship.[57] Herod exercises his kingship through deception and violence. He instructs the Magi to search diligently for the child so that he can worship the newborn king. But when the Magi do not return to Herod, the king reveals his true motives by murdering the infants of Bethlehem in order to destroy the infant king of the Jews. Herod is a violent and deceptive king who is more concerned with power than shepherding God's people and obeying the divine will. In contrast to him, Jesus comes to shepherd God's people, Israel. Therefore, he will not treat the people as though they were his own, to do with as he wills, as does Herod; for the people belong to God.[58] The total vulnerability of Jesus "the child" foreshadows the nature of his kingship; Jesus will exercise his kingship as God's chosen servant (12:18–21) and enter Jerusalem as the meek king prophesied by Zechariah (see Matt. 21:5). Jesus, not Herod, is the legitimate king of the Jews. And under the charge, "the king of the Jews" (27:37), he will die to save his people.

Throughout the infancy narrative, Matthew employs a series of scriptural quotations to persuade readers that the wondrous events of Jesus' infancy are the prophetic fulfillment of scripture.[59] Thus Jesus is born of a virgin as prophesied by Isaiah (Matt. 1:23). In accordance with a prophecy of Micah, he is born in Bethlehem (Matt. 2:6). The return of Jesus and his family from exile in Egypt fulfills the prophecy of Hosea that God called his Son out of Egypt (Matt. 2:15). Herod's slaughter of the infants in and around Bethlehem fulfills the words of Jeremiah (Matt. 2:18). Finally, when Jesus and his family settle in Nazareth, the Matthean narrator interprets this as the fulfillment of yet another scriptural quotation ("He will be called a Nazorean," 2:23), although there is no scriptural quotation that exactly corresponds to these words.[60] The constant reminder that a particular event occurred in order to fulfill scripture should persuade readers that the appearance of Jesus is the fulfillment of scripture, not an aberration of God's plan.

In addition to fulfilling the scriptures, Jesus relives the history of his people Israel. His life is threatened by a wicked king, as was the life of the infant Moses. He is forced to leave his homeland and live in Egypt, as were the people of Israel. But just as God called his son, Israel, out of Egypt, so he calls Jesus, his unique Son, from Egypt. As the genealogy makes clear, Jesus embodies the history of his people. The Son of God, he is the true Israel who, unlike Israel of old, is perfectly obedient to God.

Having narrated the wondrous events surrounding Jesus' birth, the Matthean narrator recounts the appearance of John the Baptist, the baptism of Jesus, and Jesus' testing in the wilderness (3:1–4:16). Like the infancy narrative, these events continue the narrative task of introducing and identifying Jesus before he embarks upon his ministry.

When John the Baptist makes his appearance, he proclaims the same message that Jesus will: "Repent, for the kingdom of heaven has come near" (3:2; see 4:17). But whereas John announces the in-breaking of God's rule, Jesus will effect that rule by his mighty deeds and saving death. It is not surprising, then, that John identifies Jesus as someone more powerful than himself who will baptize with the Holy Spirit and fire (3:11).[61]

When Jesus presents himself to be baptized by John, the Baptist immediately recognizes him and tries to prevent this baptism, intended for sinners, from taking place (3:13–14). But Jesus has a deeper understanding of God's will than John, for he insists that he and the Baptist must fulfill God's just demands (*pasan dikaiosynēn;* 3:15). Although he has not sinned and is greater than John, Jesus presents himself to be baptized in order to do the will of God. Thus, the Matthean narrator presents Jesus' baptism as an act of righteousness. This act of righteousness leads to the Father's declaration that Jesus is the beloved Son in whom he is pleased (3:17).

Matthew provides his readers with an important insight into Jesus' sonship in the episode that follows, the testing of Jesus in the wilderness (4:1–11). Satan begins his first two temptations with the same challenge: "If you are the Son of God" (4:3, 6), thereby recalling the Father's declaration that Jesus is his beloved Son (3:17). In each instance, Jesus shows that he is God's Son by his obedience to God's word. In the third temptation, Satan promises Jesus all the kingdoms of the world if he will worship him. But since Jesus has come to inaugurate God's kingdom, he will not worship Satan.

Jesus' period of forty days in the wilderness recalls Israel's testing in the wilderness. Although God called his son, Israel, out of Egypt (Hos. 11:1), Israel was not obedient to God's word, as it wandered for forty years in the wilderness. Instead of living by the word of God (Deut. 8:3), Israel rebelled against God (Exodus 16). Instead of trusting God (Deut. 6:16), Israel tested God (Exodus 17). Embodying the history of his people, Jesus succeeds where Israel failed. Thus the Matthean narrator presents Jesus as the obedient Son of God who perfectly fulfills the destiny of his people.

When Jesus learns that John has been handed over, he withdraws to Galilee and dwells in Capernaum by the sea.[62] Matthew interprets this withdrawal as the fulfillment of Isaiah's prophecy that a light will shine upon those dwelling in darkness (4:14–16; see Isa. 9:1–2). In the narrative that follows, Jesus brings the light of the gospel to "Galilee of the Gentiles."[63]

The beginning of Matthew's Gospel presents readers with a rich Christology. Jesus the Messiah is the son of David, the son of Abraham. He is the legitimate king of the Jews who will shepherd God's people, Israel. Conceived by the power of the Holy Spirit, he is the beloved Son of God who embodies the history of his people Israel and fulfills its prophetic scriptures. Righteous and obedient to God's word, he comes to save his people from their sins. He is Emmanuel, the one in whom God is present to his people.

The Messiah's Ministry to Israel (4:17–11:1)

In the second part of his narrative, Matthew presents Jesus the Messiah, the Son of God, as proclaiming the kingdom of heaven, teaching his disciples how to practice a greater righteousness, and healing the ills of God's people, Israel. When he sees this people troubled and abandoned like sheep without a shepherd, Jesus sends his twelve disciples on mission to the lost sheep of the house of Israel to proclaim the kingdom of heaven and cure the sick.[64] Thus Matthew identifies Jesus as the Messiah who teaches, preaches, and heals God's people.

This section of the narrative begins with a programmatic statement: "From that time Jesus began to proclaim, 'Repent, for the kingdom of heaven has come near'" (4:17). Although John the Baptist proclaimed the kingdom of heaven (3:2), it is Jesus' ministry of teaching, preaching, and healing that inaugurates the kingdom. Consequently, he is the preeminent preacher of the kingdom. All that he says and does is guided by his initial proclamation that the kingdom of heaven has come near.

In a summary of Jesus' activity, the Matthean narrator notes, "Jesus went throughout Galilee, *teaching* in their synagogues and *proclaiming* the good news of the kingdom and *curing* every disease and every sickness among the people" (4:23). On the basis of this summary, the readers of Matthew's story can now assume that these three activities characterize Jesus' messianic ministry to Israel.[65] In the narrative that follows, Matthew illustrates Jesus' ministry of teaching by recounting his Sermon on the Mount (5:1–7:29) and his ministry of healing by narrating a series of his mighty deeds (8:1–9:34). Both of these activities, in turn, illustrate what Jesus means when he proclaims that the kingdom of heaven has come near.

The Sermon on the Mount announces the blessings of the kingdom (5:3–11) and calls for a greater righteousness (5:20).[66] In announcing the blessings of the kingdom and its eschatological rewards, the Matthean Jesus shows that he stands in a unique relationship to God. He does not pro-

32

claim the sermon as a great prophet, or even as a new Moses, but as the messianic Son of God who enjoys an intimate knowledge of God's will (see 11:25–27).[67] Consequently, when he teaches his disciples the way to a greater righteousness, Jesus states his moral demands (5:22, 28, 32, 34, 39, 44) vis-à-vis those of the law (5:21, 27, 31, 33, 38, 43). In calling for a greater righteousness, however, he does not destroy or abrogate the law, for he has come to fulfill the Law and the Prophets, not to abolish them (5:17). Disciples who follow his moral injunctions will not disobey the Mosaic law; they will practice a greater righteousness by doing more than the law demands.[68] The one who proclaims the sermon knows the fullest meaning of God's will, for he is God's messianic Son.

At the conclusion of his great sermon, Jesus gives yet another indication of his identity. Warning his disciples that not everyone who calls him "Lord" will enter the kingdom of heaven but only those who do the will of his heavenly Father, he points to the day of judgment when, as God's eschatological judge, he will solemnly declare that he did not know such evildoers, even though they address him as their Lord (7:21–23). Since the title "Lord" is properly reserved for the exalted Christ, it is evident that Matthew's narrative functions on two levels. In terms of the story, it is the earthly Jesus who speaks. But in terms of the Matthean community, the risen Lord is speaking through the earthly Jesus. Thus the Matthean narrator foreshadows the role and status of the exalted Lord in the words of the earthly Jesus.

Having presented Jesus as one who teaches with an authority from God (see 7:29), Matthew highlights Jesus' ministry of healing by narrating the mighty deeds of the Messiah. The material can be structured as follows:

8:1–4	Cleansing of a leper
8:5–13	Healing of a centurion's servant
8:14–17	Healing of Peter's mother-in-law and the ills of the people, followed by a quotation from Isaiah
8:18–22	*Discipleship stories*
8:23–27	Rescue of the disciples at sea
8:28–34	Healing of two demon-possessed men
9:1–8	Healing of a paralytic
9:9–17	*Discipleship stories*
9:18–26	Healing of an official's daughter and a woman with a hemorrhage
9:27–31	Healing of two blind men
9:32–34	Healing of a mute, followed by two contrasting reactions to Jesus' mighty deeds

The structure indicates that the Matthean narrator artistically arranges the material so that stories with a discipleship theme set off stories of Jesus' mighty deeds. After Jesus' initial mighty deeds, Matthew introduces a scriptural quotation to indicate that Jesus' healing ministry is the fulfillment of prophecy: "He took our infirmities and bore our diseases" (Matt. 8:17; see Isa. 53:4). Then, after the final healing, the narrator contrasts the positive reaction of the crowd with the Pharisees' negative judgment that Jesus is in collusion with Satan (9:34).

Jesus' mighty deeds demonstrate that the one who proclaims the kingdom in word is also powerful in deed. Thus they further disclose the mystery of Jesus' person. Since the resurrection has not yet occurred, however, the characters of the narrative do not understand the full significance of their words when they address Jesus as "Lord" (8:2, 8, 25), but the reader does. For the one who heals the leper, cures the centurion's servant, and rescues the disciples from the storm-tossed sea is the exalted Lord of the church. In his earthly ministry, he bears the infirmities of his people (8:17), and guided by the words of the prophet, "I desire mercy, not sacrifice" (Matt. 9:13; see Hos. 6:6), he calls sinners to repentance in light of God's in-breaking rule. Like the Sermon on the Mount, then, Jesus' mighty deeds are a christological proclamation; they are works of the Messiah (see 11:2).

As Jesus continues to teach, preach, and heal, he sees that God's people are like sheep without a shepherd (9:35–38), because their leaders have not fulfilled their responsibilities toward them. Therefore, the Messiah summons twelve disciples whom he sends on mission to the lost sheep of the house of Israel (10:5–6). Jesus' missionary discourse (10:5–42) provides another occasion for the Matthean narrator to speak directly to the audience of his day. While Jesus' instructions are ostensibly addressed to the disciples in the story, there are several indications that the Matthean narrator intends them for the church of his day. For example, Jesus instructs the disciples to flee to another town when they are persecuted, for the Son of Man will return before they finish preaching to the towns of Israel (10:23). Yet Matthew's story never narrates the mission of the Twelve, their persecution, or the return of the Son of Man. These events will occur in the time *after* Jesus' resurrection.

Once more the Matthean narrator writes on two levels. In terms of the story, the earthly Jesus prepares his disciples for mission, but, in terms of the Matthean community, it is the risen Lord who instructs his church. Understood in this light, Jesus' missionary speech is an illustration of what it means to call him Emmanuel: the risen Lord is present to his church and continues to instruct it as once he instructed the Twelve.

In this discourse, Jesus makes statements that point to his unique relationship with God. For example, he will acknowledge before his Father in heaven everyone who acknowledges him, and he will deny before his Father in heaven everyone who denies him (10:32–33). Whoever welcomes one of Jesus' disciples welcomes him, and whoever welcomes him welcomes the one who sent him; that is, the Father (10:40). Like Jesus' statement about the greater righteousness in the Sermon on the Mount, these missionary instructions indicate a unique relationship between Jesus and the Father that is not enjoyed by another human being.

Opposition and Consolidation (11:2–16:20)

Although the crowds are astonished by Jesus' authoritative teaching (7:28–29) and exclaim, "Never has anything like this been seen in Israel" (9:33), all is not well. Marveling at the faith of a centurion, Jesus says that he has not found such faith in Israel, and he warns that the children of the kingdom will be expelled from the banquet of the kingdom of heaven (8:10–12). Then, after witnessing Jesus' mighty deeds, the Pharisees attribute them to the power of Satan (9:34). This festering opposition leads to a crisis in the Messiah's ministry that causes him to withdraw from the religious leaders and crowds in order to instruct his disciples, who will be the nucleus of a renewed Israel, the church.

Initial Opposition from All Israel (11:2–12:50)

The first note of opposition arises from a most unlikely source, John the Baptist. Having prepared the way for an end time judge who will pronounce fearful judgment upon sinners (see 3:12), the Baptist seems puzzled by the works of the Messiah. Therefore, he sends messengers to ask, "Are you the one who is to come, or are we to wait for another?" (11:3). To be sure, the Baptist does not oppose Jesus' ministry, as do the Pharisees, but he is clearly puzzled by it. A Messiah who teaches, preaches, and heals is not the Messiah he expected.

Nevertheless, Jesus takes the occasion of the Baptist's query to extol John's role in God's salvific plan and excoriate the fickleness of "this generation" that criticized John for his ascetic ways and Jesus for being self-indulgent (11:16–19). Jesus then reproaches the Galilean towns in which he performed most of his mighty deeds (Chorazin, Bethsaida, and Capernaum) for not repenting. Thus the readers of Matthew's narrative learn what was only intimated earlier: The Messiah's ministry of teaching, preaching, and healing has not led to Israel's repentance.

The opposition to the Messiah increases when the Pharisees accuse

Jesus' disciples of violating the Sabbath and then plot to destroy him because he heals on the Sabbath (12:1–14). When Jesus heals a possessed man who is also blind and mute, the crowds ask, with a tinge of cynicism, if Jesus is really the Son of David, while the Pharisees repeat their earlier charge that Jesus drives out demons by the prince of demons (12:23–24; also see 9:34). In his reply to them, Jesus exposes the weakness of their argument and the true nature of his ministry. If he is in collusion with Satan, then Satan is destroying his own kingdom! What is really happening is a conflict of kingdoms. The messianic Son of God is laying waste Satan's power by inaugurating God's rule.

When the scribes and Pharisees ask Jesus for a sign, he identifies them as an evil and adulterous generation that will only receive the sign of Jonah the prophet (12:38–39).[69] In Jesus' view, the last state of "this evil generation" will be worst than the first. For, although the Messiah has expelled demons, Israel has not repented. Therefore, Satan will rule this generation more powerfully than before, when he takes possession of it anew (12:43–45).

In the midst of this opposition from Israel and its leaders, the Matthean narrator provides his audience with two important christological statements. First, in one of the most remarkable passages of the Gospel, Jesus praises the Father and discloses the intimate relationship that the Son enjoys with the Father (11:25–27).[70] Proclaiming that the Father has handed everything over to him (see 28:18, where this will be repeated), Jesus assumes an unheard-of relationship to God: No one knows the Son except the Father, and no one knows the Father except the Son, and those to whom the Son reveals him (11:27). This statement will be confirmed at Peter's confession, when Jesus tells Peter, "flesh and blood has not revealed this to you [Jesus' sonship], but my Father in heaven" (16:17).

Second, when Jesus withdraws because the Pharisees are plotting to destroy him, the Matthean narrator introduces an extended fulfillment quotation from the prophet Isaiah (Matt. 12:18–21; see Isa. 42:1–4). Jesus the Son of God is the chosen servant who proclaims justice to the nations. Although his opponents plot his destruction, he withdraws from their machinations, for he is God's humble servant who, in accord with his own teaching, does not injure or retaliate against his enemies.

In sum, chapters 11–12 bring the crisis between Israel and its Messiah to a head. Although the Messiah has taught and preached about the kingdom of heaven and cured Israel's ills, Israel has refused to repent. Consequently, it has not recognized the Messiah to whom the Father has given all things, the servant of God who will bring justice to the nations.

Parables of the Kingdom (13:1–53)

Having encountered opposition from all segments of Israel, Jesus delivers a discourse of parables in which he reveals the mysteries of the kingdom of heaven to his disciples (13:11). Those who understand the parables also comprehend the role that Jesus plays in God's salvific plan. Two of these parables are especially important for our purposes since Jesus explains their allegorical meaning.

The first is the parable of the sower (13:1–9), which Jesus decodes for his disciples but not for the crowd (13:18–23). His interpretation reveals that although people hear his proclamation of the kingdom, they do not accept it for a variety of reasons. Some hear without understanding. In others, the message never takes root, or worldly anxieties distract them. But those who hear the message of the kingdom with understanding bear a rich harvest. Therefore, although many have rejected Jesus' ministry, others have understood and will bear fruit.

But it is the parable of the weeds among the wheat (13:24–30) with its explanation (13:36–43) that provides a new insight into Matthew's Christology. The one who sows the good seed (the children of the kingdom) is the Son of Man, and the enemy who sows the weeds (the children of the evil one) is the devil. At the present, the children of these two kingdoms live side by side. But at the end of the ages, the Son of Man will send his angels to separate the two, and the righteous will shine like the sun in the kingdom of their Father. Thus the parable reveals that there are two opposing kingdoms: the kingdom of Satan who rules this present age and the kingdom of the Son of Man who will overcome Satan's rule.[71]

Like Jesus' missionary discourse, the parable discourse can be read on two levels. In terms of the story, Jesus is explaining what is happening in his earthly ministry. But in terms of the Matthean community, he is addressing the church living in the period after his resurrection. The members of the church are the children of the kingdom presently waiting for the Son of Man to separate good and evil and rescue them from their present circumstances. Interestingly, there is no need for Jesus to explain who the Son of Man is. The readers of Matthew's Gospel know that he is the risen Lord, the Son of God, who will return at the close of the ages.

Opposition, Withdrawal, Consolidation (13:54–16:20)

Having revealed the mystery of the kingdom to his disciples, Jesus withdraws when he learns that Herod has put John the Baptist to death (14:13). Likewise, after a severe confrontation with the Pharisees and Sadducees, in which Jesus defends God's law over and against the tradition of the elders, he withdraws to the Gentile region of Tyre and Sidon (15:21). He makes these strategic withdrawals in the face of danger so that he can be with his disciples. For their part, the disciples begin to grow in their understanding of Jesus' identity. Thus, when he comes to them, walking upon the Sea of Galilee, Peter first doubts that it is Jesus and says, "Lord, if it is you, command me to come to you on the water" (14.28). Then, when Peter begins to sink and Jesus must rescue him from the sea, all the disciples worship Jesus and proclaim, "Truly you are the Son of God" (14:33). Still later, at Caesarea Philippi, when Jesus asks, "Who do people say that the Son of Man is?" (16:13), Peter responds in the name of all the disciples, "You are the Messiah, the Son of the living God" (16:16). Jesus, in turn, makes Peter the foundation of his church, indicating that a new congregation will arise out of Israel.

The Christology of Matthew's Gospel makes a major advance over that of the Gospel of Mark, in which no human character recognizes that Jesus is the Son of God until after his death. For Matthew, the earthly Jesus already foreshadows the dignity of the risen Lord. In confessing him as the Son of God, the disciples may not understand the full significance of their words, since Jesus has not yet died and risen from the dead, but they already recognize that the one who teaches, preaches, and heals in service of the kingdom has a unique relationship to God. Consequently, they rightly call him the Son of God.

The Messiah's Destiny as the Son of Man (16:21–20:34)

Peter's confession at Caesarea Philippi brings to a close the period of Jesus' teaching, preaching, and healing that was announced in 4:17. Having proclaimed the kingdom to Israel and met with opposition from Israel and its leaders, Jesus now shows his disciples what must (*dei*) befall him at Jerusalem and prepares them for the period after his resurrection when they will await his glorious return as the Son of Man. Employing a phrase reminiscent of 4:17, then, the Matthean narrator indicates that his story is taking a new turn: "*From that time on,* Jesus began to show his disciples that he must (*dei*) go to Jerusalem and undergo great suffering at the hands of the elders and chief priests and scribes, and be killed, and on the third day be raised" (16:21).

The Greek verb *dei* suggests that Jesus' passion, death, and resurrection are God's will for the Messiah, for only after Jesus has been raised from the dead can he return as the royal Son of Man, the final moment in the establishment of God's rule.[72] In trying to dissuade Jesus from his messianic destiny, Peter unwittingly plays the role of Satan (16:22–23). For if Jesus refuses to suffer and die at Jerusalem, he cannot return as the glorious Son of Man to judge the nations.

Matthew sustains this narrative line by having Jesus predict his fate on other occasions as well. For example, after the transfiguration, he instructs Peter, James, and John, "Tell no one about the vision until after the Son of Man has been raised from the dead" (17:9). Then he reminds them that the Son of Man is about to suffer, as did John the Baptist (17:12–13). On two other occasions, he informs all his disciples that the Son of Man will suffer, die, and on the third day be raised from the dead (17:22–23; 20:18–19).

In addition to speaking of himself as the Son of Man who must suffer, die, and be raised from the dead, Jesus identifies himself as the Son of Man who will come "with his angels in the glory of his Father" to repay each one in accordance with his deeds (16:27). Some of the disciples will even live to see the Son of Man coming with his kingdom (16:28). In that new age, the royal Son of Man will be seated on his glorious throne, and his disciples will be enthroned to judge the twelve tribes of Israel (19:28).

This use of Son of Man in Matthew's Gospel can be viewed from two vantage points. *Within the narrative,* it is the distinctive way that Jesus refers to himself when speaking of his destiny to suffer, die, be raised from the dead, and return at the end of the ages as God's royal eschatological judge.[73] The characters within the narrative never question Jesus' use of this expression nor do they ever employ it to identify Jesus. *From the point of view of Matthew's audience,* however, Son of Man has become a technical term which can now be used as a title to identify Jesus as God's eschatological judge. Thus, when believers refer to Jesus as the one who will return to judge the nations, they identify him as the Son of Man.

But this Son of Man is none other than the Son of God, and his kingdom is the final establishment of God's rule.[74] When the Son of Man returns, he will come with *his Father's* angels (16:27). At the transfiguration, the heavenly voice identifies Jesus as "my beloved Son" (17:5). Then, in his discourse on church life, Jesus explicitly refers to God as his heavenly Father three times (18:10, 19, 35). The one who calls himself the Son of Man, then, is preeminently the Son of God.

Because he is preeminently God's Son, Jesus promises that where two or three of his disciples gather in his name, he is present in their midst (18:20), thereby recalling the promise contained in his name, Emmanuel (see 1:23). Because he is preeminently the Son of God, it is not necessary for Jesus or his disciples (who are sons of their heavenly Father) to pay the temple tax (17:24–27). Most important, because he is the Son of God, Jesus can say that the Son of Man came to give his life as a ransom for many (20:28), thereby recalling the purpose of his mission: to save his people from their sins (1:21).

The use of "Son of Man" adds a new dimension to the Christology of this narrative because it clarifies the Messiah's destiny to suffer, die, be raised from the dead, and return at the end of the ages. From the perspective of the resurrection, believers identify Jesus as the Son of Man, for they know that the Son of Man is the Messiah, the Son of the living God (16:16).[75]

The Messiah's Rejection and Vindication (21:1–28:20)

The final portion of Matthew's story narrates the fulfillment of the events that Jesus predicted. The Messiah enters Jerusalem as its messianic king only to be rejected and put to death. Jesus' apparent defeat, however, paradoxically becomes the means by which he fulfills the commission contained in his name to save his people from their sins (1:21) since he dies for the forgiveness of sins (26:28). Therefore, God vindicates the obedience of his beloved Son by raising him from the dead and giving him all authority in heaven and on earth (28:18). Thus the stage is set for the final act of God's salvation history when, at the parousia of the Son of Man, the kingdom of heaven will be established in power.

The Messiah's Ministry in Jerusalem (21:1–25:46)

The Matthean narrator portrays Jesus' messianic entry into Jerusalem in a manner that shatters conventional messianic expectations. Although Jesus arrives as Israel's king, he enters Jerusalem as the meek and humble king foretold by the prophet Zechariah: "Look, your king is coming to you, humble, and mounted on a donkey, and on a colt, the foal of a donkey" (Matt. 21:5, quoting Zech. 9:9). The description of Jesus as the meek (*praus*) king of Israel recalls Jesus' third beatitude that the meek will inherit the land (5:5) and his description of himself as meek and humble of heart (11:29).[76] Israel's messiah will not be a powerful warrior king who will dislodge foreign invaders[77] but a servant-king who saves his people from their sins by pouring out his blood on their behalf (26:28).

When this servant-king enters Jerusalem, he cures the blind and the lame in the temple precincts (21:14), and children hail him as the Son of David, angering Israel's religious leaders. Although the Messiah is more than the Son of David, as Jesus will show (22:41–46), it is an acceptable way of addressing Jesus. Moreover, those who identify or call upon Jesus as the Son of David in Matthew's story are usually people of little social status: the blind (9:27; 20:30–31), a foreign woman (15:22), children (21:15). By having them address Jesus as the Son of David, the Matthean narrator shows that, whereas people of little account recognize Jesus as Israel's Messiah, Israel's religious leaders, who should know better, do not.[78]

Because Israel's leaders do not accept what the children proclaim—that Jesus is the Son of David—Jesus' ministry to Jerusalem is a time of conflict with its religious leaders, who question his authority (21:23). Jesus' response is a series of parables (21:28–22:14), two of which have important christological implications. One shows that Jesus is the Son sent by the Father, destined to inherit the vineyard of Israel. Because Israel has not accepted him, the kingdom of God will be taken from it and given to a nation that will bear fruit (21:33–46). The other parable shows that Jesus is the Son for whom the heavenly king has prepared the wedding feast of the kingdom. Because Israel refused the invitation to the kingdom, however, the invitation has been extended to all nations (22:1–14).

Jesus concludes his Jerusalem ministry with a severe denunciation of the scribes and Pharisees (23:1–39) and a final discourse that looks to the period between his resurrection and glorious return as the royal Son of Man (24:1–25:46). He denounces the scribes and Pharisees because their deeds do not correspond to their words. Therefore, while disciples should do what they say, disciples should not imitate their deeds. As regards teaching, however, Jesus' disciples have one teacher and instructor, and he is the Messiah (23:8–10).

Jesus has already taught his disciples by four major discourses: the Sermon on the Mount, the missionary discourse, the parable discourse, and the discourse on church life. In his fifth and last discourse, the Messiah looks to the future and instructs his followers how to conduct themselves as they await the parousia of the Son of Man. This final teaching contains an important Christology that focuses on the royal Son of Man.

The discourse is a response to the disciples' question: "Tell us, when will this be [the destruction of the Temple], and what will be the sign of your coming (*parousia*) and of the end of the ages?" (24:3). The ensuing discourse indicates that there will be a period of trial and tribulation during which pseudo-messiahs and pseudo-prophets will deceive many and the disciples will be hated on account of Jesus' name. But the end will not come as quickly as some expect since the good news of the kingdom must be preached first to all nations (24:4–14). When the Temple is finally laid waste, it will be time to flee Judea. But the disciples should not be mislead by pseudo-messiahs and pseudo-prophets (24:15–28), for the Son of Man

41

will come in a way that no one can mistake: on the clouds of heaven with power and great glory to gather the elect (24:29–31).

Despite this detailed scenario, Jesus warns that only the Father knows the exact time of the Son of Man's parousia (24:36); consequently disciples must conduct themselves as vigilant and industrious servants in the period preceding their Lord's return (see the teaching and parables of 24:37–25:30). But when the Son of Man arrives, he will come in glory with his angels. Then, seated upon his glorious throne, he will judge the nations of the earth (25:31–46). At that moment, the kingdom of heaven will be established in full power, and no one will be able to deny Jesus' authority as the exalted Lord of heaven and earth.[79]

In this final discourse, Jesus ascribes a glorious future to himself as God's eschatological judge, when he will act with God's own power and authority. Nonetheless, he remains subservient to the Father, for not even the Son knows when these events will take place (24:36). Before they occur, however, the Son of God must obediently surrender his life upon the cross.

The Messiah's Death and Resurrection (26:1–28:20)

Jesus' passion is the final testing of the Son of God. As Satan tested the obedience of God's Son in the wilderness, the Passion tests the determination of the Son to fulfill his messianic destiny.

This passion narrative is the repository of a rich Christology that portrays Jesus as the obedient Son of God who pours out his blood for the forgiveness of sins.[80] In the Garden of Gethsemane, he addresses God as "my Father" and asks that the cup of suffering be removed, but then adds, "yet not what I want but what you want" (26:39). When arrested, he knows that he can appeal to his Father for more than twelve legions of angels, but he does not do so, so that the scriptures can be fulfilled (26:53–54). Before the Sanhedrin, he does not deny that he is the Messiah, the Son of God, and he prophesies that he will return as the Son of Man at the right hand of Power, coming with the clouds of heaven (26:64).[81] After Judas betrays Jesus, he admits that he has betrayed innocent blood (27:4), and Pilate's wife calls Jesus a "righteous man" (27:19, RSV). Nevertheless, when faced with a choice between Jesus called Messiah and Barabbas, the people of Israel choose the latter (27:22–26).

As Jesus hangs from the cross, the passersby and the chief priests test the Son of God, as did Satan in the wilderness (see 4:3, 6).

If you are the Son of God, come down from the cross. (27:40)

He trusts in God; let God deliver him now, if he wants to; for he said, "I am God's Son." (27:43)

But just as Jesus, the new Israel, refused to trust in his own power while in the wilderness, so the obedient Son of God refuses to save himself by descending from the cross. Instead, he cries out to his Father with the opening words of Psalm 22 (27:46), and then dies with a loud cry (27:50). The death of God's obedient Son results in apocalyptic signs (the tearing of the temple curtain, an earthquake that opens the tombs of Israel's holy ones). The shaking of the earth leads the Gentile centurion and those about him to acknowledge that Jesus was truly the Son of God (27:51–54).

This confession is not the moment of christological disclosure that it is in Mark's Gospel, where the centurion is the first human being to confess that Jesus was God's Son (Mark 15:39). But the apocalyptic signs surrounding the confession of the centurion and those with him are more dramatic and clearly indicate that the time of the Gentiles is at hand.

The resurrection is God's vindication of Jesus' obedient death. Despite the efforts of the chief priests and Pharisees to secure the tomb, God raises Jesus from the dead. This resurrection is never described, but when the women arrive at the tomb, there is an earthquake (as there was at Jesus' death) because the angel of the Lord descends from heaven and rolls away the stone. He then tells the women that the crucified one has been raised, just as he said (28:6).

When the risen Lord meets the women, he instructs them to tell his disciples that he is going to Galilee, where they will see him (28:10). Then, at the mountain in Galilee, the eleven disciples worship the risen Lord, although some appear to have harbored doubts (28:17).

In his great commission (28:18–20), the risen Lord to whom all authority has been given commands the disciples to make disciples of all the nations by baptizing them and teaching them to keep all that he has commanded them. Then, alluding to the promise contained in the name "Emmanuel" (see 1:23), he promises to be with them until the end of the age.

This final scene resolves the remaining issues of the narrative and marks a new beginning. The time of the Messiah's exclusive mission to Israel (15:24) has ended, and the time of the church's universal mission to the nations has begun. Jesus the Messiah inaugurated the kingdom of heaven by his ministry of teaching, preaching, and healing, and he saved his people from their sins by his death and resurrection. But now his disciples must make disciples of all nations as they await the Son of Man, who will gather the elect and judge the nations at his parousia. Then the kingdom of Satan will be destroyed and God's rule established in power and glory.

Christology in Matthew's Gospel

Matthew's narrative Christology follows the main lines of Markan Christology: Jesus the Messiah is preeminently the Son of God who must suffer, die, and be raised from the dead so that he can return in glory at the end of the ages to gather his elect. But in retelling the story of Jesus, Matthew has enriched Mark's Christology in several ways.

Jesus Messiah, the Son of David

Matthew is firmly convinced that Jesus is Israel's long-expected Messiah. Consequently, he begins his narrative with a detailed genealogy that divides Israel's history into three parts: from Abraham to David; from David to the exile; from the exile to the Messiah. The appearance of the Messiah, therefore, is the culmination of Israel's history, and Jesus is this Messiah.

Although Jesus was conceived through the power of God's Spirit, Matthew insists that Jesus is a royal descendant of David since Joseph adopted him into David's royal lineage. Jesus the Messiah, then, is a royal descendant of David who was born in David's city of Bethlehem, as the prophet foretold. But this royal descendant of David is not the powerful warrior Messiah that many expected. He comes to inaugurate the kingdom of heaven and lay waste to Satan's rule. "The works of the Messiah" (11:2) are teaching, preaching, and healing, all of which promote the in-breaking of God's rule.

The Davidic Messiah of Israel comes as one who takes the infirmities of his people upon himself (8:17). He is a servant who proclaims justice to the nations (12:18–21). He does not enter the royal city of Jerusalem as a powerful warrior but as a humble and meek king (21:5). Consequently, it is people of little social status (the blind, a Canaanite woman, the children of Jerusalem), rather than Israel's leaders, who recognize Jesus as the son of David.

Jesus Messiah, the Obedient Son of God

As the Davidic Messiah, Jesus is preeminently the obedient Son of God. Conceived by the power of God's Spirit, he has a unique relationship to God that distinguishes him from all others. His relationship with God is so intimate that no one knows the Son except the Father, and no one knows the Father except the Son and those to whom the Son wishes to reveal the Father (11:27).

The Father himself identifies Jesus as his beloved Son in whom he is well pleased (3:17; 17:5). This divine pleasure is the result of the Son's obedience.

Tested by Satan in the wilderness (4:3, 6), as well as by those who deride him at his crucifixion (27:40, 43), Jesus demonstrates that he is the Son of God by obediently trusting in the power of God to save him. Even when faced with the prospect of a fearful death, he submits himself to his Father's will (26:42).

As the obedient Son of God who does the will of his Father by fulfilling all righteousness (3:15), Jesus shows his disciples how they can become sons of their heavenly Father by doing a righteousness that surpasses that of the scribes and Pharisees. To be sure, he enjoys a unique relationship to God that distinguishes him from his disciples. But if the disciples imitate Jesus' obedience, they will truly be sons of their heavenly Father.

Although the disciples confess that Jesus is the Son of God (14:33; 16:16), it is doubtful that they understand the full significance of their confession since Jesus has not yet been raised from the dead. But they have begun to recognize Jesus' unique relationship to God even if they do not comprehend its full implications.

Because it is a narrative, the Gospel of Matthew does not provide a systematic reflection upon the nature of Jesus' sonship. It does not explain the relationship between Jesus and God; instead, it describes the perfect obedience of the Son who comes to inaugurate God's rule by a ministry of teaching, preaching, healing, and by freely surrendering his life for the forgiveness of sins.

Jesus Messiah, the Teacher of Righteousness

Jesus begins his messianic ministry by proclaiming the kingdom of heaven (4:17) and providing his disciples with an extended teaching on the greater righteousness that the kingdom requires (5:1–7:28). Thus the Sermon on the Mount portrays Jesus as the teacher of righteousness par excellence. In six antitheses (5:21–48), he places his words on a par with those spoken by God to the wilderness generation through Moses, and in every instance he requires his disciples to practice a righteousness that transcends the demands of the law. When speaking of almsgiving, prayer, and fasting (6:1–18), he shows his disciples how to practice a righteousness that only their heavenly Father will see and reward. Then at the conclusion of the sermon, he warns disciples that only those who do the will of *his* heavenly Father will enter the kingdom of heaven (7:21).

Although Jesus does not make explicit christological claims in the Sermon on the Mount, his teaching on righteousness is implicitly christological.[82] On the one hand, by proclaiming the blessings of the kingdom in his beatitudes, Jesus fulfills Israel's prophetic promises. On the other, by teaching a way of righteousness that surpasses that of the scribes and Pharisees, he shows that he has an understanding of God's will that is only accessible to one who is God's Messiah. Thus it is not surprising that the crowds are astonished at his teaching, for Jesus teaches with an authority unknown to their scribes (7:29).

Jesus Messiah, the Savior of God's People

Matthew's Christology is a redemptive Christology.[83] Not only does it inform readers of Jesus' identity, it clearly explains what he has done for humanity. Put most simply, Jesus effects the forgiveness of sins by inaugurating God's kingdom through his messianic ministry and his saving death and resurrection.

The name "Jesus" indicates what the Messiah must do: save his people from their sins (1:21). To accomplish this, the Messiah calls Israel to repentance, because the kingdom of heaven is at hand (4:17), and teaches his disciples a greater righteousness than that of the scribes and Pharisees so that they can enter the kingdom of heaven (5:20). But to effect the forgiveness of sins, the Messiah must surrender his life as a ransom for others (20:28) and shed his blood for the forgiveness of sins (26:28). Thus, while the kingdom is inaugurated by Jesus' ministry of teaching, preaching, and healing, the forgiveness of sins is effected by Jesus' obediently surrendering his life on the cross.

The church plays a vital role in the drama of redemption in the period between Jesus' resurrection and parousia. Commissioned by its risen Lord to make disciples of all nations, its ministry extends the forgiveness of sins to others. Assured of the continuing presence of its risen Lord (1:23; 18:20; 28:20), the church makes disciples of all nations by baptizing them in the name of the Father, the Son, and the Holy Spirit, and teaching them all that Jesus has commanded (28:18–20).

Although the Gospel of Matthew never explicitly calls Jesus "savior," Jesus' ministry clearly effects salvation for his people. By teaching, preaching, and healing, he inaugurates God's rule and frees people from Satan's rule; by dying upon the cross he effects the forgiveness of sins. But who are the beneficiaries of this salvation? The words of the infancy narrative, "for he will save his people from their sins" (1:21) suggest the people of Israel. But the ending of Matthew's story indicates that "his people" now includes all who will become Jesus' disciples, Gentiles as well as Jews. Thus the Jewish Messiah becomes the savior of the nations.

Jesus Messiah, the Eschatological Judge

Matthew's story of Jesus is opened-ended inasmuch as the final phase of the story is not yet concluded, for Jesus the glorious Son of Man must still return at the close of the ages to gather his disciples and judge the nations.

46

Intimations of this future occur throughout the story. For example, Jesus' parable of the weeds with its allegorical explanation (13:24–30, 36–43) clearly indicates that the Son of Man will return at the close of the ages to separate the children of the kingdom from the children of the evil one. Likewise, Jesus' fifth and final discourse (24:1–25:46) teaches disciples that they must be vigilant servants because the Son of Man will return when they least expect to judge them and the nations.

Indications of Jesus' eschatological role as judge occur throughout Matthew's narrative and remind readers that the end of the story is also the beginning of a new and critical phase in God's dealing with his people: the Messiah, the Son of God, is the exalted Lord of the church who will return as the glorious Son of Man. The precise relationship between Lord and Messiah on the one hand, and the confessional titles listed above, on the other, may be explained as follows.

While Jesus' opponents regularly address him as teacher or rabbi, his disciples address him as Lord. For disciples living after the time of the resurrection, Jesus Messiah, the Son of God, is the Lord of his church because God has raised him from the dead. The use of Lord during the course of Jesus' earthly ministry, then, indicates the extent to which the Matthean narrator views the story of Jesus in light of the resurrection: the earthly Jesus already speaks and acts with the authority of the risen Lord.

The frequent references in Matthew's Gospel to Jesus as the Son of Man should be interpreted in light of Jesus' work and destiny.[84] Son of Man is not a messianic or confessional title in the way that Messiah or Son of God is, since no one confesses that Jesus is the Son of Man. Moreover, the characters of the narrative never register surprise when Jesus refers to himself as the Son of Man. Rather, Son of Man is Jesus' chosen self-designation to indicate what he does, or what he must do, as the messianic Son of God. Son of Man is especially used in conjunction with Jesus' return at the close of the ages to gather the elect and judge the nations.[85] While the characters of the story do not confess Jesus as the Son of Man, the term may well have become a title for Matthew's church, which waits for the return of Jesus, the glorious Son of Man.

Titles and terms such as "Son of God," "Messiah," "son of David," and "Son of Man" play an important role in Matthew's story, but the Gospel's Christology should not be reduced to them, as important as they are. What Jesus does is as important as the titles ascribed to him. The central focus of Matthew's Gospel is upon Jesus as the one who fulfills the scriptures of Israel, teaches his disciples a greater righteousness, inaugurates the kingdom of God, and saves his people from their sins.[86]

2

Messiah and Lord of All

*I*n the previous chapter, I suggested that old stories can generate new ones. Thus, when narrators retell stories, they are creating new stories. The Gospel of Matthew, we have seen, is more than a simple retelling of Mark's story; it is a new narrative with its own plot, characters, and setting. The same is true of the Gospel of Luke. The Lukan narrator follows the basic outline of his Markan predecessor, but in retelling the story he omits material from the old narrative, introduces new episodes, and arranges others in a different way.[1] Consequently, the story he recounts is a new narrative with a distinctive christological point of view.[2]

But in addition to retelling Mark's story of Jesus, the Lukan narrator recounts the story of the church in a second volume, the Acts of the Apostles. In doing so, he relates events to which Mark and Matthew allude but never describe: the time after Jesus' resurrection.[3] Thus, the Lukan narrator extends the story of Jesus by recounting the vital role that the risen Lord plays in the life of the early church. But is there a narrative unity between the Gospel of Luke and the Acts of the Apostles? Can we speak of a single, uninterrupted story, or do these writings represent different stories: the story of Jesus *and* the story of his church?

The modern designation of these two works as "Luke-Acts" suggests that there is a narrative unity that binds them together.[4] A good indication of this is the way in which the Lukan narrator begins his second volume: "In the first book (*prōton logon*), Theophilus, I wrote about all that Jesus did and taught from the beginning until the day when he was taken up to heaven, after giving instructions through the Holy Spirit to the apostles whom he had chosen" (Acts 1:1–2). This brief résumé of the Gospel, in which the narrator once more addresses Theophilus (see Luke 1:3), suggests that he is resuming the narrative begun in the Gospel. But is it the same story? The answer to this question is not so clear.

On the one hand, there is a narrative unity between the Gospel of Luke and the Acts of the Apostles inasmuch as Acts completes the important themes that the Gospel introduces.[5] For example, at the end of the Gospel the risen Lord instructs his disciples to remain in Jerusalem until they have been "clothed with power from on high" (Luke 24:49). Then, in the Acts of the Apostles, the disciples are clothed with power from on high when the Spirit descends upon them at Pentecost (Acts 2:1–12). Here, the Gospel clearly points to an event that finds its fulfillment in the Acts of the Apostles.

On the other hand, the Gospel, as well as Acts, can claim a literary integrity of its own.[6] For example, although the Gospel concludes with an account of Jesus' ascension on Easter Sunday (Luke 24:50–53), the Lukan narrator begins Acts with a new account of the Lord's ascension, which occurs forty days after the resurrection (Acts 1:6–11)! While this time discrepancy is confusing for anyone who tries to establish the actual course of events, it is not as confusing from a purely literary point of view. The ascension account of the Gospel brings closure to a narrative line introduced at the beginning of Jesus' journey to Jerusalem (Luke 9:51), whereas the ascension account of Acts provides the starting point of the disciples' witness to Jerusalem, Judea, Samaria, and the ends of the earth (Acts 1:8). Thus, while one account of the ascension brings literary closure, the other inaugurates a new narrative.

The story of Luke's Gospel clearly focuses upon the person of the earthly Jesus, whereas the story of Acts recounts the church's witness to the risen Lord, especially the witness of Paul and the Twelve. Both writings have their own story to tell. But Luke and Acts also possess a narrative unity, inasmuch as the person of Jesus is the indispensable character in both writings. The risen Lord to whom the church witnesses cannot be separated from the earthly Jesus who called this community into being. Thus Luke-Acts is akin to the Deuteronomistic history of the Old Testament.[7] While the individual writings of that history have their own story to tell, there is an overarching unity that holds their several stories together.

The upshot of this discussion is as follows. In Luke-Acts we are dealing with two stories that have a narrative unity rooted in the person of Jesus. One relates the ministry, death, resurrection, and ascension of the earthly Jesus;

the other recounts the church's witness to the risen Lord. Although the followers of Jesus play a greater role in one story than in the other, the risen Lord, who is one with the earthly Jesus, brings narrative unity to both writings. Luke's Christology is embedded in these stories to which we now turn.

THE GOSPEL OF LUKE

The Gospel of Luke begins with an elegant prologue (1:1–4) in which the narrator explains his purpose: to provide readers with assurance (*asphaleian*) about the events concerning Jesus that have recently transpired.[8] To accomplish this, Luke has written an orderly account, after carefully examining everything. And indeed, when compared to Mark's story of Jesus, the Gospel of Luke is a more orderly narrative that can be outlined as follows.

1:5–2:52	The birth and childhood of God's Messiah
3:1–4:13	The initial appearance of God's Messiah
4:14–9:50	The ministry of God's Messiah in Galilee
9:51–19:44	The journey of God's Messiah to Jerusalem
19:45–21:38	The ministry of God's Messiah in Jerusalem
22:1–24:53	The passion, death, resurrection, and ascension of God's Messiah

As in the Gospels of Mark and Matthew, there is a conflict between Jesus the Messiah who proclaims the kingdom of God and those to whom he announces his message. There is also a deeper, underlying conflict between the kingdom of God and the power of Satan, who holds humanity in bondage. But the plot of Luke's Gospel is not a mere repetition of the plot that controls the Gospel of Mark. The manner in which Luke has ordered the events of his story produces a narrative with a plot that can be summarized as follows.

The Messiah of God comes to his people Israel as the Spirit-anointed Son of God with a gracious offer of salvation: the forgiveness of sins. Despite this gracious offer, Israel does not repent. Nonetheless, its rejection of the Messiah paradoxically fulfills God's plan that the Messiah must suffer in order to enter into his glory so that repentance and forgiveness can be preached in his name to all nations.

The ending of this story provides the narrative line for the Acts of the Apostles, where the Messiah's disciples offer Israel a second opportunity to repent and enjoy the blessings of salvation. Although a significant portion of Israel turns to the Messiah, another remains unrepentant. As a result, the ending of Acts suggests the opening of yet another story that Luke does not tell, a further offer of salvation to the nations.

The Fulfillment of God's Promises (1:5–2:52)

The opening of Luke's Gospel raises an intriguing question: Who were the intended readers for whom the Evangelist wrote? Were they Gentile or Jewish Christians, or both? While the rest of Luke-Acts seems to indicate that Luke was writing for a predominantly Gentile audience, the atmosphere created by the Lukan infancy narrative is thoroughly Jewish.[9] The announcement of salvation occurs in the heart of Israel, the Temple of Jerusalem. Moreover, this salvation is the fulfillment of promises made to Abraham (1:55), takes place within the house of David (1:69), and is good news for those awaiting the redemption of God's people (1:68; 2:38). To be sure, there are also indications that this salvation will be extended to Gentiles (2:32),[10] but not even this overture to the nations can alter the clear message of the Lukan infancy narrative: that the birth of Jesus, the Davidic Messiah, fulfills God's promises to Israel and portends the redemption of God's people. This, it seems to me, is the proper starting point for investigating Luke's Christology.[11]

The Lukan infancy narrative reads like a writing from the Old Testament, the beginning of the final and glorious chapter in the story of Israel's monarchy. The story starts where it will end, in the Temple of Jerusalem (1:8–9; 24:53), when the angel of the Lord informs the aged Zechariah that he and his barren wife, Elizabeth, will have a child who will prepare a people fit for the Lord (1:17). The first to learn of God's coming salvation, then, are pious Israelites who have faithfully observed the commandments of the law (1:6).

The angel of the Lord announces the birth of the Messiah to the virgin named Mary, in Nazareth of Galilee (1:26–38). Mary will conceive a son whom she must name Jesus. The child will be called the Son of the Most High God, and the Lord will give him the throne of David his father so that he can rule over the house of Jacob forever. The biblically literate reader will immediately recognize that the angel's message is the fulfillment of messianic promises made to David through the prophet Nathan (2 Sam. 7:12–16).[12] Thus the narrative begins with messianic expectations that Mary's child will restore the Davidic monarchy. Exactly what this means, however, is not clear, since the throne of David had been vacant for centuries. Moreover, Mary is a virgin.

When Mary inquires how this can be, the angel informs her that the Holy Spirit will come upon her, and the power of the Most High will overshadow her. Thus her son will be called God's Son (1:34–35). Although important questions remain, it is apparent that Mary's child will not be just another Davidic king. This child will be God's Son, and his kingdom will have no end. How his enthronement will occur, however, is not yet clear.

The meeting of Mary and Elizabeth brings the two mothers together and provides further christological information. Although Elizabeth has not been privy to the angel's announcement, she already calls Mary "the mother of my Lord" (1:43), thereby anticipating the manner in which believers will address the risen Christ. Mary's canticle is thoroughly "theological," focusing on the mighty acts of the Savior God who is already effecting a reversal of fortunes. Although she does not understand all that happens, Mary recognizes that the action of God in her life is the first stage in the fulfillment of the promises made to Abraham and his descendants. The first part of the infancy narrative clearly indicates that the birth of the Messiah and his predecessor is the continuation of God's faithfulness to Israel and not a disruption of salvation history. Jesus is the Davidic Messiah who will fulfill the promises God made to Abraham.

The stories of the birth and circumcision of John and Jesus continue the process of "building up" Luke's Christology. In his prophetic canticle (1:68–79), Zechariah blesses the God of Israel who has brought redemption to his people by raising up a horn of salvation (a savior) within the house of David. The appearance of this Davidic savior will bring Israel salvation from its enemies so that it can worship God in holiness and righteousness in accordance with the covenant God made with Abraham.[13]

The birth of the Messiah in David's city of Bethlehem is the result of a royal decree from the "savior" of the secular world, Caesar Augustus. Consequently, although Jesus' parents live in Nazareth, they must go to the city of David, since Joseph, the putative father of Jesus, is of Davidic lineage (2:1–7). Thus Luke explains that even though Jesus was reared in Nazareth (4:16), he was born in David's city of Bethlehem, as befits the Messiah.[14]

The first to learn of the Messiah's birth are shepherds, as was David of old (2:8–20). Even though they are socially marginalized (or perhaps precisely because they are), the angel of the Lord announces the good news of the gospel to them: that a savior has been born for them, who is Messiah and Lord (2:11). The confluence of these three titles (Savior, Messiah, Lord) is the christological climax of the infancy narrative. Although Jesus will never again be called Savior within the Gospel narrative,[15] it is apparent that he is the true Savior of his people rather than Caesar Augustus. The language of the angel's announcement indicates that the one who is the Savior is both Messiah and Lord, a point Peter will reiterate at Pentecost (Acts 2:36). While "Messiah" indicates the specifically Jewish nature of Jesus' salvific role, "Lord" anticipates the royal enthronement of the Messiah and describes how believers view the crucified Messiah in light of the resurrection.

Because Jesus is the Jewish Messiah, his law-observant parents have him circumcised and presented to the Lord in accordance with the prescriptions of the law (2:21–24). In describing these events, the Lukan narrator makes a point the other Evangelists do not: Jesus is the circumcised Messiah! This is of no little significance given the fierce battles that Paul waged over circumcision and the decision of the Jerusalem church not to require circumcision of Gentiles (Acts 15); it is another indication that Jesus is Israel's Messiah.

The events surrounding Jesus' circumcision and presentation develop his significance for Israel further. In the Temple of Jerusalem, the aged Simeon recognizes that Jesus is the Lord's Messiah (2:26; see 9:20 where Peter identifies Jesus in a similar way), a light of revelation for the Gentiles and glory for the people of Israel (2:32). Similarly, the temple prophetess, Anna, recognizes the redemptive role that Jesus will play, and she speaks of him to all who were waiting for the redemption of Jerusalem (2:38).

The account of the twelve-year-old Jesus sitting in the midst of the Temple's teachers (2:41–52) is not part of the infancy narrative proper. But it does provide a transition between the infancy account and Jesus' adult life by showing how the child "grew and became strong, filled with wisdom" (2:40; also see 2:52). The conversation between Jesus and his distraught parents indicates that the twelve-year-old child is already aware that the Temple is his Father's house, and he is God's Son. At this point, the child only sits and asks questions of the religious leaders, but as an adult he will take possession of his Father's house and teach the people of Israel daily in its precincts (19:45–48).

The theology of the Lukan infancy narrative can be described, somewhat paradoxically, as an Old Testament Christology, for it portrays Jesus as the Lord's Messiah, the royal descendant of David, the savior and redeemer of his people Israel. Ultimately, however, it is a New Testament Christology that clearly identifies the Lord's Messiah as God's Son. Thus Luke brings forth old things as well as new. With his feet firmly planted in the story of Israel, he narrates a story that will eventually incorporate the nations as well. The Messiah of Israel will be a savior for Gentiles as well as Jews.

The Appearance of God's
Spirit-Anointed Messiah (3:1–4:13)

In a style reminiscent of the prophets, the Lukan narrator carefully dates the precise moment when the Word of God came to John, the son of Zechariah, in the desert (3:1–2).[16] While this chronological statement undoubtedly provides Luke's audience with a sense of historical reliability, it also roots the events that will follow in Israel's prophetic tradition. As his father prophesied, John is the prophet of the Most High; he has come to prepare the way of the Lord by proclaiming a baptism of repentance for the forgiveness of sins (1:76–77; 3:3). But since the people have not been privy to the events of the infancy narrative, they wonder if John is the expected Messiah (3:15). Aware of their unspoken questions, John assures them that he is not the Messiah, for one more powerful than himself will come, who will baptize them with Holy Spirit and fire, separating what is good from what is evil (3:15–17).

In order to draw a distinction between the time of John and the time of the Messiah, the Lukan narrator (before introducing Jesus) reports that Herod imprisoned John (3:19–20).[17] Consequently, even though the reader can suppose that John baptized Jesus, there is no description of this event.[18] Moreover, by omitting any direct mention of John baptizing the Messiah, the Lukan narrator forestalls any suggestion that John's baptism was responsible for the anointing of the Messiah with God's Spirit. Rather, the descent of the Spirit upon the Messiah and the Father's declaration that Jesus is his beloved Son are more closely related to Jesus' prayer than to his baptism by John.[19]

> Now when all the people were baptized, and when Jesus had also been baptized and was praying, the heaven was opened, and the Holy Spirit descended upon him in bodily form like a dove. And a voice came from heaven, "You are my Son, the Beloved; with you I am well pleased." (3:21–22)

Having described Jesus as the Spirit-anointed Messiah, the Son of God in whom the Father is well pleased, Luke provides his readers with a genealogy that begins with Joseph and traces Jesus' lineage through David and Abraham to Adam.[20] Although the genealogy is impressive in its historical sweep, the Lukan narrator subverts it with a single comment: "Jesus was about thirty years old when he began his work. He was the son (*as was thought*) of Joseph" (3:23). Jesus is not the physical descendant of Joseph since he was conceived through the power of God's Spirit. Joseph has merely adopted him into the line of David. Consequently, the genealogy identifies Jesus as a descendant of David and Abraham, but its primary purpose is to confirm Jesus' divine sonship. The Messiah who is son of Joseph, son of David, son of Abraham, son of Adam, is preeminently Son of God (3:38).

The emphasis upon Jesus' sonship continues in the account of his testing in the wilderness. Filled with the Holy Spirit (4:1), the Son of God is led by the Spirit into the wilderness where the devil tests him. To test Jesus' divine sonship, the devil begins his first and last temptations in the following way: "If you are the Son of God" (4:3, 9). As in Matthew's Gospel, Jesus shows that he is God's Son by faithful obedience rather than a display of divine power. As a result, the devil leaves him until an opportune time, the Passion, Jesus' last and greatest test (4:13; see 22:3).

The initial appearance of John and Jesus confirms what the infancy narrative has already proclaimed. John is the prophet of the Most High, the precursor of the Messiah, whereas Jesus is the Son of the Most High, the promised Messiah. These episodes also highlight the continuing role of God's Spirit, for Jesus the Son of God is the Spirit-anointed Messiah. Empowered by the Spirit, he has been anointed for a messianic ministry.

A Gracious Offer of Salvation (4:14–9:50)

After his baptism and testing in the wilderness, Jesus returns to Galilee empowered by the Spirit (4:14; also see 3:22; 4:1), where he teaches in synagogues. In the synagogue of Nazareth he reads from the prophet Isaiah and boldly proclaims that this prophetic text finds its fulfillment in his messianic ministry "today" (4:16–21).[21]

> The Spirit of the Lord is upon me, because he has anointed me to bring good news to the poor. He has sent me to proclaim release to the captives and recovery of sight to the blind, to let the oppressed go free, to proclaim the year of the Lord's favor.[22]

Several chapters later, when the disciples of John tell him all that Jesus has been doing, the Baptist (evidently puzzled by Jesus' ministry) sends two of his disciples to ask, "Are you the one who is to come, or are we to wait for another?" (7:19). In response, Jesus answers:

> Go and tell John what you have seen and heard: the blind receive their sight, the lame walk, the lepers are cleansed, the deaf hear, the dead are raised, the poor have good news brought to them. And blessed is anyone who takes no offense at me. (7:22–23)

In responding to John, Jesus is clearly recalling his messianic program described in the synagogue of Nazareth. He is God's Messiah, even though he does not immediately effect the apocalyptic judgment that John expects (3:16–17). Instead, his ministry consists of preaching good news to the poor, healing the sick, freeing people from Satan's bondage, restoring sight to the blind, and announcing a year of favor; that is, the forgiveness of sins. Because this kind of ministry has the potential of being misunderstood and falling short of messianic expectations, Jesus pronounces a beatitude upon those who are not scandalized by such a messiah.

The warning implied in this beatitude, however, is of no avail. At the very outset of Jesus' ministry, the citizens of Nazareth reject him despite his gracious words, because they only know him as "the son of Joseph" (4:22).[23] Thus the episode at Nazareth establishes a pattern for the Messiah's ministry. The Spirit-anointed Messiah comes to the people of Israel with a gracious offer of salvation but is misunderstood and rejected. From Jesus' point of view this is merely the repetition of an old pattern experienced by the prophets Elijah and Elisha, who extended salvation to foreigners because the people of Israel rejected them (4:24–27). And so this gracious offer of salvation will be given to others, if Israel rejects its Messiah.

Despite being rejected at Nazareth, the Messiah carries out his messianic ministry to Israel in the land of Galilee (4:14–9:50). He expels demons (4:31–37), cures the sick (4:38–41), proclaims the good news of the kingdom (4:42–44), calls disciples (5:1–11), cleanses lepers (5:12–16), forgives sins (5:17–26), summons sinners to repentance (5:27–32), chooses twelve of his disciples to be apostles (6:12–16), preaches a great sermon that is good news for the poor (6:20–49), and even raises the dead (7:11–17).

Israel's response to its Messiah is mixed. On the one hand, people recognize the authority and power of Jesus' word (4:36); they glorify God on behalf of him (5:26); they acknowledge Jesus as a great prophet and exclaim that God has visited his people (7:16–17). On the other hand, the scribes and Pharisees question the right of Jesus to forgive sins (5:21; 7:49), his table fellowship with tax collectors and sinners (5:30), and his behavior on the Sabbath (6:1–11). Moreover, shortly after the people proclaim that Jesus is a great prophet, Simon the Pharisee questions if Jesus is truly a prophet since he allows a sinful woman to touch him (7:39). In Jesus' judgment, Israel's response has been inconsistent. Having accused John of being possessed because he was ascetical, Israel criticizes Jesus as a drunkard and a glutton because of his table fellowship with sinners (7:31–35). Clearly, Israel has not understood the nature of Jesus' messianic ministry.

Toward the end of Jesus' Galilean ministry, therefore, the question of his identity comes to center stage. While some speculate that he is John raised from the dead, others say that Elijah has appeared, or one of the prophets of old has arisen. But Herod is perplexed. Acknowledging that he beheaded John, he asks, "who is this about whom I hear such things?" (9:9).[24]

Herod's question receives a series of answers in the rest of chapter 9. [25] First, Peter correctly confesses that Jesus is "the Messiah of God" (9:20), recalling Simeon's words about "the Lord's Messiah" (2:26). Second, Jesus teaches his disciples that as God's Messiah the Son of Man must suffer, be rejected by Israel's leaders, and be raised from the dead. Third, at his transfiguration Jesus discusses with Moses and Elijah the "exodus" he is about to accomplish at Jerusalem (9:31),[26] and the Father once more declares that Jesus is his beloved Son (9:35; see 3:22). Finally, before making his great journey to Jerusalem, Jesus instructs his disciples that the Son of Man will be betrayed (9:44).[27]

By the conclusion of Jesus' Galilean ministry, there is little doubt about his identity and the nature of his messianic ministry. He is the Spirit-anointed Messiah, a prophetic Messiah,[28] the Messiah of God, the Son of God.[29] His messianic ministry entails preaching the good news of the Gospel to the poor, curing the sick, freeing those bound by Satan, restoring sight to the blind, forgiving sins, and calling sinners to repentance. While the Lukan narrator has further clarified Jesus' identity and mission in this section, he has not yet explained how this Messiah will be enthroned and rule over the house of Jacob forever (1:33).

A Journey in Fulfillment
of God's Plan (9:51–19:44)

The account of Jesus' great journey to Jerusalem begins with a comment that signals a major turn in the Lukan narrative.[30]

> When the days drew near for him to be taken up (*analēmpseōs*), he set his face to go to Jerusalem. (9:51)

This majestic verse also suggests *how* Jesus will be enthroned over the house of Jacob forever. After his death and resurrection, he will be "taken up" into heaven (Acts 1:2, 11, 22), where he will sit at the right hand of God, enthroned as Lord and Messiah (Acts 2:34–36). Before this can take place, however, the Messiah must accomplish his "exodus" in Jerusalem (9:31); for, as the risen Lord will tell his disciples, it was necessary (*dei*) for the Messiah to suffer in order to enter into his glory (24:26) since it was written in the scripture that the Messiah would suffer and rise from the dead (24:46). The beginning of Jesus' journey to Jerusalem, then, is more than a change of direction; it indicates a profound consciousness of his messianic destiny to suffer, die, rise from the dead, and be taken up into heaven, where he will be enthroned as Lord and Messiah.[31]

Throughout the journey section, the reader finds Jesus instructing his disciples, admonishing the crowds, and fending off the attacks of the religious leaders, especially the Pharisees. Aware of God's in-breaking kingdom, Jesus requires disciples to abandon family, home, and possessions to proclaim the kingdom of God (9:57–62; 12:32–34; 14:25–33). Aware that Israel has not repented (10:13–16; 11:29–32), he warns the crowds of what will happen if they do not repent (13:1–9). And aware that the kingdom will bring a reversal of fortunes for many, Jesus cautions the Pharisees that all who exalt themselves will be humbled (14:7–24).

When he finally approaches Jerusalem, Jesus recounts the parable of the pounds (19:12–27), since some suppose that the kingdom of God will appear immediately, perhaps when Jesus enters Jerusalem (19:11). But just as the nobleman of the parable must first go to another country to obtain his kingship and then return, so the Messiah must be taken up to heaven to be enthroned before returning as the glorious Messiah, the Son of Man (see Acts 3:20). The kingdom of God, then, will not come in power when Jesus enters Jerusalem but at his parousia when he returns as Israel's royal Messiah. Before these events can take place, however, the Messiah must minister to Jerusalem.

The journey section enhances Luke's Christology in several ways. First, it presents Jesus as a *prophetic Messiah* who proceeds to Jerusalem with a profound awareness of his messianic destiny (9:51; 13:31–35; 18:31–34) and unique relationship to God (10:21–22). Second, it portrays Jesus as the *preacher of the kingdom* who understands his unique role in God's plan (10:23–24; 11:29–32) and summons Israel to repentance because the kingdom is at hand (13:1–9). Third, it depicts Jesus as the *compassionate Messiah* who calls sinners to repentance and brings salvation to those in need (13:10–17; 15:1–32; 17:11–19; 18:35–43). Fourth, it represents Jesus as *faithful to Moses and the prophets* (10:25–28; 16:16–17, 29; 18:18–23). Finally, it points to the Messiah's destiny as the *Son of Man* who will return suddenly and unexpectedly to gather the elect (17:22–37).

The Messiah in Possession of His Temple (19:45–21:38)

Jesus' journey to Jerusalem concludes with a prophetic lament that forebodes the city's destruction since it does not recognize his messianic visitation (19:41–44, also see 13:34–35). Therefore, when Jesus enters Jerusalem, he is already aware that it will not receive him as God's Messiah. Nevertheless, after cleansing the Temple, he teaches the people daily in its precincts (19:45–48).

This temple ministry recalls the episode from Jesus' childhood when his parents found him in the Temple, seated in the midst of its teachers, listening and asking questions. But it also stands in sharp contrast to that episode since the adult Jesus now instructs the people of Israel in his capacity as the Messiah and Teacher who proclaims the good news.[32] This ministry, however, meets with hostility from the religious leaders, who correctly perceive that the people hang on Jesus' every word. Consequently, they attempt to discredit him by challenging his authority (20:1–2) and posing questions regarding the payment of taxes (20:20–26) and the resurrection of the dead (20:27–40). In every instance, however, Jesus manifests his superior teaching. The religious leaders fall silent; they no longer dare to ask him any questions (20:26, 40).

Although Jesus does not tell the religious leaders by what authority he acts since they will not acknowledge that John's baptism was of heavenly origin, he tells the people the parable of the tenant farmers (20:9–18), which provides an allegorical insight to his ministry. He is the beloved Son sent by the Father (20:13), the rejected stone that will become the cornerstone. Those who stumble over him will be destroyed (20:17–18).

After the religious leaders finish their questions, Jesus asks how they can claim that the Messiah is the Son of David since David addresses the Messiah as his Lord (20:41–44).[33] The christological implication of Jesus' unanswered question is that the Messiah is not the Son of David but the Son of God. For, even though the Lukan narrator has presented Jesus as the one who will inherit the throne of David his father (1:32), the reader knows that Jesus has been conceived through the power of God's Spirit. Therefore, he is called the Son of God (1:35).

The climax of the Messiah's temple ministry is a prophetic discourse on the Temple's destruction and the coming of the Son of Man (21:8–36).[34] The discourse is occasioned by Jesus' remark that the Temple will be destroyed (21:6). Asked when this will happen and what signs will accompany it, Jesus warns his audience not to be deceived by false messiahs or terrified when they hear of wars and insurrections, as if these were the final signs of the end. First, Jesus' disciples will be persecuted and hated "on account of his name" (21:12, 17), a prophecy that will find its fulfillment in the Acts of the Apostles. When this occurs, he (presumably the risen Lord) will give them a wisdom that their adversaries will be unable to refute (21:15).[35] Then, after the destruction of Jerusalem, and when the times of the Gentiles have been fulfilled (21:20–24),[36] there will be cosmic signs that presage the coming of the Son of Man (21:25–28), and the Messiah's followers will know that their redemption is at hand (21:28).

It is somewhat paradoxical that Jesus speaks of redemption in conjunction with Jerusalem's destruction since the prophetess Anna spoke of the child Jesus to all who were awaiting the redemption of Jerusalem (2:38). The redemption of Jerusalem, however, is not coterminous with the physical preservation of the city. Rather it will occur when the Messiah returns as the glorious Son of Man.

Luke's exposition of Jesus' Jerusalem ministry presents a kaleidoscope of christological images that are rooted in his messianic theology. Jesus comes to Jerusalem as its promised Messiah to bring God's eschatological gift of peace (19:42). As Messiah, he takes possession of his Father's house, the Temple, and there he teaches Israel with an authority that threatens the leadership of the chief priests, scribes, and elders, who will eventually hand him over to the Romans.[37] Aware that he is the beloved Son whom the Father has sent, Jesus knows that Israel will reject him. But he proceeds with his prophetic mission because the final redemption of Israel can only occur when the Messiah returns as the glorious Son of Man. Before this can take place, however, the Messiah must suffer and die.

The Messiah Who Must Suffer
to Enter into His Glory (22:1–24:53)

The account of Jesus' death and resurrection is, as one would expect, the climax of the Lukan story of Jesus.[38] The Messiah who resolutely determined to journey to Jerusalem because he knew that the time for him to be taken up into heaven was drawing near is arrested, led to Pilate, and accused of misleading Israel on two counts. First, he has opposed the payment of taxes to Caesar, and second, he claims to be the Messiah, a king (23:2).[39] Although Pilate is not convinced of Jesus' guilt (23:4, 14, 22), he hands him over, and Jesus is crucified as the King of the Jews (23:38), a political charge. The manner in which Jesus suffers and dies leads a criminal to acknowledge Jesus' innocence (23:41), a Roman soldier to confess that Jesus was truly righteous (23:47),[40] and the crowds to return home beating their breasts (23:48).

The events following Jesus' death and burial provide the narrative's denouement. At the empty tomb, two angels remind the women of Jesus' words that the Son of Man had (*dei*) to be handed over to sinners and crucified, and to rise on the third day (24:7). On the road to Emmaus, the risen Lord teaches two disciples that the Messiah had (*edei*) to suffer such things in order to enter into his glory, as it is written in Moses and the Prophets (24:26–27). Finally, when the risen Christ appears in Jerusalem to the eleven apostles, he explains that Moses, the Prophets, and the Psalms had already written of the Messiah's suffering and resurrection and that repentance for the forgiveness of sins should be preached in the Messiah's name to all the nations (24:44–47).[41] Then, after leading the disciples to Bethany and blessing them, Jesus is taken up into heaven (24:50–51), thereby attaining the ultimate purpose of his journey to Jerusalem. As for the disciples, they return to the Temple of Jerusalem where the narrative began. There they praise God and wait for the coming of the Spirit (24:52–53).

The Lukan narrator explains the complication caused by Israel's rejection of the Messiah in the following way. Despite the apparent failure of the Messiah's ministry to Israel, everything happened according to a divine plan clearly outlined in Moses, the Prophets, and the Psalms; that is, in Israel's sacred writings.[42] The suffering and death of the Messiah was the necessary prelude to his entrance into glory, which the Acts of the Apostles describes as a royal enthronement at God's right hand (Acts 2:34–36). The soteriological result of this "exodus" from suffering to exaltation is the forgiveness of sins. In dying on the cross, the Messiah has given his body and shed his blood for (*hyper*) his disciples (22:19–20). Although Luke is notoriously reserved about the salvific dimensions of Jesus' death, especially when compared to Paul, he hardly envisions the Messiah's death as a senseless miscarriage of justice.[43] Rather, the death of Jesus is part of a great movement from suffering to exaltation that effects the forgiveness of sins.

When the two disciples on the road to Emmaus lament, "we had hoped that he was the one to redeem Israel" (24:21), they misunderstand the nature of Israel's redemption. Still thinking in terms of national liberation, they have not yet realized that this Messiah redeems Israel and the nations from the rule of Satan and the burden of sins. To be sure, the infancy narrative speaks of salvation in language that can be construed in terms of national restoration: namely, Jesus will restore the Davidic monarchy and expel Israel's enemies. But throughout his story, the Lukan narrator has continually refined the meaning of Jesus' messiahship and the salvation he brings. In the Acts of the Apostles, Luke will continue this process of defining and refining Jesus' messiahship, as well as its significance for Israel and the nations.

A Prophetic Messiah, the Son of God

The Gospel is not the whole of Luke's Christology, but it provides the indispensable foundation for what he will say in the Acts of the Apostles. Its main themes can be summarized in the following way. First, Jesus, the promised Messiah of Israel, comes with a gracious offer of salvation from God. As God's Messiah, he confirms that the God of Israel has been faithful to his promises, for the salvation announced in Israel's scriptures has become a reality in the person of Jesus.

Second, because Jesus is God's Messiah, he is most properly called the Son of God. While such a statement could be made of every Israelite king, inasmuch as the king was the Lord's anointed (*Christos*) and adopted by the Lord on the day of his coronation (Ps. 2:7), Luke sees a unique dimension to Jesus' messianic sonship. He is called God's Son because he has been born through the power of the Most High God; Joseph was not his biological father. After Jesus' baptism and at the transfiguration, God confirms that Jesus is his beloved Son, and Jesus exercises this sonship by faithfully trusting in God rather than by displays of divine power for his own benefit.

Third, the messianic Son of God is the Savior of his people. Anointed with the Spirit of God, he brings salvation to his people by preaching good news to the poor, freeing those under Satan's bondage, curing the sick, calling sinners to repentance, and suffering upon the cross. While this salvation is present "today" in the person of the Messiah, the fullness of salvation will only occur in the kingdom of God, when the Messiah returns at the end of the ages in his capacity as the Son of Man. At the present moment, however, people who repent can experience the forgiveness of sins.

Fourth, the Messiah of Israel is a prophetic figure who calls Israel to repentance. Like the great prophetic figures of Israel's past, he experiences opposition and, ultimately, rejection. But unlike the prophetic figures of the past, the Messiah is not simply one of the prophets; he is the Son of the Most High God. Consequently, those who refuse his offer of salvation reject the eschatological agent God sent to his people.

Finally, the Messiah is the Lord, the one who exercises divine prerogatives because he is enthroned at God's right hand. Since this enthronement as Lord only occurs after Jesus' resurrection and ascension, properly speaking it is not part of the Gospel story of Jesus. But the Lukan narrator introduces the term "Lord" in narrative comments (10:1) and even puts it on the lips of certain characters, before Jesus' resurrection (1:43). In doing so, he points to the unity of the earthly Jesus and the risen Christ. Jesus did not become the Messiah and Lord in function of his resurrection; he was already Messiah and Lord at his birth.[44]

Although the Lukan Gospel is often seen as more Gentile in its orientation than the Gospel of Matthew, it displays a Christology that is deeply rooted in Israel's scriptures. Luke firmly believes that everything in his story of the Messiah can be substantiated by Moses, the Prophets, and the Psalms. Although the Messiah of his Gospel redefines traditional messianic expectations, everything about this Messiah was already written in Israel's scripture.[45]

THE ACTS OF THE APOSTLES

In his second volume, the Acts of the Apostles, the Lukan narrator finishes the christological portrait of Jesus begun in the Gospel by completing themes introduced in the Gospel. For example, at the announcement of Jesus' birth, the angel Gabriel told Mary that God would give her son the throne of David, and he would reign over the house of Jacob forever (1:32–33). At the end of the Gospel narrative this promise remains unfulfilled, and apparently impossible to fulfill. But in the Acts of the Apostles, readers discover that Jesus' resurrection is his messianic enthronement and exaltation at God's right hand. The risen Lord who is Israel's Messiah is presently ruling over a restored Israel that has repented, and he will rule forever.[46]

But how can we employ a narrative approach to get at the Christology of Acts? Even if we argue that Acts is part of a larger work (Luke-Acts) with its own plot, there remains an important difference between it and the Gospel. Whereas the latter is clearly a story of Jesus, the former is not. In the Acts of the Apostles, the narrative focuses upon the church's witness to Jesus' resurrection, especially the witness of Peter, Stephen, and Paul. To be sure, the risen Lord plays a role by directing and encouraging the missionary work of his witnesses, but Acts is no longer the story of Jesus in the manner that the Gospel is. It is the story of the church.

Nevertheless, Acts is replete with "stories" of Jesus that recall the Gospel narrative, completing and explaining it. These stories are found in the speeches of Acts which proclaim that Jesus was truly Israel's Messiah, even though he was shamefully put to death; for God raised him from the dead. In proclaiming Jesus' resurrection, the speeches relate various aspects of the Jesus story and show that Israel's scriptures prophesied the significant events of his story. Not only do the speeches of Acts recount the story of Jesus, they reinterpret it in light of Israel's history. In doing so, they provide us with another access to Luke's narrative Christology.[47]

Speeches of Peter

As the chief spokesman of the Twelve, Peter delivers a number of speeches in the first part of Acts, especially chapters 2–5.[48] His sermons show that he has become a keen interpreter of scripture who is able to discern how Israel's sacred writings spoke of the Messiah's suffering and resurrection.[49] In the course of these speeches, Peter explains that the enthroned Messiah of Israel now rules and grants salvation to those who believe in his name. Accordingly, calling upon the name of the Lord (Jesus) and the significance of Jesus for all people are central tenets of Peter's christological proclamation; for the Messiah of Israel is the Lord of all (10:36).

From the Time of John
to the Ascension (1:16–22)

Peter's first speech occurs shortly after Jesus' ascension and is delivered to 120 believers. Peter, who has become a skilled interpreter of scripture, recognizes that David prophesied that Judas's homestead would be left desolate because he betrayed the Messiah (Ps. 69:25). Moreover, David also prophesied that another should take Judas's place among the Twelve (Ps. 109:8). But the new member of the Twelve must be someone who accompanied the original group during the whole period that the Lord Jesus was present to them: from the time of John the Baptist to the time of the Lord's ascension. The time of the Jesus story, then, is the time during which Jesus was present to his disciples: from the time of John to the ascension.[50] However, the plotted time of the narrative also includes Israel's history, since David had already prophesied these important events: Judas's end and the need to fill his office anew.[51]

The prayer of the assembled believers for guidance begins, "Lord, you know everyone's heart" (1:24). But who is this Lord to whom the assembled believers pray? God or Jesus? Acts ascribes the title *kyrios* to both God and Jesus, but in several instances, it is not clear if the term applies to Jesus or God.[52] Acts 15:8 describes God as one who knows the heart, suggesting that God may be in view here, as well. But since Peter has already identified Jesus as Lord (1:21), and since it was Jesus who first called the Twelve, here the title probably refers to Jesus. If so, the assembled believers are praying to Jesus as Lord, just as they were accustomed to praying to God.[53] This is not to say that they are identifying Jesus as God, but they are clearly ascribing God-like prerogatives to him.

Lord and Messiah (2:14–40)

The descent of the Spirit upon the community of believers serves as an occasion for Peter to deliver his first and longest kerygmatic speech. The audience consists of "devout Jews from every nation under heaven" (2:5) who have mistaken the behavior of the Spirit-filled believers as drunkenness, leading Peter to refute their charges with an extended quotation from Joel 2:28–32. Peter shows that these are the last days, and God has poured out his Spirit upon the small community of believers so that "everyone who calls upon the name of the Lord shall be saved" (2:21, quoting Joel).

After correcting the audience's misconceptions, Peter launches into an extended proof from Israel's scriptures that the one whom they crucified and killed by the hands of those outside of the law (the Romans) was none other than the Messiah (2:29–36). There are two proofs for this. First, God reversed their actions by raising Jesus from the dead in accordance with the prophetic words of Psalm 16, notably the verse that reads, "For you will not abandon my soul to Hades, or let your Holy One experience corruption" (2:27, quoting the psalm). In speaking those words, the prophetic king David was not speaking of himself, since he died, but of the Messiah's resurrection; for David was fully aware that God would put one of his descendants upon his throne (2:30).

Second, having been raised from the dead, Jesus has been exalted at God's right hand, as David prophesied: "The Lord [God] said to my Lord [the Messiah], 'Sit at my right hand, until I [God] make your enemies [referring to the Messiah's enemies] your footstool'" (Ps. 2:7). The psalm must refer to the Messiah rather than to David since David did not ascend into heaven. On the basis of this psalm, therefore, Peter concludes that God has made the crucified Jesus both Lord and Messiah (2:36). Thus Peter resolves the question raised by the infancy narrative: how will Jesus sit on the throne of David and rule over the house of Jacob forever? Although Jesus was identified as Messiah and Lord at his birth (2:11), Peter indicates that something decisive happened at the resurrection: "Jesus has been enthroned as Lord and Messiah for Israel, to fulfill all the promises made to it."[54]

When his Jewish audience asks what they must do, Peter's Christology takes a moral and soteriological turn. They must repent and be baptized in the name of Jesus Christ so that their sins can be forgiven, and they might receive the gift of the Holy Spirit (2:38). The eternally enthroned Messiah has become the source of salvation for them.

Peter's Pentecost sermon is an excellent example of a Christology that begins from below.[55] On the one hand, Peter clearly presents Jesus as a human being through whom God worked: "*a man* attested to you by God with deeds of power, wonders, and signs that God did *through him* among you" (2:22). He was handed over, crucified, and if God had not raised him from the dead, Jesus' enemies would have been victorious. But on the other hand, by exalting Jesus to his right hand, God has made him "both Lord and Messiah" (2:36), so that those who repent and believe in his name can receive the forgiveness of sins and the gift of the Holy Spirit. More than Israel's Messiah, Jesus has been exalted to the status of Lord so that the words of the prophet Joel — that once applied to God — are now ascribed to Jesus: "everyone who calls upon the name of the Lord [Jesus] shall be saved" (2:21).[56]

Central to Luke's Christology is the clear affirmation that Jesus' crucifixion and death happened "according to the definite plan and foreknowledge of God" (2:23). Marion Soards writes, "Thus, the cross is not cast as a scandal, for the crucifixion of Jesus at the hands of the lawless is viewed as part of the fulfillment of God's plan."[57] Put another way, for Luke the story of Jesus is the plan of God (*hē boulē tou theou*). While this story has a tragic element, inasmuch as a significant portion of Israel rejected the Messiah, its narrative line was not unforeseen. The story of Jesus fulfills Israel's scriptures and occurs in accordance with God's will.

The Glorification of God's Servant (3:12–26)

The occasion for this speech, which occurs in the precincts of Jerusalem's Temple, is the healing of a crippled beggar "in the name of Jesus Christ of Nazareth" (3:6).[58] Taking advantage of the crowd's amazement at this healing, Peter explains that this name has healed the crippled (3:12–16), and he summons the crowd to repentance (3:17–26).

This speech is especially rich in the manner it describes Jesus: he is God's servant (*pais*), the holy and just one (*ton hagion* and *dikaion*), the leader of life (*ton archēgon tēs zōēs*), the Messiah who has been designated for them (*ton prokecheirismenon hymin Christon*), the prophet of whom Moses spoke. Those who reject this prophet will be cut off from the restored people of Israel, whereas those who repent will experience the forgiveness of sins and times of refreshment. Several of these titles appear in other speeches, especially Peter's responses to the Sanhedrin (4:8–12; 5:29–32), as well as in the community's prayer for courage (4:24–30). Moreover, the christological import of the name "Jesus," introduced in Peter's Pentecost sermon (2:21, 38), plays a vital role in this speech, as well as those that follow. Finally, references to the prophets and the description of the people as "the descendants of the prophets and of the covenant" (3:24–25) situate the story of Jesus within the whole of Israel's story.

As Marion Soards notes, "the speech is immediately kerygmatic."[59] It begins by drawing a sharp contrast between the actions of human beings and the action of God.[60] Accordingly, two contrasts dominate the opening verses (3:12–16). First, Peter affirms that the God of Abraham, Isaac, and Jacob (see Ex. 3:6) glorified his servant Jesus, whom they handed over and denied, even though Pilate had decided to release him. Second, Peter recalls the people's behavior when Jesus stood before Pilate (see Luke 23:13–25). They denied the holy and the just one, putting to death the leader of life. But God reversed their action by raising Jesus from the dead. The name of Jesus Christ the Nazorean has healed the crippled man because God glorified his servant Jesus despite their actions.

In making his appeal for repentance (3:17–26), Peter mitigates his harsh judgment by acknowledging that the people and their leaders acted in ignorance of God's plan. They did not realize that all the prophets foretold that the Messiah would suffer (3:17–18), a clear echo of the risen Lord's teaching in Luke's Gospel (24:27, 44, 46). Calling upon the crowd to repent, Peter identifies Jesus as the Messiah designated for them. Presently, he resides in heaven, but when he appears again he will play a vital role in the restoration of all things. Thus the crowd must repent, for this is the prophet of whom Moses spoke (see Deut. 18:19). Israel, then, is receiving a second chance to repent, the first being the time of Jesus' ministry. Those who do not repent now will be cut off from the restored people of Israel.

Peter's speech concludes by reminding the crowd that they are the descendants of the prophets and of the covenant God made with their ancestors, when he told Abraham that all the families of the earth would be blessed in his offspring (3:25, quoting Gen. 22:18). That is why God raised his servant Jesus and sent him first to Israel to bless and turn the people from their wicked ways (3:26).

Peter's temple speech provides a concrete example of how the name "Jesus" saves. It has the power to restore a crippled man to perfect health (3:16) and wipe away sins (3:19).[61] Having already explained from Israel's scriptures that Jesus is both Lord and Messiah, enthroned at God's right hand (2:36), Peter employs this speech to make the crowd aware of its responsibility in the Messiah's death and the urgency of responding to God's new offer to repent. In doing this, Peter introduces a number of titles that enrich the Christology of his Pentecost sermon.

The central concept for identifying Jesus is *messiahship.* The prophets foretold that this Messiah would suffer (3:18), but Israel and its leaders acted in ignorance of God's plan (3:17–18). Nevertheless, there is still time to repent before the parousia and the restoration of all things that the prophets foretold (3:21).[62]

The Messiah is *God's servant,* as were Israel and David of old (Luke

1:54, 69). Appearing at the beginning and end of the sermon (3:13, 26), the term "servant" plays an important role in Peter's sermon. As the servant of God, Jesus is "the messianic successor of the house of David and the fulfillment of Israel's messianic expectations."[63] Rather than describe Jesus as the suffering servant portrayed in Isaiah, the term identifies him as "the eschatological, messianic prophet, the one who was sent and appointed to work miracles, to bring about conversion, and to bless."[64] This servant of God is *the holy and just one*. In the Gospel, Jesus is called holy from his birth, the Son of God because the Holy Spirit and the power of the Most High God overshadowed his mother. Even unclean spirits acknowledge that he is the Holy One of God (Luke 4:34), since he was anointed by God's Spirit.[65] At Jesus' death, the centurion praises God by saying that Jesus was righteous (Luke 23:47). That is to say, the persecuted Jesus—not his persecutors—stood in the proper relationship to God. He was the truly righteous sufferer in the full sense of the word *dikaios*.[66] But now, when Peter identifies Jesus as the holy and just one, he does so in light of the resurrection. It is the resurrection that proves beyond all doubt that Jesus is holy and just, for the risen One clearly belongs to the realm of God. Finally, Peter notes that Jesus is *the leader of life*. The term employed here, *archēgos,* denotes one who is first, who stands at the head of something, one who leads.[67] Thus, as Moses led Israel out of Egypt, Jesus leads those who believe in his name to life, for he is the one who has already made the great exodus (see Luke 9:31) from death to life.

The plotted time of the story that Peter presupposes extends from the covenant God made with Abraham to the restoration of all things at the Messiah's parousia. It is a story of hidden identity, rejection, and reversal. Although the prophets foretold that the Messiah would suffer, Israel and its leaders did not recognize that Jesus was God's holy and righteous servant, the Messiah designated for them in fulfillment of the covenant promises. Therefore, they rejected him only to have God override their judgment.

The Stone Rejected by the Builders (Acts 4–5)

Chapters 4–5 of Acts narrate the growing conflict between the risen Lord's witnesses and Israel's religious leaders. The conflict begins when the religious leaders arrest Peter and John for teaching and proclaiming that the resurrection of the dead has occurred in Jesus (4:1–3). The next day, Peter defends his behavior in a speech before the Sanhedrin (4:8–12). The result of this initial confrontation is a stern warning "not to speak or teach at all in the name of Jesus" (4:18). When Peter and John report these events to the community of believers, the community prays for courage to speak the word, that is, the message of the resurrection, with boldness (4:24–30). This prayer, to which we will return, echoes themes of Peter's earlier speeches and provides further insight into the divine plan that was at work in Jesus' passion. Next, when the apostles gather in the temple area and perform signs and wonders, the religious leaders arrest them and put them in prison (5:17–18). Miraculously delivered from their imprisonment, the apostles resume their teaching in the Temple. Brought before the religious leaders once more, Peter and the apostles deliver a defense speech (5:29–32) that echoes themes of Peter's earlier sermons. Unmoved by these words, the religious leaders have the apostles flogged and forbid them to speak in the name of Jesus anymore (5:40). It is all to no avail, however, for the apostles continue to preach that the Messiah is Jesus (5:42).

These chapters develop an important theme that was introduced in Peter's Pentecost speech: "everyone who calls on the name of the Lord shall be saved" (2:21, a quotation from the prophet Joel). In the Joel quotation, "the name of the Lord" refers to God, but in the context of the Pentecost speech the name of the Lord is the name of the Lord Jesus, a prominent theme in the first part of Acts. The speeches before the Sanhedrin (4:8–12; 5:29–32) and the prayer of the believing community for boldness (4:24–30) develop the theology of Jesus' name and its salvific power in two ways.[68] First, they reinforce christological themes of Peter's earlier speeches by repeating them in slightly different ways. Second, they introduce new christological material.

In his *first speech before the Sanhedrin* (4:8–12), Peter must defend what has just taken place in the Temple: the healing of a crippled man, which has become the occasion for teaching the people in Jesus' name. In defense of his behavior, Peter employs another contrast formula: the crippled man was healed by the name of Jesus Christ of Nazareth whom *they crucified* but *God raised from the dead* (4:10; for the previous contrast formulas, see 2:23–24; 3:13–15). Next, to verify this divine reversal of Jesus' rejection Peter enlists Ps. 118:22. But whereas the psalm reads, "the stone that the builders rejected has become the chief cornerstone," Peter says "the stone that was rejected *by you,* the builders; it has become the cornerstone" (4:11), thereby emphasizing the responsibility of the religious leaders in Jesus' rejection. He then concludes that there is salvation in no one else since there is no other name by which we must (*dei*) be saved (4:12). This last phrase recalls the Joel quotation of the Pentecost sermon (2:21) and indicates that the name of Jesus now functions with the same power and authority as the Divine Name. Thus, from an initial affirmation that the name of Jesus Christ of Nazareth healed the crippled man, Peter moves to the bold assertion that this name is the *only* source of salvation! The reason for such assurance is the resurrection whereby God reverses what the religious leaders have done.

Although *the prayer of the community* (4:24–30) is not a speech, it is important for our purposes because of its christological content. The entire community utters the prayer and so demonstrates its insight into the scriptures, as Peter has already done on numerous occasions. Recognizing that the Holy Spirit spoke through God's servant (*pais*) David, the community interprets the second psalm as a prophecy of God's preordained plan (*boulē*) for his anointed one, the Messiah. Herod, Pontius Pilate, the Gentiles, and the people of Israel were the ones David spoke of when he said:

> Why did the Gentiles rage,
>   and the peoples imagine vain things?
> The kings of the earth took their stand,
>   and the rulers have gathered together
> against the Lord and against his Messiah.
>   (Acts 4:25–26)

Those who persecuted Jesus were unwittingly carrying out God's preordained plan that his Messiah would suffer such things (see Luke 24:26, 46).

The community's prayer identifies this Messiah as the one whom God anointed, "your holy servant Jesus" (4:27; *ton hagion paida sou Iēsoun*). The use of the servant title here echoes what Peter already said of Jesus (3:13, 26) and establishes another link between Jesus and David, also identified as God's servant (4:25). Furthermore, it prepares for the climax of the prayer in which the community petitions God for boldness (4:29–30). Thus the prayer concludes with a second reference to Jesus as God's "holy servant" (4:30). Moreover, it employs the theme of Jesus' name to show that God is at work *through* the name of his holy servant Jesus to effect salvation.

The Lukan narrator identifies Peter and the apostles as the orators of *the final speech before the religious leaders* (5:29–32). While a corporate speech presents historical critical problems (how does a group give a speech?), from a literary point of view it indicates the growing boldness of the church that now speaks with a united voice about the events that have transpired. Accordingly, after explaining the necessity (*dei*) of obeying God rather than human beings, Peter and the apostles employ the now familiar contrast formula: *God* raised Jesus whom *they* [the Sanhedrin] killed by hanging him on a tree.[69] In doing so, God exalted Jesus as leader and savior (*archēgon kai sōtera*) at his right hand (an allusion to Ps. 110:1, which Peter employed earlier in his sermon at Pentecost; see 2:32–35), to give repentance and forgiveness of sins to Israel. The first of these titles (leader) was used in Peter's temple discourse, where he identified Jesus as the leader of life (3:15). The second (savior) has not yet occurred in Acts, but it clearly recalls the angel's announcement at Jesus' birth, "to you is born this day in the city of David a Savior, who is the Messiah, the Lord" (Luke 2:11). In light of this speech, the meaning of these titles is clear: Jesus the Messiah is the leader and savior of Israel inasmuch as he is the one through whom God effects repentance and forgiveness of sins.[70]

To summarize our findings thus far, in chapters 2–5 the Lukan narrator recounts *four* speeches in which Peter plays a prominent role, and a prayer of the community. While the people of Israel provide the audience for the two longer speeches, the religious leaders are the audience for the two shorter discourses. Taken as a whole, the speeches present Jesus as the Messiah who fulfills the prophets and covenant promises made to Israel. By the resurrection, God has enthroned him at his right hand and made him Lord. Seated at God's right hand, the enthroned Messiah dispenses the Spirit, and through his name God effects wondrous works that culminate in repentance and the forgiveness of sins. This Messiah can be called God's servant, God's holy servant, the righteous one, leader, the author of life, savior, the prophet of whom Moses spoke. But ultimately he is the Messiah. His exalted status, however, is best expressed by the designation "Lord," formerly reserved to God. The story of this Messiah is the culmination of Israel's story.

Lord of All, Judge of the Living and the Dead

Acts reports three more speeches by Peter: two in the extended narrative of Cornelius (10:34–43; 11:5–17), and one at the conference of Jerusalem (15:7–11). While these speeches develop some of the christological themes that Peter has already introduced, they now focus on the soteriological significance of Israel's Messiah for the Gentiles. In doing so, they present Jesus as someone with significance for the salvation of all people.

Peter's *first speech* (10:34–43) provides the most extensive outline of Jesus' earthly ministry, and this has led some to suggest that it represents the earliest kerygma of the church. The speech begins with an important insight that Peter has learned from the Cornelius incident: God shows no partiality (10:34–35). Having acknowledged this point, so central for the Gentile mission, Peter launches into his christological kerygma by summarizing the story of Jesus (10:36–43).

Although God shows no partiality, he singled out the children of Israel by sending his word to them, preaching peace through Jesus Christ who is Lord of all. Peter then explains how Jesus' ministry began in Galilee after the preaching of John the Baptist. God anointed Jesus with the Holy Spirit and power, and Jesus went about doing good. Then, employing another contrast formula, Peter explains how *the Jerusalemites killed him* by hanging him on a tree, but *God raised him* on the third day. Peter and other chosen witnesses now testify that this one (Jesus) has been destined by God as the judge of the living and the dead. The prophets testify that "everyone who believes in him receives forgiveness of sins through his name" (10:43).

While this speech manifests several points of contact with Peter's earlier discourses,[71] it is remarkable for the manner in which it focuses on the universal significance of Jesus' messiahship. The Messiah of Israel is the Lord of all, the one who will judge the living and the dead, a point Paul also makes in his speech at Athens (17:30–31). In terms of the Lukan narrative, Peter has grown in his understanding of Jesus' significance. He understands, in a way that he did not earlier, that the Messiah of Israel is Lord of all.

Peter delivers his *last two speeches* before Jewish believers who are skeptical that the God of Israel has extended salvation to the Gentiles in the same way that he offered it to Israel. In a speech before circumcised believers at Jerusalem (11:5–17), Peter summarizes the salient points of the Cornelius incident to show how God gave the Gentiles "the same gift that he gave us when we believed in the Lord Jesus Christ" (11:17). In his last speech at the Jerusalem conference (15:7–11), Peter recounts the Cornelius episode to establish that Gentile believers need not be circumcised. Speaking in language that approaches the Pauline teaching of justification by faith, he says, "we believe that we will be saved through the grace of the Lord Jesus, just as they will" (15:11).

Peter will no longer appear in the Acts of the Apostles, but he has clearly traversed a long road from the early days of Pentecost. In those first days, he needed to establish that despite Jesus' shameful death upon the cross, Jesus is Israel's promised Messiah. Now Peter becomes a defender of Gentiles and argues that the Messiah of Israel is the Lord of all.[72]

Speeches of Paul

Like Peter, Paul delivers a number of speeches in Acts: three as a missionary, and four as a prisoner for the Lord. For New Testament Christology, the most important is the first: Paul's sermon in the synagogue of

Antioch of Pisidia. Nonetheless, other speeches provide important christological material, especially Paul's final defense before Festus and Agrippa.

The Savior Whom God Brought to Israel (13:16–41)

Although readers know that Paul has been preaching about Jesus ever since his conversion (chapter 9), from a literary point of view Paul's speech at Pisidian Antioch functions as an inaugural sermon since this is the first extended speech of Paul that the Lukan narrator has chosen to report. Although the sermon is directed to a specific audience of Jews and God-fearers, readers can rightly assume that this is the *kind* of missionary discourse Paul employed in other synagogues of Asia Minor and Greece. Accordingly, it is not necessary for the Lukan narrator to recount in detail what Paul said in other synagogues. When Paul comes to Thessalonica, for example, it is sufficient to report the following:

> And Paul went in [to the synagogue], as was his custom, and on three sabbath days argued with them from the scriptures, explaining and proving that it was necessary for the Messiah to suffer and to rise from the dead, and saying, "This is the Messiah, Jesus whom I am proclaiming to you." (17:2–3)

Readers can suppose that Paul gave a much longer sermon, similar to the one he delivered at Antioch of Pisidia, the prototype of his preaching to Jews and God-fearers. With this background, we turn to Paul's speech in the synagogue of Antioch.

This speech takes place after the reading of the Law and the Prophets, when the synagogue official invites Paul and Barnabas to speak a word of encouragement to the people.[73] Accordingly, Paul begins with a brief review of Israel's history that culminates with the appearance of Jesus, whom Paul identifies as the savior whom God sent to Israel in fulfillment of the promise made to David (13:16–25). The story of Israel includes the deliverance of the people from Egypt, the period of their wandering in the wilderness, the inheritance of the land, the time of the judges until the prophet Samuel, the people's request for a king, the removal of Saul, and the establishment of David, a man who did God's will. Although the people are called descendants of Abraham (13:26), there is no mention of Abraham, nor is there any reference to the giving of the law at Sinai. There is, however, a significant reference to the Mosaic law at the end of the sermon (13:39).

Paul begins the first part of his speech by referring to the election of the ancestors (13:17) and concludes with God's choice of David, the ideal king (13:22). In light of this election theology, he then presents Jesus as the descendant of David, the promised savior whom God sent to Israel. In the second part of his speech (13:26–41), Paul employs scripture to show that Jesus is Israel's promised savior, and he clarifies the nature of the salvation Jesus brings.

The argument that Jesus was Israel's savior begins when he reminds the synagogue audience that the message of salvation was sent to them (13:26). Contrasting the work of humans and God, Paul notes that the inhabitants of Jerusalem and their leaders did not understand the prophetic scriptures but unwittingly fulfilled them by asking Pilate to have Jesus killed. God, however, counteracted what they did by raising Jesus from the dead (13:27–30). In doing so, the Lord fulfilled what he promised their ancestors. As did Peter in his Pentecost sermon, Paul employs Psalms 2 and 16 to prove that David foresaw the resurrection of one of his descendants (13:33–37). The Lukan Paul then concludes with an important soteriological statement that makes use of the vocabulary of justification. Through this man there is forgiveness from all those sins from which people could not be freed by the law of Moses; everyone who believes in this man is justified (13:38–40).

The Christology of Paul's inaugural sermon can be summarized as follows. Jesus is the descendant of David, who fulfills the promise God made to Israel. This promise is the resurrection of the dead, as Paul will explain in his defense speeches (23:6; 24:14–15; 26:6 8). By raising Jesus from the dead, God has fulfilled this promise and made Jesus a source of salvation: the forgiveness of sins that the Mosaic law could not effect. Paul does not explicitly identify Jesus as the Messiah in this speech, but readers familiar with Peter's Pentecost sermon now realize that the one God raised from the dead is, by that fact, the Messiah. The description of Jesus as Savior, however, recalls Peter's speech before the Sanhedrin (5:31) as well as his words at the conference of Jerusalem, "we believe that we will be saved through the grace of the Lord Jesus" (15:11). In sound Pauline fashion, then, the inaugural speech of the Lukan Paul focuses on the soteriological role of Christ.

The Man Whom God Has Appointed Judge (17:22–31)

The Lukan narrator recounts Paul's speech at Athens in detail since it presents an example of how Paul the missionary spoke outside the synagogue setting to Gentiles who were not God-fearers.[74] Since Paul cannot presuppose the heritage of Israel's sacred history that he could in the synagogue, he begins with the God who made the world and everything in it to convince his audience that this is the true God. Only at the end of the speech does Paul introduce his christological kerygma, and he does this without identifying Jesus by name. In past times, he says, the Creator God overlooked human sinfulness, but now he has fixed a day when he will judge the world in righteousness by a man whom he has appointed for this task. To give assurance of this, God has raised this man from the dead.[75]

The christological kerygma is at a minimum here, and the brief manner in which Paul presents it presupposes a fuller understanding of why Jesus died and God raised him from the dead. It is not surprising, then, that the Athenian audience is put off by the speech, although some are persuaded (17:32–34). But the speech does develop the role of Jesus as God's eschatological judge, a theme absent from other speeches apart from Peter's sermon to the household of Cornelius (10:42).

The Whole Purpose of God (20:18–35)

Paul's speech to the elders of Miletus is a farewell discourse rather than a missionary or kerygmatic sermon. Therefore, it is not surprising that it does not contain a major christological statement. It does, however, summarize how Paul views his ministry among the churches of the Mediterranean basin. He has testified to Jews and Greeks about repentance toward God and faith in the Lord Jesus Christ (20:21). Most important, he did not shrink from declaring to them "the whole purpose of God" (tēn boulēn tou theou; 20:27). The phrase is another way of referring to the story of Israel in its most recent version, which now includes the appearance of the Messiah. There is a divine purpose in Israel's history, and this history culminates in the Messiah and the salvation he has effected. The speeches that we have already discussed have indicated this divine purpose by showing how Israel's history and scripture prepared for, and pointed to, the Messiah.[76]

Because Paul has declared the whole purpose of God's plan to the elders of Ephesus, they must shepherd the church of God which God obtained dia tou haimatos tou idiou (20:28). While this difficult phrase could mean God's own blood, it is more probable that it refers to the blood of Jesus. Thus the translation of the New Revised Standard Version ("with the blood of his own Son") is helpful, even though the word "Son" does not appear in the text. Most important, if the text has the blood of Jesus in view, it points to the soteriological dimension of his death, a theme that Luke-Acts does not develop elsewhere.

The Hope and Promise of Israel (Acts 22–26)

In the final part of Acts, Paul delivers a number of speeches in which he defends his ministry before Jews and Gentiles.[77] Although his primary purpose is to show that he has not violated the laws of his people, these speeches provided him with an occasion to proclaim his christological kerygma. He argues that he is on trial because he upholds the promise God made to Israel: that there would be a resurrection of the dead (23:6; 24:21; 26:6–8). For, in Paul's view, by raising Jesus from the dead, the God of Abraham, Isaac, and Jacob inaugurated the general resurrection of the dead. As Paul writes in his first letter to the Corinthians, Jesus is the first fruits of a general resurrection yet to occur (see 1 Cor. 15:20).

The Lukan Paul insists that he has remained a faithful member of his people and preaches "nothing but what the prophets and Moses said would take place: that the Messiah must suffer, and that, by being the first to rise from the dead, he would proclaim light both to our people and to the Gentiles" (26:22–23). This faith in the resurrection allows the Lukan Paul to affirm that he is a Pharisee on trial for his hope in the resurrection of the dead (23:6). There is only one point of difference between him and other Pharisees. Whereas they hope for the resurrection of the dead, Paul maintains that God has initiated the general resurrection of the dead by raising Jesus from the dead.

In two of his defense speeches (22:3–21; 26:2–23), Paul recounts his conversion on the road to Damascus to explain how he came to this faith.[78] Previous to his conversion, he explains, he zealously persecuted the way he now preaches as the hope and promise of Israel (22:3–5; 26:9–11). But the risen Lord appeared to him and identified himself with those whom Paul persecuted (22:6–11; 26:12–18). Ignorant of the one who appeared to him in glorious light (22:6; 26:13), Paul asked, "Who are you, Lord?" The one shrouded in glory identified himself as Jesus (22:8; 26:15).

Paul narrates the events that occurred after this encounter in two ways. When speaking to the Jerusalemites, he recounts the role of Ananias, who identified Jesus as "the Righteous One" to whom Paul must now bear witness (22:12–16).[79] Then Paul explains how the Lord appeared to him while he was praying in the Temple and commissioned him to preach to the Gentiles (22:17–21).

Having recounted these events in chapter 22, Paul does not repeat them when defending himself before Agrippa and Festus in chapter 26. Instead the commissioning now occurs on the Damascus road where the risen Lord explains why he has appeared to Paul.

> I have appeared to you for this purpose, to appoint you to serve and testify to the things in which you have seen me and to those in which I will appear to you. I will rescue you from your people and from the Gentiles—to whom

I am sending you to open their eyes so that they may turn from darkness to light and from the power of Satan to God, so that they may receive forgiveness of sins and a place among those who are sanctified by faith in me. (26:16–18)

Paul then explains that he preached repentance to those in Damascus, Jerusalem, Judea, and to the Gentiles, in obedience to this vision. His preaching is nothing more than what Moses and the prophets foretold: that the Messiah would suffer (26:22–23). This statement echoes the words of the risen Lord at the conclusion of the Gospel (Luke 24:26, 46) and establishes that Paul's preaching is the continuation of Israel's redemptive history. In raising Jesus from the dead, God was fulfilling Israel's hope.

Although Paul's defense speeches do not contain the rich christological kerygma of Peter's earlier sermons, or of Paul's sermon at Antioch of Pisidia, they make an important contribution to the Christology of Acts. First, they clearly identify the central role that Jesus plays in the hope of Israel, which is the resurrection of the dead. Prior to Jesus' resurrection, the general resurrection of the dead was merely a hope. By raising Jesus from the dead, however, God has begun to fulfill the promise he made to Israel. Second, in recounting his conversion, Paul draws attention to the active role that the enthroned Messiah plays in salvation history. Although he has been taken up into heavenly glory, the risen Lord has not been removed from the story of Acts. While the risen One normally works through witnesses empowered by his Spirit, there are moments when he still plays an active role within the narrative. The outstanding example of the risen Lord's active role is the conversion of Paul, but one should not forget the other moments when the Lord appears to Paul: in Corinth (18:9–10), and twice in Jerusalem (22:17–21; 23:11). Consequently, although the enthroned Messiah remains in heaven until the universal restoration (3:21), he appears in heavenly glory to commission and strengthen Paul.

Finally, all the accounts of Paul's conversion draw a relationship between the enthroned Messiah and his followers. Those who persecute Jesus' followers persecute him (9:4, 22:7; 26:14). Although the Lukan narrative does not explain how the persecution of Jesus' followers can affect the risen Lord, this statement suggests an intimate relationship between the risen Lord and his disciples that approaches a mystical union. Although Jesus is enthroned in heaven as God's Messiah king, he stands in solidarity with his followers, just as the Son of Man stands in solidarity with the oppressed of the earth (Matt. 25:31–46). This solidarity is appropriate to the one the church now acclaims as *kyrios,* a title normally reserved for God.

Stephen's Story of Israel

Thus far, we have seen that the speeches of Peter and Paul presuppose a narrative of Jesus' career, and that this narrative is the latest and most important chapter in God's dealings with Israel. Accordingly, we could say that the story of Israel is the story of Jesus, inasmuch as Israel's history foreshadows the story of Jesus. In this regard, Stephen's speech to the Hellenists (7:2–53) plays a central role since it is the most detailed presentation of Israel's history.

Unlike the speeches of Peter and Paul, this speech does not contain an extended christological kerygma. Its explicit Christology is reserved to a question and harsh accusation: "Which of the prophets did your ancestors not persecute? They killed those who foretold the coming of the Righteous One, and now you have become his betrayers and murderers" (7:52). Nonetheless, this speech plays a central role in the Christology of Luke-Acts because of the unrelenting manner in which it portrays Israel as repeatedly rejecting the savior figures God sent to redeem it. Like the episode of Jesus' inaugural sermon (Luke 4:16–30), this speech functions as a story within the story that provides the key to unlocking the meaning of the larger narrative. To anticipate our results, the whole of Israel's history foreshadowed the rejection of Jesus, thereby frustrating the promise God made to Abraham, "they shall come out and worship me in this place" (7:7). This promise will only be fulfilled when Israel repents and worships God by calling upon the name of Jesus.

Stephen makes this speech in response to the accusations of false witnesses that he purportedly speaks against "this holy place and the law" (6:13). Instead of directly defending himself, Stephen recounts Israel's history and shows that the people have never worshiped God as they ought, or observed the law, even though God promised that Israel would worship him "in this place"[80] and gave Abraham "the covenant of circumcision" (7:7–8). Israel has always been "stiff-necked" and "uncircumcised in heart and ears" (7:51), as its history has repeatedly shown.

To prove his accusation, Stephen rehearses Israel's history. This history, as recounted by Stephen, includes the call of Abraham (7:2–8), the rejection of Joseph by his brothers (7:9–16), and the repudiation of Moses by his kinsmen (7:17–34). Stephen also recalls the period of Israel's wandering in the wilderness, as well as the time of Joshua, David, and Solomon (7:35–50). The leading figures of the speech, however, are Joseph and Moses, and their repudiation prefigures the rejection of Jesus.

The parallels between Joseph and Moses on the one hand, and Jesus on the other, are striking. Joseph's brothers sold him into slavery, but God rescued him from all of his afflictions so that he could save his brothers and their families from famine. Similarly, Jesus was rejected by his people, but God raised him from the dead so that he could save them from their sins. Moses was instructed in all wisdom and was powerful in word and deed. He came to his own people to rescue them, but they rejected him, asking, "Who made you a ruler and a judge (*archonta kai dikastēn*) over us?" (7:27). Although they had rejected Moses, God sent him forty years later as ruler and liberator (*archonta kai lytrōtēn*) of his people, and Moses led them out of Egypt, performing wonders and signs (7:35–36). After these events, Moses told the Israelites, "God will raise up a prophet for you from your own people as he raised me up" (7:37). Jesus is the prophet like Moses whom God raised up (3:22). He was filled with wisdom (Luke 2:40), and he performed deeds of power, wonders, and signs among his people (Acts 2:22). Although the people repudiated Jesus, God effected redemption through him (Luke 2:38; 24:21), despite his death on the cross.[81]

Because Israel repeatedly rejected the savior figures God sent to redeem it, what God spoke to Abraham ("they shall come out and worship me *in this place*," 7:7) was not fulfilled, even though Solomon built God a temple (7:47). Only when Israel calls upon the name of the Lord (Jesus) will it worship God *in this place*, as God promised Abraham. In this regard, the words of Zechariah's canticle are illuminating:

> and to be mindful of his holy covenant, and of the oath he swore to Abraham our father, and to grant us that, rescued from the hand of our enemies, without fear we might worship (*latreuein*) him in holiness and righteousness before him all our days. (Luke 1:72–73, RNAB)

From the point of view of the Lukan narrator, Israel cannot worship God in holiness and righteousness without calling upon the name of the Lord, who is Jesus. If Stephen has spoken against *this place* (the Temple), as his accusers charge, it is because Israel will worship God in holiness and righteousness only when it calls upon the name of the Lord. Stephen's perspective on Israel's history, then, provides a framework within which to understand the story of Jesus. As Israel's last and greatest savior figure, the Righteous One (7:52), Jesus the Messiah enables Israel to worship God in holiness and righteousness, as God swore to Abraham.

Christology in Luke-Acts

Although Luke writes with Gentiles in view,[82] his two-volume work presents one of the most traditional Christologies of the New Testament. In the infancy narrative and the speeches of Acts, the Lukan narrator portrays Jesus as the fulfillment of Israel's traditional messianic hopes. Jesus is the royal descendant of David who will rule over the house of Jacob forever. Thus, even after the resurrection, the apostles ask the risen Jesus if he is going to restore the kingdom to Israel. Moreover, Paul insists that his own preaching is no different from that of the prophets and Moses, who foretold that the Messiah must suffer. Far from disqualifying Jesus as the Messiah, Jesus' sufferings authenticate his messiahship, for those who know how to read what is written in Moses and the Prophets. Of the many terms that Luke employs to identify Jesus, then, "Messiah" is among the most important. Indeed, one could argue that it is *the* title in reference to which all others are to be understood.

Like other writings of the New Testament, however, Luke-Acts presents Jesus' messiahship in light of the resurrection. It insists that Jesus' messianic enthronement occurred at the resurrection, when God exalted him in royal dignity at his right hand. From his exalted station at God's right hand, the enthroned Messiah sends forth the Spirit, and God effects powerful deeds in the name of Jesus. Those who call upon this name will be saved from their sins. The enthroned Messiah, therefore, is properly addressed as Lord, a title normally reserved for God. This heavenly Lord directs the mission of his church and watches over the welfare of his witnesses. Still able to participate in the life of his church, though enthroned in heaven, he calls Paul, the persecutor, to conversion. Enthroned at God's right hand, the Messiah of Israel has become the Lord of all who repent and believe in his name, Gentile as well as Jew.

The designation of Jesus as the Messiah of Israel, therefore, must be viewed within the context of Jesus' exalted status. By calling upon the Messiah as its Lord, the church attributes a godly status to Jesus, as does the Gospel when it identifies him as the Son of God. However, whereas "Son of God" occurs with some frequency in the Gospel, it all but disappears from Acts, except for its use in 9:20 and 13:33. The virtual absence of the "Son of God" title does not mean that it has become less important for Luke-Acts. After all, it is God who identifies Jesus as his Son at Jesus' baptism and transfiguration. But now that Jesus has been raised from the dead and exalted at God's right hand, believers address him with the name that is above every other name, *kyrios*.

In addition to calling Jesus "Lord," the church continues to address God as Lord. Moreover, in several places it is not clear if *kyrios* refers to Jesus or God.[83] While these ambiguous designations are bothersome to those seeking precise information, they suggest that the boundaries between

Jesus and God have become fluid in the narrative of Acts since the risen One enjoys a unique relation with God. The enthroned Messiah *is* the Son of God, and it is proper for believers to address him as *kyrios,* even as they address God.

Like the Gospel of Matthew, Luke-Acts places the story of Jesus within the broader story of Israel so that the story of Jesus becomes the story of Israel. In doing this, Luke-Acts witnesses to continuity in God's dealing with Israel. The God of Jesus is the God of Israel, and this God effects salvation through his anointed one, the enthroned Messiah. By making use of the story of Israel to clarify the story of Jesus, Luke-Acts prepares readers for the Christology of Paul who, like Luke, presupposes the story of Israel in his presentation of Jesus.

3

The Climax of Israel's Story

$\mathcal{E}$ ven the casual reader of the New Testament recognizes that the genre of Paul's writings is different from that of the Gospels. Whereas the Gospels are narratives that recount the events of Jesus' ministry, death, and resurrection, Paul's writings belong to the genre of the Hellenistic letter.[1] As such, their purpose was to strengthen, encourage, admonish, advise, and, when necessary, rebuke the congregations he had established, or, in the case of Romans, he was about to visit. Consequently, although his writings contain a great deal of theology, they are not theological treatises on Christology, soteriology, and ecclesiology. Rather, Paul addressed specific situations in the congregations to which he wrote, and in this regard, his correspondence was "occasional."[2]

Although his letters were occasional in nature, when Paul responded to queries from the churches or problems within them, he grounded his responses in the gospel he received when God revealed his Son to him (Gal. 1:11–12). That gospel is the good news of what God has done in his Son, Jesus Christ: reconciled the world to himself through the death and resurrection of Christ (2 Cor. 5:19). To use the vocabulary of J. Christiaan Beker, the "contingency" of Paul's letters is grounded in the "coherency" of his gospel.[3] Consequently, his writings are thoroughly theological, even though he did not compose them as theological treatises.

Given the nature of Paul's writings, how can we uncover the Christology that he develops in them? Theoretically, there are several ways of proceeding. For example, we could study the major titles Paul applies to Jesus, such as "Lord," "Christ," and, "Son of

God."[4] This approach, however, leaves something to be desired since Paul is more interested in soteriology (the benefits that Christ obtains for believers) than in titles.[5]

Therefore, it might be more profitable to examine the soteriological concepts that Paul uses to explain Christ's benefits. For example, Christ justifies, sanctifies, redeems, liberates, and reconciles believers.[6] This approach is an improvement over the first, for what Christ has done is an essential component of his identity. For example, the one who redeems is the Redeemer. But it also raises a question. How are the benefits of Christ (justification, sanctification, redemption) related to each other? Accordingly, many have tried to systematize Paul's Christology.[7] However, while a synthesis of Paul's thought is desirable, it runs the risk of neglecting the occasional and contingent character of his writings. Moreover, a Pauline synthesis may give the impression that Paul was a systematic thinker akin to a contemporary theologian, when, in fact, he was a pastor responding to the needs of his congregations. Without neglecting or disparaging these approaches, I propose to investigate Paul's Christology from a narrative perspective by focusing on the underlying story of Israel and Christ that his letters presuppose. Since this approach has only recently been introduced into the study of Pauline Christology, it requires some explanation.[8]

Stories or narratives play an important role in our lives. As individuals we make sense of our lives by understanding them as continually unfolding stories. The past tells us where we have been. The present indicates where we are, and the future provides us with goals and ideals to be attained. However, since the future is yet to unfold, the story by which we interpret our lives is ever in need of revision. New events provide perspective on the past and require us to reformulate the story anew. Our individual stories, however, are not the whole story. To understand who we are, we place the story of our lives within greater stories, such as the story of our family or nation. Thus national and family epics also identify who we are. But even then, the story is not complete, and we must continually revise it as new events unfold and provide greater perspective on the past.

If this brief analysis is correct, we can assume that Paul understood himself in terms of at least two interrelated narratives: the story of his own life and the story of his people Israel. Previous to his call and conversion, Paul comprehended both stories in light of the Mosaic law, the sign of Israel's covenant status before God. Thus Paul writes that prior to his call he surpassed his contemporaries in zeal for the law (Gal. 1:14; Phil. 3:4–6). We can assume, then, that the covenant God made with Israel at Sinai played a central role in Paul's pre-Christian story of Israel.

But stories are not complete until they have ended, and, before they have ended, they are liable to change and adjustment. In the case of Paul, the story by which he understood his life—the story of Israel—was dramatically altered when God revealed to him that the crucified Jesus was God's Son (Gal. 1:16). This dramatic disclosure did not mean that the old story was no longer true, for Paul never concluded that God had been unfaithful to Israel (see Romans 9–11). But it did require Paul to rethink and reread the old story in light of its most recent event: the sending of God's Son, whom the law identified as cursed because he died the shameful death of crucifixion (Gal. 3:13). To put it another way, the story of Christ gave new meaning to the story of Israel and required Paul to reinterpret Israel's story as well as the story of his own life.

Since Paul's correspondence is occasional in nature, he never gives a full account of his personal story, the story of Israel, or the story of Christ.[9] Nevertheless, his letters suggest that there is an underlying narrative by which he understands the story of his life and the story of his people Israel. In each of Paul's letters, I submit, there is an implied story, which I will call "the story of Christ" or "the Christ story." This story provides a profitable starting point for studying Paul's Christology since it clarifies the grammar of Paul's thought. Before proceeding further, however, two concepts must be clarified here: "the story of Christ," and "the grammar of Paul's thought."[10]

As regards the first, the story of Christ, I do not mean a narrative of Jesus' career, such as the Gospels present. Apart from the events surrounding Jesus' death and resurrection, Paul tells his readers very little about Jesus' life.[11] Rather, by this expression I am signifying *the story of God's dealings with Israel and the Gentiles in light of what God has done in his Son, Jesus Christ.* Thus the story of Christ includes the story of Israel with its most recent chapter, the sending of God's Son. If one were to synthesize the different events of this story as found in Paul's letters, it might read something like this.

Adam, the first human being, initiated a history of sin by his disobedience, and this resulted in death and condemnation for all. To reconcile the world to himself and rescue humanity from its sinful plight, God sent his Son, whose obedience unto death upon a cross inaugurated a new history of grace and acquittal. God had always determined that he would justify the Gentiles as well as the Jews on the basis of faith. Therefore, before sending his Son, he made a covenant with Abraham that would be fulfilled in Christ, Abraham's singular descendant. In the period between this covenant and the sending of Christ, Israel received the law, which made it aware of its transgressions. But

85

God did not intend the law to bring justification and life. The goal of the law was Christ, and God proposed to reconcile the world to himself through his Son, whom he set forth as an expiation for sins. In the fullness of time, God sent his preexistent Son to reconcile the world to himself. Justified, reconciled, and at peace with God, believers now await the fullness of salvation that God will effect when he sends his Son at the end of the ages to rescue believers from the coming divine wrath. At Christ's parousia, the general resurrection of the dead will occur, and then death, the last and greatest enemy, will be destroyed. So, God will be all in all.

Some readers will recognize that this *composite* story draws heavily upon Paul's letters to the Galatians, Romans, and Corinthians, and to a lesser extent upon those to the Thessalonians and Philippians. The complete story does *not* exist in any single letter, and Paul never formulated the whole story as I have. Moreover, it is not at all evident that the story of Abraham and Christ found in Galatians fully coheres with the story of Adam and Christ found in Romans and 1 Corinthians. Thus it may well be that Paul's Christ story shifted as he encountered new challenges in the churches to which he wrote. For example, while it was crucial for Paul to relate *the end* of the Christ story to the Thessalonians because they were concerned about those who died before the parousia, it was more important for him to relate *the beginning* of the Christ story to the Galatians because they were unsure of their relationship to Abraham, Israel, and the law.

As regards the second point, the grammar of Paul's thought, this expression refers to the manner in which Paul's concepts about God, Christ, Israel, the Gentiles, and creation are interrelated.[12] Narratives, like sentences, have a grammar whereby a series of discrete events are related to each other to form a plot, "the principle of interconnectedness and intention."[13] If one removes the verb from a sentence, the remaining words no longer form a sentence. Similarly, if one removes the principle that connects one event to another from a narrative, there is no story. For example, conflict is the principle that connects the several incidents of Mark's Gospel so that they form a story. If we do away with the conflicts between Jesus and the religious leaders, and Jesus and his disciples, the Markan Gospel no longer functions as a narrative. It becomes a series of discrete events, and it is impossible to determine how Jesus, the disciples, and the religious leaders are related to one another.

Can we reconstruct the story or stories that underlie Paul's letters? The answer to this question is important for Pauline Christology, for if we do not know how the story coheres, then we do not understand how Christ functions in Paul's Christology, or the meaning of the titles and benefits that he attributes to Jesus. A grasp of the grammar of Paul's thought is essential for comprehending his Christology. Therefore, we must determine how Christ functions in the story that underlies Paul's thought.[14]

I am proposing, then, that Paul's Christology is embedded in an underlying narrative just as the Christology of the Gospels is encoded in the narratives they relate. This underlying narrative gives coherence to the several christological and soteriological statements Paul makes in his letters. However, whereas the narratives of the four Gospels are explicit, those underlying Paul's letters are implicit. Consequently, we must uncover and reconstruct the narrative of each letter as best we can. Only then will the coherence of Paul's thought become apparent, despite the contingent and occasional nature of his letters.

I am not proposing that there is a defined and unchanging Christ story that we can easily reproduce, as my earlier summary might suggest. We do not know the full extent of Paul's Christ story since he never recounts it in any letter. Moreover, Paul's story of Christ probably underwent change and adaptation as he grew in his understanding of what God accomplished in Christ; for new circumstances surely required Paul to rethink his story. But it is not unreasonable to assume that there is a narrative that undergirds his writings and that we can know something of it.

Rather than begin with a reconstruction of the Christ story drawn from Paul's letters,[15] I propose to uncover the Christ story presupposed in each letter, thereby respecting the occasional nature of his writings. In this chapter I deal with those letters whose Pauline authorship is not disputed: Romans, 1 and 2 Corinthians, Galatians, Philippians, 1 Thessalonians, and Philemon. The one exception to this is 2 Thessalonians, which I treat with 1 Thessalonians since the subject matter of the two letters and the story they presuppose are similar. Philemon is not treated since it does not present a significant Christology. In considering these letters, I proceed chronologically, beginning with the earlier letters and concluding with Paul's later correspondence. Since there is considerable dispute about the dating of Philippians and Galatians, I recognize that not all will agree with the chronology I have adopted: 1 and 2 Thessalonians, 1 and 2 Corinthians, Galatians, Romans, and Philippians.

Uncovering the story of Christ that undergirds Paul's correspondence will not be an easy task, and a project such as this runs the risk of reading more into the text than is there. But it is possible to know something of Paul's underlying Christ story if one pays attention to the several statements Paul makes about Christ's work and the manner in which he views Christ in relationship to the story of Israel. Paul develops a narrative grammar whereby he relates Christ to God, Israel, and humanity. The principal actor of his Christ story is God; the recipient or beneficiary of God's salvific work is humanity, Gentile as well as Jew; and the agent by which God accomplishes this work is Christ, the Son whom the Father sent into the world to rescue it from the coming wrath.

THE LETTERS TO THE THESSALONIANS

First Thessalonians is a paraenetic letter that exhorts and encourages a Gentile Christian community suffering affliction and persecution from its Gentile neighbors.[16] It was occasioned by a report Paul received from Timothy about the community (3:6). Overall the report was positive, and Paul employs this letter to recall former teaching and exhort the Thessalonians to remain faithful to their call and election as a sanctified community that must stand blameless before the Lord on the day of his parousia (5:23). Paul also takes the occasion of this letter to provide the community with further teaching about the Lord's parousia, since the death of some members of the community has disturbed the Thessalonians and caused them to ask if deceased believers will share in the salvation the Lord's parousia will bring.

Second Thessalonians is also a paraenetic letter that exhorts the Thessalonians to remain steadfast in the face of affliction and persecution. Whether it was written by Paul, or by one of his coworkers with his approbation, it describes a deepening crisis at Thessalonica.[17] Persecution has become more severe, and this has led some to assert that the day of the Lord is at hand (2 Thess. 2:2). Consequently, Paul must provide the community with further instruction about the Lord's parousia. He writes that before the parousia there will be a general apostasy and the appearance of "the lawless one" who, at the present time, is being restrained by someone or something (2 Thess. 2:1–12).

Traces of a Story

The Christ story of the Thessalonian correspondence says very little about Jesus' earthly life or the story of Israel. Moreover, the events that it does relate tend to focus upon the conclusion of the story: the day when God's Son will return in glory to gather his elect.[18] Nevertheless, there are traces of a more comprehensive story in its references to the election of the Thessalonians, Jesus' death and resurrection, the parousia, and the coming wrath of God.

When Paul reminds the Thessalonians that they have been called, elected, and chosen by God (1 Thess. 1:4–5; 2:11–12; 4:7; 5:9, 23–24; 2 Thess. 1:11; 2:13), he implicitly associates them with the people of Israel. Just as God called Israel, so he called the Gentile Thessalonians, through Jesus Christ, to be his chosen people. In effect, Paul makes the Thessalonians part of a history of election that began with Israel.[19]

Another indication of a more comprehensive story occurs in the moral exhortation of 1 Thess. 4:1–12. Toward the end of that exhortation, Paul says that there is no need for him to write to the Thessalonians on the subject of mutual charity, for they have been "taught by God" (4:9). While there is no unanimity on the meaning of this term, the passage is reminiscent of Jeremiah's promise that God will establish a new covenant with Israel, whereby the law will be written in people's hearts so that there will be no need for one person to teach another (Jer. 31:33–34). If Paul is alluding to the text of Jeremiah, then the Thessalonians, who have been "taught by God," are the beneficiaries of a new covenant.[20] Although Paul does not explicitly mention Christ here, he presupposes his work, as does the election theology that occurs throughout 1 Thessalonians. The Thessalonians are God's chosen people and have received the promised gift of the Spirit (4:8; see Ezek. 36:27; 37:14) because of what Christ has done for them.

A further indication of a more encompassing story occurs when Paul commends the Thessalonians for imitating him and the Lord when they received the word in great affliction (1 Thess. 1:6). He notes that the Thessalonians have become imitators of the churches of God in Judea by enduring the same things from their compatriots that the Judean churches are suffering from the Jews, who killed the Lord Jesus and the prophets and are presently persecuting Paul, for which reason the wrath of God is coming upon them (2:14–16).[21] From this text, we can surmise the following narrative: Jesus was a prophetic figure who was persecuted as were the prophets before him. And just as the Jewish people killed the prophets, so they killed him. At present his followers are enduring a similar fate, but the period of persecution is coming to an end because the wrath of God is about to be revealed.

This wrath of God plays an important role in Paul's story. In 1 Thess. 1:9–10, he reminds the Thessalonians how they turned from idols to the living and true God to await his Son, Jesus, whom he raised from the dead. Jesus, God's Son, will deliver the Thessalonians from the divine wrath when he returns as God's eschatological agent. In 2 Thessalonians Paul describes how God will exercise his wrath. Jesus will return in blazing fire with his mighty angels to inflict punishment on those who do not acknowledge God or obey the gospel of the Lord Jesus Christ (1:5–10). In both 1 and 2 Thessalonians, Jesus is God's eschatological agent who will play a crucial role at the end of the ages. But whereas 1 Thessalonians portrays Jesus as the one who delivers the elect from the wrath of God, 2 Thessalonians depicts him as punishing those who persecuted the elect.

The theme of God's wrath also occurs in 1 Thess. 5:9–10, where Paul writes that God did not destine the Thessalonians for wrath but for salvation through Jesus Christ who died for (*hyper*) them. Consequently, whether they are alive or dead, they will always be with Christ. The death of Christ clearly plays a central role in the story that Paul presupposes, and it indicates that Jesus was more than a prophet. He died *for* others (1 Thess. 5:10), and God raised him from the dead (1 Thess. 1:10). As God's eschatological agent he will deliver believers from God's wrath at his parousia.

When Paul speaks of this parousia, he is telling the Thessalonians the final chapter of the story, a chapter that has not yet unfolded. Reminding them of what they should already know, he supplements their understanding by further teaching (1 Thess. 4:13–18). For example, death cannot separate believers from the risen Lord since there is an intimate connection between the resurrection of Christ and the resurrection of believers. When the Lord returns, those who died believing in him will be raised, and those who are alive will be snatched up to meet him in the air.

In 2 Thess. 2:1–12, Paul warns the community that the parousia will not come as soon as some expect, despite the severe persecution the Thessalonians are undergoing. Before the parousia takes place, there will be a great apostasy and the appearance of the lawless one. Then the parousia of the Lord will occur, and the Lord Jesus will destroy the lawless one with the breath of his mouth. At the present time, however, someone or something is restraining the lawless one. Consequently, while the Lord's parousia is imminent, it is not at hand.[22]

The Christ Story

Although Paul does not explicitly narrate his Christ story, the Thessalonian correspondence presupposes a story or narrative that may be summarized as follows.

> Jesus, the Son of God, endured a life of affliction. His afflictions were similar to those endured by the Jewish prophets of old. Just as the Jewish people killed the prophets, so they killed Jesus. The death of Jesus, however, played a significant role in God's plan of salvation, for he was God's Son,

and God raised him from the dead. Christ died on behalf of others, and when he returns he will rescue believers from God's wrath and lead them to salvation. Because of Jesus' death, believers enjoy the gift of the Spirit; they are the sanctified and elect people of God.

The story of Jesus is part of a larger story: the story of God's plan for salvation. Previously, humanity worshiped idols rather than the living and true God. Because of this, humanity is destined to suffer God's wrath, unless it turns to the living and true God. Those who turn from idols and wait for the coming of God's Son are an elect and chosen people like Israel of old. At present, this sanctified congregation experiences severe affliction, but this will end at the parousia. Then the Lord will descend from heaven, the dead will be raised, and believers who are alive will be gathered to the Lord forever. The parousia, however, will not take place as quickly as some suppose. Certain events must occur first: the great apostasy and the appearance of the lawless one. Nevertheless, it will come like a thief in the night. Therefore, all must be prepared so that they can stand blameless in holiness before the Lord on the day of his parousia.

The Thessalonian correspondence presupposes a minimal Christ story that is heavily weighted toward the events of the end time: The one whom the Jews put to death will return as God's eschatological judge, the Son of God. But as brief as the story is, it discloses an important Christology. First, Jesus is God's eschatological agent of salvation. His death accomplishes something that the death of the prophets could not. It provides a way for believers to escape God's wrath and makes them members of the called and sanctified congregation. Second, God vindicated Jesus by raising him from the dead. In turn, Jesus' resurrection is the first in a series of resurrections that will occur at the parousia. God will bring to life, through Jesus, those who have believed in his son. Third, Jesus enjoys a godly status. He is the "Lord," "the Lord Jesus Christ," "the Lord Jesus."[23] Presently, he dwells in heaven with God, his Father, waiting for the word of command that will inaugurate his parousia. Fourth, although Paul does not develop an extensive Son of God Christology in Thessalonians, he clearly presupposes that Jesus is God's Son. The nature of this sonship, however, is not defined. Fifth, although Paul knows the traditional significance of *Christos* ("Messiah"), he does not dwell on Jesus' messianic status so much as he presupposes it. The one who saves the elect from God's wrath is the Messiah, the Son of God. In sum, though the Thessalonian correspondence does not provide a complete Christology, it is an overture to a Christology that Paul will develop more fully in other writings.

THE LETTERS TO THE CORINTHIANS

There are several indications that Paul presupposes a story of Christ in his Corinthian correspondence. For example, he relates how, on the night he was handed over, Jesus instituted the Eucharist (1 Cor. 11:23–26). In reminding the Corinthians of the gospel that he preached to them, he recalls that Christ died for our sins, was buried, was raised on the third day, and that he appeared to numerous witnesses: Cephas, the Twelve, five hundred brethren, James, all the apostles, and finally, to Paul himself (1 Cor. 15:1–11).[24] Then, in a discussion about the resurrection of the dead, Paul describes Christ's parousia and the events of the end time (1 Cor. 15:20–28, 50–57). In addition to these texts which focus on Christ's death, resurrection, and parousia, Paul alludes to Jesus' teaching on divorce (1 Cor. 7:10–11) and his instruction that those who preach the gospel should be supported by it (1 Cor. 9:14). If we add to these a series of texts that intimate Christ's preexistence (1 Cor. 8:6; 10:4, 9; 2 Cor. 8:9), the Corinthian correspondence suggests a rather extensive story that can be plotted in terms of his preexistence, death, resurrection, and parousia.

Although Paul seems to suggest that Christ enjoyed some sort of preexistence, he is more concerned with Christ's postexistence than his preexistence,[25] just as he is more interested in Jesus' death and resurrection than in the events of his earthly ministry. There is an important similarity, then, between the stories of Paul's Thessalonian and Corinthian correspondence inasmuch as Christ's death, resurrection, and parousia remain focal events.

But since Paul must respond to new issues in 1 and 2 Corinthians that range from difficulties besetting the community to a personal defense of his apostolate, this correspondence highlights new aspects of the Christ story. For example, in dealing with the danger of party strife at Corinth (1:10–4:21), Paul discusses the nature of God's wisdom, arguing that the crucified Christ is the power and wisdom of God (1 Cor. 1:24). When responding to a Corinthian inquiry about the legitimacy of participating in sacral meals at which the food to be consumed has been sacrificed to idols (1 Cor. 8:1–11:1), Paul refers to Israel's experience in the wilderness (10:1–13) and reminds the Corinthians how Israel committed idolatry, even though it drank from "the rock" who is Christ (10:4, 9). When discussing the resurrection of the dead and the nature of the resurrection body (1 Cor. 15:1–58), Paul draws a comparison between Adam, in whom all died, and Christ, who brings the resurrection of the dead (1 Cor. 15:20–28) so that believers might bear his image just as they bore the image of the first man (1 Cor. 15:45–49). Finally, when defending his apostolic ministry before the Corinthians (2 Cor. 2:14–5:21), Paul recounts the story of Moses' veil (Ex. 34:29–35) and argues that God made him the minister of a new covenant (2 Cor. 3:6). As a minister of this new covenant, he lifts the veil that prevented Israel from looking upon the glory of God, the glory that shines on the face of Christ, the image of God (2 Cor. 4:4–6). In a word, the questions and issues that Paul faced at Corinth required him to rethink and draw upon new aspects of his Christ story.

But did Paul have a single, neatly defined narrative about Christ that he employed as occasion demanded? The answer to this question is not a simple yes or no. To be sure, there is a certain consistency to Paul's Christ story when it deals with Christ's death, resurrection, and parousia. Paul's Christ story, however, was intimately related to the story of Israel, a story he reinterpreted in light of what God had done in Christ. Consequently, Paul's Christ story had the potential for growing and developing as the apostle reread the story of his people in light of Christ. To use Paul's metaphor, the veil that once lay over his heart had been lifted (2 Cor. 3:14–16) so that he understood the story of his people as the story of Christ. Therefore, while the essential core of his Christ story is constant, it was also a developing narrative. As Paul read old texts with an "unveiled heart," his story of Christ grew and developed. Thus he learned to call Christ the wisdom and power of God, the rock from which Israel drank in the wilderness, the new Adam in whom God was at work reconciling the world to himself, the image of God whose face reflects the glory of God.

Christ the Wisdom of God

At the beginning of his Corinthian correspondence, Paul calls Christ the wisdom of God (1:24, 30). To what extent he thought of Christ in terms of wisdom prior to his Corinthian correspondence, we do not know. But even if he had come to this understanding of Christ earlier, the danger of factions at Corinth was surely the crucible in which he further developed his wisdom Christology.[26]

The Corinthian community was in danger of disintegrating into rival factions because its members identified themselves too closely with the ministers of the gospel who had baptized them (1:12), claiming, perhaps, that the one who baptized them imparted a particular wisdom to them. In responding to this problem, Paul does not dispute that the gospel brings a certain wisdom, but he does insist that there is an essential difference between the wisdom of this age and the wisdom of God. The wisdom of God is the crucified Christ, a wisdom the world cannot understand. Thus Paul establishes a fundamental opposition between the wisdom of this age and

the wisdom of God. To the world the wisdom of God (Jesus Christ crucified) is folly and weakness, but to those who are being saved, Christ crucified is the power and wisdom of God. Conversely, what the world counts
as wisdom and power, God views as weakness and folly.

Paul says that the wisdom he proposes is for the mature and spiritual
since it is the revelation of the mystery of God (2:1), hidden from human
wisdom but determined by God before the ages for our glory (2:7). Paul
presupposes that the world has gone astray and is no longer capable of
knowing God. Therefore, since the world did not know God through its
own wisdom, God revealed his wisdom in the folly of the cross so that the
crucified Christ has become the power and wisdom of God (1:24). For
those who believe the gospel, Christ is their wisdom, righteousness, sanctification, and redemption (1:30).

The central event in this drama is the crucifixion of Jesus. For the
Jewish world, that event was the stumbling block that prevented it from
accepting Jesus as the Messiah. For the Gentile world, the proclamation
of a crucified savior was the height of folly (1:23). Paul understood this
all too well from his preaching among Gentiles and Jews. But his proclamation of the crucified Christ also taught him the paradoxical nature of
power, wisdom, and strength: namely, what the world understands as
wisdom, God calls folly, and what the world views as strength, God calls
weakness. Paul learned that God paradoxically manifested his power
and wisdom in the weakness and folly of the cross, so that the crucified
Christ has become the ultimate manifestation of God's wisdom and
power.

This revelation of God's power and wisdom is "the mystery of God"
(2:1), hidden but foretold in scripture. Thus, in quoting the prophet Isaiah
(2:9; see Isa. 52:15; 64:4), Paul shows that the message of the cross is
God's predetermined plan for humanity's glory. The rulers of this age,
however, did not know or recognize this wisdom, otherwise they would
never have crucified "the Lord of glory" (2:8).

There is no other place in Paul's letters where he identifies Christ so explicitly as the wisdom of God. But in doing so, is he implying that Christ
is the preexistent wisdom of God? There are intimations of Christ's preexistence in Paul's Corinthian correspondence. For example, in 1 Cor. 8:6,
he speaks of one God who is Father and one Lord, Jesus Christ, "from
whom are all things and through whom we exist." In 1 Cor. 10:4, he says
that Christ was the spiritual rock from which the congregation of Israel
drank during its sojourn in the wilderness, and that Israel tested Christ in
the wilderness (10:9). Finally, in 2 Cor. 8:9, Paul reminds the community

of Christ who became poor for their sake even though he was rich, which suggests an act of self-emptying similar to that described in Phil. 2:5–11.

On balance, however, Paul is more concerned with the post-resurrection existence of Christ than with his preexistence. Thus, although Paul seems to presuppose some sort of preexistence in the texts listed above, he never focuses upon or discusses this preexistent state. Rather, the concept is always in the service of other goals. For instance, his enigmatic remark that Israel tested Christ during the period of its wilderness wandering warns the Corinthian community not to fall into idolatry as did Israel (1 Cor. 10:9). To encourage the Corinthians to be generous in the collection for Jerusalem, he reminds them that Jesus impoverished himself for their sake. In neither case does Paul discuss or explain the nature of Christ's preexistence.

In the opening chapters of 1 Corinthians, there is no indication that Paul thinks of Christ as preexistent wisdom. Rather, he argues that the shameful death of Christ upon the cross was the manifestation of God's wisdom, righteousness, sanctification, and redemption to a recalcitrant world that did not know God through its own wisdom. Thus it is unlikely that in identifying Christ as the wisdom of God, Paul has Christ's preexistence in view. His argument in the opening chapters of 1 Corinthians is remarkably theocentric. He does not simply speak of Christ, nor does he engage in speculative discussions about Christ's person. Rather, he relates Christ to God and humanity. God is the Father of the Lord Jesus Christ who was crucified for us. Christ is wisdom, righteousness, holiness, and redemption from God for humanity's sake. Paul's story of Christ, the wisdom of God, then, is a story about God's dealings with and for humanity.

Christ the New Adam

There are two places where Paul explicitly employs a comparison between Adam and Christ. The first is Rom. 5:12–21, where he contrasts the destructive results of Adam's disobedience with the salvific effects of Christ's obedience, and the second is 1 Cor. 15:1–58, where he contrasts the first Adam who brought death into the world with Christ, the new Adam, who has become the source of resurrection life. In both cases Paul's "Adam Christology" is in the service of his soteriology. By casting Christ in the role of a new Adam, Paul shows that the obedience of Christ resulted in acquittal for all (Rom. 5:18), and through his resurrection all are brought to life (1 Cor. 15:22). Thus Paul's Adam Christology must not be isolated from his soteriology.

95

Some have argued that the roots of Paul's Adam Christology are the call or conversion he experienced on the Damascus road, when God revealed his Son to him (Gal. 1:15–17; also see Acts 9; 22; 26).[27] The glory shining on the face of the risen Christ (2 Cor. 4:6) led Paul to identify him as the image (*eikōn*) of God. As the image of God, Christ is a new Adam, what God intended humanity to be (see Gen. 1:26, where God creates humanity in his image and likeness).

Whether or not Paul's call/conversion experience was the origin of his Adam Christology, this Christology appears for the first time in 1 Corinthians 15, where the apostle must show the Corinthians the intimate connection between the resurrection of Christ and their resurrection, as well as clarify the nature of the resurrection body. This Christology, then, is not developed for its own sake but to resolve an urgent problem within the Corinthian community.

To Paul's dismay, some are saying that there is no resurrection of the dead (1 Cor. 15:12). After reminding the Corinthians that the gospel he preached to them rests on the death and resurrection of Christ (1 Cor. 15:1–11), the apostle draws out the intimate connection between Christ's resurrection and the resurrection of all believers (1 Cor. 15:13–19). Christ is the "first fruits" of a general resurrection still to occur (1 Cor. 15:23). Because there is an essential similarity between Christ's resurrection and the resurrection of believers, Paul argues that if there is no general resurrection of the dead, then not even Christ has been raised from the dead. For Paul, the resurrection of Christ is not an isolated event, unrelated to the resurrection of believers, but the beginning of the general resurrection of the dead.[28] Thus the resurrection of Christ implies the resurrection of all who believe in him.

Having established that Christ's resurrection implies a general resurrection of the dead, Paul introduces his Adam Christology and explains the events that will precede and follow the general resurrection of the dead (1 Cor. 15:20–28). Paul's discussion presupposes an understanding of the human predicament that he will develop at length in Romans 5. Here, however, he only foreshadows that discussion when he notes that death entered the world through a human being and all died in Adam, therefore the resurrection of the dead must also come through a human being. This is why all receive life in Christ (1 Cor. 15:21–22).

Later, as he explains the nature of the resurrection body, Paul draws a second contrast between Adam and Christ (1 Cor. 15:45–49). Referring to Genesis, he notes that the first man, Adam, was a living being formed from the dust of the earth (see Gen. 2:7), whereas the eschatological man, Christ, is a living spirit from heaven. Because the first human was the ancestor of all human beings, all bear his image (*eikōn*), and they possess a mortal and corruptible body. At the resurrection of the dead, however, this body will be transformed and bear the image (*eikōn*) of the heavenly one, the new Adam (1 Cor. 15:49).

When Paul speaks of Christ as the man from heaven, the heavenly one (vv. 47–48), he is referring to the risen Lord, who is a life-giving spirit because he has been raised from the dead. Previous to his resurrection, Jesus also bore the image of Adam. But now, risen and transformed, he is the heavenly one, the image of God, and he will confer upon believers the image of his resurrection body at the general resurrection of the dead.

Paul employs this Adam-Christ comparison to explain the destiny of humanity in light of what God has done in Christ. Although he does not speak of a "fall" in 1 Corinthians 15, he says that death came through a human being (v. 21), and since then humanity has been under the power of death, bearing the image of the earthly Adam. To be freed from its predicament, therefore, humanity must be freed from death. Although this liberation began with Christ's resurrection, it will not be complete until the general resurrection of the dead.

The order in which this final victory will occur is outlined in 1 Cor. 15:23–28. The victory has begun with the resurrection of Christ, which marks the first phase of the general resurrection of the dead. At Christ's parousia, the dead will be raised. Then Christ will hand over the kingdom to his Father. The Son himself will be subjected to God, and God will be all in all. During the period between Christ's resurrection and the resurrection of the dead, Christ reigns as God subjects all enemies to Christ. But the last and greatest enemy, "death," will not be overcome until the general resurrection of the dead. Then, when the dead are raised, God will have subjected everything to Christ, thereby fulfilling the words of Psalm 8. Originally applied to humanity, the psalm is applied to Christ, the new Adam: "For God has put all things in subjection under his feet [referring to Christ]" (1 Cor. 15:27, alluding to Ps. 8:6). The events of the end time can be summarized as follows.

> Christ has been raised from the dead.
> Christ is now reigning, and God is subjecting all enemies under Christ's feet.
> Christ will return at the parousia, and the dead will be raised.
> Death, the last enemy, will be destroyed, when the dead are raised, and God will have subjected everything to Christ.

Then Christ will hand over the kingdom to God his Father.
Christ will be subjected to God, his Father.
God will be all in all.

Paul's Adam Christology, as presented in 1 Corinthians, is in the service of soteriology. Breathtaking in its sweep, it provides a way to understand how Christ functions in relationship to God and humanity. In relationship to God, he is the Son who fulfills the destiny of humanity as described in Psalm 8. This is the perfect human being to whom God intended to subject all things. In relationship to humanity, Jesus is the beginning of a new creation, and he makes it possible for those who bear the image of the earthly one to bear his own image, the image of the heavenly one. In 2 Corinthians, Paul will develop this theme of Christ, the image of God, who transforms others into the same image.

Christ the Image and Glory of God

In 2 Corinthians, Paul calls Christ the image of God (4:4). As noted above, he may have come to this conclusion in light of his Damascus road experience, when God revealed his Son to him. Thus, if Paul is referring to his call in 2 Cor. 4:6 ("For it is the God who said, 'Let light shine out of darkness,' who has shone in our hearts to give the light of knowledge of the glory of God in the face of Jesus Christ"), he may have understood Christ as the *eikōn* of God, because he saw the glory of God on the face of the risen Lord. Whatever the origin of this expression, "glory" and "image" play an important role in Paul's Christology.[29] But, as with his Adam Christology, Paul's view of Christ as the image of God who radiates God's glory is closely tied to his soteriology.

The occasion for this Christology is Paul's defense of his apostolic ministry as developed in 2 Cor. 2:14–5:21. While there is uncertainty about the precise circumstances surrounding 2 Corinthians, it is clear that Paul must defend his ministry to the Corinthians because other preachers, who came to Corinth with "letters of recommendation," have criticized the apostle. Exactly who they were, and how their gospel differed from Paul's, is difficult to say. But on the basis of what Paul writes in 2 Cor. 3:1–4:18, it would appear that, in addition to possessing letters of recommendation from other churches (3:1–4), they interpreted their ministry in relationship to the Mosaic law.

The Mosaic law does not play an important role in Paul's Corinthian correspondence, especially when compared to his discussions of the law in Romans and Galatians. But in 2 Cor. 3:7–11, Paul draws a contrast between the old covenant and the new covenant of which he is a minister, thereby suggesting that others may have legitimized their preaching on the basis of its relationship to the Mosaic law.

Already hinting at the new covenant, Paul writes that he does not need any letters of recommendation to the Corinthians since the community itself is his letter of recommendation, not written on tablets of stone (as was the old covenant) but on their hearts of flesh. This last expression is an allusion to Jer. 31:33; Ezek. 11:19; 36:26, and it prepares for Paul's claim that he is the minister of a new covenant (2 Cor. 3:6).[30]

Having established that he has no need for letters of recommendation to the community that he founded, Paul draws a contrast between the old and new covenants to show the surpassing glory of the latter (3:7–11). He recognizes that the old covenant was glorious since the Israelites were not able to look upon the face of Moses, which reflected the glory (*doxa*) of God. Then, arguing from the lesser to the greater, Paul asks how much more glorious is the glory (*doxa*) of the new covenant since it is a ministry that derives from the Spirit rather than a ministry that leads to death. Accordingly, Paul's ministry leads to righteousness rather than condemnation.

Drawing upon the story of Moses' veil (Ex. 34:29–35), Paul affirms that he acts with greater boldness than Moses did. To understand what he means, it is necessary to review the story of Moses' veil as recounted in Exodus 34. According to that narrative, after Moses descended from Mount Sinai, the skin of his face shone with the reflected glory of God. When Aaron and the Israelites saw the glory of God shining on Moses' face, they were afraid to approach him. Consequently, Moses put a veil on his face lest the Israelites see God's glory shining on his face. Whenever Moses spoke with God, however, he removed the veil.

Paul's exegesis and application of this passage is greatly disputed. While many commentators argue that Moses veiled his face to prevent the Israelites from seeing that the glory on his face was fading, this interpretation does not accord with the plain sense of the story in Exodus 34, where Moses veils his face to prevent the Israelites from seeing the glory of God reflected on his face. For this reason, I find the explanation of Richard Hays satisfying.[31] Paul means that Moses veiled his face lest the Israelites see the glory of God. In a similar way, the ministry of the old covenant, as exemplified by Moses veiling his face, veiled the glory of God from the Israelites.

Contrasting himself with Moses, Paul says that he acts with greater boldness than Moses did since his ministry reveals the glory of God shining on the *face* of Christ (2 Cor. 4:6) who is the *eikōn* of God (4:4). Consequently, all who look upon Christ and see the glory of God are being transformed from glory to glory into the same image (3:18; also see Rom. 8:29; 1 Cor. 15:49). Whereas the veiled face of Moses prevented the Israelites from seeing the glory of God, the face of Christ reveals the glory of God. This is the ministry of the new covenant of which Paul is a minister.

The identification of Christ as the *eikon* of God who reveals God's glory recalls Paul's earlier statement that Christ is the "Lord of Glory" crucified by the rulers of this age (1 Cor. 2:8), as well as his comment that as we have borne the *eikōn* of the earthly one, the first Adam, so we will bear the *eikōn* of the heavenly one, the new Adam (1 Cor. 15:49). Christ, the wisdom of God, is the crucified Lord of Glory, and the crucified Lord of Glory is the *eikōn* of God, the new Adam. As the *eikōn* of God, Christ transforms believers into his image because, in gazing upon him with unveiled faces, they are gazing upon the glory of God (2 Cor. 3:18).

Paul does not explicitly deal with the human predicament in his discussion of glory since he is primarily concerned to establish that he is the minister of a new covenant in which believers can view the glory of God with unveiled faces shining on the face of Christ. But in Romans, where he describes the human predicament at length (Rom. 1:18–3:20), he says that all are deprived of the glory of God because all have sinned (Rom. 3:23). Although Paul has not made any reference to sin thus far, he makes a major statement about sin and reconciliation in 2 Corinthians 5, where he describes himself as Christ's ambassador who carries God's offer of reconciliation.

Once more, Paul insists that he is not trying to commend himself to the Corinthians. The love of Christ controls his ministry because Paul has come to the conviction that one man died for all with the result that all died (5:14). Here, Paul views Christ as a representative figure, as he did in 1 Corinthians 15, where he developed his Adam Christology. But whereas 1 Corinthians 15 focused on the resurrection, this text looks to Christ's death. The one man is Christ, the new Adam, whose death was vicarious and atoning because he died for all (*hyper pantōn apethanen*) so that they might live for him who died and rose on behalf of them (*tō hyper autōn apothanonti kai egerthenti;* 5:15).

Because Christ is a representative figure who died for humanity, Paul affirms that those "in Christ" are a new creation (5:17). He does not identify Christ as the new Adam in this text, but the reference to "a new creation" recalls 1 Cor. 15:49 in this way: just as humanity bore the image of the earthly one, so it will bear the image of the heavenly one (Christ the new Adam) at the general resurrection of the dead. For Paul, the death-resurrection of Christ is the central event in God's work of establishing a renewed creation. This renewal of creation was necessary because human-ity was at enmity with God. Therefore, God was in Christ reconciling the world to himself, "not counting their trespasses against them" (2 Cor. 5:19). In a paradoxical statement that stands in sharp contrast to his earlier description of Christ the *eikōn* of God, Paul writes that God made the sin-less Christ sin for our sake (*hyper hēmōn*) so that in Christ we might be-come the righteousness of God (5:21).

Paul's qualification that Christ was sinless ("did not know sin") fore-stalls any misunderstanding along the lines that Christ committed sin. Rather, Paul once more portrays Christ as a representative figure who stands in the place of humanity. Whereas Christ, the image of God, enjoyed the righteousness of God because he stood in the correct relationship to God, errant humanity was at enmity with God because of its transgressions. To reconcile the world to himself and renew creation, God put the sinless Christ in the place of sinful humanity so that sinful humanity could stand in the place of the sinless Christ. Once more, Christ functions as a repre-sentative figure, completely associating himself with the human condition so that humanity might be reconciled to God.

Paul does not tell a story in this section, nor does he allude to any bibli-cal narrative, but he clearly presupposes a story of humanity hostile and gone astray from God. Because humanity was unable to reconcile itself to God, God reconciled the world to himself in Christ. Consequently, anyone who is in Christ is a new creation.

The Christ Story

Although Paul does not explicitly relate a story about Christ in his Corinthian correspondence, he clearly presupposes such a Christ story in his response to the situation he confronted at Corinth. He identifies the cruci-fied Christ as the power and wisdom of God, "secret and hidden, which God decreed before the ages for our glory" (1 Cor. 2:7). The world did not un-derstand this wisdom, and its rulers crucified "the Lord of glory" (1 Cor. 2:8). This Lord of glory is the *eikōn* of God (2 Cor. 4:4), the one on whose face shines the glory of God (2 Cor. 4:6). Because of its trespasses, hu-manity was at enmity with God (2 Cor. 5:19), deprived of his glory (see Rom. 3:23). To reconcile the world to himself, God put the sinless Christ in the place of sinful humanity (2 Cor. 5:21). Christ died as the representative of all, the one for the many (2 Cor. 5:14). Thus he is the new Adam, the be-ginning of a new creation, and all who are in Christ are a new creation (2 Cor. 5:17). At present, humanity groans as it waits to be fully transformed

(2 Cor. 5:1–10). But even now, believers are being transformed from glory to glory as they gaze, with unveiled faces, upon the glory of God present in Christ, the image of God. At the general resurrection of the dead, believers will bear the image of the heavenly one, the new Adam. Then the plan of God's wisdom, predetermined for the glory of humanity, will be completed (1 Cor. 2:7), and God will be all in all (1 Cor. 15:28).

THE LETTER TO THE GALATIANS

Paul's letter to the Galatians is the apostle's response to a community crisis fraught with profound social and theological implications. Although Paul established the churches of Galatia on the basis of faith and did not require his converts to adopt the prescriptions of the Mosaic law, Christian missionaries of a strong Jewish bent came to Galatia preaching another version of the gospel: namely, those who believe in Christ, even if they are Gentiles, must be circumcised and observe the prescriptions of the Mosaic law. These "agitators," as Paul calls them, argued that Gentiles must observe the works that the Mosaic law prescribed, especially circumcision, dietary regulations, and Sabbath observance; otherwise, they will not be justified—that is, they will not stand in the proper covenant relationship to God. The social implication of this "other gospel," as Paul calls it, required non-Jewish people to adopt a way of life that would identify them as Jews before they could share in the inheritance of Christ. The theological implication was no less profound since the requirement that non-Jews be circumcised and adopt the prescriptions of the Mosaic law called into question the sufficiency of what God had done in Christ. Faced with this challenge to the gospel he preached among the Gentiles, Paul finds it necessary to persuade the Galatians not to have themselves circumcised. In doing so, he recapitulates and defends the "truth of the gospel" that he preached to the Galatians.[32]

As in Paul's other letters, Jesus' death is the central moment in the Christ story that underlies his letter to the Galatians. However, the narrative presupposed in Galatians is different from that which we have uncovered in Paul's Thessalonian and Corinthian correspondence because Paul must address a new issue: how Gentiles share in the promises God made to Abraham. Accordingly, since the crisis at Galatia revolved around the Mosaic law and the covenant God made with Abraham, Paul relates the story of Christ to the promises God made to Abraham and finds it necessary to discuss the role of the Mosaic law. Thus Galatians presents readers with a new aspect of Paul's underlying Christ story that begins with Abraham and finds its climax in the death of Christ,[33] whereas the story that underlies Paul's Corinthian correspondence begins with Adam. However, whereas in his Corinthian correspondence the plotted time of the Christ story explicitly includes the parousia, this is not the case in Galatians. To be sure, Paul has not abandoned hope for the future (see Gal. 5:5, 21), but Galatians does not describe the events that will occur at the end of the ages as he does in the Thessalonian and Corinthian correspondence.[34] The new situation at Galatia required Paul to focus on other aspects of his Christ story.

Christ the Singular Descendant of Abraham

Galatians makes extensive use of narrative material. For instance, in chapters 1–2 Paul presents a narrative of the events before and after his call to persuade the Galatians that he received his gospel through a revelation of Jesus Christ (1:12) and that James, Peter, and John recognized the grace bestowed on him (2:9), even though he later rebuked Peter at Antioch for betraying the truth of the gospel (2:11–14).

In Galatians 3–4 Paul does not narrate a series of events as in chapters 1–2, but it is evident that he presupposes an underlying narrative that includes the covenants made with Abraham and Moses. Paul employs this underlying narrative to establish his thesis that a person is justified by the faith of Jesus Christ rather than by the works of the law (2:16).[35] His rereading of Israel's sacred story, in contrast to that of the agitators, however, marks a departure from Israel's traditional understanding of its story.

Employing Genesis 17 as their starting point, the agitators probably reminded the Gentile Galatians that circumcision was the sign of the eternal covenant that God made with Abraham and his descendants. Thus any uncircumcised male will be cut off from God's people (Gen. 17:14). Likewise, the agitators may have reminded the Galatians that those who do not observe the prescriptions of the law put themselves under a curse (Deut. 27:26), whereas those who obey God's statutes and ordinances will live (Lev. 18:5). If the Gentile Galatians wish to participate in the covenant blessings of Abraham, therefore, they must accept circumcision, the sign of God's eternal covenant with Abraham, a sign that implies observance of the Mosaic law. It was inconceivable for the agitators that the Messiah would abolish God's law. Although we do not know the full scope of the argument they proposed, we can suppose that they reverenced the law.

Paul, however, reasoned in a way that altered his pre-Christian understanding of Israel's story. First, and most important, if righteousness could be attained through the law, then why did Christ die (Gal. 2:21)? Because God sent his Son into the world (4:4), and because the Son had freely given himself for humanity's sins (1:4), Paul reasoned that the law was unable to give righteousness and life (2:21; 3:21). Therefore the law must have played a different role in Israel's history than Paul previously supposed.

Forced to rethink the story of Israel in light of the story of Christ, Paul returned to the story of Abraham, especially as narrated in Genesis 12 and 15. He concluded that God had announced the gospel in advance to Abraham, when he promised the patriarch that the nations would be blessed in him (Gal. 3:8; see Gen. 12:3). Furthermore, Paul noted that the promises God made to Abraham were intended for the patriarch's seed (Gal. 3:16; see Gen. 12:7). Taking advantage of the grammatical point that "seed" is singular rather than plural (*sperma*), Paul concludes that God's promises to Abraham had a singular "seed" or descendant in view, Christ (Gal. 3:16).

To summarize the story thus far, God had always intended to justify the Gentiles and had previously announced this to Abraham. Participation in the blessings of Abraham, however, was to take place by means of Abraham's singular descendant, Christ. But if Christ is the seed of Abraham, Abraham's singular descendant, of what benefit is this to the Gentile Galatians?

Paul answers this question at the conclusion of chapter 3. Those who have been baptized into Christ have clothed themselves with Christ. Because they belong to Christ, they are Abraham's seed, heirs in accordance with the promise God made to Abraham (3:26–29). Thus Paul presupposes a story that begins with Abraham and finds its climax in Christ. Most important, this rereading of Israel's history allows him to bypass the need for circumcision, for it argues that those in Christ are Abraham's descendants.

Paul's rereading of Israel's history, however, downplays the covenant that God made with Israel at Sinai, and Paul argues that this covenant, based on legal observance, is subservient to the promises God made to Abraham (3:15–18). In Paul's new understanding of Israel's story, the Mosaic covenant was a latecomer that appeared 430 years after God made his promises to Abraham. Since these promises constituted a legally ratified will or covenant (*diathēkē*) with Abraham, the covenant based on the law could not annul or alter them. Thus the basis of one's relationship to God is not the legal observance prescribed by the Mosaic law but the faith exemplified by Abraham and Christ (3:9).

The law's role was quite different from what Paul had previously thought. In light of the promises God made to Abraham and their fulfillment in Christ, Paul now sees that the law had a temporary role in Israel's history. Unable to give life, it was ordained as Israel's disciplinarian (*paidagōgos*). Its purpose was to make Israel aware of the transgressions it committed, until Abraham's singular descendant, Christ, should appear. The appearance of Christ initiates the period of humanity's maturity, when it is no longer necessary to be under the guidance of this disciplinarian. Having attained maturity, believers are endowed with the Spirit, who leads and guides them to fulfill the law by the love commandment. In a word, because Abraham's descendant, Christ, has appeared, believers are no longer under the law. Children of Abraham, because they are in Christ, believers are led and guided by the promised Spirit.

Christ the Son of God

By his rereading of Israel's story, Paul establishes that Christ is the legitimate heir of Abraham who inherits the promises God made to the patriarch and ends the law's role as Israel's disciplinarian. But how is Christ able to do this? Paul received the answer to this question in a "revelation of Jesus Christ," when God revealed his Son to him (1:16). At that moment, Paul learned that the crucified one was none other than God's Son, whose shameful death upon the cross rescued humanity from this present evil age (1:4). Thus, the story of Christ's saving death upon the cross is the climax of the Abraham-Christ story and the hermeneutical key that unlocks the meaning of Israel's history.

Paul does not narrate the story of Christ's life and death, but he alludes to, and presupposes, it throughout this letter. In chapter 4, for instance, he presents the whole sweep of the story when he writes:

> But when the fullness of time had come, God sent his Son, born of a woman, born under the law, in order to redeem those who were under the law, so that we might receive adoption as children. And because you are children, God has sent the Spirit of his Son into our hearts, crying, "Abba! Father!" So you are no longer a slave but a child, and if a child then also an heir, through God. (4:4–7)

In terms of plotted time, the story of Christ's mission began when the Father sent him, at a specific historical moment. Previous to this moment, there was an extended period of waiting. Paul describes this period as the time between the promises God made to Abraham and the coming of Christ, the descendant of Abraham. With the appearance of Abraham's singular descendant, believers have received the promised Spirit because they are God's children.

Although the Son's preexistence does not play an explicit role in this letter, I suggest that it is part of the story Paul presupposes for the following reasons. First, it makes little sense for Paul to speak of Christ being born of a woman, under the law, in Gal. 4:4, if he does not presuppose that Jesus is different from other human beings since the same statement could be made of any other Jewish person. Paul's remark that Jesus was born of a woman, under the law, points to a change of status that later theology would call the incarnation. When Paul writes that Jesus was born of a woman, under the law, therefore, he implies preexistence, even though he does not develop the notion.[36]

Second, although Paul's notion of preexistence is more implicit than explicit, it identifies a unique aspect of Jesus' sonship. Jesus was not merely exalted to, or adopted to, the status of being God's Son, he was God's Son previous to his resurrection, indeed, previous to his earthly existence. Consequently, while "Son of God" can be applied to human beings such as Israel's king or the righteous person, Jesus enjoyed a unique status as God's Son since he was always the Son of God.

Third, it is Christ's status as God's preexistent Son that endows his work with salvific value. While other human beings died for the sake (*hyper*) of their friends or nation, their deaths did not justify or redeem others. Christ's death, however, was redemptive because the one who gave himself on behalf of others was God's unique Son. The preexistence of Christ, then, allows Paul to situate the origin of Christ's redemptive work in God.[37]

For Paul, Christ's salvific death is inseparable from his identity. Therefore, while Paul is deeply concerned about Christ's work, he does not neglect the question of Christ's identity. For this reason, I propose that the concept of preexistence is at work in Paul's understanding of Christ in Galatians.

To summarize, the text of Gal. 4:4–7 is the Christ story in miniature. Because it implies preexistence, it encompasses as well as overlaps with the Abraham story. Thus the Christ story of Galatians includes the following elements:

> The preexistence of Christ
> God's promises to Abraham
> A time of waiting for Abraham's singular descendant
> The interlude of the law, Israel's disciplinarian
> The time of fulfillment when God sends his Son
> The time of the Spirit, when believers are no longer under the law.

The sending of God's Son is the turning point in the narrative and the resolution of the human predicament. In Galatians, Paul alludes to this predicament several times. For example, he explains that God sent his Son "to redeem those who were under the law" (4:5). Shortly after this, he describes the preconversion situation of the Gentile Galatians as enslavement "to beings that by nature are not gods" (4:8). In another part of this letter, he writes that Christ "gave himself for our sins to set us free from the present evil age" (1:4). He reminds the Galatians that "Christ redeemed us from the curse of the law by becoming a curse for us" (3:13). Thus, Paul describes the human predicament as a situation of sinfulness and enslavement to other powers representative of this present evil age. While this condition afflicted the whole of humanity, those under the law needed Christ to redeem them from the curse with which the law threatened them if they did not fulfill it. Accordingly, Paul presents Christ, the singular descendant of Abraham, as the one who redeems humanity from its predicament of sin and enslavement and frees those under the law from the threat of its curse.

Christ accomplishes this redemption through his death upon the cross, the focal point of Paul's preaching to the Galatians. When rebuking the Galatians, for example, he asks, "Who has bewitched you? It was before your eyes that Jesus Christ was publicly exhibited as crucified!" (3:1). This verse suggests that when Paul came to Galatia, he told the story of Christ's death in such vivid detail that it was as if Christ were crucified before their eyes. Although Paul does not say as much, we can suppose that the occasion of his initial preaching was the moment when he told the Galatians his story of Christ, a narrative that focused on the shameful death of the Son of God upon the cross.

Although Paul does not retell the story of how Christ was crucified, there are indications of the story Paul presupposes. First, it is clear that Christ was not merely the object of God's action. In an unusual turn of phrase, Paul writes that Christ "gave himself for our sins" (1:4). Then, in a more personal vein, he writes of the Son of God "who loved me and gave himself for me" (2:20), underlining the personal manner in which Christ's death affected him, as well as the freedom with which Christ surrendered his life. Although Paul does not explicitly speak of Christ's death as a sacrifice in Galatians, the use of the preposition *hyper* ("for, on behalf of") and the active use of *paradidōmi* ("to give, to hand over") indicate that Christ willingly and actively handed himself over for the sake of others. To that extent, his death was a sacrifice for the sake of others.

The Faith of Jesus

Thus far, I have not discussed one of the most important concepts of Galatians: justification by faith rather than by works of the law. Although justification primarily concerns soteriology, Paul's soteriology always implies a Christology, just as his Christology always implies a soteriology. Thus, we have seen that the christological concept of "Christ the descendant of Abraham" includes an explicit soteriology; namely, those who are in Christ become descendants of Abraham and heirs of the promised Spirit, empowered by that Spirit to call God "Father."

Paul's teaching on justification by faith finds its fullest expression in 2:15–21, especially in 2:16, where he writes:

> yet we know that a person is justified not by the works of the law but through *the faith of Jesus Christ.* And we have come to believe in Christ Jesus, so that we might be justified *by the faith of Christ,* and not by doing the works of the law, because no one will be justified by the works of the law.

In this translation, I have chosen the alternate reading found in the footnote of the New Revised Standard Version, "the faith of Christ" in place of "faith in Christ." In doing so, I am not denying that Paul calls his converts to believe *in* Christ since he clearly says that "we have come to believe in Christ Jesus" (2:16). Rather, with a number of scholars, I have chosen to interpret *pisteōs Iēsou Christou* and *pisteōs Christou* as subjective genitives: the faith, or faithfulness, of Jesus Christ.[38] Thus, Paul is saying that believers are justified on the basis of the faithfulness that Christ manifested in surrendering his life upon the cross rather than on the basis of legal observance. The faith of Christ is the ground for the believer's justification and the reason one believes *in* Christ.

This interpretation seems to accord with what Paul has already said about Christ's death in 1:4 and 2:20; namely, Christ, the Son of God, freely gave himself for us because he loved us. It also finds support in Romans 5, where Paul contrasts the disobedience of the first Adam with the obedience of Christ the new Adam. In my view, Christ manifested this obedience by surrendering his life upon the cross. Paul's teaching on justification in 2:16, then, implies a Christology that views Jesus as the obedient Son of God. This, in turn, accords with Paul's description of Christ as the descendant of Abraham. It is the faithful Son of God who is faithful Abraham's descendant: Christ, who gave himself for our sins.

The Christ Story

The underlying story of Galatians can be summarized in this fashion. God always intended to justify the Gentiles on the basis of faith. Thus he told Abraham, well in advance of the gospel, that all nations would be blessed in him. To accomplish this, God made a covenant with Abraham and his seed, Christ. Thus Christ was Abraham's singular descendant and the beneficiary of the promises God made to Abraham. The period between the time of the promises and the coming of the heir was a period of minority and enslavement for humanity. Gentiles found themselves enslaved to beings that were not gods, while the Jewish people were under a law that served as their disciplinarian, until the promised descendant should come. Since this law was given through the mediation of angels, 430 years after the promises God made to Abraham and his seed, it did not alter the covenant God made with Abraham, a covenant based on promises and faith. The role of the law was temporary, and its purpose was to make those under it aware of their transgressions. It did not alter or annul the covenant promises God made with Abraham.

In contrast to the covenant God made with Abraham, the law was based on the principle of doing its prescriptions, and it threatened those who did not observe all that was written in it with a curse. Consequently, those under the law found themselves threatened with a curse, if they did not do its prescriptions. Of itself, the law could not justify or give life. Therefore, in the fullness of time, God sent his preexistent Son to redeem those under the law and make Gentiles, as well as Jews, sons and daughters of God. Born of a woman, under the law, God's Son shared the human condition of those he redeemed. The moment of redemption occurred when the Son of God freely gave himself for the sake of others by dying a shameful and scandalous death upon the cross. Because he was "hung upon a tree," the law identified the Son of God as being under a curse (Deut. 21:23). But by accepting the curse of the law, the Son of God freed those under the law from the threat of its curse and brought to completion the promises God made to Abraham.

The death of Christ upon the cross was a climactic act of faithfulness which made it possible for Gentiles as well as Jews to share in the promises God made to Abraham. Because of this death, Gentiles as well as Jews have become children of God, capable of addressing God as "Father," through the power of the promised Spirit. By his death, the Son of God gave himself for our sins to rescue us from the present evil age. His death was an act of personal love so that each individual can say, "Christ loves me and lives in me." Those baptized into Abraham's singular descendant, Christ, are Abraham's descendants, even if they are not circumcised. They have been set free and given their majority; they are justified. Having received the promised Spirit, they are a new creation, the Israel of God (Gal. 6:16), which awaits the hope of righteousness and the kingdom of God.

THE LETTER TO THE ROMANS

There is a continuing scholarly discussion about the situation and circumstances that occasioned Paul's letter to the Romans.[39] In this section, I presuppose that Paul wrote to the Christians at Rome for several reasons: (1) to introduce himself to an important community of believers whom he had never visited but which had heard of the law-free gospel Paul preached among the Gentiles; (2) to seek support for his coming missionary work in Spain; (3) to ask the Roman community for its prayers so that the Jewish Christians of Jerusalem would not refuse the collection of money from his Gentile converts that he was bringing to Jerusalem as a sign of unity between Gentile and Jewish believers; and (4) to address some concrete problems at Rome between the "weak" and the "strong."[40] Thus there is an "occasional" dimension to Romans, making it similar to Paul's other correspondence. But the genre of the letter is also akin to an extended essay, inasmuch as the letter provides Paul with an opportunity to present his teaching about justification by faith, apart from the polemically charged atmosphere that characterizes his letter to the Galatians. Thus Fitzmyer's description of Romans as an "essay-letter" is apt.[41]

In my discussion of Paul's Christ story thus far, I have suggested that when writing to the Thessalonians, Corinthians, and Galatians, the apostle adapted his story of Christ in response to the questions and problems he encountered. Accordingly, in writing to the Thessalonians, his Christ story focused on the Lord's parousia, since the Thessalonians were concerned about the fate of those who had died before the Lord's return (1 Thessalonians), and there were rumors that the parousia was at hand (2 Thessalonians). But in writing to the Corinthians, the apostle presupposed a story that included Adam since it was necessary to explain the nature of the resurrection body and the restoration of the divine image that Adam had lost. Then, in Galatians, Paul's underlying story began with God's promises to Abraham in order to show that those in Christ are Abraham's descendants. But in Romans, while Paul must still respond to specific questions about, and charges against, his gospel, he is not as constrained by circumstances. Thus he can present the gospel that he preaches in a more orderly and systematic fashion. Consequently, the underlying Christ story of Romans is more developed.

This does not mean that the story of Christ underlying Romans is *the* Christ story into which all others neatly fit. There are striking differences between the underlying stories of Galatians and Romans, even though the two letters deal with a similar theme: justification by faith. The reason for this is simple. Although Paul may not be as constrained by circumstances in Romans as in other letters, the need to present his gospel of justification by faith determined what aspects of the story he would draw upon. The underlying story of Romans, then, is not necessarily the full story of Christ, but it is a clearly developed account, and a knowledge of this story is helpful for understanding the stories we have already uncovered.

The Human Condition

Ultimately, a complete story of Christ should explain why God sent him into the world. Although Paul provides answers to this question in his earlier correspondence, his answer is most fully developed in the opening chapters of Romans, where he describes the universal condition of human sinfulness. This clearly defined section (1:18–3:20) begins with the announcement that God's wrath is being revealed against all ungodliness and wickedness (1:18), and it concludes with a solemn pronouncement that no one will be justified in God's sight "by deeds prescribed by the law" (3:20). Between these two statements, Paul indicts the Gentile world of sin (1:18–32) by demonstrating that even though the Gentiles knew something of God, they did not accord God the glory God was due but exchanged the glory of the immortal God for the image of created things. Paul concludes his description of Gentile sinfulness by saying that they hate God and deserve death, for, although they knew God's just decrees, they did not observe them (1:32).

Having indicted the Gentile world, Paul accuses his Jewish compatriots of committing the very sins for which they condemn others (2:1–29). For, although the Jews possess the law and the sign of circumcision, they, like the Gentiles, do not do what the law commands. On the day of God's wrath, therefore, they will be deprived of glory, honor, and immortality because they did not observe the law.

Paul concludes that all human beings are under the power of sin (3:9). Therefore, even though he has said that God would give eternal life to those who seek glory, honor, and immortality by doing good (2:6–7), in reality, no one is just, and all have gone astray (3:10–12) since "all have sinned and fall short of the glory of God" (3:23). Accordingly, when Paul writes that no one will be justified in God's sight by the deeds of the law, he means that no one will be justified by the law since no one has completely fulfilled its prescriptions. All have violated God's law, Jew as well as Gentile.

However, perhaps there is one exception to this tragic state of affairs: the great patriarch Abraham. After all, did not the book of Sirach proclaim that Abraham kept the law of the Most High (Sirach 44:20). While the author of Sirach and other pious Jews viewed Abraham as fulfilling the Mosaic law, even before it was given, Paul does not. He insists that God did not reckon righteousness to Abraham on the basis of his works but on the basis of faith, indicating that even Abraham could not produce the works necessary to be justified in God's sight. The God who justified Abraham is the God who justifies the ungodly, crediting righteousness to Abraham on the basis of his faith (4:2–5).

Paul provides further insight into the human condition when he describes the result of justification as reconciliation and peace with God, to whom believers now have access (5:1–11). This new situation implies that prior to being justified and reconciled, humanity was at enmity with God (see 1:30, where Paul describes Gentiles as hating God). Therefore, Paul notes that Christ died for the ungodly; he died for humanity at the precise moment when all were sinners in God's sight (5:7–8), for prior to being reconciled to God, humanity could only be described as God's enemy (5:10).

Later, in chapter 8, when describing the glorious destiny that awaits the children of God, Paul notes that even creation had been subjected to futility, inasmuch as it was enslaved to corruption (8:20–21). Although the precise meaning of this text is disputed, Paul implies that it was God who subjected the created order to futility (*mataitēs*); that is, to an existence that continually leads to the corruption which is death.[42] As a result, the sinful human condition affects the whole of the created order so that neither humanity nor the created order is able to attain the goal for which God destined them: participation in his immortal glory. Engulfed and enslaved by sin, creation (and so humanity) finds itself destined for corruption and death rather than immortality and eternal life.

The Origin of the Human Condition

Although Paul has provided an insightful description of the sinful condition that infects humanity, he has not explained its origin: why have human beings sinned and fallen short of God's glory? In 1 Cor. 15:21, Paul alluded to the role of Adam in the human condition when he noted that just as death came through a human being, the resurrection of the dead came through a human being, Jesus Christ. This text, however, did not discuss the reason for human sinfulness. But in Rom. 5:12–22 Paul returns to the figure of Adam to explain how sin entered the world, and condemned all human beings to death. Adam's transgression brought sin into the world, which, in turn, led to death. Thus, in Rom. 5:12, Paul goes beyond the statement made in 1 Cor. 15:21, where he said that death came through a human being, namely, Adam.

In Romans 5, Paul attributes the presence of death in the world to Adam's transgression. Then, in one of the most disputed phrases of Romans, he adds, "and so death spread to all *eph' hō* all have sinned" (v.12). While the New Revised Standard Version translates *eph' hō* as "because," thereby implying that death spread to other human beings because they sinned after the pattern of Adam, Joseph Fitzmyer suggests that a better translation is "with the result that." Thus the phrase points to *the result of Adam's sin* as well as to the personal responsibility that human beings bear for their sinful actions.[43] Paul's thought in Rom. 5:12, then, may be summarized as follows: Adam transgressed God's commandment, thereby introducing the power of sin into the world. As a result of sin, death (understood as separation from God as well as physical destruction) entered the world and spread to all human beings who sinned *as a result* of Adam's transgression.

Although Paul does not fully explain the connection between Adam's transgression and the sinful actions of his descendants, he assumes that there is a relationship between the transgression of the first human being and his descendants when he notes that many were made sinners by the one man's transgression (Rom. 5:19). Not only is Adam the first human being but he stands at the origin of a sinful history that all other human beings have ratified as a consequence of Adam's transgression.

In his comparison between Adam and Christ, Paul shows how one man's transgression affected the many. First, one trespass led to death for many (5:15); second, one trespass brought condemnation for many (5:16); third, one trespass put the many under the tyranny of death (5:17). The origin of the sinful condition that infects the whole of humanity, then, is Adam's transgression with the attendant entry of sin and death into the world.

When Paul speaks of sin and death, he is not merely referring to a single transgression of the law and the physical end of one's life, respectively. In Pauline discourse, sin and death are powerful forces that enslave human beings to a way of life opposed to God's will. Sin is the power, unleashed by Adam's transgression, that enslaves others to a way of life opposed to God. Likewise, death is a power that not only ends life but eternally separates one from God. Consequently, when Paul speaks of a violation of God's commandment, he usually employs the vocabulary of "transgression" rather than "sin." And when he speaks of death, he has more in mind than the termination of life.

Paul discloses his understanding of sin and death further in chapter 7, where he discusses the law. Approaching the law in a more positive manner than he did in Galatians, he affirms that it is holy, and its commandments are holy, just, and good (7:12). But despite the goodness of the law and its divine origin, it cannot remedy the sinful human condition, which is one of being sold into slavery under the power of sin. Thus the power of sin unleashed by Adam's transgression uses the opportunity of the commandment to frustrate the purpose of the commandment; for when the law says "you shall not covet," human desire is aroused (7:8–12). Not only does the power of sin frustrate the purpose of the commandment, it leads one to death, inasmuch as those who transgress the commandment condemn themselves to separation from God. Humanity finds itself in a predicament, then, from which it cannot extricate itself. Aware of God's will in the commandment, it cannot obey the very commandment of which it approves because of the in-dwelling power of sin (7:17), which leads to death. Because of Adam's transgression, humanity has been enslaved to sin (6:17) and destined for the eternal separation from God that is death (6:21).

The Solution to Humanity's Predicament

Paul's detailed description of the human predicament provides the proper framework for understanding his soteriological Christology. Having described the sinful condition that infects humanity and explained its origins as Adam's transgression, Paul presents God's solution as the sending of his own Son "in the likeness of sinful flesh" (8:3). In describing the effects of the Son's work, Paul employs a number of concepts such as justification, salvation, reconciliation, expiation, redemption, freedom, new life, sanctification, and glorification.[44] All of these concepts suppose an underlying narrative, to which we now turn.

This narrative begins with Adam, whom Paul identifies as the *typos,* the "pattern," the "example," or the "model" of the one who is to come, namely, Christ (5:14). Adam and Christ mark the beginning and climax of the story that Paul presupposes, respectively. The narrative time of the story, however, is not limited to the period between these two figures, for Paul understands Christ as God's preexistent Son whose work will not be completed until the parousia. Thus, while the narrative moves from Adam to Christ, it also looks forward to God's final victory that will occur at Christ's parousia.

As already noted, sin entered the world through Adam's transgression, and through sin death ruled over all (5:12, 17). Paul insists that death even reigned in the period between Adam and Moses, before the Mosaic law entered the stage of human history. For even though people of that period could not knowingly transgress specific commandments of God's law as Adam did (since the Mosaic law had not yet been given), human beings died nevertheless because death reigned. When, at last, the law made its appearance, those under the law transgressed God's commandments knowingly, as did Adam. Thus, as holy and good as the law was, it increased transgressions (5:20) since at least part of humanity now knew the law's just commandments.[45] For this reason God sent his own Son in the likeness of "sinful flesh" as an offering for sin, to do what those under the power of sin could not do, obey the commandment of God.

As in 2 Cor. 5:21, where Paul speaks of God making Christ to be sin so that humanity might become the righteousness of God, and Gal. 3:13, where he writes that Christ became a curse to redeem those under the curse of the law, the jolting expression "sinful flesh" does not mean that Jesus was a sinner. Rather, it emphasizes that the Son of God took on the human condition to redeem those under the power of sin and death.[46] In Christ, God accomplished what humanity could not do: observe the just commandment of the law. Representing humanity before God, therefore, Christ effected a "divine interchange"[47] whereby humanity becomes the righteousness of God (2 Cor. 5:21), is freed from the curse of the law (Gal. 3:13), and fulfills its just requirements in Christ (Rom. 8:3).

Drawing a contrast between Adam and Christ, Paul notes that whereas Adam's singular transgression, an act of disobedience, led to a judgment and resulted in condemnation for all, Christ's righteous act of obedience led to acquittal and life for all. Thus Adam and Christ are the progenitors of two opposing histories. Whereas Adam initiated a history of sin that led to condemnation and death, Christ initiated a history of grace that leads to life and acquittal. As for the Mosaic law, it stands between these two figures. And, even though it reveals God's will, it is unable to redeem humanity from sin since sin frustrates its purpose.

Just as Adam inaugurated a history of sinfulness by a single transgression, Christ initiated a history of grace leading to life by a singular act of obedience: his death upon the cross. Paul describes this act of obedience and its consequences in Rom. 3:21–26, where he recapitulates the central theme of this letter, the righteousness of God, or, as the New English Bible translates *dikaiosynē theou*, "God's way of righting wrong" (1:17). In 3:22, Paul writes that God manifested his righteousness *dia pisteōs Iēsou Christou* for all who believe. The interpretation of this phrase is disputed. Does it mean that God manifested his righteousness "through faith *in* Jesus Christ for all who believe," as the majority of commentators argue, or does Paul mean "through the faith *of* Jesus Christ for all who believe"? As with Gal. 2:16, where we encountered a similar problem, I propose, in light of what Paul says in Romans 5 about the obedience of Jesus Christ, that it is preferable to construe the phrase as "the faith of Jesus Christ"; that is, the faithful obedience that Christ manifested in surrendering his life upon the cross.[48] The righteousness of God, which begins and ends with faith (1:17), then, was revealed upon the cross, when the Son of God obediently accomplished the will of his Father, thereby canceling the disobedience of Adam.

Although the law and the prophets witness to the righteousness of God, when read in the light of Christ, it was necessary for God to deal with human sinfulness apart from the law since all sinned and fell short of the divine glory. Therefore, God freely justified humanity by his grace through the redemption (*apolytrōseōs*) that comes through Christ Jesus, whom God set forth as an atoning sacrifice (*hilastērion*). God effected this atonement through the blood of his own Son to prove his own righteousness. This was necessary since, in his great mercy, God previously overlooked humanity's transgressions (3:21–26).

This compact statement of God's righteousness (3:21–26), paraphrased above, comes immediately after Paul's description of humanity's sinfulness (1:18–3:20). It clearly indicates that (1) God is the primary actor of Paul's underlying story, (2) sinful humanity is the recipient and beneficiary of God's saving justice, and (3) Jesus Christ is the agent by which God effects this saving justice. Thus the God who was active throughout Israel's history is the primary actor of Paul's redemptive story, and Christ is his redemptive agent.

Through Christ's faithful act of obedience, God accomplished the following. First, all are freely justified through the redemption effected in Christ (3:23–24). That is to say, humanity stands in the proper covenant relationship to God because, in Christ, God redeemed humanity from the sinful situation described in 1:18–3:20, thereby restoring the glory Adam lost. Second, God wiped away sin by setting forth his own Son as an atoning sacrifice (*hilastērion;* 3:25). Here, Paul draws upon the imagery of the Day of Atonement and presents Christ as the "mercy seat" smeared with blood for the purpose of wiping away sin. But whereas the old mercy seat was sprinkled with the blood of a goat, the new mercy seat, Christ, is smeared with his own blood, thereby doing away with sin. This was necessary since, in his great mercy, God had previously overlooked humanity's transgressions. But now, to show his saving righteousness, God has finally dealt with sin by the death of his own Son.

To summarize, Christ's singular act of obedience was his death upon the cross, an act of faithfulness that manifested God's righteousness. By this faithful act of obedience of his Son, God justified humanity and dealt with sin, once and for all.

In 5:1–11, Paul summarizes the benefits of Christ's death in terms of justification, peace with God, access to God, reconciliation, deliverance from God's wrath, and assurance of final salvation. In doing so, he remarks that Christ died for us, the ungodly, while we were still weak (5:6). Noting that one would hardly die for a just person, although one might possibly die for a truly good person, Paul says that Christ died for us while we were still sinners (5:7–8). At this point, one might expect Paul to draw the conclusion that Christ's death manifested his love for us, much as Paul concluded in Gal. 2:20. Instead, he writes: "*God* proves his love for us in that while we were still sinners Christ died for us" (5:8). This unexpected conclusion indicates the unique relationship between God and Jesus. The act of Jesus upon the cross becomes an act of God, so that the love Jesus manifests by dying for the ungodly is the love of God for sinful humanity.

In the following verses (5:9–10), Paul asks two rhetorical questions that are dependent on what he has just said. First, if we have been justified by the blood of Christ, then how much more will we be saved *through* him from God's wrath? Second, if we were reconciled to God when we were God's enemies, how much more will we be saved *by* Christ's life now that we have been reconciled? Paul concludes that we can boast *through* the Lord Jesus Christ, *through* whom we have received reconciliation.

Paul's emphasis on God's love and his frequent use of prepositions such as "through" and "by" recall what we noted above: God is the primary actor of Paul's story and Christ is God's agent of salvation. Thus the theme of the letter is *God's* justice, *God's* righteousness, *God's* way of acquitting sinful humanity. *Through Christ,* humanity is justified, redeemed, reconciled, and saved. *In Christ,* humanity finds grace and life.

None of this would be possible, however, if Christ were merely another human being. Thus, when Paul says that God sent his Son (8:3), he intends something more than the sending of a prophet into the world. Although Paul does not explicitly speak of preexistence, he implies that the Son of God underwent a change of status. In this regard, the text of Rom. 8:3 is similar to Gal. 4:4, where Paul says that in the fullness of time God sent his Son, born of a woman, to redeem those under the law. In both instances, Paul is thinking of something akin to what later theology would call the incarnation, although Paul does not develop that concept here. Thus, when he writes that Jesus "was declared to be Son of God with power according to the spirit of holiness by resurrection from the dead" (1:4), he does not mean that Jesus *became* God's Son at the resurrection. Rather, at the resurrection, Jesus was shown to be who he always was, the Son of God, whom the Father sent into the world.

Although many of his contemporaries would not have agreed with his reading of Israel's story, Paul is firmly convinced that his gospel, which is the story of God's salvific work in Christ, is the prophetic fulfillment of Israel's story. So he describes the gospel of God, which he preaches among the Gentiles, as promised beforehand through the prophets in the holy scriptures (1:2). He affirms that God's righteousness, although disclosed apart from the law, is attested to by the law and the prophets (3:21). And he points to the justification of Abraham (4:1–25), to show how the gospel establishes the law (3:31). As regards Jesus' earthly origin, Paul identifies him as a descendant of David (1:3), who ministered to his own brethren, the circumcised, to show God's truthfulness (15:8). And although Paul usually employs "Christ" as part of Jesus' name, rather than as a messianic title, he clearly recognizes that Jesus was the promised Messiah (9:5). Paul narrates Israel's story differently than his contemporaries because he reads it in light of its ending, the sending of God's Son into the world.

Christ the End of the Law

As in Galatians, Paul's reading of Israel's story in light of Christ puts the law in a new perspective. To be sure, Paul presents the law in a more positive light in Romans than in Galatians. Nonetheless, his story has little room for the covenant that God made with Israel at Sinai. The reason for this is as follows. Since Paul is interested in the salvation that Christ offers to Gentiles as well as Jews, his story must focus on those figures who include rather than exclude Gentiles from what God has done in Christ. Therefore, the story of Galatians is plotted in terms of Abraham and Christ in order to show that the Gentiles are Abraham's descendants through faith rather than circumcision, while the story of Romans is plotted in terms of Adam and Christ to show that God has rescued humanity from a situation of universal sinfulness through faith in Christ rather than the prescriptions of the law. In contrast to Adam and Abraham, Moses could not play such a role since the Mosaic law draws a sharp distinction between Gentile and Jew.[49]

Paul does not dismiss the role of Israel and its law; for if the appearance of Christ makes Israel and its history irrelevant, then God's integrity and faithfulness to his promises are in question. After all, the oracles of God were entrusted to Israel (Rom. 3:2), and to Israel belong the adoption, the glory, the covenants, the giving of the law, the worship, the promises, the patriarchs, and the Messiah (9:4–5).[50] Therefore, it is inconceivable to Paul that God has rejected his people (11:1). But something has gone awry since the majority of Israel did not accept Jesus as the Christ. Aware of this, and probably accused by some of minimizing the role of Israel in his gospel,

Paul addresses the question of Israel's destiny in Romans 9–11. In the midst of that discussion, he indicates the fundamental problem that has bedeviled Israel: it did not recognize that the purpose and goal of the law was Christ. Christ was the end (*telos*) of the law (10:4). Here, as commentators have pointed out, *telos* means end in the sense of goal. Understood in this way, Paul is saying that the law was given with Christ in view. Its purpose was to bring Israel to Christ and to the righteousness that comes from God. Thus Paul is expressing a thought that he has already developed in Galatians: the law was Israel's disciplinarian, leading it to Christ, so that Israel might be justified by faith (Gal. 3:24). Unfortunately, Israel misunderstood the purpose of the law, and when God sent his Son, Israel stumbled over the stone that causes offense, that is, Christ (Rom. 9:2). Instead of accepting Christ and the righteousness that comes from God, Israel sought to establish its own righteousness on the basis of a law that already attained its goal in Christ (10:3–4). It is as if Israel had continued to run a race after it had crossed the finish line.[51] Thus, in Paul's view, Israel is now running in vain since the race is over, and the law has reached its goal in Christ.

In making this critique of his people, Paul is also making an important christological statement, for if Christ is the *telos* of the law, then it has found fulfillment in him. Christ now assumes the central place that the law once played in Israel's history. Previous to his call, Paul undoubtedly viewed the law as the revelation of God's will and wisdom, and so the means by which one maintains a proper covenant relationship with God. The law was the source of justification, and ultimately of salvation. But now Paul understands that the central role he once attributed to the law belongs to Christ in a surpassing manner. It is Christ who reveals the will and wisdom of God. It is Christ who establishes people in the proper covenant relationship to God. It is Christ who is the source of righteousness and salvation. Christ is the end of the law because the law prophetically points to him. Now that he has come, the law has completed its salvation-historical role. To attribute a further salvation-historical role to the law is to misunderstand its significance.

The Christ Story

The Christ story of Romans is similar and different from the stories that we have already uncovered from other Pauline letters. It does not focus on the parousia, as does the Thessalonian correspondence, but it clearly presents Christ as the Son of God who rescues humanity from the coming wrath of God by his death upon the cross. Like the story in the Corinthian correspondence, it draws an important relationship between Adam and Christ, but it goes further in its description of the human predicament and Christ's role in extricating humanity from it. As in Galatians, questions about righteousness and the law play a central role in this story, but whereas the underlying story of Galatians moves from Abraham to Christ, that of Romans is more universal in scope, beginning with Adam and moving to Christ. In all these stories, however, the death resurrection of Christ remains the focal event; for the one who died on the cross was none other than the Son of God. In all of the letters examined thus far, except the Thessalonian correspondence, there are intimations that Paul viewed God's Son as preexistent, although he never employs this term nor does he dwell on the concept. In Philippians, the letter to which we now turn, that concept plays a more central role.

THE LETTER TO THE PHILIPPIANS

For some, the Christology of Paul's letter to the Philippians is coterminous with what is often identified as "the Christ hymn" (2:5–11). In these verses scholars, as well as everyday readers, find an important text for the doctrines of Christ's preexistence and incarnation. It is little wonder, then, that this poetic text has played such an important role in the history of New Testament interpretation, especially as regards Christology. But the Christology of Philippians need not, and should not, be limited to this text since there is a rich Christology in the rest of this letter as well. Therefore, before considering the Christ hymn, I propose to identify the story of Christ that underlies this letter.

Philippians is a letter of friendship with a paraenetic goal.[52] Paul writes from prison[53] to thank the Philippians for their financial support (4:10–20) and to assure them that, despite his imprisonment, his difficult circumstances have furthered the preaching of the gospel (1:12–26). The central portion of this letter contains an extended paraenesis (1:27–2:18) in which Paul encourages the Philippians to conduct themselves in a way worthy of the gospel of Christ (1:27–30) by living as a united community in which members consider the interests of others as more important than their own (2:1–4). In the midst of this paraenesis, Paul introduces the so-called Christ hymn (2:5–11).

Following this paraenesis, Paul warns the Philippians of other Christian preachers whom he calls evil-workers because they would require Gentile converts, such as the Philippians, to submit to circumcision (3:1–11). Calling upon the Philippians to imitate him because he has imitated Christ, Paul reminds them that their citizenship is in heaven (3:12–4:1). He then entreats two feuding women, Syntyche and Euodia, to be reconciled with each other (4:2–9).

On first reading, it might appear that a letter of moral exhortation such as this would have little to say about Christ, apart from its famous hymnic passage. But Paul grounds this moral exhortation in a story of Christ that, while it is most explicitly stated in the Christ hymn, can be found in other parts of this letter as well.

The Story of Israel Continues

There is no place in Philippians where Paul makes extensive use of Israel's story as he does in 1 Corinthians 10 or 2 Corinthians 3. Nor is there any place where he explicitly relates Christ to Adam or Abraham, as he did in Romans and Galatians, respectively. But there are moments when it becomes apparent that the story of Israel, read in light of Christ, underlies this letter and, one suspects, Paul's earlier preaching to the Philippians.

A first instance occurs in the letter's greeting (1:1–2), when Paul reminds the Philippians of their elected status, addressing the letter "to all the saints (*tois hagiois*) in Christ Jesus who are in Philippi with the bishops and deacons." The designation of the Philippians as "saints" or "holy ones" does not point to the moral quality of their lives so much as it reminds them that they have been consecrated and set apart by God, numbered among his people, as was Israel of old. Thus, even though Paul does not mention Israel, he presupposes that the story of Israel continues in the community life of the Gentile Philippians.

This becomes more explicit in the letter of thanksgiving (1:3–11) when Paul writes of his confidence "that the one who began a good work among you will bring it to completion by the day of Jesus Christ" (1:6). The good work to which Paul refers is "the harvest of righteousness that comes through Jesus Christ for the glory and praise of God" (1:11); the one who began this good work is God the Father; and the day of Jesus Christ is the parousia, when the Philippians must stand pure and blameless (1:10). Thus the whole scope of Paul's underlying story can be found in the opening verses of this letter and summarized as follows: Through Christ, God began the work of establishing the Philippians in righteousness, consecrating them to himself as he did Israel of old. But this work will only be completed by God at Christ's parousia. In the meantime, the sanctified Philippians must prepare themselves for that day so that they can stand pure and blameless. The primary actor of this story is God who is Father; the agent of salvation is Jesus Christ who is Lord; and the beneficiaries are Gentiles such as the Philippians who have been granted an elected status formerly reserved for Israel of old.

121

A second example occurs in the midst of Paul's great paraenesis (1:27–2:30). There, shortly after the Christ hymn, he encourages the Philippians to do everything "without murmuring and arguing, so that you may be blameless and innocent, children of God without blemish in the midst of a crooked and perverse generation, in which you shine like stars in the world" (2:14–15). Here, Paul's language echoes a number of texts that recall the wilderness story of Israel. For example, while the Israelites were in the wilderness, they murmured against Moses and Aaron because they had no food (Ex. 16:1–9).[54] Later, when Moses recalled this wilderness period, he described the community of Israel as a perverse and crooked generation because of its disobedience (Deut. 32:5). In exhorting the Philippians to do everything without murmuring and arguing, then, Paul warns the newest members of God's people not to repeat the errors of the wilderness generation. In contrast to Israel of old, the Philippians are to shine like stars in the world. With this simile, Paul recalls the eschatological destiny of the wise and just as portrayed in the book of Daniel, 12:3 ("Those who are wise shall shine like the brightness of the sky, and those who lead many to righteousness, like the stars forever and ever"). Although they are Gentiles, the Philippians have been incorporated into Israel's story through Jesus Christ.

The incorporation of the Philippians into Israel's story becomes even more explicit in a third example. Warning the Philippians of the Judaizing preachers whom he calls dogs, evil-workers, and those who mutilate the flesh (Phil. 3:2), Paul assures the Philippians that they are the circumcision (3:3). Here, Paul seems to presuppose the argument developed in Galatians: Those who are in Christ are Abraham's descendants, even if they are not circumcised. Paul paradoxically asserts that the uncircumcised Philippians are the circumcision, by which he means something akin to "the Israel of God" (Gal. 6:16). Thus, while Jewish-Christian missionaries urged Paul's Gentile converts to become circumcised in order to attach themselves to Israel, Paul counters that his converts are the truly circumcised because they have been made righteous through Christ. The Philippians belong to Israel as reconstituted by God's work in Christ.

To summarize, although Paul does not narrate the story of Israel in this letter, a story of Israel underlies his preaching. He presupposes that his Gentile converts know their new status as God's elected people, the Israel of God.

Through the Faith of Christ

In his warning to the Philippians not to be taken in by Jewish-Christian preachers who require circumcision (chapter 3), Paul offers himself as a model for the Philippians to imitate. More than anyone else he could and did trust in the external signs that identified him as a member of the people of Israel (3:4–6). But everything that he once considered as a gain, he now reckons as a loss on account of something he now considers of far greater value: knowledge of Christ, whom he identifies as his Lord (3:7–8). Paul's purpose in pursuing this knowledge is to gain Christ and be found in him so that he might have the righteousness that comes from God and attain to the resurrection of the dead (3:9–11). Rather than be taken in by Judaizing preachers of the gospel, therefore, the Philippians should follow Paul's example.

In calling upon the Philippians to forsake everything to attain the righteousness that comes from God, Paul draws a striking contrast between a righteousness based on the Mosaic law and a righteousness based on faith. He writes:

> For his sake I have suffered the loss of all things, . . . that I may gain Christ and be found in him, not having a righteousness of my own that comes from the law, but one that comes *through the faith of Christ,* the righteousness from God based on faith. I want to know Christ and the power of his resurrection and the sharing of his sufferings by becoming like him in his death, if somehow I may attain the resurrection from the dead. (3:8–11)

As was the case in Gal. 2:16 and Rom. 3:22, I have chosen to translate the Greek phrase *dia pisteōs Christou* as a subjective genitive, "through the faith *of* Christ," even though most translations employ the objective genitive, "through faith *in* Christ."[55] I make this decision in light of the underlying story of Philippians, especially as it unfolds in the Christ hymn (Phil. 2:6–11) that will be considered below. In this underlying story Christ is the agent of God's salvation. Thus Paul looks forward to the day of Christ when the Philippians will have produced the harvest of righteousness that comes *through* Jesus Christ *for* the glory and praise of God (1:11). Christ's agency in the work of salvation is clearly expressed by reading *dia pisteōs Christou* in 3:9 as a subjective genitive: The righteousness that comes from God and depends on faith (*epi tē pistei*) is mediated *through* the faith of Christ.[56] But what does Paul mean by the faith of Christ? And, if Christ is God's preexistent Son, as the Christ hymn intimates, how can one speak of the faith of Christ?

It should be clear that Paul is not talking about faith as a virtue whereby one subscribes to creeds or doctrines. In our discussions of Galatians and Romans, I suggested that the faith of Christ is the faithful obedience that the Son of God manifested in freely surrendering his life on the cross. In this regard, the presentation of Christ as the new Adam who followed a path of obedience (Rom. 5:12–21) illustrates what I mean by the faith of Christ.

The Christ hymn, as we shall see, provides a further example of Christ's faith since it celebrates the humble obedience of the one who took on the status of a slave and died on the cross rather than take advantage of his equality with God. Therefore, when Paul writes that he wants to participate in Christ's sufferings and be conformed to his death (Phil. 3:10), he expresses his desire to pattern himself after the one who emptied himself for the sake of others. So Morna Hooker writes, " 'conformity to Christ's death' means conformity to those attitudes which led Christ to submit to death."[57]

To summarize, as he warns his readers of Judaizing missionaries and offers the example of his own behavior as a model for his converts to imitate, Paul presupposes an underlying Christ story.[58] Central to this story is "the faith of Christ," which mediates God's righteousness to the Philippians and makes them "the circumcision" (3:3), by which Paul means the people of God.

Awaiting a Savior

Although the decisive moment in the Christ story was Jesus' death-resurrection, Paul knows that the story has not been concluded. And so, on several occasions, he points to what still lies ahead. For example, in the thanksgiving of this letter, he writes that the work God began in the Philippians will be brought to its conclusion on "the day of Jesus Christ" (1:6), and he indicates that believers must be pure and blameless in "the day of Christ" (1:10). Paul exhorts the Philippians to live blameless and innocent lives in the midst of a crooked and perverse generation, so that he can boast of them on "the day of Christ" (2:16). This "day of Jesus Christ" or "day of Christ" is the parousia, which Paul describes in greater detail in his Thessalonian and Corinthian correspondence. Although Paul now reckons with the possibility of his own death before the Lord's coming (1:23), he remains confident that the Lord is near (4:5).

The concluding portion of the Christ story plays an important role in Phil. 3:12–21, where the apostle continues to present himself to the Philippians as an example worthy of imitation. Having said that he hopes to attain to the resurrection of the dead (3:11), he immediately concedes that he has not yet reached the goal. In his pursuit of the "upward calling" of God that comes in Christ, Paul is like an athlete who forgets what lies behind and strains to reach the goal (3:13). But Paul recognizes that all do not view the world in this way. Many live as "enemies of the cross of Christ" (3:18), inasmuch as they live merely for this life.[59] So he reminds the Philippians that their citizenship is in heaven and that they are waiting for a savior,[60] who is Jesus Christ the Lord (3:20). It is this Christ who will transform their lowly bodies and conform them to his own glorious body, in accordance with the power that enables him to subject all things to himself (3:21).

Although Paul does not employ the vocabulary of "parousia" or "resurrection" in 3:12–21, there is little doubt that these are the topics of his exhortation. Indeed, the whole section presupposes what Paul has written about Christ's parousia and the resurrection of the dead in his Thessalonian and Corinthian correspondence.[61] What is new is Paul's emphasis upon the heavenly citizenship of the Philippians and his description of Jesus as a savior from heaven. But the essential elements remain constant: at his parousia, the moment that marks the general resurrection of the dead, Christ will transform the earthly bodies of believers so that they will conform to his resurrection body. Although Paul does not explicitly employ a Christology based on the figure of Adam here, as in 1 Corinthians 15, it seems to underlie what he says. Christ, the savior from heaven, is the new Adam.

To summarize, we have uncovered a narrative in Philippians that presupposes the story of Israel, the faith of Christ, and the coming day of the Lord. The Philippians were drawn into the story of Israel when God began his work in them through Christ. Through the faith of Christ, the Philippians received the righteousness that comes from God. Since their true home is in heaven, they must wait for the final harvest of righteousness, when a heavenly savior will transform their bodies to conform to his glorious resurrection body. It is God who will accomplish this, through Christ.

Having spoken of the Christ story that underlies the whole of Philippians, it is time to turn to the story in the Christ hymn.

Jesus Christ Is Lord (2:6–11)

Philippians 2:6–11 stands in the midst of Paul's paraenesis to the Philippians to live a life worthy of the gospel (1:27–2:18), and it marks a high point in Pauline Christology. It is not surprising, then, that this passage, often called "the Christ hymn,"[62] has been at the center of scholarly discussion, especially as regards Paul's Christology. This discussion has focused on questions such as the following: (1) What are the genre and origin of this text? Does it represent an early Christian hymn from the church's liturgy that Paul incorporated into this letter, or is Paul the author of this poetic passage? (2) What is the appropriate religious background for understanding the Christology of this text? Does it presuppose a comparison of Christ with Adam, with wisdom, with the servant of Isaiah, or with some combination of these concepts? (3) What does the Greek word *harpagmos* (2:6) mean? (a) That Christ did not consider equality with God as an act of usurpation on his part but as his inherent right? (b) That Christ did not consider equality with God as something to be clung to, or, if he did not possess such equality, as something to be sought after? (c) That Christ did not consider equality with God as something he should take advantage of?[63]

All of these questions are interrelated, and the answer to each determines how one views the Christology of this passage. For example, if Phil. 2:6–11 is an early Christian hymn that Paul inherited, then we know little of its original context or *Sitz im Leben,* and it is difficult, if not impossible, to determine the appropriate background against which to understand the Christology of the text, although we can suppose that Paul would have agreed with the basic Christology of a hymn that he adopted. But if this text is Paul's own composition and not a hymn that he inherited, we might be more inclined to interpret it in light of other Pauline statements about Christ. As for the difficult word *harpagmos,* it is crucial to the debate about Christ's preexistence and the christological background of this hymn. For if there is an Adam-Christ comparison in this text, as many have recently maintained,[64] then Phil. 2:6–11 is not necessarily speaking of a preexistent being, and *harpagmos* refers to an equality with God that Christ could have grasped at, as did Adam, but did not. In a word, although a great deal has been written about the Christ hymn, the scholarly consensus about its meaning is not as strong as one might expect.

In addition to the questions raised above, it is important to note what this passage does *not* say. First, it says very little, if anything, about soteriology. Although it refers to Jesus' death on the cross, it does not say how Jesus saved humanity. Second, it does not explicitly identify Jesus as the Son of God, the new Adam, or the Servant of God, although scholars have argued that one or more of these christological concepts underlies this passage. Rather, it employs the simple name "Jesus" and the more christologically oriented name "Jesus Christ," as well as the title "Lord."

The many difficulties that I have noted and the narrative approach of my work suggest that it may be more helpful to study the Christ hymn within its present literary context. For even if this passage represents earlier hymnic material that Paul incorporated into this letter, the present literary context of the letter is the only context we possess. Most important, it is the context within which Paul himself wants us to read and understand this text. This context, as already mentioned, is an extended paraenesis (1:27–2:18) in which Paul summons the Philippians to conduct themselves in a manner worthy of the gospel by striving to live as a united community in which all consider the needs and interests of others as more important than their own. Thus, Paul introduces this passage in the following way, "Let the same mind be in you that was in Christ Jesus" (2:5).

This translation, taken from the New Revised Standard Version, is already an interpretation of a text that, when translated literally, reads: "Think this in/among you which even in Christ Jesus." As can be seen from this wooden translation, a verb needs to be supplied. But what verb? Translations such as the King James Version, the New American Standard Bible, the New International Version, and the Douay Rheims understand the text as referring to an attitude of humility found in Christ that the Philippians should imitate; accordingly, they supply the verb "to be." Thus the King James Version reads, "Let this mind be in you, which *was* also in Christ Jesus." In contrast to this, the New American Bible and the footnote of the New Revised Standard Version highlight an attitude that the Philippians should have because they are in the realm of Christ; accordingly, they supply the verb "to have." So the New Revised Standard Version footnote reads, "Let the same mind be in you that you *have* in Christ Jesus."

Although subtle, the difference in these translations is important. Translations represented by the King James Version suggest that Paul calls upon the Philippians to imitate Christ, whereas translations represented by the footnote of the New Revised Standard Version suggest that Paul is reminding the Philippians that they can and should adopt a new attitude because they live in the realm of Christ. That new attitude is outlined in the so-called Christ hymn.

However, many have argued that it is impossible to imitate Christ, as portrayed in this passage, since the text presents him as the preexistent Son of God who empties himself only to be exalted by God and given the name above every other name. While it is true that believers cannot imitate Christ in every aspect of his career, as described in the Christ hymn, in my view the paraenetic context of this passage indicates that Paul employs this text for the purpose of moral exhortation.[65] Thus after calling the Philippians to a corporate unity that requires them to humble themselves before each other (1:27–2:4), Paul employs the Christ hymn to strengthen his exhortation since this passage presents the story of Christ who was vindicated by God, *precisely because he humbled himself.* Consequently, Paul says to the Philippians, if you follow my moral exhortation, you can be sure of final vindication by God; for just as Christ humbled himself and was exalted by God, so will you be. Consequently, although the translations of the New Revised Standard Version footnote and the New American Bible do not explicitly counsel imitation in the manner that the King James Version does, they do not necessarily exclude it. Rather, they present Paul's meaning more clearly: because you are in the realm of Christ, you can act in a particular way that is exemplified in Christ, with the full assurance that the one who vindicated Christ will vindicate you.

If it is true that the literary context of Phil. 2:6–11 is paraenetic and the purpose of the text is to provide an example and assurance of divine vindication, then it is not surprising that Christ's salvific work does not play an explicit role in this text since the Christology of this text is in the service of moral exhortation. The Christology of this text, therefore, must be interpreted in light of its literary and pastoral purposes.

This passage can be divided into two parts. In verses 6–8, the narrative focuses on the humility of Christ who was obedient to the point of dying on the cross. Then, in verses 9–11, it explains how God vindicated Christ for his humility and obedience: God exalted Jesus by giving him the name *Kyrios*. Thus the passage is a brief narrative that can be summarized in terms of humiliation and vindication. But who is the one who humbled himself? How did he humble himself? And how did God exalt him?

There is no doubt that Jesus Christ is the subject of these verses since Paul prefaces them by exhorting the Philippians to have the same mind that they have in "Christ Jesus" (Phil. 2:5). But what is not clear are the underlying claims that the text makes for Jesus, when it says that (1) although he was in the form of God (*morphē theou*), (2) he did not consider equality with God as *harpagmon*.

Although "form" is a correct translation of *morphē*, it can give the impression that the one called Christ merely had the external appearance of divinity but did not possess the inner reality of what it means to be divine. This, however, is not the meaning of the Greek word, as nearly all commentators indicate. In Greek, *morphē* refers "to the specific form on which identity and status depend,"[66] and the term might better be rendered as "nature" or "status." Thus Paul's initial point that Christ Jesus was in the form of God means that he possessed a divine status.[67] The claim that one who possessed this divine status took the *morphē* of a slave establishes the basic contrast of the text and confirms what is said above. Christ who had a divine status now takes on the status of a slave. The reference here is to real status and position rather than mere outward appearance.

Although Christ enjoyed the status of God, he did not consider this equality with God (*to einai isa theō*) as *harpagmon*. The Latin Fathers interpret this word in terms of "plundering," "robbery," or "usurpation," yielding the meaning that Christ knew that equality with God was his inherent right, not something he had stolen or usurped.[68] The difficulty with this interpretation, however, is that it disrupts the logic of Paul's exhortation, which depends upon Christ's humility. Therefore, most commentators prefer an interpretation along the lines of the Greek Fathers who understood *harpagmon* in terms of a prize or treasure to be held onto, yielding the meaning that Christ did not treat his divinity as something to be greedily clung to. Both the Latin and Greek Fathers, however, agreed that equality with God was something Christ already possessed.

In more recent discussions some who favor an Adam-Christ comparison have argued that this text does not refer to Christ's preexistence nor does it claim that he possessed equality with God before he was exalted. Rather, authors such as James Dunn claim there is an implicit comparison between Adam and Christ at work here.[69] Whereas Adam tried to grasp at equality with God, Jesus did not. Others, however, have criticized this view, especially since "Dunn gives no account of what glory Christ could have had which was not available to other men and how he surrendered it up."[70] Still others have argued that the phrase *harpagmon hēgēsato* should be rendered in terms of taking advantage of something already possessed.[71] According to this reading, Paul is saying that although Christ had a divine status, he did not think his equality with God was something he should take advantage of, or exploit, in dealing with others. Instead, he emptied himself (*heauton ekenōsen*) by assuming the status of a slave (*morphēn doulou*).

In saying that Christ emptied himself by taking the status of a slave, the text does not mean that Christ divested himself of divinity so that he no longer enjoyed a divine status. Were that the case, it is difficult to see how there could be any continuity between the preexistent one who enjoyed a divine status and the one who assumed the status of a slave. Rather, *ekenōsen* ("he emptied") is best understood in light of not taking advantage of something. Thus, in emptying himself Christ refused to take any advantage of his divine status. Rather, being born in human likeness (*en homoiōmati anthrōpōn*), the preexistent one finds himself in human form as regards his specific appearance (*kai schēmati euretheis hōs anthrōpos*). Again, Paul is not referring to a mere external form in contrast to a true inner reality. The specific human appearance of Christ indicates a real human being who humbled himself and became obedient to the point of dying a slave's death of crucifixion.

The first part of this text, then, points to a preexistent being who had a divine status and enjoyed equality with God. Nonetheless, he did not think his status and equality represented something he should insist upon or take advantage of. Therefore, he set aside these advantages and took on the status of a slave so that he was born as a human being with a specific human appearance. As such, he humbled himself to the point of dying the death of crucifixion. An amplified version of this passage might read as follows:

> Although he was in the form of God—that is, he already enjoyed godly status—he did not consider his equality with God something that he should insist upon or take advantage of in dealing with others. Rather, he set aside his divine prerogatives by assuming the status of a slave. Being born in the likeness of a human being, he was found to be in the specific likeness of a human person. He humbled himself by becoming obedient to the point of dying a slave's death upon the cross.

In these few verses Paul proclaims what later theology would call preexistence and incarnation, but he does not develop or explain either concept since his primary purpose is moral exhortation. Thus his main point is as follows: if the preexistent one did not take advantage of his status, neither should the Philippians take advantage of theirs. Instead, in humility (*tē tapeinophrosynē*), they should regard others as better than themselves (2:3), thereby following the pattern of the one who humbled himself (*etapeinōsen heauton*) by his obedient death on the cross (2:8).

The second part of this text (2:9–11) provides the Philippians with the necessary motivation for not acting from selfish ambition or conceit, but in humility, regarding others as better than themselves (2:3). When Christ acted in this way, God vindicated him by exalting him above every other creature. Thus God super-exalted Christ and graciously granted him the name reserved to God himself, *Kyrios*. Alluding to the text of Isa. 45:23, Paul writes that at the name of Jesus, every knee must bend in heaven, on earth, and under the earth.

To grasp the full significance of this statement, one must recall that the text of Isaiah 45 is one of the strongest claims for monotheism in the Old Testament.

> Turn to me and be saved, all the ends of the earth! *For I am God, and there is no other.* By myself I have sworn, from my mouth has gone forth in righteousness a word that shall not return: "*To me every knee shall bow, every tongue shall swear.*" (Isa. 45:22–23)

What was once spoken of God is now attributed to Christ because God has exalted him by giving him the name *Kyrios*. Does this mean that the preexistent one has become something he was not before, or that he received a divine status he did not formerly enjoy? In my view, the answer must be no. The first part of this text (2:6–8) speaks of the preexistent one who was born in the human likeness of the man Jesus. The second part of this text (2:7–11) describes the exaltation of that human one so that at his name, "Jesus," every knee should bend because Jesus has been given the name that once belonged exclusively to God, namely, *Kyrios*. Thus, the second part of this text speaks of the super-exaltation of the incarnate one, whereas the first part begins by referring to the one who becomes human in Jesus. An amplified version might be translated as follows:

> Because Jesus humbled himself and obediently accepted the death of a slave, God more than exalted him by granting him his own divine name, the name *Kyrios,* which is above every other name. So whenever the name of "Jesus" is heard, every being in heaven, on earth, and under the earth should "bend the knee," as it says in the prophet Isaiah, and every tongue should confess that Jesus Christ is *Kyrios* unto the glory of God the Father.

But who is the one who has become human in the person of Jesus? Although there are no explicit references to Jesus as the Son of God in this letter, the text coheres with Paul's Son of God Christology, especially if Paul presupposes preexistence, as I have indicated.[72] This does not necessarily exclude the influence of other motifs such as the servant of Isaiah, wisdom, or even Adam.[73] But the primary motif, though never explicitly expressed, would appear to be Paul's Son of God Christology.[74] Notice, for example, the similarity between Rom. 8:3 ("by sending his own Son in the *likeness* of sinful flesh") and Phil. 2:7 ("being born in human *likeness*"). Whereas texts such as Rom. 8:1–3 and Gal. 4:4 speak of God *sending* his own Son into the world, however, Philippians focuses on the initiative of the preexistent one who assumes the status of a slave. The text of Philippians does not explain why he did this, since *its primary function is paraenesis,* but, if one recalls what Paul said of Christ's faithfulness, this text may be viewed as another example of what Paul means by the faith of Jesus Christ.

To conclude, Phil. 2:6–11 is a story within a story. While the whole of Philippians provides us with a story that presupposes the story of Israel and looks forward to Christ's parousia when God's plan will be complete, the Christ hymn focuses on the central and most important aspect of that story, the humiliation and exaltation of the preexistent Son of God. Since this story begins with the preexistence of Christ and looks forward to the universal acclamation of his majesty, it encompasses the Christ story we have already uncovered in Philippians.

Christology in Paul's Letters

No one of Paul's letters contains a systematic presentation of his Christology, nor does any letter embody the whole of his Christology. Writing in response to specific pastoral situations, Paul undergirds his arguments and admonitions by reminding readers of what Christ has done for them. Consequently, like his letters, his Christology is occasional in nature. This is not to say, however, that it is minimal or unimportant. Paul's understanding of Christ and his work is integral to the gospel he preaches. Paul may not systematize his christological thought, but certain concepts are crucial for understanding what he says.

First, the central event of Paul's gospel is the death and resurrection of Christ. Everything that the apostle preaches hinges on this event. In the words of Romans, Jesus "was handed over to death for our trespasses and was raised for our justification" (4:25). By this event, believers are freed from the curse of the law (Gal. 3:13), the righteousness of God is communicated to them (2 Cor. 5:21), and sin has been condemned (Rom. 8:3). By this event, believers have been ransomed, reconciled, justified, sanctified, and they confidently await the fullness of salvation. Christ's death and resurrection is the central event of God's salvific work, and it, more than anything else, qualifies Christ as the agent of God's salvation.

Second, while the death and resurrection of Christ is the central event of God's salvific work, it is not the final event, nor the only event that defines Christ's identity. Paul is firmly convinced that Christ will return again (1 Thess. 4:13–5:11) and, when he does, the general resurrection of the dead will take place. Then death will be definitively defeated, Christ will hand over the kingdom to his Father, and God will be all in all (1 Cor. 15:28). Thus Christ the justifier is also the final agent of God's eschatological salvation. Christ is the first fruits of the general resurrection, and his resurrection anticipates the destiny of all who entrust themselves to him.

Third, while the fulcrum of Paul's Christ story is the death and resurrection, and while the story is heavily weighted to what is yet to come, there are important intimations of preexistence in Paul's Christology. Paul never develops these at length, nor does he speculate about what kind of preexistence Christ enjoyed, but he does suggest that Christ played a role in God's creative work (1 Cor. 8:6), that God sent him into the world (Gal. 4:4; Rom. 8:3), and that Christ acted in Israel's history (1 Cor. 10:4, 9). Moreover, on two occasions he appears to employ the notion of preexistence to underline the humility and self-abasement of God's Son (2 Cor. 8:9; Phil. 2:6–11). From a theological point of view, the notion of preexistence establishes that the Christ event is the invasion of God's divine grace from the realm of God.[75]

Fourth, Christ's obedience unto death and his exalted status as the first fruits of the general resurrection identify him as the new Adam. The sinless and obedient Christ (Rom. 5:1–11) is everything Adam and his descendants were intended to be but failed to be because of sin. Christ, the new Adam, is the perfect image of God (2 Cor. 4:4) who reflects the glory of God. He has become "a life-giving spirit," and, at the general resurrection of the dead, believers will bear the image of this man from heaven (1 Cor. 15:45–49).

Fifth, because God has raised Christ from the dead, believers enjoy a unique relationship to their risen Lord. Believers are in Christ; they are members of his body (1 Cor. 12:27); and Christ dwells in them (Gal. 2:20). Put another way, Christ is no longer bound by time or space.

Sixth, titles do not play a major role in Paul's Christology. But three titles occur with some frequency: "Christ," "Lord," and "Son of God." The first, for all practical purposes, has become a name. Thus, Paul can speak of Jesus Christ, Christ Jesus, Christ, the Lord, or simply Christ. "Christ" is rarely used in a titular sense (but see Rom. 9:5). Moreover, Paul never tries to prove that Jesus was the Messiah. There is no need to, for Paul defines messiahship in light of Christ's death and resurrection. That is to say, the one who died on the cross for the sins of all, and whom God raised from the dead, is God's Messiah. There are no other qualifications.

As for Jesus' identity, Paul's preferred title seems to be "Son" or "Son of God," even though "Lord" occurs more frequently. Put most simply, Jesus Christ is God's Son and our Lord (1 Cor. 1:9). Thus, when God called Paul, he revealed that the crucified Jesus is his Son (Gal. 1:16). If we ask what it means to say that Jesus is the Son of God, the answer is found in what has been said thus far. He is the preexistent one whom God sent into the world to die *for* our sins, the one whom he raised for our justification, the new Adam, the image of God's glory. Because the relationship of believers to God's Son is one of servants to their lord, they rightly address him as "Lord," fully aware that this is the name above every other name (Phil. 2:9), the name that properly belongs to God, and now to God's Son.

Finally, Christ is the climax of Israel's history. That is to say, the Christ event was not an aberration or midstream correction in God's plan. The story of Christ is the story of Israel, its climactic and closing chapter. It was with Christ in view that God made the promises to Abraham (Gal. 3:6–9) and the law was given to Israel (Rom. 10:4). To be sure, Paul tells his story of Christ and Israel in different ways. Despite his several revisions, however, the essential point remains the same: Christ is the climax of Israel's story.

4

The Revelation of the Mystery

*M*ost New Testament exegetes classify the letters that we will consider in this chapter (Colossians, Ephesians, 1 and 2 Timothy, and Titus) as deutero-Pauline. This terminology indicates that, in their opinion, others wrote these letters in Paul's name.[1] While I agree with those who view Colossians, Ephesians, and the pastoral epistles as deutero-Pauline, that classification does not play a significant role in this chapter since this work is primarily concerned with the Christology *in* the Pauline letters rather than in establishing the Christology of the historical figure Paul. Moreover, since the deutero-Paulines claim Pauline authorship, I refer to the authors of these letters as "Paul." This claim to Pauline authorship is important since the authors who identify themselves in this way stand in a theological tradition indebted to the great apostle. Only a careful study of the deutero-Paulines will determine if these authors have been faithful to that tradition. But I am of the opinion that these letters represent authentic developments of Paul's thought rather than aberrations or distortions of it, even though their authors introduce new christological perspectives.[2] As in the previous chapter, I will investigate the Christology of these letters in terms of their underlying Christ stories.

THE LETTER TO THE COLOSSIANS

More than a century ago, J. B. Lightfoot wrote of Colossians: "The doctrine of the Person of Christ is here stated with greater precision and fullness than in any other of St. Paul's epistles."[3] While many contemporary Pauline students may not concur with Lightfoot's judgment that "The Christology of the Colossian Epistle is in no way different from that of the Apostle's earlier letters,"[4] nearly all will agree that Christology plays a central role in this letter. This is especially evident in the hymnic passage of 1:15–20, which presents Christ as the one in, through, and for whom all things were created (1:15–18a) and reconciled (1:18b–20).[5] Thus it is not surprising that scholars have devoted as much attention to this passage as to the famous Christ hymn of Philippians.[6] Moreover, as in the case of Philippians, many maintain that an early Christian hymn underlies this passage of Colossians.[7]

As important as this passage is, studies that focus on reconstructing an original hymn, or those that interpret the passage apart from its literary context, fail to do justice to either the Christology of Colossians or its hymnic passage. Consequently, I begin with some general observations about the Christ story of this letter before proceeding to its celebrated hymnic passage.

The content of Colossians can be summarized somewhat briefly.[8] First, Paul and Timothy, the coauthors of this letter, greet the Colossians as holy and faithful brethren in Christ (1:1–2). Second, in an extended thanksgiving (1:3–23) that consists of several subsections, Paul gives thanks for the faith of the Colossians (1:3–8), makes a prayer-wish on their behalf (1:9–20) that recalls the creative and redemptive work of God's Son (1:15–20), and relates the Son's work to the Colossian community (1:21–23). Third, Paul explains the special role that he plays in the economy of salvation: he is making known the mystery hidden for ages (1:24–2:5).[9] Fourth, Paul exhorts and rebukes the Colossians because they are in danger of succumbing to a "philosophy" based upon merely human tradition rather than upon Christ (2:6–23).[10] In this section, Paul employs the Christology of the letter's thanksgiving, especially its hymnic passage, to undergird his argument. Fifth, there is an extended moral exhortation (3:1–4:6) that derives its force from the Christology Paul has developed. Sixth, Paul concludes with final greetings (4:7–18).

This summary indicates that the Christology of Colossians is in the service of moral exhortation. Paul must persuade the Colossians that there is no need to submit to a philosophy that extols the "elements of the world" because the fullness of God resides in Christ, the sole mediator in the orders of creation and redemption.

Transferred to the Kingdom of the Beloved Son

Paul summarizes how the story of Christ affected the lives of the Colossians in the thanksgiving of this letter: "He [God the Father] has rescued us from the power of darkness and transferred us into the kingdom of his beloved Son" (1:13). This verse highlights two distinct periods in the life of the Colossian community: Once (*pote*) they were estranged and hostile toward God, doing evil deeds, but now (*nyni*) Christ has reconciled them through his death in order to present them blameless and irreproachable on the day of his appearance (1:21–22; see 3:4). From the point of view of the Colossians, then, the story of Christ narrates how they were rescued from the powers of darkness. Previous to Christ they were in bondage to these forces and alienated from God because of their transgressions, but now they are saints and faithful brothers and sisters in Christ (1:1), God's chosen ones, holy and beloved (3:12) because Christ has reconciled them to God.

Unlike Romans, Colossians does not explain the origin of the human predicament presupposed in this letter. But it clearly indicates that, previous to Christ, humanity was in need of redemption, which Paul defines as the forgiveness of sins (1:14). Therefore, it continually reminds the Colossians what has occurred through Christ. They have been raised with Christ (3:1), and because they have died with him by associating themselves with him in baptism, their lives are hidden with Christ, in God, so that when Christ appears they will also appear in glory with him (3:3–4). Once, the Colossians walked in a sinful way of life that Paul calls the old self (3:9; *ton palaion anthropon*), but now they must put on the new self that has been renewed according to the image (*eikōn*) of God who created it (3:9–10).

Although Colossians does not relate this Christ story to the story of Israel, as Paul does in other letters, there are echoes of that story.[11] For example, Paul writes that the Colossians were circumcised by a circumcision that was not carried out by human hands but by the stripping away of their carnal bodies, an act that he identifies as "the circumcision of Christ" (2:11). By this metaphor, Paul indicates that Christ's death was the authentic circumcision that freed the Colossians from the power of the flesh. Thus, even though they have not been physically circumcised, they were spiritually circumcised by Christ, who made them God's holy and elect people.[12]

Paul suggests a similar point when he explains that in the new self "there is no longer Greek and Jew, circumcised and uncircumcised, barbarian, Scythian, slave and free; but Christ is all and in all!" (3:11). This couplet recalls the climactic ending of Galatians 3, where Paul declares, "There is no longer Jew or Greek, there is no longer slave or free, there is no longer male and female; for all of you are one in Christ Jesus. And if you belong to Christ, then you are Abraham's offspring, heirs according to the promise" (Gal. 3:28–29). Thus, although the story of Israel is not an explicit part of the underlying Christ story of Colossians, Colossians suggests that its Gentile converts have undergone a spiritual circumcision that has made them God's holy and elect people. In the language of Galatians, they are descendants of Abraham.

Although the Colossians have been rescued from the powers of darkness and transferred into the kingdom of God's Son, they have not yet attained the final victory, even though Paul speaks of them as already raised with Christ (Col. 3:1). This expression, like so many others in Colossians, is metaphorical. The Colossians have been raised with Christ insofar as they have associated themselves with him in baptism, but they are not yet in heaven. Indeed, as the moral exhortation of this letter shows, they are still capable of falling into old ways of living. Thus Paul writes of the hope stored up for the Colossians in heaven (1:5), of Christ reconciling the Colossians so that he can present them holy, blameless, and irreproachable (1:22), and of Christ appearing and their appearance with him (3:4).

The Paul of Colossians never uses the word "parousia," and he is more inclined to employ spatial rather than temporal imagery when speaking of salvation.[13] But what he says about the future of believers does not contradict what is found in the undisputed Pauline letters; for although God has transferred the Colossians from one realm to another, the final victory has not been attained. For example, Colossians distinguishes between the kingdom of God (4:11) and the kingdom of God's beloved Son (1:13). While the kingdom of God points to God's eschatological victory, the kingdom of Christ anticipates that victory. A similar view is found in 1 Cor. 15:23–28, where Paul writes that Christ will reign until his enemies have been put under his feet. Then, when the end comes, he will hand over the kingdom to God his Father, and everything will be subjected to God, who will be victorious. The broad strokes of the Christ story we have uncovered can be summarized in this way.

> The Colossians, like the rest of humanity, were once enslaved to the powers of darkness and alienated from God because of their transgressions. But now God has reconciled them through Christ's death upon the cross. This death was their circumcision, and it transferred them to the messianic kingdom of God's Son. Consequently, the Colossians are God's holy and elect people as was Israel of old, and they now await the appearance of God's Son. On that day they will appear in glory because the Son will present them blameless and irreproachable to his Father.

Mediator of God's Creative and Redemptive Work

The story we have uncovered thus far presents Christ in two ways. First, he is the agent through whom God reconciled believers to himself. Second, he is the Son of God, seated at God's right hand, who already rules over a kingdom into which believers have been transferred (Col. 1:13; 3:1). But this is not the whole of the Colossian Christ story. In the hymnic passage of 1:15–20, Paul presents Christ as the one mediator of God's creative (1:15–18a) and redemptive work (1:18b–20).

Most exegetes divide the passage into two parts. In the first (1:15–18a), Paul proclaims that Christ is the *eikōn* of the unseen God and the *prōto-tokos* of all creation because all things were created in (*en*), through (*dia*), and for (*eis*) him. He concludes the first part by identifying this agent of God's creation as the head (*kephalē*) of the body, which is the church. Except for this final statement, which some view as a gloss to an earlier hymn, the focus is exclusively upon the singular role Christ played in the creation of all things. And except for this reference to the church, the focus is upon creation rather than specific historical events.

In the second part of the passage (1:18b–20), which some think the author of Colossians modeled and composed after an earlier hymn supposedly found in the first part, Colossians identifies Christ as the *archē* and the *prōtotokos* from the dead, in whom the fullness (of God) dwelt. Thus Christ is the one through whom God reconciled all things to himself by making peace through the blood of the cross. Here, the singular role of Christ in reconciling all things to God holds center stage, and the historical event of Christ's death upon the cross plays a prominent role.

This hymnic passage identifies Christ in several ways and deals with his role in creation and redemption, emphasizing that Christ is the sole mediator of creation and redemption.[14] In doing so, the passage develops the scope of the Christ story we have already uncovered; for, in addition to reconciling the Colossians, God has reconciled to himself all things in heaven and on earth as well. This cosmic reconciliation was foreshadowed in God's work of creation since the one through whom God reconciled all things was the one in whom, through whom, and for whom all things were created.

This story of creation and redemption is the divine economy of salvation (1:25), the mystery hidden for ages but now revealed to God's holy ones (1:26). The mystery is the presence of Christ among Gentiles such as the Colossians (1:27). The mystery of God is Christ in whom are all the treasures of hidden wisdom and knowledge (2:2–3).[15]

The language of mystery and reconciliation, and the emphasis upon Christ's mediating role in creation, are not entirely new.[16] In 1 Cor. 2:1 Paul refers to "the mystery of God." In 2 Cor. 5:19 he writes, "in Christ God was reconciling the world to himself" (also see Rom. 5:10–11). And in 1 Cor. 8:6 he affirms, "yet for us there is one God, the Father, from whom are all things and for whom we exist, and one Lord, Jesus Christ, *through whom* are all things and *through whom* we exist." But in Colossians, Christ's singular role in creation and redemption is more fully integrated into the Christ story, and the disclosure of this role unveils God's mystery, hidden for ages.

I have arranged the hymnic passage of Colossians in a way that highlights its structure and key phrases. For the purpose of representing the Greek text as closely as possible, the translation and word order is slavishly literal.

The One Mediator of Creation
who is the representation of the unseen God,
the *firstborn* of all creation
because *in him* were created *all things*
in the heavens and on the earth
things seen and things unseen
whether thrones or lords
whether rulers or powers
all things through him and *for him* were created
And he is before *all things*
And *all things,* in him, hold together
And he is the head of the body, the church

The One Mediator of Reconciliation
who is the beginning, the *firstborn* from the dead,
in order that among all things he might be first,
because *in him* was pleased all the fullness to dwell
and *through him* to reconcile *all things for him,*
making peace through the blood of his cross
whether things on earth
or things in heaven.

To understand the meaning of this passage *as it now stands in Colossians,* one must pay careful attention to its literary context, especially to the verses that immediately precede it. It is then evident that the subject of the passage (twice introduced by the phrase "who is") is God's beloved Son "in whom we have redemption, the forgiveness of sins" (1:14). Accordingly, the attributes "representation," "firstborn of all creation," "the beginning," and "the firstborn" are applied to the Son of God, whom Paul portrays as the singular mediator of God's creative and redemptive work.[17]

140

In the first section of this passage (vv. 15–18a), Paul identifies the Son as the *eikōn* ("representation") of the unseen God and the *prōtotokos* ("first-born") of all creation. Those familiar with Paul's Christ story as related in 2 Corinthians will recall that the apostle identified Christ as the *eikōn* of God on whose face the glory of God shines (2 Cor. 4:4, 6). While the accent is slightly different here, the thought is essentially the same: Christ, the Son of God, is the perfect representation or manifestation of the God who cannot be seen by human beings. Therefore, only the Son of God mediates authentic knowledge of God.

The designation of the Son as *prōtotokos* is more problematic since the term can refer to the first in a series of like beings (such as the firstborn of many brothers and sisters), as well as indicate the superiority of someone or something.[18] In the first instance, the Son would be viewed as the first created being of creation, in which case the Son would be a creature of God. In the second, the term would emphasize the superiority of the Son to all creation, intimating that the Son belongs to a different order of being. The question is complicated by the theological issue of preexistence. Does the Paul of Colossians view the Son of God as preexistent? If so, what does he understand by this concept?

While most commentators maintain that this passage implies some sort of preexistence, even if the precise nature of that preexistence is not specified, James Dunn argues that, rather than viewing Christ as the preexistent agent of creation, this passage affirms that *"Christ now reveals the character of the power behind the world."*[19] If I have understood Dunn correctly, he means that the experience of Christ led the author of Colossians to declare that the creative power of God which was at work in creation as divine wisdom has now been revealed in Christ. While this is a powerful statement, it is not the same as saying that the Son of God is the preexistent agent of God's creation.

In my view Colossians implies some sort of preexistence since its author insists that all things were created in, through, and for the Son. Therefore, even though the passage does not set out to explain or develop a notion of preexistence, the Son's preexistence lies in the background, much as it does in 1 Cor. 8:6; 2 Cor. 8:9; Gal. 4:4; and Phil. 2:6.

The Son is the *eikōn* of the unseen God and superior to all creation (Col. 1:15), because all things were created in (*en*) him, through (*dia*) him, and for (*eis*) him (1:16). These prepositional phrases indicate that God created the world in the sphere of, through the agency of, and for the purpose of the Son, who is the goal of creation (1:16).[20] Lest there be any misunderstanding about the comprehensive role of the Son in God's creation, Paul defines "all things" (*ta panta*) by two couplets that embrace the whole of creation: (1) whatever is in heaven or on earth, (2) whether it is visible or invisible. Then, lest there be any confusion about the things that are not seen, he introduces two further couplets that embrace the whole of the unseen heavenly order: whether thrones or dominions, whether rulers or powers. Accordingly, there is no creature in whose creation the Son did not have a mediatorial role.

In the final verses of this part (1:17–18a), Paul makes three affirmations about the Son. First, he is before (*pro*)[21] all things. Second, all things cohere in him, thereby finding their meaning in him. Third, he is the head of the body, which is the church. While the first two statements expand on what has already been said about the Son's role in creation by emphasizing his priority to creation as well as his ultimate significance for it, the third narrows the cosmic scope of this passage and highlights a historical entity, the church. The one who is before all things and in whom all things cohere is the authoritative ruler of a historical community to which the Colossians belong.

In light of this abrupt change of perspective, it is not surprising that those who argue for an earlier hymn view this reference to the church as a later addition.[22] But in its present literary setting, the phrase makes perfect sense, even though it departs from the theme of creation. The church is that portion of humanity which acknowledges that the mediator of God's creative work is the one who has authority and headship (*kephalē*) over it.

The identification of the Son as the head of the church serves as a transition to the second part of this passage (vv. 18b–20) in which Paul turns to the Son's redemptive role in God's creative work. In terms of the Christ story this represents a significant change: from a creation in which there is perfect harmony because everything coheres in the Son, to a creation in dire need of being reconciled to God. Thus the passage presupposes a rebellion on the part of creation but does not specify when or how this occurred.[23] There is no reference to Adam's transgression or Israel's disobedience. The scope of the rebellion envisioned here includes the human community, but it also goes beyond it, for God reconciled all things through and for the Son, whether on earth or in heaven. Accordingly, Colossians supposes some sort of cosmic rebellion that affected humanity as well.

The passage begins by identifying the Son as the beginning (*archē*), the firstborn (*prōtotokos*) from the dead, a clear reference to the Son's resurrection from the dead. Here, Colossians echoes Rom. 8:29, "For those whom he [God] foreknew he also predestined to be conformed to the image of his Son, in order that he might be the firstborn (*prōtotokon*) within a large family." Whereas Romans focuses on the Son's relationship to other human beings, Colossians emphasizes the preeminence of the Son.

He is the firstborn from the dead *in order that* he might hold the first or chief place.

Just as Colossians explains why Christ is the representation of the unseen God and firstborn of all creation, so it also clarifies why he is the beginning and firstborn from the dead: because "all the fullness" was pleased to dwell in him and to reconcile all things through him and for him. "All the fullness" is best taken as a circumlocution for God, especially the wisdom and glory of God; it anticipates Paul's comment, "in him [Christ] the whole fullness of deity dwells bodily" (2:9). The purpose of this statement, however, is not so much to identify the Son as it is to explain his role in reconciling creation: God was pleased to dwell in the Son and reconcile all things through and for him. Thus there is a clear parallel between the creative and redemptive roles of the Son.

Order of Creation	Order of Redemption
"All Things"	
created in him	all the fullness dwells in him
created through him	reconciled through him
created for him	reconciled for him

Paul further specifies the Son's role in God's redemptive work when he writes that God made peace through the blood of the Son's cross. Although the language is metaphorical, it indicates that reconciliation occurred in the sphere of human history. This historical act reconciled heavenly as well as earthly creatures to God. Consequently, just as the Son played a universal role in creation, so he enjoyed a similar role in restoring creation.

The hymnic passage of Colossians is not a complete story, but it implies an underlying narrative of creation, rebellion, and restoration. This narrative serves as a framework for understanding the story of redemption and reconciliation discussed above. The reconciliation the Colossians have experienced in Christ is part of a cosmic reconciliation that involves all things, and is related to God's work of creation, also mediated by the Son. The implicit Christ story of Colossians allows Paul to rebuke, correct, and exhort those who might be led away by a "philosophy" founded on deceptive human traditions rather than on Christ.

The Fullness of God

I have already noted that the various presentations of Paul's underlying Christ stories are closely related to the situations that occasioned his letters. What is true of the undisputed Pauline letters is valid for the deutero-Paulines

143

as well. For although these letters may not have been written by Paul, they respond to real situations in the life of the church. In the case of Colossians, the circumstances that occasioned this writing are greatly disputed, and I will not rehearse that debate.[24] It will be sufficient to provide a general description of the letter's background to see how the community's circumstances affected the shape of Paul's underlying Christ story.

In 2:6–23, a section in which Paul exhorts, warns, and rebukes the Colossians, there are several indications of the "philosophy" that occasioned this letter, even though the precise nature of this "false teaching" remains elusive. First, Paul describes this teaching as a "philosophy," by which he means a religious teaching, rather than some aspect of Greco-Roman philosophy. In Paul's view, this erroneous teaching is based upon empty and human traditions corresponding to *ta stoicheia tou kosmou* rather than Christ (2:8). The identity of *ta stoicheia tou kosmou* is one of the unsolved questions of Pauline studies. The expression could refer to elementary teaching, the basic physical elements that make up the world, or spiritual powers or forces associated with the elements that make up the world. Given the emphasis upon unseen things in the hymnic passage we have just discussed (1:16, 20) and the penchant of the Colossian Paul for metaphorical language, I understand *ta stoicheia tou kosmou* as an expression for spiritual powers to whom the Colossians were tempted to attribute a mediating role in their efforts to enter the heavenly realms. Because of the erroneous teachings of "the philosophy," the Colossians had already adopted certain ascetical practices in order to worship, or worship with, these intermediary powers (2:16–23).

This summary sketch leaves several questions unanswered. For example, were the powers benevolent or malevolent? Are they to be associated with the "rulers and authorities" mentioned in 1:16 and 2:10, 15? Did they cause the cosmic rebellion presupposed by the poetic passage of 1:15–20? None of these questions can be answered with full confidence, in my judgment. But we can affirm with some assurance that Paul's underlying Christ story is his response to any religious teaching that requires a mediator, or mediators, in addition to God's Son.

In warning and admonishing the Colossians, Paul makes a number of christological statements that echo what he has already written in the hymnic passage about God's Son. For example, he reminds the Colossians that the fullness of deity (*to plērōma tēs theotētos*) dwells bodily in Christ (2:9; see 1:19, where he says that all the fullness was pleased to dwell in him). He calls Christ the head (*kephalē*) of every ruler and authority (2:10; see 1:16, which affirms that the powers and authorities were created in, through, and for the Son). And he reminds the Colossians that Christ is the head of the body, the source of its support and growth (2:19; see 1:18, where Paul calls Christ the head of the body, which is the church).

Next, in one of the most remarkable metaphors of the New Testament, Paul turns to the nature of Christ's redemptive work upon the cross. After describing Christ's death as the act whereby the Colossians were spiritually circumcised (2:11), he says that Christ canceled the debt (*cheirographon*) that was held against the Colossians, with the list of particulars detailing this debt (*dogmasin*), by nailing this bond of indebtedness to the cross (2:14). In this metaphor, Paul portrays Christ's death as an act of power whereby the one in whom the fullness of deity dwells crucifies the legal debt of sinfulness that threatened the Colossians.[25] In a striking reversal of images, the Crucified becomes the Crucifier! As a result of his victorious death upon the cross, Christ leads the powers and authorities in triumphal procession. Thus the mediator of creation becomes the one mediator of redemption.[26]

Pauline Christology in a New Key

The Christ story of Colossians introduces new elements that were mentioned but not fully developed in Paul's other letters. Thus Colossians emphasizes Christ's role as mediator in creation as well as redemption and insists that his redemptive and creative roles extend to all things, unseen as well as seen, in heaven as well as on earth. The seeds for these concepts, however, are present in Paul's writings. For example, Paul insists that there is only one God and Father, "from whom are all things and for whom we exist, and one Lord, Jesus Christ, through whom are all things and through whom we exist" (1 Cor. 8:6). He affirms that even creation was subjected to futility and waits for the day when it will be set free from its bondage to decay (Rom. 8:20–21). In the climactic ending of Romans 8, Paul triumphantly proclaims that no power in heaven or on earth can separate the elect from the love of God (8:38–39). And in 2 Cor. 5:19 he affirms that God was in Christ reconciling the world to himself.

The emphasis that Colossians places on Christ's unique role as the one in, through, and for whom God created and reconciled the world is the response of the Colossian Paul to a situation that the Paul of the undisputed letters did not face. No longer is the question the fate of the dead, the relation of Gentiles and Jews, or the origin of human sinfulness. Colossians must address and explain the uniqueness of Christ. Is he the sole mediator between God and creation capable of establishing peace between God and all things? Or must believers call upon other mediators in addition to Christ? Paul's answer in Colossians is clear: Christ, and only Christ, for the one active at the creation of all things has redeemed all things by the blood of his cross.

THE LETTER TO THE EPHESIANS

Ephesians presents contemporary readers with several literary and theological problems. Its structural and literary similarity to Colossians, for example, raises the question of literary dependence. Did the author of this letter know and make use of Colossians, or did the author of Colossians know and make use of Ephesians?[27] As regards theology, both writings emphasize that Christ plays the central role in God's plan of reconciling all things, in heaven and on earth, thereby opening the way for a Christology that is cosmic in scope. In Ephesians, however, the church plays a more central role than it does in Colossians, and this leads Ernst Käsemann to comment:

> Wherever ecclesiology moves into the foreground, however justifiable the reasons may be, Christology will lose its decisive importance. . . . That very thing has already happened in the letter to the Ephesians. Here, as the opening hymn already brings out, the church has become the central eschatological event.[28]

For Käsemann, Ephesians is the New Testament writing that "most clearly marks the transition from the Pauline tradition to the perspectives of the early Catholic era."[29] It is a document in which Christology is in danger of becoming subservient to ecclesiology.

Although Käsemann overstates his case, his pointed remarks highlight the distinctive nature of Ephesians vis à vis Colossians and the other Pauline writings we have investigated. In Ephesians the church is more than a localized community of believers, it is the church universal, the body of Christ in which Jewish and Gentile believers are united. The church is the new humanity (*kainos anthropos*) that must grow into mature manhood (*eis andra teleion*), "the full stature of Christ" (4:13). Consequently, the Christology of Ephesians is inextricably bound to its ecclesiology, but without becoming subservient to it; for, as Ephesians clearly states, the church is subject to Christ, its head and savior (5:23–24).[30]

Ephesians differs from Colossians in another respect. Whereas Colossians responds to a crisis that threatened the life of a particular congregation, there is little indication that Ephesians addresses a crisis situation. Indeed, it is doubtful that its audience is a particular congregation since the words "in Ephesus" are absent from several important manuscripts of this letter (1:1).[31] The omission of these words and the content of this writing

146

suggest that it was intended for a number of Gentile congregations in Asia Minor to remind them of their new status in Christ and exhort them to live accordingly. If so, then the name of each congregation would have been inserted when the letter was read to it.

In all likelihood, the author of Ephesians was a Jewish Christian familiar with the Pauline tradition, and his intended recipients a new generation of Gentile Christians. The battles Paul fought at Antioch, Jerusalem, and Galatia on behalf of his Gentile converts had been won, and uncircumcised believers now enjoyed a secure place within the church. A new generation of Gentiles, however, needed to be reminded that they and Jewish believers formed one body in Christ who had broken down the dividing wall that once separated them from each other.[32] Consequently, the author of Ephesians writes in the name of the great apostle to remind his audience of the mystery of Christ (3:4). In doing so, he presupposes a story of what God has done in Christ and continues to do for the church. "Paul" plays a central role in the telling of this story, and I refer to him as the author of this letter and the Ephesians as its recipients, even though the letter was probably written by another, in his name, to a more general audience.

In chapter 3, Paul reminds this new generation of Gentile believers of the mystery made known to him by revelation (3:3).[33] He tells them that if they read what he has written, they will perceive his understanding of "the mystery of Christ."[34] This mystery—the unity of Jewish and Gentile Christian believers in Christ—is at the heart of the Christ story that Ephesians presupposes.[35] Because of what God has done in Christ, Gentile believers are "fellow heirs, members of the same body, and sharers in the promise" (3:6) with Jewish believers, for they belong to the same body, the body of Christ, which is the church. This mystery of reconciliation, then, is at the heart of the story that underlies Ephesians.

Summing Up All Things in Christ

The letter to the Ephesians begins with an extended blessing in which Paul outlines his story of Christ in bold strokes (1:3–14). Most commentators note the similarity of this blessing to the *berakhah,* the Jewish blessing whereby one gives praise and thanks for God's mercies.[36] In this case, Paul employs the form of the blessing to praise and thank the God and Father of Jesus Christ for the redemption bestowed upon the Ephesians *in Christ.* Although the blessing is divided into twelve verses, it is a single Greek sentence overloaded with participles and genitive constructions. It supposes a story that can be summarized as follows.

In accord with the mystery of his will, God determined to gather all things in Jesus Christ, his beloved Son.[37] Therefore, before the creation of the world, God had already chosen the recipients of this letter and destined them for adoption as his sons and daughters. Before the mystery of God's will could be accomplished, however, it was necessary for Christ to redeem the elect from their trespasses by shedding his blood. Because of God's work in Christ, the elect already enjoy adoption, redemption, and the forgiveness of their trespasses. Moreover, they have been sealed with God's Spirit, their pledge of the inheritance for which God destined them.

Although this narrative is rather general, it offers a number of christological insights that the rest of the letter will develop in greater detail. Foremost is the central role of God, who is identified as the God and *Father* of our Lord Jesus Christ (1:3).[38] Salvation begins with a divine initiative; for God chose the Ephesians *before* establishing the foundations of the world and destined them to be his adopted sons and daughters (1:5). This work of salvation is a mystery that has been disclosed to the elect; it is the mystery of God's will (1:9).[39]

For Ephesians, the role of Christ is absolutely integral to the mystery of God's will. Repeatedly employing the preposition "in" (*en*), Paul notes that God blessed the Ephesians *in* Christ (1:3), and elected them *in* him (1:4). *In* his Beloved he bestowed his grace upon them (1:6), and *in* him they received redemption (1:7). *In* Christ, God has set forth his favor (1:9), for he had determined to sum up everything *in* Christ, whether in heaven or on earth (1:10). Therefore, *in* Christ the Ephesians were chosen (1:11), for they first hoped *in* him (1:12), and *in* him they heard the word of truth (1:13).

Although the precise nuance of this preposition is disputed, it is probably to be taken in this sense: Christ is the sphere where, and the agent by whom, God effects salvation.[40] Since God's work of salvation takes place in the sphere or realm of Christ, Ephesians views Christ as one who enjoys more than a human status, as is already implied when Paul identifies him as "our Lord" (1:3). Moreover, although Ephesians never discusses the question of preexistence, that people can be chosen *in* Christ before the foundations of the world intimates a notion of preexistence, however imperfectly formed that notion might be.[41]

The Christ of Ephesians, however, is not a mythical figure. Echoing Rom. 3:24–25 ("through the redemption that is in Christ Jesus, whom God put forward as a sacrifice of atonement by his blood"), the author carefully notes that redemption was effected through the blood of Christ (1:7).[42] Thus, even though the death of Christ does not play as prominent a role in Ephesians as it does in other Pauline writings, it is hardly neglected, and chapter 2 will de-

148

velop it further.[43] Indeed, it is the death of Christ that enables God to effect his plan of summing up, or gathering together, all things in Christ (1:10).

The verb "to sum up" (*anakephalaioō*) occurs only one other time in the New Testament, in Rom. 13:9, where Paul writes, "The commandments . . . are *summed up* in this word, 'Love your neighbor as yourself.'" Here, Paul means that the love commandment summarizes all the others since it gathers them in a single commandment from which they can be deduced.[44] In an analogous manner, Ephesians proclaims that the Christ is the unique individual in whom God has chosen to gather together all things—whether they be in the heavens or on earth—so that all things are gathered and given their meaning in him.[45] The richness of this concept can be seen from the several ways that translators render it: "to gather up all things in him" (NRSV); "to sum up all things in Christ" (NAB); "everything in heaven and on earth, might be brought into a unity in Christ" (REB). Although the word is not repeated in Ephesians, the remainder of the letter clarifies its meaning by describing the unity, peace, and reconciliation God effects in Christ. It is not surprising, then, that Ephesians identifies Christ as "our peace" (2:14), and the gospel as "the gospel of peace" (6:15).

One of the striking aspects of the Ephesian Christ story is the manner in which it plots the time of salvation. The events of the story begin in eternity, focus on Christ, and then celebrate the present experience of believers: election, adoption, redemption, and forgiveness. Ephesians gives little indication, however, that there will be a future apocalyptic intervention such as Christ's parousia.[46] The Spirit is the pledge or down payment (*arrabōn*) of an inheritance toward redemption (1:14) that lies in the future, but it is not at all apparent that an apocalyptic event inaugurates that future.[47]

Christ's Enthronement and Headship

In his blessing, Paul wrote that the purpose of God's plan was to sum up all things in heaven and on earth in Christ, but he did not explain how God accomplished this. In the prayer of thanksgiving (1:15–23) that immediately follows the great blessing, however, Paul provides an initial answer. As in the blessing, Paul begins with God, whom he now identifies as "the God of our Lord Jesus Christ, the *Father of glory*" (1:17; compare with 1:3). By calling God "the *Father* of glory," Paul reminds his readers that God is the Father who adopted them in Jesus Christ (1:5–6). He then prays that his audience will be enlightened to know the hope that is integral to the election they have received and the riches of the *glory*, which is their inheritance among God's holy ones (1:18).[48]

149

Because Paul wants the Ephesians to be mindful of the power that the Father of glory works on their behalf, he recalls the supreme act of power that God exercised in Jesus Christ.

God put this power to work in Christ when he raised him from the dead and seated him at his right hand in the heavenly places, far above all rule and authority and power and dominion, and above every name that is named, not only in this age but also in the age to come. And he has put all things under his feet and has made him the head over all things for the church, which is his body, the fullness of him who fills all in all. (1:20–23)

Although these verses function primarily as the conclusion to Paul's thanksgiving prayer, they also provide further insight into the Christ story that underlies this letter. The essential points are: (1) The Father of glory raised Christ from the dead and enthroned him at his right hand above every spiritual being; (2) God subjected everything to Christ; (3) God gave Christ as head over the church, his body, which is filled by Christ who fills all things.

The first of these affirmations is the most traditional: God raised Christ from the dead (see Rom. 4:24; 1 Cor. 15:4) and enthroned him at his right hand, a strong allusion to Ps. 110:1. Ephesians, however, emphasizes that the God of glory enthroned Christ in the heavenly places, *above every spiritual being*. Although Ephesians does not identify these spiritual beings, there are indications of their hostility to humanity; for, in a later passage, Paul exhorts his audience to put on the armor of God, for their struggle is not against flesh and blood but "the spiritual forces of evil in the heavenly places" (6:12).[49] The resurrection of Christ, therefore, includes Christ's enthronement, whereby God established his Messiah[50] as ruler over spiritual as well as human beings.

Paul's second statement—that God has subjected all things to Christ—is an allusion to Ps. 8:6, and it is reminiscent of 1 Cor. 15:25–27, which makes use of the same psalm in its discussion of the resurrection of the dead. However, whereas 1 Corinthians 15 views the process of subjecting everything to Christ as still under way, Ephesians gives the impression that the process has been completed. Compare the two texts.

For he [Christ] must reign *until* he [God] has put all his enemies under his feet. The last enemy to be destroyed is death. For "God has put all things in subjection under his [Christ's] feet." (1 Cor. 15:25–27)

And he [God] has put all things under his feet [Christ's] and has made him [Christ] the head over all things for the church. (Eph. 1:22)

Thus, even though Ephesians employs apocalyptic language ("this age," "the age to come"), it does not anticipate an apocalyptic event that will usher in the new age. The new age has begun with Christ, and the powers have already been subjected to him. It is left to believers to claim their inheritance by living in accordance with this new situation.

It is Paul's final statement, however, that introduces the most distinctive aspect of Ephesians' Christology: the enthroned Christ, to whom the heavenly powers have been subjected, is the head of the church, which is his body. As the body of Christ, the church has been filled by the one (Christ) who is filling all things.

A description of the church as the body of Christ is not new to Paul's writings. In Rom. 12:4–5, Paul writes, "For as in one body we have many members, and not all the members have the same function, so we, who are many, are one body in Christ, and individually we are members of one another." And in 1 Cor. 12:12–26, Paul compares the church to a body with many members, each member making its distinctive contribution to the body. He then concludes, "Now you are the body of Christ and individually members of it" (1 Cor. 12:27). In these texts, Paul employs the concept of the body functionally and theologically. In terms of function, he draws a comparison between the human body and the church to show that just as the parts of a human body have diverse functions for the good of the whole, so the members of a local congregation have diverse functions for the good of the entire congregation. The theological underpinning of this functional comparison is Paul's conviction that believers are "one body in Christ" (Rom. 12:5), for they have been baptized "into one body" (1 Cor. 12:13). Thus, Paul conceives of Christ as a living being into whom believers can be incorporated. In the words of C. F. D. Moule, Christ is "a living, transcendent, inclusive, more-than-individual Person."[51]

Rather than focus on the functional dimension of the body metaphor, however, Ephesians stresses the corporate and cosmic dimension of Christ.[52] In doing so, it enriches the metaphor of the church as the body of Christ with the metaphor of Christ as the head of the church. This new metaphor, also found in Col. 1:18, allows Ephesians to explore the relationship between Christ and the church in a manner that the body metaphor of Romans and 1 Corinthians does not. For example, by identifying Christ as the head of the church, Ephesians can present him as the one into whom the church is growing in order to attain its full stature.

But speaking the truth in love, we must grow up in every way *into him who is the head,* into Christ, from whom the whole body, joined and knit together

151

by every ligament with which it is equipped, as each part is working properly, promotes the body's growth in building itself up in love. (4:15–16)

In another place, Paul employs the metaphor of Christ the head of the body to exhort Christian wives to be subject to their husbands, "For the husband is the head of the wife just as Christ is the head of the church, the body of which he is the Savior" (5:23). But in doing so, Ephesians makes an important christological point. Since Christ is the head of the church, the church must be subservient to him, just as a human body is subservient to the head that guides and directs it. This metaphor, however, does not make Christ another part of the body, albeit the most important. Rather, it clarifies the relationship between him and the church. As the head of the body, Christ rules over and directs the church. As the body of Christ, the church draws its strength and nourishment from him into whom it is growing. This metaphor, therefore, should dispel any suspicion that Christology is subservient to ecclesiology in Ephesians.

In identifying the church as the body of Christ, Ephesians also notes that it is the fullness (*plērōma*) of him who fills all things.

And he has put all things under his feet and has made him the head over all things for the church, which is his body, the fullness of him who fills all in all. (1:22–23)

Exactly what Ephesians means at this point is disputed since the Greek text can also be translated, " . . . the fullness of him who *is filled* all in all" (Douay Rheims New Testament).[53] These alternate translations have important implications for ecclesiology and Christology. In the first instance, as represented by the New Revised Standard Version and most other translations, the sense is that the church is filled by Christ who also fills all things. In the second, the church completes Christ as members are incorporated into it.[54] However, the explicit mention of Christ filling all things in 4:10 ("so that he might fill all things") suggests that a similar interpretation should be adopted here. Thus, the enthroned Christ, to whom the heavenly rulers have been subjected, is filling all things, and in a special manner, he is filling the church. But what does it mean to say that Christ is filling all things, and what does Ephesians understand by fullness (*plērōma*)?

Colossians clearly states that the fullness of God was pleased to dwell in Christ (Col. 1:19), and in Christ the fullness of deity (*theotētos*) dwells bodily (Col. 2:9). The situation in Ephesians, however, is not so clear, unless we presuppose that its author knew and adopted the terminology of

Colossians. However, there are some helpful indications of what Ephesians intends. In chapter 3, Paul prays that his audience may be filled with the fullness of God (3:19), and in chapter 4 he speaks of "attaining to the whole measure of the fullness of Christ" (4:13, NIV).[55] On the basis of these texts and the related texts of Col. 1:19 and 2:9, it appears that "fullness" refers to God's own being, especially as God manifests himself through his wisdom, Spirit, and glory. Christ already enjoys this fullness and communicates it to the church, which is filled by the fullness of Christ, in whom the fullness of God dwells (see Col. 1:19; 2:9). In addition to filling the church with his fullness, Christ also fills all things. Thus, Ephesians suggests that Christ's role is not limited to the sphere of the church.

To summarize, the thanksgiving of this letter (1:15–23) adds detail to the Christ story outlined in the opening blessing (1:3–14). The Father of glory raised and enthroned his Beloved Son in the heavenly places and made him head of the church, which is his body. Consequently, all things in heaven and on earth find their point of convergence in Christ, who rules over all. In him all things are gathered together and summed up. Enthroned in heaven, he fills all things with the wisdom, spirit, and glory of God that fills him.

Christ the Reconciler

In his opening blessing, Paul praised God for the redemption and forgiveness he effected through the blood of Christ (1:7), indicating thereby that the Gentile recipients of this letter had been alienated from God. But Paul did not describe in detail either the former situation of his audience or Christ's redemptive work. In chapter 2, however, he draws a sharp contrast between the present and former condition of his Gentile audience.[56] In doing so, he fills out his underlying Christ story by reminding his audience of their former condition "without Christ" and contrasting it with their new situation "in Christ."

The condition of the Ephesians without Christ can be described in two ways. First, they were dead in their sins and transgressions because they lived according to the dictates of the age and the desires of their carnal nature rather than according to God's will. Consequently, they were alienated from God and destined to experience the wrath of God (2:1–3; compare Rom. 1:18 and 1 Thess. 1:10). As Gentiles, they also experienced another kind of alienation; they were separated from the commonwealth of Israel.

So then, remember that at one time you Gentiles by birth, called "the uncircumcision" by those who are called "the circumcision" . . . remember that

153

you were at that time without Christ, being aliens from the commonwealth of Israel, and strangers to the covenants of promise, having no hope and without God in the world. (2:11–12)

Writing from a Jewish perspective, Paul notes that "the law with its commandments and ordinances" (2:15) divided his Gentile audience from the commonwealth of Israel. While Jews looked upon Gentiles as being without God because they were ignorant of the law, Gentiles looked upon Jews as arrogantly separating themselves from the rest of humanity for the sake of their law. This description of the Gentile predicament supposes Israel's story of covenant, promise, and law.

Contrasting this former situation with the present status of his Gentile readers, Paul reminds them that they have been saved by grace (2:5, 8) and made "citizens with the saints and also members of the household of God" (2:19). They are part of a plan that has been hidden for ages and has now been revealed to the holy apostles and prophets: the mystery of Christ (3:4). Simply stated, the mystery is this: "the Gentiles have become fellow heirs, members of the same body, and sharers in the promise in Christ Jesus through the gospel" (3:6). It was always God's plan that Gentile and Jewish believers should form one new person in Christ (2:15), but only now have they been gathered in Christ. The narrative that Paul presupposes, then, makes Christ the one in whom the Father of glory reconciles humanity to humanity, as well as to himself.

The manner in which Paul describes this reconciliation is rather interesting. In discussing reconciliation between God and humanity, he notes that when humanity was dead in its own trespasses, God brought it to life *with* Christ by raising Christ and seating humanity *with* him in the heavenly places (2:5–6). This co-resurrection and exaltation occurs *in Christ* and recalls Paul's earlier statement that God raised and seated Christ at his right hand in the heavenly places (1:20).[57] It surely does not mean that those in Christ are *already* in heaven, for Paul is keenly aware of his audience's failings, but it does suggest that those who are *in* Christ, as members of his body, already participate in the power of his resurrection and exaltation. They are saved by grace through faith in what God did when he raised and exalted Christ. The resurrection and exaltation of Christ, then, play an important role in reconciling humanity to God.

When Paul discusses the reconciliation that God has effected between Gentile and Jew, however, he gives greater attention to Christ's saving death. The Gentiles who were alienated from the commonwealth of Israel "have been brought near by the blood of Christ" (2:13). Drawing upon Isa.

57:19 ("Peace, peace, to the far and the near, says the LORD"), Paul identifies Christ as "our peace" (2:14). He came and proclaimed peace to the Gentiles, who were far off, and to Israel, who was near (2:17). This peace is the reconciliation Christ effected between Gentile and Jewish believers when he abolished the dividing wall of hostility, the law, through his death upon the cross (2:16).

To explain the effects of reconciliation, Paul employs two metaphors. First, Jewish and Gentile believers form a new person, or a new humanity, in Christ. This new humanity is a third race that incorporates Gentiles as well as Jews. The new humanity is already present in the church, the body of Christ, which is growing into its head, Christ (4:15). Second, the church is a holy temple in the Lord, and the cornerstone of this temple is Christ, the one who holds the entire structure together (2:20–21).

This rich Christology presents Christ as God's agent of reconciliation. In doing so, it builds upon the theology of reconciliation found in Rom. 5:1–11 and 2 Cor. 5:17–21. Like those texts, Ephesians highlights the importance of Christ's death upon the cross (2:13, 16). Ephesians, however, gives greater prominence to the reconciliation that God effects in Christ between Jewish and Gentile believers. Whereas Paul fought for the right of Gentiles to share in the blessings of Abraham on the basis of their faith in Christ, the author of Ephesians sees the emergence of a new people composed of Gentile and Jewish believers. This people is not a new or restored Israel but the church, the body of Christ. Incorporated into Christ's body, believers are reconciled to each other and to God because they have been raised and seated with Christ in the heavenly places. This Christology presents an exalted Christ in corporate and even cosmic images, but it is firmly rooted in a historical event: the death of Christ upon the cross. Suggesting the paradoxical image of an individual in whom God gathers together the whole of humanity, it is akin to Paul's Adam Christology.

The Love of Christ for His Church

The underlying story of Ephesians presents the God and Father of the Lord Jesus Christ as the one who initiates the work of salvation in Christ. Christ, however, is not merely the passive instrument of God's work. To the contrary, he plays an active role in God's work of salvation. We have already seen, for example, the role Christ played in reconciling Jewish and Gentile believers in his body by abolishing the law with its commandments and ordinances and proclaiming peace to Jew and Gentile alike. But there are other indications in Ephesians of Christ's work. One of the most striking occurs in the household code of chapter 5, where Paul exhorts Christian wives to subject themselves to their husbands. To support his exhortation, he draws an analogy between Christ and the church on the one hand, and Christian husbands and wives on the other. But in addition to exhorting wives to subject themselves to their husbands, he uses the body-head metaphor to exhort Christian husbands to love their wives.

> Husbands, love your wives, just as Christ loved the church and gave himself up for her (*heauton paredōken hyper autēs*), in order to make her holy by cleansing her with the washing of water by the word, so as to present the church to himself in splendor, without a spot or wrinkle or anything of the kind—yes, so that she may be holy and without blemish. (5:25–27)

Making use of the body-head metaphor, Paul then exhorts Christian husbands, as the heads of their wives, to love their wives as their own bodies. To undergird this exhortation, he turns to the example of Christ who loves his body, the church (5:28–29).

Paul also employs the example of Christ when he calls upon his audience to be imitators of God and to live in love "as Christ loved us and gave himself up for us (*paredōken heauton hyper ēmōn*), a fragrant offering and sacrifice to God" (5:1–2). Once more, the warrant for this moral exhortation is the self-sacrificing love of Christ. In the undisputed Pauline letters, Paul frequently speaks of Christ dying for us, or being handed over for us, but only rarely does he say that Christ gave or handed himself over for us (Gal. 1:4; 2:20). Given the few references that Ephesians makes to the death of Christ, this emphasis on his love and role in handing himself over is all the more striking. To use the language of Arland J. Hultgren, it points to the redemption won by Christ.[58]

But it was not only when he willingly died for us that Christ played an active role in God's plan of salvation. Paul also reminds his audience that when Christ ascended, he distributed gifts (apostles, prophets, evangelists, pastors, and teachers) to the church "for building up the body of Christ" (4:12).

> Therefore it is said, "When he [Christ] ascended on high he made captivity itself a captive; he gave gifts to his people." (4:8)

Here, Paul quotes from Ps. 68:18. However, whereas the psalm reads, "You [the Lord God] ascended the high mount, leading captives in your train and *receiving gifts* from people," Ephesians applies the psalm to Christ who *gave gifts* to his people. Interpreting the text in light of Christ,

Paul explains that the one who ascended (Christ) is the one who descended to the lower parts of the earth, and that he ascended so that he might fill all things (4:9–10). Thus Ephesians presents Christ in a manner reminiscent of the Son of Man in the Fourth Gospel who descends from heaven and then ascends to the Father.[59] We can summarize the underlying story of Christ in Ephesians as follows.

> Christ descended from the heavenly places to reconcile humanity to God and to itself in accord with God's hidden plan. To accomplish this, he offered himself as a pleasing sacrifice to God, shedding his blood on the cross for the sake of the church, his body, which he loved, so that he might present the church to himself as a spotless bride. The Father of glory raised his Son from the dead and seated him at his right hand, subjecting everything in the heavens and on the earth to him. In ascending to God so that he might fill all things, Christ gave gifts to the church for building up the body of Christ.

Christology in Ephesians

Ephesians clearly makes overtures to a cosmic Christology when it says that God intended to sum up all things in heaven and on earth in Christ (1:10) and proclaims that Christ is the one who fills all things (1:23; 4:10). Moreover, it is quite emphatic that God has enthroned Christ at his right hand and subjected all things to him. Viewed from this perspective, Christ already rules over the cosmos, so that the parousia falls into the background. Ephesians, however, is more interested in Christ's relationship to the church than to the cosmos. Christ is the head of the church, and the church is his body. There are good reasons, then, to characterize the Christology of Ephesians as an ecclesial Christology, but not in the sense that Christology is at the service of the church, or that Christ has become subservient to the church. It is the church that must subject itself to Christ, for God has enthroned him above all things in heaven and on earth. Moreover, it is Christ who shed his blood and handed himself over for the sake of the church that he loved. The church, however, plays a vital role in the Christology of this writing since believers experience Christ as members of his body. As members of that body they are at peace with each other, for Christ has broken down the dividing wall of hostility between Gentile and Jewish believers. Thus, this ecclesial Christology presents Christ as the great reconciler of humanity to God and to itself. Christ is the one who continues to fill all things and reconcile them to God.

THE PASTORAL EPISTLES

New Testament scholarship is in the process of reassessing the Christology of the pastoral epistles (1 and 2 Timothy, Titus).[60] Until relatively recently, most scholars agreed that there was little, if any, unity to the Christology of these letters. For example, Martin Dibelius and Hans Conzelmann, in their influential commentary on the Pastorals, write:

> there is a diversity of Christological perspectives which must not be combined to reconstruct "the" Christology of the Pastorals. The unity does not lie in a particular Christological conception (several types stand side by side with no sign of theological reflection). Rather unity results from the constant emphasis upon the meaning of salvation for the present.[61]

And, in an equally influential commentary on these letters, A. T. Hanson makes the following judgment about their author:

> He does not have any doctrine of his own, but makes use of whatever comes to him in the sources which he uses. Indeed one could legitimately claim that his way of teaching doctrine is to quote liturgical and confessional formulae.[62]

In other words, the author of the Pastorals merely adorned his writings with christological statements from the creeds and liturgy of the early church, but he did not successfully integrate this material into his letter, in part, because he did not possess a unified Christology.

In recent years, this negative assessment of the Pastorals has given way to a more positive evaluation of their Christology. While nearly all commentators agree that the Pastor (a common designation for the author of these letters) employed traditional christological formulae in his letters, recent studies emphasize the manner in which the author of the Pastorals has integrated these formulae.[63] Moreover, they propose that the Pastor is a creative theologian in his own right. His Christology may not rival that of the great apostle in whose name he writes, but it does represent an important contribution that is indebted to the Pauline tradition.

The Christology of these letters is rooted in an underlying story of Christ which supposes the important moments in the divine economy of salvation. It can be summarized as follows:

> Before the beginning of time, God, the Savior, willed the salvation of all people. The Savior God revealed this plan at the right time: at the epiphany of Christ Jesus, the Savior, the one mediator between God and human beings, who appeared in the realm of the flesh. Christ Jesus came into the world to

save sinners and give himself as a ransom for all. Manifested in the realm of the flesh, he was vindicated in the realm of the spirit, and now he is preached to all nations. At present, believers await a second epiphany of this great Savior God, Christ Jesus, our Lord, the just judge. When he appears, they will attain the fullness of the salvation they already enjoy.

The Christ story I have recounted is an artificial narrative composed of elements from each of the Pastorals. All of these letters, however, presuppose a narrative akin to this story, even if a particular letter emphasizes one aspect more than another.[64] Thus the Pastorals develop an epiphany Christology whereby the Savior God manifests himself in the epiphany of the Savior, Christ Jesus, who came into the world to save sinners. To verify this, we must turn to the texts that constitute this story.

First Timothy

First Timothy supposes that Paul has left Timothy in charge of the church at Ephesus to combat false teachers and safeguard the sound teaching entrusted to him (1:3–7; 6:20–21). To assist Timothy, Paul writes this letter, which consists of moral instruction and codes of conduct for promoting piety and order in "the household of God" (3:15). False teachers have already disturbed the church with myths and endless genealogies (1:4), forbidding marriage and demanding abstinence from foods God created (4:1–4). To combat their erroneous teaching, Timothy must hold fast to the sound teaching that has been entrusted to him, the *paratheke*.[65] Since the proclamation of God's work of salvation is at the heart of what has been entrusted to Timothy, Paul reminds his young associate of God's salvific plan in four statements (1:15; 2:5–6; 3:16; 6:13–16) to which we now turn.

The One Who Came into the World to Save Sinners

The first of these statements occurs at the beginning of the letter, where Paul recalls what Christ Jesus did in his own life (1:12–17). Previous to his conversion, Paul was a blasphemer and persecutor, an arrogant man. He was the foremost (*protos*) sinner. But despite Paul's sinfulness, Christ Jesus had mercy on him so that Paul might serve as pattern (*hypotyposin*) for future generations of what Christ Jesus can do for those who believe in him. Thus, Paul points to his life's story as a model for all who will come to faith. If Christ Jesus acted so mercifully toward Paul, the foremost sinner, he will do the same for those who believe in him. Filled with this confidence, Paul writes:

> The saying is sure and worthy of full acceptance, that Christ Jesus came into the world to save sinners—of whom I am the foremost. (1:15)

159

This saying, upon which Timothy can rely, suggests the outline of a story that can be summarized in this way: The world was filled with sinners alienated from God; therefore Christ Jesus came into the world to save them; Paul's own life exemplifies this work of salvation.

This "faithful statement," the first of several in the pastoral epistles,[66] is similar to material in the Synoptic and Johannine traditions. For example, in the Gospel of Luke, Jesus describes his mission in terms of saving sinners (Luke 5:32; 19:10), but he does not say that he "came into the world," as if from another realm. On the other hand, the Gospel of John contains several sayings that speak of Jesus coming into the world (John 1:9; 3:19; 9:39; 11:27; 16:28; 18:37), but none of these speak of Jesus coming into the world to "save sinners."[67] Thus 1 Timothy presents us with a saying that is related to other traditions but formulated in a new way.

This faithful saying recasts these traditions in several ways.[68] First, it identifies the one who came into the world as "Christ Jesus." While the nondisputed Pauline letters also use this formula, the Pastorals employ it with a regularity that makes it their preferred and distinctive manner of referring to Christ, to the point that they never call Christ the Son of God.[69] "Christ Jesus," however, does not merely function as a personal name, for even if the recipients of the Pastorals did not understand the full implications of *Christos,* it is difficult to imagine that their author did not.[70] When he writes, "Christ Jesus," therefore, he means something such as the following: God's Savior (Christ) who is Jesus, or, the Savior Messiah (Christ), who is Jesus. In other words, "Christ Jesus" refers to the one who accomplishes God's work of salvation. Christ Jesus is not simply another person, then; he is *the* savior figure who came into the world.

In addition to employing the Christ Jesus formula, the Pastorals join a statement of Christ's soteriological work (to save sinners) to one that suggests preexistence (came into the world).[71] The description of Christ's soteriological work associates him with God, whom the Pastorals describe as "God our Savior" (1:1), "God our Savior, who desires everyone to be saved" (2:3–4), "the living God, who is the Savior of all people" (4:10). The coming of Christ Jesus into the world intimates that Christ Jesus enjoyed a preexistent status, although this is neither explicitly stated nor developed. As we progress through the Pastorals, however, it will become evident that some notion of preexistence is at work in the Christ story that underlies these letters, even if it is never explicitly stated or explained.

The statement that Christ Jesus came into the world to save sinners, then, provides a starting point for the Christology of the Pastorals, for it anchors God's salvific plan in a historical event, the coming of Christ Jesus into the world. Moreover, it alerts us to the human predicament of sinfulness and suggests the preexistence of Christ Jesus.[72]

God's Will to Save All People

Having explained how the salvific work of Christ Jesus has been exemplified in his own life as a pattern for future generations, Paul urges that "prayers, intercessions, and thanksgivings be made for everyone" (*hyper pantōn anthrōpōn*; 2:1). He says that this is acceptable in the sight of God our Savior, who wants *everyone* to be saved and come to the knowledge of the truth. To support this claim, he writes:

there is *one* God;
there is also *one* mediator between God and humankind,
Christ Jesus, himself human,
who gave himself a ransom for all
—this was attested at the right time.

(2:5–6)

Thus the Pastorals argue in this fashion: It is fitting to offer prayers for all since there is one God who wants all human beings to be saved and one mediator who gave himself as a ransom for all (*hyper pantōn*) so that they might be saved. This brief formula also serves as the outline for a narrative. Namely, humanity was in need of redemption, but it was unable to bridge the gulf between itself and the one God. Therefore, at the right time in a history of salvation, the sole mediator between God and humanity, himself human (*anthrōpos*), gave himself as a ransom for all.

Once more the Pastorals stand in continuity with older traditions that they juxtapose in order to create a new formula. In this case, the formulation echoes statements from Paul and Mark.

yet for us there is one God, the Father,
from whom are all things and for whom we exist,
and one Lord, Jesus Christ,
through whom are all things and through whom we exist.

(1 Cor. 8:5)

For the Son of Man came not to be served but to serve,
and to give his life a ransom for many.

(Mark 10:45)

In addition to these traditions, the emphasis upon Christ Jesus' initiative in surrendering himself recalls similar statements in other Pauline writings.

161

who *gave himself* for our sins to set us free from the present evil age, according to the will of our God and Father. (Gal. 1:4)

the Son of God, who loved me and *gave himself* for me. (Gal. 2:20)

as Christ loved us and *gave himself* up for us, a fragrant offering and sacrifice to God. (Eph. 5:2)

But whereas 1 Cor. 8:6 focuses on the one God who is creator, and the one Lord Jesus Christ, the agent of his creation, the addition of the ransom tradition allows the Pastorals to present Christ Jesus as the mediator of redemption who freely surrenders himself for the sake of all. In adopting the ransom tradition, however, the Pastorals also modify it. It is Christ Jesus (rather than the Son of Man) who gives himself as a ransom for all (rather than many).[73] Likewise, whereas Gal. 2:20 and Eph. 5:2 speak of the Son of God giving himself up for us, the Pastorals speak of Christ Jesus, which suggests that "Christ Jesus" is as significant for them as "Son of God" is for Paul.

But what does the Pastor mean when he notes that Christ Jesus was himself human (*anthrōpos*)? To answer this question, we must recall how the Pastor portrays God. God is the King of the ages, immortal and *invisible* (1:17). He dwells in *unapproachable* light, and no one has ever seen or can *see* him (6:16). Because God is invisible and unapproachable, humanity needs a mediator[74] between itself and "the blessed and only Sovereign, the King of kings and Lord of lords" (6:15). The statement that Christ Jesus is the one mediator between God and humanity, therefore, implies a godly status on the part of Christ Jesus, whereas the statement that he is human explains how this mediator can represent a humanity that cannot see or approach God.[75] Christ Jesus is such a mediator because he is human as well as divine. The author of the Pastorals is on the way to a doctrine of incarnation. Moreover, his presentation of Christ Jesus as the one who is able to mediate between humanity and the unseen God (because he is divine and human) may be a further intimation of preexistence.

Manifest in Flesh

The christological crescendo of 1 Timothy occurs in the hymnic passage of 3:16.[76]

He was revealed in flesh,
   vindicated in spirit,
seen by angels,
   proclaimed among Gentiles,

believed in throughout the world,
    taken up in glory.

Although this text may have once enjoyed a liturgical setting, it has long since received a literary one in which it plays a role in the Pastor's assault against the false teachers.

According to this literary setting, Paul hopes to see Timothy soon. But if he is delayed, he wants his young assistant to know how one ought to behave in the household of God. Therefore, he reminds Timothy of "the mystery of our religion" (3:16), the text quoted above. Immediately following this passage, he warns Timothy of the false teachers whose ascetical practices urge believers to reject as evil what God created as good (4:1–5). Thus, this hymnic passage may be functioning as part of an argument against teachers who misrepresent the created order as evil.[77]

The passage consists of three stanzas, each of which contains two lines that establish a fundamental contrast. In the first stanza, the contrast is between the realm of the flesh and the realm of the spirit; in the second, between the sphere of the angels and the sphere of human beings; and in the third, between this world and the realm of God's glory. These contrasts suggest that the salvific work of Christ is cosmic in scope since it unites these different realms.[78]

The first stanza affirms that the one who appeared in flesh (*ephanerōthē en sarki*) was vindicated in spirit (*edikaiōthē en pneumati*). This epiphany in the realm of the flesh points "to the totality of Christ's earthly historical existence,"[79] the appearance of Christ Jesus in the realm of human weakness and sinfulness. Thus, it is closely related to the statement of the Fourth Gospel, "and the Word became flesh and lived among us" (John 1:14). Despite dwelling in the realm of the flesh (or perhaps precisely because he dwelt in the realm of the flesh), Christ Jesus was vindicated in the realm of the spirit; that is to say, "What Christ has accomplished in the human realm is now confirmed and corroborated by God's declaration."[80] The opening stanza, then, encompasses the whole of the Christ story, from incarnation to exaltation. Moreover, while the epiphany language of this text does not explicitly mention preexistence, it intimates that the one who appeared in the realm of the flesh preexisted in the realm of the spirit.[81]

The second stanza moves from the heavenly realm where Christ was seen by angels to the earthly where he is preached among the nations.[82] In effect, this stanza elaborates on the first by showing that Christ's vindication in the spiritual realm was made known to the heavenly beings that inhabit it. Moreover, this vindication has led to a proclamation in the earthly realm that includes all nations. What is seen in heaven is preached among the nations; namely, God vindicated the one who appeared in the realm of the flesh.

The third stanza begins where the second left off, in the earthly realm, and from there it moves to the heavenly. Thus the hymn concludes with a reference to the heavenly realm.[83] The one who was preached among the nations is believed in throughout the world and has been taken up into glory. This last phrase is best understood in general terms rather than as referring to a specific event such as the ascension; that is to say, Christ was taken up into God's sphere, the realm of glory.

The mystery of religion that Paul communicates to Timothy can be summarized in this way. What angels have seen and what has been preached throughout the world is the vindication of Christ Jesus who appeared in flesh. Those who denigrate the realm of creation misunderstand the mystery of religion: that Christ effected salvation in the realm of the flesh.

Final Epiphany

The final text occurs within Paul's last charge to Timothy. It highlights two events of the Christ story, only one of which has already occurred.

> In the presence of God, who gives life to all things, and of Christ Jesus, who in his testimony before Pontius Pilate made the good confession, I charge you to keep the commandment without spot or blame until the manifestation (*epiphaneia*) of our Lord Jesus Christ, which he [God] will bring about at the right time—he who is the blessed and only Sovereign, the King of kings and the Lord of lords. (6:13–15)

Although the pastoral epistles never explicitly mention the death of Christ, the story that underlies these writings presupposes this salvific death. Thus the Pastorals affirm that Christ Jesus came into the world to save sinners, gave himself as a ransom for all, appeared in the realm of the flesh, and made his confession before the Roman governor, Pontius Pilate, who ordered his execution.[84] Reminding Timothy of this confession, Paul calls upon him to render similar testimony on behalf of Christ. Moreover, he assures him that there will be another "manifestation of our Lord Jesus Christ" at the "right time." Thus, the Savior God who determined the time when Christ Jesus would give himself as a ransom for all has also set the time for Christ Jesus' final epiphany.

Although 1 Timothy makes use of earlier traditions, its Christology manifests a remarkable unity that focuses on the will of God the Savior to save all. To effect this salvation, the one mediator between God and humanity, Christ Jesus, came into the world to save sinners by giving himself as a ransom for all. Thus, he appeared in the realm of the flesh. Vindicated by God in the heavenly realm, he is preached throughout the world until "the right time," when he will appear again. God is the author of this plan for salvation, but Christ is the principal agent who actively executes it.[85] Although there is no explicit statement of Christ's preexistence, references to his coming into the world, the portrayal of him as the unique mediator between the unseen God and humanity, and his manifestation in the realm of the flesh intimate prior existence with God.

Second Timothy

According to this letter, Paul's circumstances have changed dramatically. The apostle is no longer a free man but a prisoner, perhaps at Rome. He has already undergone a first hearing, and those who should have supported him did not (4:16).[86] The great apostle knows that the time for his departure from this life has come (4:6), and so he writes a farewell testament to Timothy to encourage him to "share in suffering like a good soldier of Christ Jesus" (2:3). Although it is not explicitly stated, Timothy seems to be in Ephesus, where Hymenaeus and Philetus are claiming that the resurrection has already taken place (2:17–18).[87] The letter presents Paul as the model apostle who has suffered and is about to die for the gospel. To persuade Timothy to follow his example, Paul employs a number of texts that are central to the Christology of this letter.

Before proceeding to those texts, two points should be noted. First, whereas 1 Timothy reserves the title "Savior" for God (1 Tim. 1:1; 2:3; 4:10), 2 Timothy applies it to Christ Jesus (2 Tim. 1:10), thereby associating him with God.[88] Second, this letter uses the title "Lord" (in reference to Jesus) with unusual frequency in an absolute manner ("the Lord").[89] Since "Lord," like "Savior," is a title for God, its application to Christ Jesus highlights his unique relationship to God.[90]

Through the Epiphany of Our Savior Christ Jesus
To persuade Timothy to bear his share of hardship for the gospel, as the imprisoned Paul is already doing, Paul reminds him of God's saving plan in which Christ Jesus played the decisive role.

> who saved us and called us with a holy calling,
>> not according to our works
>> but according to his own purpose and grace.
> This grace was given to us in Christ Jesus

before the ages began,
but it has now been revealed through the appearing of our Savior
Christ Jesus,
    who abolished death
    and brought life and immortality to light
        through the gospel.

(1:9–10)

Paul then says that he has been appointed a herald, teacher, and apostle of this gospel for which he now suffers. If Timothy understands what God has done through the appearance of Christ Jesus, he must also suffer for the gospel.

These few verses can be put into narrative form. Humanity was in desperate need of salvation, but it could not save itself by its own works. Because of its plight, God saved humanity according to his purpose and grace. Before the ages of human history began, God already determined to give this grace in Christ Jesus. But it is only now, through the epiphany of the Savior, Christ Jesus, that this grace has been revealed. He has destroyed death and brought life and immortality to light.

If we inquire about the role of Christ in this story, we find an answer in the author's coordinating of God's salvific plan with the work of the Savior, Christ Jesus. God is the one who *saves* and calls us, and Christ is the *Savior* who enables this to take place, since God's eternal plan is manifested (*phanerōtheisan*) through the manifestation (*epiphaneia*) of Christ Jesus. While the Greek noun *epiphaneia* normally refers to Christ's second epiphany or manifestation[91] (what Paul calls the parousia), in this instance it refers to the earthly manifestation or appearance of the Savior, what later theology would call the incarnation. But whereas that doctrine focuses on the enfleshment of the Word, this *epiphaneia* embraces the earthly career of Christ Jesus, from birth to death. The earthly manifestation of the Savior is the manifestation of the saving God. Christ Jesus is both the agent of salvation and the Savior, and his epiphany suggests the revelation of one who already existed with God.[92]

The Faithfulness of Christ Jesus
To strengthen the young Timothy, Paul reminds him of Christ Jesus who was raised from the dead (2:8). He then draws upon another "faithful saying," to assure Timothy that those who die with Christ will live with him (2:11–13). Andrew Y. Lau puts it well when he writes of this saying, "It also serves to remind Timothy of the fact that before Christ was exalted and began to reign at the Father's right hand, he lived and remained faithful to accomplish the task entrusted to him."[93]

Remember Jesus Christ, raised from the dead, a descendant of David—that is my Gospel. (2:8)

As nearly all commentators point out, the statement recalls the opening of Paul's letter to the Romans:

the gospel concerning his Son, who was *descended from David* according to the flesh and was declared to be Son of God with power according to the spirit of holiness by *resurrection from the dead, Jesus Christ* our Lord. (Rom. 1:3–4)

However, there are important differences between the two statements. Whereas the text of Romans employs the "Son of God" title and speaks of the Son's Davidic descent before mentioning his resurrection, the text of 2 Timothy mentions the resurrection first and then identifies "Jesus Christ" (not the Son) as a descendant of David. The reversal of what is the normal word order for the Pastorals (Christ Jesus), and the reference to Davidic descent at the end of the text underlie Jesus' messiahship. Jesus, who is called Christ, was a descendant of David because he was the Messiah. Thus, although the Pastorals do not otherwise refer to Israel's history, they envision continuity between Israel's messianic expectations and the epiphany of Christ Jesus.

The purpose in recalling the resurrection of Jesus Christ, however, is more paraenetic than doctrinal. Paul wants to remind Timothy that he will share in Christ's resurrection if he dies with him. Thus, he introduces yet another tradition.[94]

If we have died with him,
   we will also live with him;
if we endure,
   we will also reign with him;
if we deny him,
   he will also deny us;
if we are faithless,
   he remains faithful—
      for he cannot deny himself.
         (2:11–13)

The structure of the material is not difficult to discern, for it consists of four conditional clauses, each with its consequence. The fourth conditional clause, however, breaks the pattern of the first three, necessitating the final line, "for he cannot deny himself." The point of this hymnic passage, then, is twofold. First, if believers are united with Christ in his death, they will participate in the life that comes from his resurrection. Second, Christ remains faithful, even if believers do not, since faithfulness is integral to his identity.

The first of these points — sharing in Christ's death leads to life — is reminiscent of what Paul writes in Rom. 6:8, "But if we have died with Christ, we believe that we will also live with him." Moreover, it adds a new dimension to the christological thought of the Pastorals: the participation of believers in Christ's final victory. The second point — Christ's faithfulness — is reminiscent of Paul's statement in 2 Cor. 1:19, "For the Son of God, Jesus Christ, whom we proclaimed among you, Silvanus and Timothy and I, was not 'Yes and No'; but in him it is always 'Yes.'" For the author of the Pastorals, Christ Jesus is the example of faithfulness to God, and even if believers are unfaithful, he remains faithful. As a result, even those who have denied him can repent.

The Just Judge

The last texts we will consider are related by the theme of judgment. They occur in chapter 4 and remind Timothy that the Lord will render judgment at his second epiphany. Consequently, Timothy must persevere in his faith.

> In the presence of God and Christ Jesus, who is to *judge the living and the dead,* and in view of his appearing (*epiphaneian*) and his kingdom, I solemnly urge you. (4:1)

> From now on there is reserved for me the crown of righteousness, which the Lord, *the righteous judge,* will give me on that day, and not only to me but also to all who have longed for his appearing (*epiphaneian*). (4:8)

> Alexander the coppersmith did me great harm; the Lord will pay him back for his deeds. (4:14)

Although these texts function as moral exhortation rather than as doctrinal statements, they contribute to our understanding of the Pastorals' Christology. First, they explain what will occur at the final manifestation or epiphany of Christ Jesus; he will come with his kingdom as the judge of the living and the dead. Second, they indicate that the one who exercises judgment has a divine status since judgment is a divine prerogative. It is appropriate, therefore, that the Pastor employs the *Kyrios* title in 4:8, 14. In the case of 4:14, there is even an allusion to Ps. 62:12, which describes how God will judge, "For you repay to all according to their work." But whereas the psalm attributes judgment to God, the Pastor ascribes it to the Lord, Christ Jesus.

Although 2 Timothy follows the main lines of 1 Timothy, it discloses new facets of the Pastor's Christology: the use of the title "Savior" for Christ Jesus; the absolute use of the title "Lord," especially in conjunction with judgment; the recognition of Christ's Davidic descent; and the presentation of the Christ story in terms of two epiphanies or manifestations: the earthly appearance of Christ Jesus in the realm of the flesh and his future appearance when he will judge the living and the dead. This Christology begins with God's divine initiative and presents Christ Jesus as the agent of his salvific work. But it also portrays him as the Savior, Lord, and Judge who actively effects salvation.

Titus

Paul's letter to Titus is similar to 1 Timothy in form and content. The circumstances of this letter presuppose that Paul has left Titus on the island of Crete for the purpose of appointing presbyters in every town, just as Paul directed him (1:5). As for Paul, he plans to spend the winter at Nicopolis and hopes that Titus will soon join him (3:12). To assist Titus in his work, Paul writes this letter in which he outlines the qualifications for a presbyter/bishop (1:7–9),[95] warns Titus of false teachers (1:10–16), and provides him with instructions for moral behavior (2:1–3:11). To strengthen this moral teaching, Paul reminds Titus that the saving grace of God has appeared in, and through, the person of Jesus Christ, the Savior, who will appear again (2:11–14; 3:4–7). These texts are the christological climax of the pastoral epistles.

While Titus is similar in form and content to 1 Timothy, it is also distinctive, especially in its use of christological titles. Whereas 1 Timothy regularly refers to Christ as "Christ Jesus," Titus employs this usage once (1:4). Moreover, it never refers to Jesus as "Lord." The preferred title for Christ in this letter is "Savior," which the author applies both to Christ (1:4; 2:13; 3:6) and God (1:3; 2:10; 3:4). For example, Savior is applied to God and Christ in the letter opening.

> in due time he revealed his word through the proclamation with which I
> have been entrusted by the command of *God our Savior,*
> To Titus, my loyal child in the faith we share:
> Grace and peace from God the Father and *Christ Jesus our Savior.*
>
> (1:3–4)

The use of this title for both God and Christ within the space of two verses clearly identifies Christ with God and prepares for the climactic statement of 2:13, where Jesus Christ is identified as "our great God and Savior."

While each of the Pastorals focuses on the theme of salvation, that theme reaches a christological high point in this letter.

Our Great God and Savior

The first great christological statement of this letter functions as the theological justification for the moral instruction that Titus must give to various groups within the church. After outlining these instructions (2:1–10), Paul explains why they should be observed.

> For the grace of God has appeared,
> bringing salvation to all,
> training us to renounce impiety and worldly passions,
> and in the present age to live lives that are
> self-controlled, upright, and godly,
> while we wait for the blessed hope
> and the manifestation of the glory
> of our great God and Savior, Jesus Christ.
> He it is who gave himself for us
> that he might redeem us from all iniquity
> and purify for himself a people of his own
> who are zealous for good deeds.
>
> (2:11–13)

This passage focuses on two epiphanies or manifestations, only one of which has occurred. The first is the manifestation of God's saving grace (*epephanē gar hē charis tou theou sōtērios*), which has already taken place. The second is the manifestation (*epiphaneia*) of the glory of our great God and Savior Jesus Christ, which has not yet occurred. The first epiphany took place when Jesus Christ gave himself for us (*hyper hēmōn*) to redeem us from every iniquity so that he might purify for himself a people zealous for good works. Thus, one of the purposes of this epiphany was to train people to live justly and devoutly in this age as they await the second epiphany, at which Jesus Christ will gather to himself the people he has purified for good works.[96]

This rich text contains allusions to other texts, as well as a major problem for interpretation. As regards the allusions, the following should be noted. The appearance of God's saving grace *for all* clearly recalls the statement of 1 Tim. 2:4 that God our Savior "desires everyone to be saved," as well as 1 Tim. 4:10, that the living God is "the Savior of all people." The description of Jesus Christ as the one who gave himself for us to redeem us recalls a similar description in 1 Tim. 2:6 that Christ Jesus "gave himself as a ransom for all." Finally, the description of Jesus Christ purifying a people for his possession (*laon periousion*) echoes Deut. 7:6, "the

LORD your God has chosen you out of all the peoples on earth to be his people, his treasured possession." However, whereas Deuteronomy identifies this people as God's possession, Titus makes the bold claim that Jesus Christ purified a people for himself, and so he ascribes one of God's prerogatives to Christ.[97]

This description of Christ who purifies a people for himself, as did God, leads us to the major interpretive problem of this text. Should the Greek phrase *tou megalou theou kai sōtēros hēmōn Iēsou Christou* be translated "the great God *and our* savior Jesus Christ" (NAB), or "our great God *and* Savior Jesus Christ" (NRSV)?[98] While there is a clear distinction between God and Jesus Christ in the first translation, the second identifies Jesus Christ as our great God and Savior. The solution to this problem does not rest solely on grammatical grounds alone but must take into consideration the theology of the Pastorals.[99]

There is no other instance in the Pastorals where Christ is called God. However, two considerations make it likely that in this instance the Pastorals ascribe the phrase "our great God" to Jesus Christ. First, every other occurrence of *epiphaneia* in the Pastorals refers to a single manifestation, be it the past (2 Tim. 1:10) or future epiphany of Christ (2 Tim. 4:1, 8). If the text is interpreted as referring to *both* God and Christ, then we are faced with the anomaly of two independent epiphanies, one of God and one of Christ. The Pastorals, however, present the epiphany of Christ as an epiphany of God in and through Christ. Second, the ascription of "Savior" to Christ, the same title the Pastorals employ for God, suggests a Christology that can support the remarkable phrase, "our great God and Savior."

What then does the author mean when he writes "our great God and Savior"? Given the unambiguous statement that God is one and Christ is the mediator between God and the human race (1 Tim. 2:5), the author does not mean that Christ is a second God. A more fruitful approach is that of Andrew Y. Lau, who has investigated the conceptual background of the epiphany language in the Pastorals.[100] The epiphanies of Christ Jesus (past and future) are the visible manifestation of God in and through the person and work of Jesus Christ. Because God has been manifested in Christ's person and salvific work, and will be manifested through the future epiphany of Christ, the author can call Christ "our great God and Savior." Christ has not replaced God, nor is he a second God alongside of God. He is the manifestation of God, past and future. Although the author has not yet developed a doctrine of the incarnation, there is continuity between his teaching and that of later theology that identifies Jesus Christ as God incarnate.

171

Through Jesus Christ Our Savior

The Pastorals are insistent that believers must do good works since Jesus Christ has purified a people for himself who are eager to do such works. Thus, people must devote themselves to good works (3:8, 14). But in addition to emphasizing good works, the Pastorals remind their audience that salvation is rooted in what God has done through Christ. Thus, after recalling the former condition of his readers (3:3), the author writes:

> But when the goodness and loving kindness of *God our Savior* appeared, he *saved us*, not because of any works of righteousness that we had done, but according to his mercy, through the water of rebirth and renewal by the Holy Spirit. This Spirit he poured out on us richly *through Jesus Christ our Savior,* so that, having been justified by his grace, we might become heirs according to the hope of eternal life. (3:4–7)

The essence of this rich and complex text is summarized in the words I have italicized: God our Savior saved us through Jesus Christ our Savior. Thus, God initiates the work of salvation, and Jesus Christ is the agent *through whom* he accomplishes salvation. God saves people *through* a regenerative washing which is the renewal that comes from the Spirit, whom the Savior God poured out *through* the Savior Jesus Christ. The manifestation of God's goodness and loving-kindness, then, comes *through* Christ. The epiphany of Jesus Christ *is* the manifestation of God for the salvation of all.

Epiphany Christology

The underlying narrative of the pastoral epistles is a story of epiphany or manifestation. Christ Jesus appeared in the realm of the flesh and gave himself to redeem all people. In doing this, he manifested the Savior God who wills the salvation of all people. Christ Jesus will appear again to judge the living and the dead, and when he does, the saving power of the Savior God will be manifested. Who then is Christ Jesus? He is the great God and Savior, the Lord, the Mediator between God and human beings. He is the one who manifests God's saving intention through his saving work.

5

Victory through Suffering

*T*he major Christologies of the New Testament are found in the Synoptic tradition, the Johannine tradition, and the Pauline tradition.[1] But in addition to these great traditions, the New Testament contains three other writings with significant Christologies: 1 Peter, Hebrews, and Revelation. Their Christologies represent three other traditions, each with a distinctive perspective. First Peter focuses on the sufferings of Christ, Hebrews on the high priesthood of Christ, and Revelation on the victory of the slaughtered Lamb. Although they share some common themes, these writings are not related to one another, and each presupposes a different story of Christ. Central to their stories, however, is the death and resurrection of Christ.

My decision to deal with these writings in one chapter is a matter of convenience since the scope of this work does not allow for an extended treatment of each. Nonetheless, there is some justification for treating them together since each employs Christology to encourage and strengthen the audience it addresses. The author of 1 Peter, for example, presents the suffering Christ as a paradigm of the Christian life: what happened to Christ (he suffered unjustly) is happening to believers (they are suffering unjustly), and the glory he now enjoys will soon be theirs. In order to exhort a community that is in danger of forsaking its original commitment, the author of Hebrews presents Christ as a high priest according to the order of Melchizedek, who purified believers from their sins by a perfect offering of himself to God. Finally, in order to strengthen believers facing persecution, the author of Revelation portrays Christ as the slaughtered Lamb who has won the victory for God's saints. In all of these writings, Christology is in the service of the Christian life.

THE FIRST LETTER OF PETER

The author of 1 Peter identifies himself as "Peter, an apostle of Jesus Christ," who writes to "the exiles of the Dispersion in Pontus, Galatia, Cappadocia, Asia, and Bithynia" (1:1), from "Babylon" (5:13). While some modern scholars accept the Petrine authorship of this letter, most believe that someone from a Petrine circle wrote this letter in Peter's name.[2] The circumstances surrounding the composition of this letter have been vigorously debated during the past half century, and until somewhat recently, there was a consensus that the letter addressed Christians in Asia Minor suffering from an official persecution by the Roman state. Moreover, many argued that the remnants of a baptismal homily had been incorporated into this letter. In recent years, however, this consensus has broken down and another has taken its place.

According to this newer consensus, 1 Peter is a literary unity and originated in a Petrine circle, probably situated at Rome. Its recipients were not necessarily recent converts, nor were they enduring an official state persecution, but they were suffering ridicule and social harassment on account of their faith. In the eyes of their nonbelieving contemporaries, they were social deviants. To strengthen them during this period of hardship and suffering, therefore, a member of the Petrine circle wrote to these Christians living in the Roman provinces of Asia Minor (modern-day Turkey).[3]

The rhetorical strategy of this letter is straightforward. Believers should not be surprised when others ridicule and insult them, for Christ endured similar treatment. Rather, they should be confident of future glory since they are the people of God. At present, they are dispersed as exiles, but they will be glorified after their suffering, as was Christ.

A letter of moral exhortation, the purpose of 1 Peter is to encourage believers to live in a particular way. Consequently, it is not primarily concerned with Christology, but it does employ christological traditions to support its moral exhortation and supposes an underlying narrative comprising the following events: preexistence, suffering, death, resurrection, ascension (during which Christ preaches to the spirits), exaltation at God's right hand, final visitation, and judgment.[4] This story can be summarized as follows.

At one time, the recipients of this letter were not the people of God, nor could they expect mercy from God, for they were burdened by their sins. But now, they are a chosen people, a royal priesthood, a holy nation, God's people. Christ suffered for their sins, bearing them in his body, on the cross, and redeemed them from their former way of life by his precious blood. Founded on "the living stone" that is Christ, they are being built into a spiritual house. But this did not happen by chance.

God always knew that the recipients of this letter would be his people. Thus, Israel's prophets prophesied about the grace destined for them and already knew of the sufferings destined for Christ since the Spirit of Christ revealed those sufferings to the prophets. When Christ appeared, he suffered maltreatment without retaliating. Put to death, he was raised from the dead and went to heaven. As he journeyed through the heavens, he proclaimed the victory he had won to the spirits who had rebelled previous to the great Flood, thereby sealing their doom. Christ now sits at God's right hand, with every angel, authority, and power subject to him. Although believers suffer at present, they can be confident that Christ, whom they have never seen, will be revealed, for these are the last times. The end of all things is approaching and the day of visitation is at hand. When the chief shepherd is revealed, judgment will begin with the household of God. Then it will be visited upon those who rejected Christ, the chosen and precious cornerstone of God's spiritual house.

For a fuller understanding of this story, we must turn to the text of 1 Peter.

The Sufferings Destined for Christ

First Peter begins with a blessing (1:3–12) similar to the great benediction of Eph. 1:3–14, in which Peter[5] reminds his audience that God has given them a living hope, an imperishable inheritance, and a salvation ready to be revealed.[6] Although the recipients of this letter are presently suffering harassment and have not seen the one in whom they believe, Peter assures them that their salvation is at hand. He concludes this blessing by disclosing that Israel's prophets served them by testifying to the sufferings destined for Christ.

This benediction leads to the first part of the letter, in which Peter describes the task and nature of the Christian community (1:13–2:10).[7] Believers must be holy because God is holy (1:13–16); they must conduct themselves with reverence, because they were ransomed by the blood of Christ (1:17–21); they must love one another because they have been born anew by God's word (1:22–25); and they must rid themselves of all malice because they are God's people (2:1–10). This section, then, serves as a powerful exhortation, for those suffering on account of their faith, to live in a manner worthy of the redemption they have received and to conduct themselves in accordance with their new status as the people of God.

The author of 1 Peter roots this moral exhortation in a Christology that focuses on the sufferings of Christ, which the opening blessing has already announced:

> Concerning this salvation, the prophets who prophesied of the grace that was to be yours made careful search and inquiry, inquiring about the person or time that the Spirit of Christ within them indicated when it testified in advance to the sufferings destined for Christ and the subsequent glory. (1:10–11)

Peter's immediate task was to make sense of the suffering that believers were enduring in the Roman provinces of Asia Minor. Faced with this challenge, he explains the continuity between the prophetic message of Israel's prophets, the sufferings of Christ, and the present circumstances of believers. The prophets foretold the sufferings Christ was to endure and the glory he now enjoys. Presently they suffer as Christ did, but in the future they will share in his glory, if they persevere in their suffering.

This text raises the question of Christ's preexistence. Is "the Spirit of Christ" the preexistent Christ? Or is "the Spirit of Christ" to be taken in another sense? For example, is it the one who reveals things about Christ, the Spirit that was later revealed in Christ, or perhaps, the Spirit that Christ received at his baptism? Since 1 Peter is not a systematic or speculative writing, it does not always provide the answers contemporary readers ask. The plain sense of the text, however, suggests that 1 Peter assumes that Christ was active before his historical appearance.[8] More specifically, it was the preexistent Christ who revealed to Israel's prophets the sufferings destined for him (*ta eis Christon pathēmata*). This notion of preexistence is similar to that in 1 Cor. 10:4 (Christ was the rock in the wilderness from which Israel drank). Although this is not the profound notion of preexistence found in the Johannine prologue, the affirmation that the Spirit of Christ revealed the sufferings of Christ to Israel's prophets is, at the least, an emerging notion of preexistence.

Having established the centrality of Christ's suffering and glory in the opening blessing, Peter reminds his audience of Christ's redemptive work on their behalf in order to strengthen them in their task as a Christian community.

> You know that you were ransomed from the futile ways inherited from your ancestors, not with perishable things like silver or gold, but with the precious blood of Christ, like that of a lamb without defect or blemish. He was destined before the foundation of the world, but was revealed at the end of the ages for your sake. Through him you have come to trust in God, who raised him from the dead and gave him glory, so that your faith and hope are set on God. (1:18–21)

This text is one of three christological passages that deal with Christ's suffering and death in 1 Peter, the others being 2:21–25 and 3:18–22. Like those christological texts, it is in the service of moral exhortation.

The passage contains several elements of the Christ story outlined above. First, Christ was known by God before the foundation of the world.[9] While this may mean that God knew that Christ would be part of his salvific plan, Peter's earlier statement about the Spirit of Christ revealing the sufferings of Christ to the prophets suggests the notion of preexistence noted above. Second, though Christ existed before the foundation of the world, it is only in this last period of time that he was revealed by God for the sake of believers such as the recipients of this letter.[10] He was manifested (*phanerōthentos*) by God,[11] because it was necessary to redeem people from the futile way of life their ancestors handed on to them. While Peter does not describe their former way of life, other statements suggest that they were burdened by sin (2:24; 3:18). Third, he shed his blood and died as a lamb without defect or blemish (*amnou amomou kai aspilou*). While some authors interpret the imagery of the lamb in terms of the paschal lamb,[12] the more immediate reference may be to the unblemished lamb of Israel's sacrificial cult.[13] Thus Numbers 28–29 repeatedly employs the adjective used here (*amōmos*, "unblemished," "without defect") to describe what kind of lamb was appropriate for temple sacrifice. Fourth, God raised Christ from the dead and granted him glory.

The language 1 Peter employs in this passage is similar to that found in a number of New Testament writings. For example, Paul reminds the Corinthians that they have been redeemed at a price (1 Cor. 6:20; 7:23). Other texts speak of the redemptive power of Christ's blood (Acts 20:28; Rom. 3:24–25; Eph. 1:7; Col. 1:20; Heb. 9:12–14). And John 1:29 describes Jesus as the Lamb of God who takes away the sin of the world. Thus, 1 Peter draws upon common traditions and imagery to exhort believers who must practice their faith in a hostile environment, rather than introducing new christological motifs. In doing so, it focuses on the redemptive value of Christ's death, comparing the offering of Christ to the sacrifice of an unblemished lamb, such as was offered in the temple sacrifice. But whereas

those sacrifices were offered repeatedly, 1 Peter insists that Christ suffered
once for sins (3:18). Moreover, 1 Peter introduces one notion that we have
not yet encountered in our study: it was the Spirit of the preexistent Christ
who revealed the sufferings and glory destined for Christ.[14] These sufferings are the focal point of the texts to which we now turn.

The Sufferings of Christ

The moral exhortation in the second part of 1 Peter (2:11–4:11) is more specific, as Peter calls upon believers to endure even unjust treatment so that they
will silence their opponents by doing what is good. The exhortation urges believers — whom Peter calls "aliens and exiles" — to be subject to civic institu-
tions for the Lord's sake (2:11–17).[15] Next, it addresses slaves (2:18–25),
wives (3:1–6), husbands (3:7), and then all believers once more (3:8–4:11).[16]
In the midst of this exhortation, Peter employs the second (2:21–25) and third
(3:18–22) of his christological passages to support his exhortation.

The first of these passages provides a christological rationale for Peter's
admonition that slaves should subject themselves to their masters, even to
those who are harsh.[17]

> For to this you have been called,
> because Christ also suffered for you,[18]
> leaving you an example,
> so that you should follow in his steps.
>
> "He committed no sin,
> *and no deceit was found in his mouth*" [Isa. 53:9].
> When he was abused, he did not return abuse;
> when he suffered, he did not threaten;
> but he entrusted himself to the one who judges justly.
>
> He himself *bore our sins* [Isa. 53:4, 12].
> in his body on the cross,
> so that, free from sins,
> we might live for righteousness;
> *by his wounds you have been healed* [Isa. 53:5].[19]
>
> For you were *going astray like sheep* [Isa. 53:6],
> but now you have returned to the shepherd and guardian
> of your souls.   (1 Peter 2:21–25)

Although this text employs more allusions to the servant passage of Isaiah
53 than any other passage of the New Testament does, it does not use Isaiah

53 as a proof from prophecy that Jesus was the suffering servant.[20] Having already stated that the Spirit of Christ revealed the sufferings of Christ to Israel's prophets, Peter assumes that Isaiah was speaking of Christ's sufferings and then applies several texts of Isaiah 53 to Christ to show that as suffering was integral to the life of Christ, so it is integral to all who follow in his footsteps. Thus, even in this christological passage, Peter is more interested in exhortation than christological reflection. What he writes, however, has christological import.

First, Peter asserts that Christ suffered "for you." The preposition he employs—*hyper* ("for")—occurs frequently in the New Testament in conjunction with Jesus' death, and in this case with his suffering.[21] In most instances a person or group of persons stands as the object of the preposition ("for me," "for us," "for all," "for the wicked"), thereby highlighting the vicarious nature of Christ's death or suffering. His suffering or death accomplishes something others could not do by their suffering or death. He "bore our sins in his body on the cross," freeing people from their sins and enabling them to live a new way of life characterized by righteousness. Christ's sufferings, then, play a decisive role in healing humanity's sinful condition (2:24). True to its interest in moral exhortation, however, 1 Peter insists that by his suffering Christ left believers with a pattern to follow.

Second, 1 Peter says that Christ suffered even though he did not commit any sin. Thus Peter reinforces what he wrote in the first christological passage: that Christ was like a lamb without defect or blemish (1:19). The primary purpose of this statement, however, remains paraenetic: namely, if Christ did not sin and refused to retaliate, how much more ought believers, who have sinned, refuse to seek revenge? Nonetheless this passage and the first, which portrays Christ as an unblemished lamb, suggest that Christ was sinless.[22]

Third, viewed as a whole, these verses tell a story about Christ that is intended to sustain believers in their time of suffering. It reminds them that they had gone astray like sheep, and there was nothing they could do to redeem themselves from their sinful condition. Because of this, Christ suffered for them, even though he had not committed sin as they did. By his death on the cross, he bore their sins and healed their wounds. Consequently, they have turned to Christ, the shepherd and guardian of their lives.[23]

This passage, more than any other, focuses on the innocent suffering of Christ. It does not speak of his preexistence, or even of his resurrection. But it does present readers with one of the most vivid portraits of Christ's sufferings in the New Testament, apart from the passion narratives. Christ is the one who, in accordance with his own injunction of nonretaliation, did not return insult for insult, because he trusted in the God who judges justly. More important, his suffering is redemptive and provides an example for others to follow. Although this passage does not explicitly explain why Christ's suffering was redemptive, it suggests that the redemptive value of his suffering is dependent upon his person: he was God's unblemished lamb, the one without sin. In following the suffering Christ, believers will undoubtedly find redemptive value in their own suffering, but only because the sinless and unblemished Christ redeems them from their sins.

The Victory of the Suffering Christ

The third christological passage of 1 Peter that deals with the suffering and death of Christ (3:18–22) undergirds the moral exhortation, central to this letter, that it is better to suffer for doing good than for doing evil (3:17).[24] To support this exhortation, which is addressed to *all* members of the community, Peter reminds his audience of the righteous one who suffered for (*hyper*) the unjust to lead them to God. But unlike the passages we have already examined, this text describes the victory of the suffering Christ in greater detail and gives further insight into the human condition prior to Christ.

> For Christ also suffered for sins once for all,
>> the righteous for the unrighteous,
>> in order to bring you to God.
> He was put to death in the flesh,
> but made alive in the spirit,
> in which also he went and made a proclamation to the spirits in prison,
>> who in former times did not obey, when God waited patiently in the
>> days of Noah, during the building of the ark, in which a few, that is,
>> eight persons, were saved through water.
> And baptism, which this prefigured, now saves you—not as a removal of
> dirt from the body, but as an appeal to God for a good conscience, through
> the resurrection of Jesus Christ,
>> who has gone into heaven
>> and is at the right hand of God,
>>> with angels, authorities, and powers made subject to him.
>
> (3:18–22)

This passage begins with a simple statement that summarizes what 1 Peter has already said, "Christ suffered for sins." However, in place of the preposition *hyper,* the author uses *peri* ("for"),[25] and then adds a note of finality to this suffering by introducing an adverb that Hebrews frequently employs when describing Christ's sacrificial death: *hapax* ("once").[26] Although this adverb is not used again in 1 Peter, it suggests what Hebrews will make explicit; there is no further need for Christ to suffer for sins. What he did *once* was sufficient to reconcile humanity to God.

Next the passage describes Christ as righteous (*dikaios*); that is, one who stands in the proper relationship to God. As one who was righteous, he suffered for (*hyper*) the unrighteous (*adikōn*). Although this is the only application of *dikaios* to Christ in 1 Peter, other writings describe him in this way.[27] But in 1 Peter, it reinforces what the author has already said about Christ as the unblemished lamb (1:19), the one who suffered even though he did not sin (2:22). Thus, in each of its major christological passages 1 Peter suggests what later theology would call the "sinlessness of Christ." [28]

As in the other passages we have studied, this text clarifies the purpose and outcome of Christ's suffering: he suffered for sins to lead us to God (see Eph. 2:18; 3:12). Thus, 1 Peter presents the soteriological effect of Christ's suffering in slightly different ways in each of its three christological passages: Christ redeemed humanity from its futile ways (1:18); he died so that we might live for righteousness (2:24); and he suffered in order to lead us to God (3:18). Central to this soteriology is the recognition that Christ bore and suffered for the sins of others (2:24; 3:18) at the price of his blood (1:19).

Having summarized Christ's salvific work in the opening verse of this passage, Peter outlines the significant events in this work of salvation: (1) Christ was put to death; (2) he was raised from the dead; (3) *as he went to heaven,* he made a proclamation to the spirits who were in prison; (4) he has been enthroned at God's right hand and the heavenly powers have been subjected to him. I will comment on each of these events, especially the third, momentarily.

Finally, Peter introduces the figure of Noah and draws a comparison between the events of the great Flood and the baptism of Christians: just as the flood waters saved a few people during Noah's day by carrying them away in the ark from a wicked generation, so the waters of baptism save believers, who are also few, from a wicked generation. The introduction of this comparison suggests that the story of the Flood plays a role in 1 Peter's Christ story, a point to which I will return.

Although the manner in which the Greek text expresses the first two events (death and resurrection) is open to interpretations, the essential meaning is clear. The one who was put to death in or by the flesh (*thanatōtheis men sarki*) has been made alive in or by the Spirit (*zōopoiētheis de pneumati*). Here, the Greek clearly establishes a contrast between "flesh" and "spirit," understood as two different modes of being: the realm of what is purely human and destined for corruption, and the realm of God's Spirit that is incorruptible. The Greek phrase, however, could be taken in several ways. For example, Christ was put to death in the sphere of, or in reference to, purely human existence, but he was made alive in the realm of, or in reference to, the incorruptible sphere of God's Spirit. Or, as Paul Achtemeier suggests, Christ was put to death by humans but raised by God's Spirit.[29] In both cases, the text refers to the events of Christ's death and resurrection.

What is not so clear is the meaning of the third event: Christ's preaching to the spirits in prison.[30] Are these spirits human or angelic beings? Did Christ preach salvation or judgment to them? Where and when did he preach? There have been three major responses to these questions.[31] First, the spirits are the souls of Noah's deceased contemporaries to whom Christ preached the good news during the period between his death and resurrection. Second, they are Noah's contemporaries to whom the preexistent Christ preached repentance through Noah but to no avail. Third, the spirits are the angels mentioned in Gen. 6:1–4, the "sons of God" who had intercourse with human women. *First Enoch* 6–12 develops this incident in great detail and views these rebellious spirits as responsible for increasing the wickedness that led to the Flood. While some authors argue that Christ preached salvation to them, others maintain that he proclaimed their final doom (as did Enoch to the fallen angels, according to *1 Enoch*) as he ascended through the heavens.

In my view, the most probable interpretation is the last, for the following reasons. First, the natural meaning of "spirits" in 3:19 is angelic beings rather than the souls of human beings. Second, the misbehavior of the angels mentioned in Gen. 6:1–4 is closely associated with the story of the Flood in both Genesis and *1 Enoch.* Third, in *1 Enoch,* Enoch is sent to the imprisoned spirits to preach their judgment rather than their salvation (*1 Enoch* 16:3).

The narrative that underlies this passage has been outlined by William Dalton in this way.[32] First, long ago God saved Noah and his family, by the Flood, from a wicked generation that was under the power of rebellious spirits. Second, God's definitive act of salvation occurred through the death and resurrection of Christ, who preached to the spirits their final doom, as he ascended through the heavens. Third, by the waters of baptism the tiny community of believers is presently being saved from a wicked generation, as were Noah and his family. Fourth, Christians can endure suffering in the present time because Christ has been victorious over these angelic powers, a victory in which baptized believers share.

If this interpretation is correct, then Christ's preaching to the spirits was not a descent into the realm of the dead to preach good news to the dead but the victorious message of his triumph to the doomed spirits who instigated wickedness prior to the Flood. But what are we to make of 1 Peter 4:6?

> For this is the reason that the gospel was proclaimed even to the dead, so that, though they had been judged in the flesh as everyone is judged, they might live in the spirit as God does.

While some interpret this text in tandem with 3:19, because they see both as referring to a common event (Christ's descent to the realm of the dead), this text (4:6) does *not* say that Christ preached to the dead but that the gospel *was proclaimed* even to the dead. Moreover, 3:19 never speaks of a descent.[33] While this text has a long history of interpretation,[34] the most probable interpretation is that the gospel was preached to Christians who, at the writing of this letter, are dead. Thus, the dead heard the gospel when they were alive and will be vindicated before their enemies. But the text is not related to 3:19 and does not speak of Christ's descent to the realm of the dead to preach the gospel.

The final event of this passage is Christ's exaltation at God's right hand and the submission of all spiritual powers to him. Such powers have not played a role in 1 Peter thus far, and the author of this letter does not dwell on them, as do the authors of Colossians and Ephesians. Nonetheless, 1 Peter stands in the mainstream of the New Testament tradition about Christ. In raising Christ from the dead, God established him over every spiritual power. Consequently, while Christ's proclamation to the spirits distinguishes 1 Peter from other New Testament writings, it does not make this writing idiosyncratic. The proclamation to the spirits, as interpreted above, is another aspect of a traditional New Testament motif: the resurrected Christ has been exalted over every spiritual power.

A Christology of Suffering unto Glory

It is difficult to find an adequate phrase to summarize the Christology of 1 Peter.[35] In fact, one might ask if there is a Christology in 1 Peter. To be sure, this letter says a great deal about the sufferings of Christ, but it never identifies Christ for its audience. Christ is not called "Son" or "Son of God," although his sonship is implied when God is identified as the Father of our Lord Jesus Christ (1:3). First Peter assumes that its audience already knows who Christ is. Thus there is no need to explain his identity. Instead, it simply speaks of Christ (twenty-two times) or Jesus Christ (nine times) but never of Christ Jesus, as do the Pauline letters. Among the images applied to Christ, the most prominent are the spotless and unblemished lamb (1:19); the living stone that is elect and precious in God's sight and forms the cornerstone of a spiritual house (2:4–6); the shepherd and guardian of our lives (2:25); the chief shepherd (5:4). But 1 Peter does not develop any of these images so that one overpowers the others or becomes the dominant motif of this letter. The image that 1 Peter most impresses upon its readers is that of the suffering Christ.

The Christology of 1 Peter is a Christology of suffering. It affirms that the sufferings of Christ were uniquely redemptive and the necessary prelude to his glory. These sufferings were already revealed to Israel's prophets by the Spirit of Christ and were necessary to redeem humanity from its sins and the spiritual powers, just as Noah and his family needed to be saved from the wicked generation of their day and the spiritual powers that led them astray. Because Christ suffered, he was brought into God's glory, and the glory he now enjoys serves as a pledge that the present sufferings of believers will not be in vain, if they suffer for what is good in the name of Christ. This portrait of Christ presumes his preexistence and sinlessness, but it never develops either concept. It also points to the uniqueness of Christ who suffered once, but it never explains why Christ is unique.

The contribution of 1 Peter to Christology is more practical than speculative, and while its Christ story is similar in its main lines to those found in the Pauline writings (preexistence, death, resurrection, ascension, and exaltation), it is not as fully developed, especially in regard to Israel's history. Nonetheless, by focusing on the sufferings of Christ, 1 Peter shows the intimate relationship between Christology and the Christian life: the *past* suffering of Christ is the *present* condition of believers, while the *present* glory of Christ is the *future* glory of those who follow in the steps of the suffering Christ.[36] While the Christology of 1 Peter may not be the most developed of the New Testament, it is among the most pastorally sensitive.

THE LETTER TO THE HEBREWS

Although this writing is traditionally called "the Letter to the Hebrews," questions about its genre, author, place of origin, intended audience and date of composition remain unresolved. As regards genre, Hebrews concludes as if it were a letter (13:22–25), but it begins with an artful and rhetorical introduction (1:1–4) rather than with a letter opening. Moreover, its author describes what he has written as a "word of exhortation" (*tou logou tēs paraklēseōs;* 13:22), leading many to view Hebrews as a sermon or homily rather than as a letter.[37] Although the Eastern Fathers maintained the Pauline authorship of Hebrews, they were aware that its literary style differed from that of the great apostle. The masculine participle *diēgoumenon* (11:32) suggests that its author was a man, but since he never reveals himself further, all attempts to identify this anonymous figure, for example, with Apollos, Barnabas, or Luke, are educated guesses. As regards place of origin, the greeting in 13:24 ("Those from Italy send you greetings") could mean that the author writes from Italy, or that he writes from outside Italy and extends the greetings of his associates from Italy to his audience. As regards this audience, the title "to the Hebrews" does not belong to the original text but was added by a later editor. Therefore, it does not provide conclusive evidence that Jewish Christians composed the original audience, although a later editor probably thought they did. The audience could have consisted of Gentile Christians living in the diaspora. Finally, as to the time of composition, there is little agreement among commentators. In some passages the author writes as if the Jewish temple cult is still in existence (9:9, 25; 10:1–3, 11), thereby implying a date before the Temple's destruction by the Romans in A.D. 70. But this may be irrelevant since the author seems to be referring to the tabernacle in the wilderness rather than to the Jerusalem Temple (9:2–5). In a word, Hebrews is as strange as the figure of Melchizedek, whom it describes as being "without father, without mother, without genealogy, having neither the beginning of days nor end of life" (7:3). Its author, its recipients, its place of origin, and its date of composition are unknown.

Although the literary origins of Hebrews are unresolved, there are several clues about the situation of its recipients. First, they did not know the Lord directly (2:3), although they have been Christians for some time (5:12). Second, they have already endured suffering and persecution (10:32–34). Third, new problems are plaguing the community. For example, some are absenting themselves from the assembly (10:25). More important, some may soon apostatize. Thus the author cautions his listeners not to harden their hearts as unfaithful Israel did in the wilderness (3:7–4:11), and, on two occasions, he severely warns them that there is no further repentance for those who knowingly apostatize (6:4–8; 12:14–17). Hebrews, then, addresses a situation in which an established community of believers is in danger of falling away from its original confession.[38]

To meet this pastoral situation, the author employs a unique blend of doctrinal exposition and moral exhortation to strengthen the resolve of his audience. The doctrinal exposition presents Jesus as the Son of God, an eternal high priest according to the order of Melchizedek, who entered the heavenly sanctuary by his death to make a perfect sacrifice for sins. In this regard, Hebrews presents the most explicitly christological and soteriological teaching of the New Testament. Interspersed with this christological material, however, are a series of exhortations intimately related to the doctrinal exposition. Drawing out the moral and practical consequences of this doctrinal exposition, these exhortations summon the community to greater faithfulness, for if the community has received so great a salvation, it is more important than ever to remain faithful to the original confession of faith.[39]

This artful juxtaposition of doctrinal exposition and moral exhortation raises the question of how the two are related. Is moral exhortation at the service of doctrinal exposition, or is doctrinal exposition at the behest of moral exhortation?[40] While it is tempting to adopt the first position, given the careful manner in which Hebrews develops its Christology and soteriology, the pastoral needs of the community suggest that the christological exposition of Hebrews is at the service of moral exhortation. The author of Hebrews develops a Christology in which he presents Christ, the Son of God, as the eternal high priest who has effected the forgiveness of sins once and for all. This Christology provides the listeners of Hebrews with a powerful motivation to remain faithful to their confession of faith. If they do not, there is no further forgiveness of sins available to them. As with 1 Peter, Hebrews does not develop Christology for its own sake. Rather, Christology is in the service of the Christian life.

God's Plan for Salvation

In addition to being in the service of the Christian life, the Christology of Hebrews is intimately related to soteriology since the primary purpose for identifying Christ as Son of God and high priest according to the order of Melchizedek is to establish the significance of his redemptive work. This redemptive work—the forgiveness of sins—was the crucial moment in God's plan of salvation. Thus Hebrews, like the other writings we have studied, presupposes an underlying narrative or story of Christ. The movement of this story is already outlined in the elegant sentences that open this work (1:1–4).

> Long ago God spoke to our ancestors in many and various ways by the prophets, but in these last days he has spoken to us by a Son, whom he appointed heir of all things, through whom he also created the world. He[41] is the reflection of God's glory and the exact imprint of God's very being, and he sustains all things by his powerful word. When[42] he had made purifica-

tion for sins, he sat down at the right hand of the Majesty on high, having become as much superior to angels as the name he has inherited is more excellent than theirs.

From the outset, Hebrews divides history into two periods: a time when God spoke in "many and various ways" to our ancestors and "these last days" when he has spoken through a Son.[43] While the first period includes the whole of human history, the history of Israel receives special attention. Thus the rest of Hebrews refers to significant portions of Israel's history. For example, in 3:7–4:11, the author recalls the time of Israel's sojourn in the wilderness, and in 11:1–39 he summarizes the full sweep of Israel's history. Beginning with Abel, Enoch, and Noah, he moves to the times of the patriarchs, Moses, the judges, David, Samuel, the prophets, and then he concludes by recalling a host of unnamed martyrs of more recent vintage. This history, in his view, culminates in Jesus, the perfecter of faith (12:2). Despite this impressive historical review, the underlying narrative of Hebrews is not a story of salvation history with a clear pattern of promise and fulfillment.[44] Rather, it presents elements of Israel's past as foreshadowing the salvation of these last days. The priesthood of Melchizedek, for example, foreshadowed the eternal priesthood of Christ, while the earthly sanctuary, the high priest, and the offering of the Day of Atonement presaged the heavenly sanctuary that the true high priest, Jesus the Son of God, entered when he atoned for sins once and for all.

The second period of human history, "these last days," began with the priestly work of the Son of God, who made "purification for sins" and now sits "at the right hand of the Majesty on high," until his enemies have been overcome and subjected to him (10:13). The period of these last days will end when Christ appears "a second time, not to deal with sin, but to save those who are eagerly waiting for him" (9:28).

The Christ story of Hebrews, however, embraces more than these periods of human history. The narrative of Hebrews reaches back to a timeless period before the creation of the world. However, it does not move from this timeless period to the period of human history in a chronological or logical fashion. Rather, as John Meier has noted, Hebrews begins its story with the exaltation of the Son, moves back to the Son's role in creation, moves further back to his relationship with God, then moves forward to the Son's role in conserving creation, forward again to his earthly work of redemption, and concludes where it began, with the Son's exaltation and its consequences.[45] The opening verses of Hebrews (1:1–4) contain all of these events. First, God appointed the Son as "heir of all things" when he exalted him, who, for a little while, was made lower than the angels. Second, the Son whom he exalted was the one "through whom he created the world." Third, this Son is "the reflection of God's glory" and "the exact imprint of God's very being." Fourth, the Son "sustains all things by his powerful word." Fifth, during his earthly life he made "purification for sins." Sixth, he has been exalted and sits at "the right hand of the Majesty." Seventh, he has inherited a more excellent name than have the angels, for he is called Son of God.[46]

While all of these moments are important for the implied story of Hebrews, Hebrews deals primarily with the Son's purification for sins and his exaltation at God's right hand rather than with his preexistence. This is not surprising since Hebrews is most interested in those things that affect the lives of its readers. For example, humanity was in need of purification from sins, but the sacrifices of the Levitical priesthood could not adequately deal with sin. Moreover, the devil had enslaved humanity through its fear of death (2:15). With the Son's exaltation at God's right hand, however, humanity can now see the outcome of its destiny as foretold in Psalm 8 (2:5–8), provided that it follows the path of obedient suffering that Jesus, the pioneer and perfecter of faith, has blazed (12:2). The Christ story of Hebrews can be summarized as follows.

In his divine plan, God intended to crown humanity with glory and honor, subjecting all things to it. But humanity was in servitude to the devil because of its fear of death. The old covenant that provided the legislation for the Levitical priesthood could not bring humanity to perfection, since it did not provide a suitable offering for sin. Consequently, the Son of God, through whom the universe was created and is sustained, shared in the blood and flesh of humanity. In doing so, he was made perfect through his obedience to God and made a perfect offering of himself to God that robbed death of its power and purified humanity from its sins. By his sacrificial death, Christ entered the true sanctuary, the heavenly sanctuary, as the eternal high priest of a new covenant. Seated at the right hand of the Majesty where he continues to make intercession for his brothers and sisters, he inherited the name "Son." Having already made purification for sins, he will come a second time to bring salvation for all who await him. Then his sisters and brothers who follow in his path of perfection will reign with him, and all things will be subjected to humanity, as God intended.

Told from the point of view of Christ's exaltation, this story of Christ presupposes three moments in the "career" of Christ: his preexistence with God; his earthly life in solidarity with humanity; and his heavenly exaltation.[47] To fill in the details of this story, we must turn to the text of Hebrews.

The Son of God

If one were to ask the author of Hebrews to identify Jesus, he would respond, "Jesus is the Son of God." Thus, at the beginning of an important summary statement, he writes, "Since, then, we have a great high priest who has passed through the heavens, Jesus, *the Son of God,* let us hold fast to our confession" (4:14–16). Although Hebrews speaks more frequently of Christ as a high priest and only employs the full title, "Son of God," four times (4:14; 6:6; 7:3; 10:29), Christ would not be an eternal high priest according to the order of Melchizedek if he were not the Son of God.[48] The divine sonship of Christ, then, is foundational for all that Hebrews says about him. To that extent, Hebrews is in continuity with most other New Testament writings. But Hebrews makes a unique contribution when it further identifies the Son of God as a high priest. Moreover, it spends more time than any other New Testament writing in establishing the preeminence of the Son. This is not to say that its Christology is the most developed of the New Testament. The Christology of the Fourth Gospel and certain aspects of Paul's Christology surpass that of Hebrews.[49] But there is little doubt that this Son of God Christology has made important overtures to what later writers would call preexistence and the incarnation.

Because the divine sonship of Christ is foundational to Christ's high priesthood, the author of Hebrews devotes the opening chapters of his epistle to establishing the superiority of Christ, the Son of God, to the angels. The purpose of this exposition is to encourage his audience to pay even greater attention to what they have heard, for if the message given through angels was valid, how much more important is the word of salvation delivered by God's Son (2:1–4). The first part of Hebrews can be outlined in this way.[50]

1:5–14	*Exposition:* The Son of God is greater than the angels of God.
2:1–4	*Exhortation:* Therefore, pay even greater attention to the word of salvation you have heard from the Son.
2:5–18	*Exposition:* God subjected the coming world to humankind, but at the present time we only see Jesus, who for a time was made lower than the angels, crowned with glory.

The point of departure for the opening exposition that the Son is greater than the angels (1:5–14) is the final phrase of the epistle's introduction: "as much superior to angels as the name he has inherited is more excellent than

189

theirs" (1:4). Having stated that the Son is superior to the angels because he has inherited a greater name, Hebrews employs seven scriptural quotations to confirm its claim.[51] Since the author views these citations as words of God spoken to the Son at the moment of the Son's exaltation, God himself verifies the christological claims of Hebrews!

In the first three quotations, taken from Ps. 2:7; 2 Sam. 7:14; and Deut. 32:43 (conflated with Ps. 97:7), Hebrews makes its audience privy to the words God spoke to the Son on the occasion of his exaltation.[52] The author, of course, was not present at the Son's exaltation, but he confidently interprets the words of scripture as God's speech to the exalted Son.[53]

You are my Son; today I have begotten you. (Ps. 2:7)

I will be his Father, and he will be my Son. (2 Sam. 7:14)

Let all God's angels worship him. (Deut. 32:43/Ps. 97:7)

Since God never addressed any angel as his Son and calls upon the angels to worship the Son, the author can assert the Son's superiority to the angels.

In the fourth, fifth, and sixth quotations, taken from Pss. 104:4; 45:6–7; 102:25–27, all according to the Septuagint, Hebrews establishes the superiority of the Son to the angels by pointing to the Son's creative activity and eternal rule. Again, the author presents these quotations as the words of God spoken to his Son, presumably on the day of the Son's exaltation, when God calls upon the angels to worship the Son.

He makes his angels winds, and his servants flames of fire. (Ps. 104:4)

Your throne, O God, is forever and ever, and the righteous scepter is the scepter of your kingdom. You have loved righteousness and hated wickedness; therefore God, your God, has anointed you with the oil of gladness beyond your companions. (Ps. 45:6–7)

In the beginning, Lord, you founded the earth, and the heavens are the work of your hands; they will perish, but you remain; they will all wear out like clothing; like a cloak you will roll them up, and like clothing they will be changed. But you are the same, and your years will never end. (Ps. 102:25–27)

Although the first and third citations, Psalms 104 and 102, originally referred to God's creative activity and permanence, and the second, Psalm 45 to the Israelite king, Hebrews applies them to Christ, the Son of God. Thus, it is the Son of God who made the angels (1:7), a bold statement that recalls the earlier claim of the introduction that God created the worlds through a Son (1:2). Then, in one of the most daring statements of the New Testament, Hebrews employs scripture to identify the Son as God. And yet, it is not the author of Hebrews who calls the Son "God" but God himself, when he says, "Your throne, *O God,* is forever and ever" (1:8).[54] Moreover, God himself addresses the Son as "Lord," the one who founded the earth (1:10).[55] It is as if the author of Hebrews knows that the claims he makes for Christ are so bold that God himself must substantiate them by his holy word.

In the final quotation, taken from Ps. 110:1, the author returns to the period of the Son's exaltation and employs the same formula with which he began his chain of citations:

> But to which of the angels has he ever said, "Sit at my right hand until I make your enemies a footstool for your feet?"

Like Psalm 2, Psalm 110 played an important role in the Christology of the early church. But whereas Ps. 2:7 ("today I have begotten you") was usually applied to Christ's resurrection, Ps. 110:1 ("Sit at my right hand") was interpreted in light of the risen Lord's exaltation, just as Hebrews employs it here. Thus the chain of quotations ends where it began, with the exaltation of the Son, the starting point for the Christ story of Hebrews.

On the basis of the scriptural quotations, there is no doubt of the Son's superiority to the angels of God. First, the exalted one inherited the name "Son" on the day of his enthronement, when God called upon his angels to worship the Son. Second, God provides a series of reasons why the angels should worship the Son: the Son created the angels and endures forever. Third, God addresses the Son as "God." Fourth, the Son sits at the right hand of the Majesty, a place of honor no angel could occupy, and he waits for his enemies to be made subject to him. On the basis of this christological exposition, the author introduces his first exhortation: if every disobedience to the message delivered by angels was justly punished, how much more ought the audience pay attention to the word of salvation delivered by the Son of God (2:1–4).

Following this exhortation, the author returns to an expository mode in 2:5–18. However, whereas his earlier exposition focused on the superiority of the Son to the angels, this one introduces the Son's earthly career and explains why "Jesus" was made lower than the angels for a little while (2:9). This initial use of the Son's earthly name ("Jesus") is striking, given the previous discussion about the name that the Son inherited at his exaltation, but it is necessary since Hebrews has moved from a discussion of the Son's exaltation to a consideration of his incarnation.[56] This is not to say that the author explicitly develops a teaching on the incarnation, for he does not say, as does the Fourth Evangelist, that the Word—or in this case the Son—became flesh (John 1:14). But, as we shall see, Hebrews makes a significant overture to what later theology would call the incarnation.

The author links this passage to his previous discussion about the superiority of the Son to the angels by the word "angels," when he writes, "Now God did not subject the coming world about which we are speaking to *angels*" (2:5). Then, to substantiate his thesis, he draws upon Psalm 8.

What is man that you are mindful of him,
or the son of man that you care for him?
You have made him for a little while lower than the angels;
You have crowned him with glory and honor,
subjecting all things under his feet.[57]

The author employs this text to substantiate his statement that God intends to subject all things to humanity rather than to the angels. Thus Hebrews affirms that the destiny of the Son is the destiny of humanity. But, whereas the exaltation of the Son has already occurred, the exaltation of humanity has not. Nonetheless, Hebrews reminds its audience of what has already happened. Jesus, who was made lower than the angels for a little while (2:9), has been crowned with glory and honor because he endured suffering and death for the sake of all.[58] Thus, without using the word "Adam," Hebrews develops a Christology similar to the Christology of Paul's letters. Jesus, the Son of God, is the perfect human being who embodies the destiny of humankind.[59]

For humanity to be brought to its destiny, however, Jesus had to lead the way to exaltation by his suffering and death; he had to be made perfect through what he suffered.[60] Thus Hebrews calls him the pioneer (*archēgon*) of salvation since he is the first of many sons and daughters to pass through suffering and death to exaltation, thereby fulfilling God's plan as announced in Psalm 8.[61] To accomplish this, however, he had to become like his brothers and sisters.

It is at this point that the author makes an important overture to a theology of the incarnation when he writes, "Since, therefore, the children share flesh and blood, he himself likewise shared the same things, so that through death he might destroy the one who has the power of death, that is, the devil" (2:14). Although Hebrews has been speaking about the earthly Jesus, it would be redundant to say that Jesus shared in flesh and blood unless there was a period when he enjoyed an existence apart from flesh and blood. On the basis of what Hebrews has already said in its opening chapter about the Son, it would appear that the author has the eternal and preexistent Son in view. In other words, without explicitly saying so, Hebrews supposes what later theology would call the incarnation; for the one who shared in the flesh and blood of human beings was the Son, "the reflection of God's glory and the exact imprint of God's very being" (1:3).

Sharing in flesh and blood was the brief moment when Jesus, the Son of God, "was made lower than the angels" (2:9). It was the essential moment in the career of God's Son, if he was to be a "merciful and faithful high priest" who would make atonement for the sins of his people. If the Son did not share the flesh and blood of human beings, he would not be able to endure suffering or taste death on behalf of his brothers and sisters. Nor would he be a high priest who understood their human condition. Consequently, he had to become like them (*homoiōthēnai*) in every respect (2:17).[62]

The first two chapters of Hebrews present a sophisticated Son of God theology that begins with the exalted and preexistent Son and moves to Jesus, the incarnate Son, who has become like his brothers and sisters in every way so that he might be a merciful and faithful high priest. This Christology presupposes three phases in the Son's career—preexistence, incarnation, and exaltation—though the first two concepts are not fully developed. For Hebrews, the incarnate Son of God embodies the destiny of humanity. Having inherited the name "Son," because he was made perfect through suffering, Jesus was exalted by God, who will subject all things to him. This is why the Son is greater than the angels, even though he was made lower than the angels for a brief while. What has happened to the Son explains how and why God will subject the coming world to humanity rather than to angels. This is a bold Son of God Christology that presents the Son as having been made perfect through suffering and having inherited the very name that identifies his being.

An Eternal High Priest

The author of Hebrews introduces the theme of Christ's priesthood at the end of chapter 2, when he explains that it was necessary for the Son to become like his brothers and sisters in every way so that he might be a "merciful and faithful high priest" (2:17).[63] Before developing this theme in chapters 5–10, however, Hebrews makes a second exhortation in 3:1–4:13 that warns its audience not to harden its heart as did unfaithful Israel during the period of its sojourn in the wilderness.[64] To avoid the error of unfaithful Israel, the recipients of this letter should consider the example of Jesus, the apostle and high priest whom they confess.[65] While Moses was faithful in God's house as a servant, Jesus was faithful over God's house as a son.[66] In chapter 11, Hebrews will develop this theme of faithfulness at length, and then present Jesus as the pioneer and perfecter of faith (12:2).[67] For the moment, however, Hebrews is content to present Jesus as a high priest who was faithful as a son, so that it can exhort its audience to persevere in faith.

Hebrews broaches its high priestly Christology slowly. Its exhortation leads to an important transitional statement that summarizes the Christology already presented and points the way to what will be developed.[68]

> Since, then, we have a great high priest who has passed through the heavens, Jesus, the Son of God, let us hold fast to our confession. For we do not have a high priest who is unable to sympathize with our weaknesses, but we have one who in every respect has been tested as we are, yet without sin. Let us therefore approach the throne of grace with boldness, so that we may receive mercy and find grace to help in time of need. (4:14–16)

In its opening chapters, Hebrews has already identified Jesus as the Son of God, a high priest able to sympathize with human weakness. But it has not yet explained how and why this sinless high priest has passed through the heavens.[69] Before doing so, Hebrews must show that Jesus possesses the qualifications to be such a priest.

The author summarizes these qualifications in 5:1–4. First, a high priest is chosen from among human beings to offer gifts and sacrifices for sins (*hyper hamartiōn;* 5:1). Second, he is able to deal with the weaknesses and sinfulness of others, because he has experienced the same. Third, a high priest is called by God since no one takes this honor upon himself. In the following verses (5:5–10), Hebrews shows that Jesus fulfills these qualifications. Drawing upon two of his favorite psalm texts, the author establishes that God appointed Christ as high priest when he said, "You are my Son, today I have begotten you" (Ps. 2:7), and "You are a priest forever, according to the order of Melchizedek" (110:4). The author does not give any indication of when God spoke these words to his Son, but in light of the opening chapters, he may have in mind the moment of the Son's exaltation. Next, he gives an extended description of the suffering the Son endured during the days of his flesh in order to show that the Son can sympathize with human weakness.[70] There is no reference to sinfulness, however, since Hebrews has already proclaimed the sinlessness of Christ (4:15). Therefore, though the Son is qualified to be a priest, he differs from other high priests in two ways. First, because he is sinless, he need not offer sacrifices for his sins. Second, his priesthood is "according to the order of Melchizedek."[71]

In chapter 7 the author explains what it means to be a priest according to the order of Melchizedek. Before doing so, he issues a stern warning as well as words of comfort (5:11–6:20) so that his audience will pay even greater attention to what he is about to say. Hebrews warns its recipients that those who apostatize will be crucifying again (*anastaurountas;* 6:6) the Son of God and holding him up to contempt. This is an unusual turn of phrase since one would expect the author to speak of crucifying Jesus or Christ. But by introducing the "Son of God" title, Hebrews reminds its readers that the one who suffered in the days of his flesh was the Son who is superior to the angels.

The author, however, has confidence in his listeners and reminds them that their hope is like an anchor firmly planted in the heavenly shrine from where it draws them forward. Jesus, their forerunner (*prodromos*), a high priest according to the order of Melchizedek (6:20), has already entered that inner shrine behind the curtain.[72]

Having shown that Christ is qualified to be a priest, the author undertakes a rather esoteric discussion to confirm that Christ, the Son of God, exercises a priesthood superior to the Levitical priesthood. The final words of chapter 6 ("a high priest forever according to the order of Melchizedek") provide him with the occasion to discuss Melchizedek (7:1–10) and explain why it was necessary for Christ to assume this greater priesthood.

The discussion opens with a rereading of a story from Genesis in which Melchizedek, king of Salem and priest of God Most High, brings bread and wine and blesses Abraham, who defeated Chedorlaomer and the kings in league with him (Gen. 14:17–24). Then someone gives a tenth of all that he has.[73] In retelling the story, the author of Hebrews makes several interpretative comments, two of which are important for our purposes. First, since the sacred text never speaks of Melchizedek's genealogy or death, the author concludes that his priesthood is eternal, a point that Ps. 110: 4 also suggests ("You are a priest *forever* according to the order of Melchizedek").[74] Moreover, in noting this, he remarks that Melchizedek resembles the Son of God who is eternal (see 1:12). Second, the author leaves no doubt that it was Abraham who paid tithes to Melchizedek, thereby showing the superiority of Melchizedek. Since the descendants of Levi were still in the loins of Abraham (Abraham being their progenitor), the author concludes that even the sons of Levi paid tithes to Melchizedek through Abraham! The eternal priesthood according to Melchizedek, therefore, is superior to the Levitical priesthood.

Having shown the superiority of a priesthood according to the order of Melchizedek, Hebrews demonstrates why there was need for a change of priesthood (7:11–28). Simply put, the Levitical priesthood could not bring about perfection (*teleiōsis*), for the sacrifices of the Levitical cult did not effect the permanent forgiveness of sins (see 10:1–4). Accordingly, there is need for another priesthood that was not legislated by the Mosaic law with its requirement of Levitical descent. Such a priesthood could only arise from an oath spoken by God: "The Lord has *sworn* and will not change his mind, 'You are a priest forever'" (7:21). With this change of priesthood, the earlier command of the law, which required Levitical descent for priesthood, has been abolished. Moreover, this oath makes Christ an eternal priest ("you are a priest *forever*"), unlike the Levitical priests who were prevented from continuing in office because of death (7:23). The one who is a priest according to the order of Melchizedek lives forever. Hebrews concludes that Christ is such a high priest, "holy, blameless, undefiled, separated from sinners" (7:26), for he is the Son "who has been made perfect forever" (7:28).

The Mediator of a Better Covenant

Hebrews summarizes all that it has been saying thus far in an important transitional statement.

> Now the main point in what we are saying is this: we have such a high priest, one who is seated at the right hand of the throne of Majesty in the heavens, a minister in the heavenly sanctuary and the true tent that the Lord, and not any mortal, has set up. (8:1–2)

Like the earlier transitional statement in 4:14–16, these verses emphasize the christological point that Hebrews has been driving home: those who believe in Christ have a superior high priest according to the order of Melchizedek.[75] However, even though Hebrews has shown the superiority of the Son's priesthood, it has not explained how the Son became a minister in the heavenly sanctuary where he is seated at God's right hand. In the material that follows (8:1–10:18), therefore, the author directs his attention to the superior ministry that Jesus exercises as high priest according to the order of Melchizedek.

Since a more excellent priesthood implies a better ministry, there is no comparison between the gifts and sacrifices of the Levitical priesthood and the priesthood of Christ. Anticipating what he will explain in detail, the author writes that the Levitical priests "worship in a sanctuary that is a sketch and shadow of the heavenly one" (8:5), whereas Jesus has become the "mediator of a better covenant" since he enjoys a more excellent ministry (8:6).[76]

This reference to a better covenant is the occasion for Hebrews to introduce an extended quotation from Jer. 31:31–34 that speaks of a new covenant: "The days are surely coming, says the Lord, when I will establish a new covenant with the house of Israel and with the house of Judah" (8:8). Hebrews concludes that in speaking of a new covenant, scripture has made the old obsolete (8:13), including its priesthood and worship. Thus the need for the mediator of a new and better covenant.

In chapter 9, Hebrews describes the earthly sanctuary in which the Levitical priests continually offered sacrifices and then discusses the singular sacrifice that Christ offered when he entered the heavenly sanctuary. The earthly sanctuary consisted of the Holy Place and the Holy of Holies. The latter was separated from the former by a curtain, and only the high priest could enter it, once each year, on the Day of Atonement.[77] For Hebrews, this earthly sanctuary and the sacrifices of its priests were merely "a sketch and a shadow" (8:5) of the heavenly sanctuary. Moreover, the very existence of this cultic system was the Holy Spirit's way of showing that the way into the heavenly sanctuary had not yet been broached (9:8).

The appearance of Christ, the high priest, changed all of this, since he entered the heavenly sanctuary by shedding his own blood (9:11–14). Because Christ entered the true and heavenly sanctuary, he is the mediator of a new covenant and his ministry is superior to the Levitical ministry in every way. First, whereas the Levitical priests continually offered animals in bloody sacrifice, Christ offered his own blood in sacrifice. Second, whereas the high priest entered the Holy of Holies once a year, by his sacrificial death Christ entered the heavenly sanctuary, the Holy Place, once and for all.[78] Finally, whereas it was necessary for the Levitical priests to offer repeated sacrifices because their sacrifices could not adequately deal with sin, Christ dealt with sin by offering himself once (*hapax*).

To explain why the sacrifice of Christ was able to accomplish what the Levitical cult could not, in 10:1–10 the author employs a quotation from

Psalm 40. He interprets the psalm text as the words of the Son spoken to God. Upon entering the world, the Son proclaims that God wants a perfect offering of self rather than the sacrificial offerings of animals incapable of sacrificing themselves. This is why God prepared a body for the Son, and the Son responds, "'See, God, I have come to do your will, O God'" (10:7).[79] The singular sacrifice of Christ deals adequately with sins, because it is the Son's perfect offering of himself to God. By this offering the Son has become the mediator of a new covenant with its promise, "I will remember their sins and their lawless deeds no more" (10:17). Thus, there is no further need for offerings on behalf of sin.

The great central section of Hebrews (5:1–10:18) presents the most detailed and systematic presentation of Christ's priesthood found in the New Testament. Its essential ideas can be summarized in four points. First, Christ was qualified to be a priest because he was called to be a priest by God and lived in solidarity with humanity. Second, Christ enjoys an eternal and superior priesthood according to the order of Melchizedek. Third, Christ exercises a superior ministry because he entered the heavenly sanctuary. Fourth, Christ's sacrifice adequately deals with sin because it was a perfect sacrifice of self to God.

The Perfected Son and High Priest

The author of Hebrews clearly identifies Jesus as the Son of God and high priest according to the order of Melchizedek. In doing so, he writes from the point of view of the Son's exaltation. He proclaims that the one who entered the heavenly sanctuary inherited a name superior to that of the angels and now sits at the right hand of the Majesty, a high priest according to the order of Melchizedek. Because Hebrews views the story of Christ from this point of view, it may appear that it espouses an adoptionist Christology; that is, Jesus became the Son of God at his exaltation. For the author of Hebrews, however, there was never a moment when Jesus was not the Son of God. Nonetheless, there is a tension in Hebrews, for if the Son is the one through whom God made the worlds (1:2), then what does it mean to say that the Son inherited a name ("Son") more excellent than that of the angels at his exaltation (1:4)? To answer this question we must say something of what it means for Jesus, the Son, to be made perfect through suffering.

The identity of Jesus is never in question for the author of Hebrews. He is, was, and forever will be the Son of God. Moreover, previous to the incarnation, the Son already existed, albeit in a way that Hebrews does not explain. The earthly Jesus was the Son of God, as Hebrews implies when it says, "Although he was a Son, he learned obedience through what he suffered" (5:8). But then the author adds, "and having been made perfect, he became the source of eternal salvation for all who obey him, having been designated by God as a high priest according to the order of Melchizedek" (5:9–10). Thus, through his earthly life, Jesus the Son of God was made perfect, and God designated him a high priest according to the order of Melchizedek.

When the author of Hebrews says that Jesus was made perfect (2:10; 5:9; 7:28), he does not mean that he underwent a moral conversion, for Jesus was sinless (4:15; 7:26). But the moral dimension of being made perfect is not entirely absent since Hebrews emphasizes that Jesus learned obedience through what he suffered (5:8). This is not to say that Jesus was disobedient to God at any point in his life. Rather, the incarnate Son of God learned something that the preexistent Son could not learn; for, in solidarity with his brothers and sisters, the Son experienced the suffering that obedience to God entails. As Albert Vanhoye notes, there is a difference between an inner disposition to be obedient and the docility that is imprinted upon one's inner being by a lived experience of obedience.[80]

His obedience was a lifelong task that culminated in a perfect offering of himself in death to God. By that final act of obedience, the Son was made perfect in his relationship to humanity and God. In relationship to God, he exemplified perfect obedience to the point of surrendering his life. In relationship to humanity, this obedience made him one in suffering with his human brothers and sisters.[81] Perfected in this way, he was appointed high priest according to the order of Melchizedek. More specifically, he became high priest through his death, whereby he entered the heavenly sanctuary, where God affirmed that he is a priest forever, according to the order of Melchizedek.

There is an implicit distinction between identity and role in the Son of God Christology of Hebrews.[82] From the point of view of *identity,* Christ was Son of God. But from the point of view of his *role* in God's plan for salvation, he becomes the enthroned Son of God, an eternal high priest, at his exaltation. Moreover, it is as the enthroned Son of God and eternal high priest that he brings his brothers and sisters to perfection. Having been made perfect by suffering and death, he has become the pioneer of their salvation (2:10), the forerunner on their behalf (6:20), the guarantee of a better covenant (7:22), and the perfecter of faith (12:2). Having been made perfect, he can show them the way into the heavenly sanctuary. In Jesus, then, humanity sees its destiny as announced in Psalm 8, "You have crowned him with glory and honor, subjecting all things under his feet" (see 2:5–8). In sum, the Christology of Hebrews is a story of salvation in which the Son of God shares in the flesh and blood of humanity to show his brothers and sisters the way to the heavenly sanctuary.

THE BOOK OF REVELATION

Like 1 Peter and Hebrews, the book of Revelation seeks to strengthen and encourage believers who are suffering, or are about to suffer, for their faith. However, the manner in which Revelation accomplishes its goal is different, as is the Christology that it develops. Whereas 1 Peter and Hebrews function as letters, the book of Revelation is a prophecy with strong overtones of apocalypticism.[83] It presents itself as "the revelation of Jesus Christ, which God gave him to show his servants what must soon take place" (1:1). Disclosed to "John" (1:1, 9; 22:8), this prophecy reveals "what is, and what is to take place" (1:19). Although John is the one who writes down the words of the prophecy, Jesus Christ is its author as well as its subject matter.[84] From a narrative point of view, then, Christ tells his own story in the book of Revelation!

The relationship of this prophecy to history has been a topic of constant discussion.[85] While some argue that Revelation merely depicts the perennial struggle between good and evil and should be read in a nonhistorical manner, others maintain that it provides a detailed outline of future events. In my view, the correct approach lies somewhere in the middle. Revelation is concerned with the struggle between good and evil, but this struggle occurs in human history.[86] Thus Revelation is concerned with historical events. It does not, however, provide its audience with a detailed outline or chronology of what will occur between now and the end. Instead, its focal point is the victory that the slaughtered Lamb has *already* won, for Revelation is as interested in the past and the present as it is in the future. Thus there is a surprising kinship between this writing and the Fourth Gospel, inasmuch as both highlight the victory that Christ has already won for believers. The book of Revelation describes this victory and its consequence in the stories that it tells.

The Stories of Revelation

The book of Revelation is a rich and complicated narrative in which stories are embedded in stories.[87] For example, there is the story of what happens to John on the island of Patmos (1:9), where this vision occurs. This is the macro story, the story within which all other narratives are embedded. Then there is the story that the Lamb (the risen Christ) reveals when he opens the seven-sealed scroll. The opening of the seven seals, which leads to the revelation of the seven trumpets, the seven bowls, the fall of Babylon, and the appearance of the new Jerusalem is the story of the church and the world. Embedded in this narrative are other stories such as the victory of the one hundred forty-four thousand, the death and vindication of the two witnesses, and the account of the dragon who pursues the woman with child. All of these stories relate the struggle and ultimate triumph of the messianic community. All of them, however, presuppose a story of Christ, and only those who know this implied story can decode the meaning of this esoteric writing. Before proceeding to this implied story, however, we must review the stories of Revelation.

Stories of John, the World, and the Church

The story of John takes place on the Lord's Day, on the island of Patmos, where he finds himself because he has proclaimed God's word and given testimony to Jesus.[88] While John is on Patmos, the risen Christ appears to him as a cosmic figure, standing in the midst of seven gold lampstands and holding seven stars. The risen Lord commands John to write down seven messages for the churches of Ephesus, Smyrna, Pergamum, Thyatira, Sardis, Philadelphia, and Laodicea.

After the risen Lord communicates these messages to John, John has a vision of heaven in which he sees the throne room of God, where four living creatures and twenty-four elders worship the one sitting on the throne. John sees a scroll in the right hand of the one sitting on the throne, but there is no one worthy to open it. When John weeps because no one is found worthy to open the scroll, he is told that the lion of the tribe of Judah, the root of Jesse, has triumphed, enabling him to open the scroll with its seven seals.

Surprisingly, the lion of the tribe of Judah appears as a Lamb who seems to have been slain. Declaring that the Lamb is worthy to receive the scroll, the heavenly court offers blessing, honor, glory, and might to the one who sits on the throne, and to the Lamb.

John now watches as the Lamb opens the first six seals of the scroll.[89] Before the Lamb opens the seventh seal, however, John has a vision of one hundred forty-four thousand people, from every tribe of Israel, who are sealed for God. John is then given a further vision of one hundred forty-four thousand from every nation, race, people, and tongue who stand before the throne of the Lamb because they have survived the time of great distress. The Lamb shepherds them and leads them to springs of life-giving water.

When the Lamb opens the seventh seal, there is silence in heaven for one half hour. Then seven angels with seven trumpets appear. The first six angels blow their trumpets,[90] but before the seventh does, John has a vision of a mighty angel with a small, opened scroll. John is told to eat the scroll and to prophesy, as was Ezekiel of old. Next, he is given a measuring rod with which to measure the temple of God. Then two witnesses are commissioned to prophesy. Although they are killed where their Lord was crucified, for bearing witness, they are raised from the dead, and the inhabitants of the earth repent. Thus, their witness bears fruit.

When the seventh angel blows his trumpet, there is a song of praise. Then a great sign appears in the sky: a woman about to give birth to a son and a huge red dragon. The woman gives birth, and her child is taken up into heaven. There, war breaks out between the dragon and Michael, who eventually casts the dragon out of heaven. Cast out of heaven, the dragon wages war on earth against the woman's offspring. In this war, two beasts assist the dragon. John then sees the Lamb on Mount Zion with the one hundred forty-four thousand mentioned earlier, and an angel informs him that Babylon has fallen. Then, one like a son of man reaps the harvest of the earth, and another angel casts the vintage of the earth into the winepress of God's wrath.

Suddenly seven angels appear with seven bowls of God's wrath, which they pour out in rapid succession.[91] As a result, Babylon is destroyed, and there is great lamentation among the kings of the earth. In heaven, however, there is great rejoicing as the celestial court prepares for the wedding feast of the Lamb.

A rider on a white horse appears, and the thrones of the beast and false prophet (the second beast) are cast into a fiery pool. An angel then imprisons Satan for a thousand years, while the souls of those who died for Christ reign with him. After this, Satan is released, but only to be definitively defeated at a final great battle. The earth is judged; Death and Hades are destroyed. As a result, there is a new creation, and the new Jerusalem, the heavenly city, comes to meet its bridegroom, the Lamb.

When the vision ends, John is told *not* to seal up its prophetic word, since Christ is coming soon. In response to the vision he has seen, John cries out, "Amen! Come, Lord Jesus!"

This story can be read on several levels. On one level, it is the story of what happened to John on Patmos. He received messages and visions from the risen Christ, who instructed him to communicate this prophecy to others, before Christ comes. On another, these messages and visions are the story of the world and the church: At present, the dragon, who is Satan, afflicts the church through his agents, the two beasts (Rome, and those who promote its emperor cult). Satan, however, has already been cast out of heaven, and the church can be confident of victory because the slaughtered Lamb who has been enthroned in heaven has already won the victory by shedding his blood. God's wrath (dramatized by seven seals, trumpets, and bowls) is already being poured out against those who refuse to repent. The climactic event of the parousia, symbolized by the rider on the white horse, is in the process of occurring. Satan and the beasts will be destroyed, the dead will be judged, and death will be no more. Thus, there will be a new creation.

Although I have told this story chronologically, the narrative of Revelation should not be interpreted in such a linear way, as if the seven bowls follow the seven trumpets, which, in turn, follow the seven seals. Revelation is better seen as a story that is told, then retold, and then retold again, each telling complete in itself.[92]

For example, after the first six seals, Revelation tells the story of the triumph of the elect, the one hundred forty-four thousand. After the sixth trumpet, it narrates the vision of the small scroll with the narrative of the two witnesses whose death and resurrection leads the inhabitants of the earth to repentance. Following the seventh trumpet, Revelation tells the story of the woman with child, and the expulsion of the dragon from heaven. Finally, after the seventh bowl, Revelation narrates the fall of Babylon and the defeat of Satan. The story, then, is more cyclic than linear; Revelation repeatedly tells the story of God's victory, each telling growing in intensity. As each cycle grows in intensity, the story moves to its inexorable conclusion, the new creation.[93]

The Story of Christ

In addition to narrating stories, Revelation presupposes a story of Christ, and it is this story that gives meaning to its prophetic message.

Like all narratives, this implied story of Christ consists of a past, a present, and a future. As regards the past, the narrative is traditional, inasmuch as it focuses on Christ's death and resurrection. The slaughtered Lamb who opens the scroll, so that John can know what is happening and what will be, is the crucified Christ who is now enthroned in heaven with the one who sits on the throne. This slaughtered Lamb is the fulfillment of Israel's messianic expectations. Thus, before presenting the Lamb, Revelation identifies him as the lion of the tribe of Judah and the root of David (5:5). The mythic story of the woman with child pursued by the dragon (12:1–17) is a messianic narrative that proclaims that the people of God has given birth to the Messiah despite the assaults of Satan.

As regards the present, the book of Revelation presupposes that the Messiah has already been "taken to God and his throne" (12:5). The long-expected Messiah, then, is the slaughtered Lamb enthroned with the one who sits on the throne. Although exalted to the heavenly sphere, the Messiah is still present to his people. This is why he appears to John as one like a son of man (1:13), so that he can encourage as well as admonish his churches. The risen One knows their situation; therefore, he reveals this prophetic message of hope and victory to his servant John.

As regards the future, Revelation is again traditional, despite its esoteric symbolism, for it proclaims that Christ will come again. Thus, he is the one like a son of man who reaps the harvest of the earth (14:14–16); he is the rider on the white horse who is called Faithful and True, the King of kings, and the Lord of lords (19:11–16). This victory of Christ, however, has already been won by the blood of the Lamb.[94] Thus the future is contained in the past, and, for those who bear faithful witness, it is already experienced in the present. The story of Revelation can be summarized in this way.

> Although he has been cast out of heaven by Michael and his angels, the great serpent, the dragon, who is Satan, continues to afflict and accuse humanity, as he did in the past. At present, he afflicts the witnesses of Jesus through two beasts who are his servants: Rome, and its emperor cult. Although Satan is still a powerful accuser, his power was effectively destroyed when Israel's Messiah, the slaughtered Lamb, shed his blood upon the cross. That death was a victory that is already celebrated in heaven because it resulted in Satan's expulsion. On earth, the followers of Jesus share in his victory by bearing witness on behalf of him, even to the point of death. As they endure such trials, they can be confident that God's wrath is coming to a climax. When it does, the victory that the Lamb has already won will be manifested; Satan and his allies will be definitively defeated; and there will be a new creation.

Few writings of the New Testament focus so intently on Christ's relationship to God, the church, the powers of evil, and the new creation. To verify this we must examine the text of Revelation more closely.

Christ and God

Nothing is more important in the study of New Testament Christology than determining how a particular writing relates Christ to God since this relationship defines who Christ is. The book of Revelation is no exception, and, in this regard, it manifests one of the most sophisticated Christologies of the New Testament.[95] Revelation discloses Christ's relationship to God in a number of ways. For example, whereas it was Yahweh who spoke to the prophets, it is the risen Christ who speaks to John, thereby putting Christ in a role normally reserved for God.[96] The manner in which Revelation describes Christ at the beginning of this prophecy also initiates a process of closely identifying him with God, not in the sense that Christ becomes God, but in a way that clearly indicates that he shares in God's being.[97] At the outset of this prophecy, for example, Revelation describes God as the one "who is and who was and *who is to come*" (1:4). Revelation then applies the language of Dan. 7:13 to Christ, "Look! *He is coming* with the clouds" (1:7), thereby suggesting the intimate relationship between the coming of God and the coming of Christ. Later, the parousia of Christ, symbolized by the rider on the white horse (19:11–21), plays a crucial role in the coming of the new creation.

In one of the few instances when God speaks in Revelation, he proclaims, "I am the Alpha and the Omega" (1:8). The risen Lord makes a similar claim when he says of himself, "I am the first and the last" (1:17; also see 2:8), a clear allusion to Isa. 44:6, where God says: "I am the first and I am the last; besides me there is no god" (also see Isa. 48:12). At the end of the book of Revelation, God repeats his earlier statement, this time adding the claim that Christ made for himself, "I am the Alpha and the Omega, the beginning and the end" (21:6). Then, Christ says of himself, "See, I am coming soon; my reward is with me, to repay according to everyone's work. I am the Alpha and the Omega, the first and the last, the beginning and the end" (22:12). In effect, the book of Revelation describes God and Christ with similar language. God is the one who was, the one who is, and the one who is coming (1:4), the Alpha and the Omega, the beginning and the end (1:8; 21:6). Christ is the one who is coming with the clouds (1:7), the first and the last (1:17; 2:8), the one who is coming soon, the Alpha and the Omega, the beginning and the end (22:12). By the end of this prophecy, therefore, readers should understand that Christ has been taken up into the very being of God. Moreover, since he, like God, is the beginning and the end, the Alpha and the Omega, it is not unreasonable to think of him as preexistent, even if Revelation does not explicitly develop this teaching.[98]

Revelation employs other strategies to draw Christ into the being of God. For example, John describes the risen Christ as having hair as "white as white wool" (1:14), an allusion to the Ancient of Days (God in Dan. 7:9) whose hair was like pure wool. Consequently, while Revelation describes the risen Lord in language reminiscent of the one like a son of man (Daniel 7), it also portrays him in language that the book of Daniel applies to God. In another instance of a similar phenomenon, Revelation describes Christ as "the holy one, the true one" (3:7), a description it later applies to God (6:10). Such examples could be multiplied, but these are sufficient to show that there is a consistent pattern of associating Christ as closely as possible with God in the book of Revelation. This pattern is most apparent in chapters 4–5, where John enters the heavenly throne room.

In chapter 4, John has a vision of heaven in which he sees the throne of God and witnesses the heavenly liturgy. The entire scene focuses on God's throne, and God is described as "the one who is seated on the throne" (4:2, 9, 10).[99] In effect, Revelation establishes that the throne belongs to God, and all others who claim godlike authority, for example, the dragon and the beast, each with its throne (13:2; 16:10), are false claimants to an authority that belongs to God. The heavenly court acknowledges this, and the four living creatures sing, "Holy, holy, holy, the Lord God the Almighty, who was and is and is to come" (4:8). Similarly, the twenty-four elders cast their crowns before the throne and sing, "You are worthy, our Lord and God, to receive glory and honor and power, for you created all things, and by your will they existed and were created" (4:11).

The purpose of John's vision in chapter 4 is to prepare for the enthronement of the Lamb in chapter 5.[100] In that chapter, John sees a scroll with seven seals in the right hand of the one seated on the throne, but there is no one worthy in heaven, on earth, or under the earth (thus, in the entire cosmos) to open the scroll. When John weeps because of this, one of the twenty-four elders tells him that the lion of the tribe of Judah (Gen. 49:9), the root of Jesse (Isa. 11:1, 10) can open the scroll because he has conquered. But instead of a lion, a Lamb appears, one who seems to have been slain, standing in the midst of, or between, the throne (*en mesō tou thronou;* 5:6) and the four living creatures and the elders. This Lamb has seven horns symbolizing the fullness of power and seven eyes that are the seven spirits of God (see 1:4), symbolizing the fullness of knowledge.[101]

The first appearance of the Lamb in the book of Revelation, therefore, identifies him as a messianic figure (the lion of the tribe of Judah, the root of Jesse), who stands closer to the throne of God than the four living creatures and the twenty-four elders. An all-powerful and all-knowing figure, even the seven spirits of God, first mentioned in 1:4, are attributed to him. The victory of the Messiah that enables him to open the scroll, however, is his death; for when he finally appears in the heavenly throne room, it is not as a lion but as a slaughtered Lamb.[102]

When the Lamb Messiah enters the throne room, he receives the scroll from the one who sits on the throne, and the four living creatures and the twenty-four elders fall before the Lamb singing:

> You are worthy to take the scroll and to open its seals, for you were slaughtered and by your blood you ransomed for God saints from every tribe and language and people and nation; you have made them to be a kingdom and priests serving our God. (5:9–10)

Countless heavenly hosts add their voices and sing a second hymn.

> Worthy is the Lamb that was slaughtered to receive power and wealth and wisdom and might and honor and glory and blessing! (5:12)

Thus, two hymns of praise are sung to the Lamb, just as two hymns of worship are sung to the one sitting on the throne (4:8, 11). However, whereas the first two hymns focus on the eternal being and *creative power* of God, the last two celebrate the *redemptive death* of the Lamb.

The whole of God's creation then sings a fifth and final hymn to the one sitting on the throne *and* to the Lamb:

> To the one seated on the throne and to the Lamb be blessing and honor and glory and might forever and ever! (5:13)

The four living creatures respond "Amen," and the twenty-four elders fall down and worship. This final hymn celebrates the enthronement of the Lamb, who now receives blessing, honor, and glory with God (see 4:11, where God received glory, honor, and praise). Thus Christ, the slaughtered Lamb, receives the same praise and worship as does God.

Revelation never presents the Lamb seated upon the throne apart from God. In 7:17, the Lamb is at the center of God's throne (*ana meson tou thronou*) from where he shepherds the elect. Then, in the final chapter of Revelation, the water of life flows from "the throne of God and of the Lamb" (22:1), and "the throne of God and of the Lamb" is in the heavenly city (22:3). Thus, the purpose of the throne imagery is to associate Christ as closely as possible with God without explicitly calling him God.

Christ and the Church

The underlying Christ story of Revelation supposes an intimate relationship between Christ and the church, the people whom he has redeemed. The first hymn to the Lamb, for example, proclaimed that he was worthy to open the scroll because he was slaughtered and he ransomed by his blood those from every tribe, language, people, and nation to be a kingdom and priests serving God (5:9–10). This relationship to the redeemed provides yet another vantage point from which to investigate the Christology of Revelation.

In the opening chapters of this prophecy, the risen Christ appears to John and instructs him to write what he sees on a scroll and send it to the seven churches in Ephesus, Smyrna, Pergamum, Thyatira, Sardis, Philadelphia, and Laodicea. This Christophany (the most detailed description of the risen One in the New Testament) presents Christ as one like a son of man (*omoion hyion anthrōpou;* 1:13) standing in the midst of seven golden lampstands, holding seven stars in his right hand, with a sharp two-edged sword coming from his mouth (1:12–16). The description of Christ as one like a son of man clearly associates him with the figure of Daniel 7, but without developing a Son of Man Christology, such as is found in the Gospels.[103] The seven golden lampstands are the seven churches and the seven stars their angels (1:20). The two-edged sword is the word of God with which Christ conquers the nations at his parousia (19:15, 21). Thus this Christophany presents Christ in three ways. First, he has been vindicated, as was the figure in Daniel. He is truly the firstborn from the dead (1:5). Second, although risen from the dead and exalted to God, he is present to the churches in whose midst he walks and whose angels he holds, for he "loves us and freed us from our sins by his blood, and made us to be a kingdom, priests serving his God and Father" (1:5–6). Third, he conquers by the power of his word, the sword of his mouth; he is "the ruler of the kings of the earth" (1:5).

When the risen One speaks, he identifies himself to John in this way:

> Do not be afraid; I am the first and the last, and the living one. I was dead, and see, I am alive forever and ever; and I have the keys of Death and of Hades. (1:18)

This self-affirmation is, for all practical purposes, an exposition of God's words, "I am the Alpha and the Omega" (1:8).[104] Like God, Jesus is the beginning and end of all things because he is the living one. Like God, he has power over Death and Hades (see Job 38:17). The one who will speak to the churches, then, has the power to give them life if they conquer.

Because Christ is present to and cares for his churches, he commands John to deliver seven messages, each one tailored to the needs of a particular church. The messages follow a set pattern: a command to write; a statement in which Christ identifies himself; an affirmation that he knows what is occurring in the church, with appropriate instruction; a call to hear what the Spirit says, with a promise to those who are victorious. While these messages are often called "letters," they are more akin to imperial edicts since the one who speaks to the churches is the King of kings and Lord of lords. [105]

The most significant aspect of these messages, for our purposes, is the manner in which Christ identifies himself to each church.

Ephesus	These are the words of him who holds the seven stars in his right hand, who walks among the seven golden lampstands. (2:1; recalls 1:16 and 1:12, 13)
Smyrna	These are the words of the first and the last, who was dead and came to life. (2:8; recalls 1:17, 18)
Pergamum	These are the words of him who has the sharp two-edged sword. (2:12; recalls 1:16)
Thyatira	These are the words of the Son of God, who has eyes like a flame of fire. (2:18; recalls 1:14)
Sardis	These are the words of him who has the seven spirits of God and the seven stars. (3:1; recalls 1:4 and 1:16)
Philadelphia	These are the words of the holy one, the true one, who has the key of David, who opens and no one will shut, who shuts and no one opens. (3:7; recalls 1:18; foreshadows 6:10; 19:11)
Laodicea	The words of the Amen, the faithful and true witness, the origin of God's creation. (3:14; recalls 1:5)

In most instances, Christ's self-description recalls what has already been said of him in chapter 1, thereby reminding the churches that the one who speaks to them is the risen Lord. In his message to Thyatira, however, the risen Lord identifies himself as "the Son of God" (2:18). Moreover, in three instances, the risen Christ explicitly refers to God as his Father (2:28; 3:5, 21).[106] In the third of these statements (3:21), Christ says, "To the one who conquers I will give a place with me on my throne, just as I myself conquered and sat down with my Father on his throne." Thus, the one who appears to John like a son of man, and later as a slaughtered Lamb, is the Son of God. This is why Revelation says that the one hundred forty-four thousand have the name of *the Lamb and his Father* written on their heads (14:1); for the slaughtered Lamb *is* the Son of God.

In addition to these explicit christological statements, four other points should be noted. First, the sevenfold use of "I know" (2:2, 9, 13, 19; 3:1, 8, 15) indicates the omniscience of the risen One who is fully aware of his churches' strengths, failures, and struggles, for he is the Lamb with seven eyes, the seven spirits of God (5:6). Second, Christ can make his sevenfold promise to those who conquer (2:7, 10, 17, 26; 3:5, 12, 21) because he is the victorious one who has conquered by shedding his blood (5:5–6). Third, the risen Lord who promises to vindicate the church is coming quickly, even as a thief in the night (3:3, 11). Finally, although Christ appears as a transcendent figure, he is close to, and loves, his church (3:9, 19).

To summarize, though enthroned in heaven with God, Christ is present to his churches. The risen One is the Messiah, the Son of God, who shed his blood (1:5; 5:9; 7:14; 12:11) to redeem a people for God. Because he has died, he now lives and is ever present to the church, which must be victorious in suffering and death, as was the slaughtered Lamb.

Christ and the Enemies of God

A plot of conflict underlies the Christ story of Revelation. The fundamental conflict is between God and Satan. Only God is worthy of worship (19:10; 22:9), but Satan employs his servants (the two beasts) to deceive humanity into worshiping him by worshiping the beast who represents Rome, the harlot Babylon. In this conflict, Christ plays an essential role. By his death the slaughtered Lamb has already won the decisive victory over Satan. This is why Michael and his angels have been able to expel Satan from heaven (12:7–9), and the heavenly chorus can sing: "Now have come the salvation and the power and the kingdom of our God and the authority of his Messiah, for the accuser of our comrades has been thrown down, who accuses them day and night before God" (12:10).

The conflict between God and Satan, however, has not yet been resolved; for having been expelled from heaven, Satan wages war on earth against the offspring of the woman who bore the Messiah (12:13–18). In this war, Satan makes use of two beasts. To the first, the Roman Empire, whom the inhabitants of the earth worship (13:1–10), Satan gives his own power and throne (13:2). The second beast represents the false prophets who serve the first beast (16:13; 19:20; 20:10); it also wields great authority (13:11–17). Thus the church, the offspring of the woman who bore the Messiah, finds itself in a life-and-death struggle with Satan, who exercises his authority through the beasts.

Enthroned in heaven, Christ plays a central role in resolving the final conflict between God and Satan by opening the scroll with its seven seals. The scroll tells the story of God's victory over Satan, which comes to its climax in the victory of the one hundred forty-four thousand who stand before the throne of God and worship him day and night, with the Lamb at the center of God's throne shepherding them to springs of life-giving water (7:15–17).

Revelation insists that only the slaughtered Lamb is worthy to break open the seals of the scroll, and it carefully notes how the Lamb opens each of the seven seals (6:1, 3, 5, 7, 9, 12; 8:1). Thus Revelation portrays Christ as the one to whom God has entrusted the future of the world, for the Lamb initiates God's final victory over Satan by opening the scroll.

The opening of the scroll narrates God's victory, for when the Lamb opens the sixth seal, the inhabitants of the earth realize that the great day of the wrath of God and the Lamb has come (6:16–17).[107] But instead of concluding its story with this day of wrath and the victory of the one hundred forty-four thousand, Revelation tells its story again. Thus, when the Lamb opens the seventh seal, seven angels with seven trumpets appear (8:1–2). Like the opening of the seals, the blowing of the trumpets is the story of God's victory over Satan. This time, however, Revelation recounts the victory in the allegory of the two witnesses (11:1–13).

The two witnesses stand for the church, which must bear witness to God against Satan.[108] Like their Lord who was crucified (11:8), the witnesses are put to death. After three and a half days, however, they are raised to life, and their witness leads others to glorify God (11:13).[109] Thus, when the seventh trumpet blows, there is rejoicing in heaven: "The kingdom of the world has become the kingdom of our Lord and of his Messiah, and he will reign for ever and ever" (11:15). The blowing of the seven trumpets, like the opening of the seals, tells the whole story.[110] Instead of concluding the narrative, however, Revelation begins it once more by recounting how seven angels pour out the seven last plagues, the seven bowls of God's wrath (chapters 15–16). The destructive force of these plagues is even greater than that of the seals and trumpets, and when the seventh angel pours out his bowl, he cries, "It is done!" (16:17), and Babylon (Rome) is destroyed (16:19). Revelation then describes the destruction of Babylon (chapters 17–18) and the victory of God (19:1–10).

The Lamb does not play an active role in this section as he did in the opening of the scrolls. He does not blow the trumpets or pour out the bowls of God's wrath. But, by opening the seventh seal, the Lamb initiates these events; for the slaughtered Lamb has been entrusted with inaugurating God's eschatological victory.

Revelation does ascribe an active role to Christ in 19:11–21. The heavens are opened and John sees a rider on a white horse, who is identified by three names. First he is called "Faithful and True" (19:11), a name that recalls an earlier description of Jesus Christ as the faithful witness (1:5), as well as Christ's description of himself to the church of Laodicea, "the faithful and true witness" (3:14). The one who rides on the white horse, then, is the Christ who has been a faithful witness to God, even unto death. Thus, he is clothed in a robe dipped in blood like the figure in Isa. 63:1–6. But whereas that figure is covered with the blood of the enemies he slaughtered, the rider on the white horse is covered with his own blood that he shed on the cross, for he is the slaughtered Lamb.

Second, he is called "The Word of God" (19:13; see Wisd. Sol. 18:15). Thus, when he rides into battle with the armies of heaven following him, he strikes down the nations with a sharp sword that comes from his mouth; namely, the word of God. This sword recalls the sharp two-edged sword that came out of the mouth of the one like a son of man who first appeared to John (1:16), as well as the manner in which Christ identifies himself to the church of Pergamum (2:12).

Finally, the one seated on the white horse has a name inscribed on his thigh, "King of kings and Lord of lords" (19:16). This name also recalls how Christ was first identified in Revelation, "Jesus Christ, . . . the ruler of the kings of the earth" (1:5). When the rider on the white horse goes into battle, the beast and the kings of the earth make war against him but to no avail. The beast and the false prophet (the second beast) are captured, and the kings of the earth are killed by the sword coming from the mouth of the rider on the white horse.[111]

Although this scene is filled with military imagery, Christ wins his victory by the sword of his mouth, which is the word of God, and by his own blood shed on the cross. The final battle, then, is not a military defeat of God's enemies but the final working out of the victory that the slaughtered Lamb has already won on the cross. The triumphal King of kings and Lord of lords is none other than the crucified Messiah.[112] The victory of God has already been won, even though it has not been fully worked out in history.

Christ and the New Creation

God's victory over Satan results in a new creation, in which Christ plays a central role. When Satan is finally cast into the lake of fire and sulfur with the beast and the false prophet (20:10), and when the dead are judged and Death and Hades are thrown into the lake of fire (20:12–15), there is a new creation (21:1). The holy city, a new Jerusalem, comes down from heaven. On the one hand, this city is described as the place where God will dwell with his people (21:3). On the other, it is portrayed as the bride of the Lamb (21:9). Thus the city is simultaneously God's people and the Lamb's bride, another indication of the intimate relationship between God and Christ. This city has no need of a temple since its temple is "the Lord God the

Almighty and the Lamb" (21:22). Nor has it any need of sun or moon since the glory of God is its light, and the Lamb its lamp (21:23). Only those whose names are inscribed in the Lamb's book of life can enter the city (21:27).[113] Within the city is the throne of God and of the Lamb, "and his servants will worship him" (22:3).[114]

For the author of Revelation, it is impossible to conceive of the new Jerusalem apart from the Lamb. The Lamb plays a central role in this city because, with God, he forms the temple of the new Jerusalem. Thus the ending of this story portrays Christ as the one who is most central to God's work of salvation, the one whom God's servants worship, even as they worship God.

Although Revelation is one of the most puzzling books of the Bible, it presents a rather clear and unified portrait of Christ. Christ is the fulfillment of messianic expectation, for he is the lion of the tribe of Judah, the root of Jesse. He is the King of kings, and the Lord of lords, for he is the slaughtered Lamb who has won the decisive victory by shedding his blood on the cross. He is the one who knows the destiny of the world, for he is worthy to open the scroll. He is present to the church; for he is the firstborn from the dead. He was dead, but now he is alive. He is the Alpha and the Omega, the beginning and the end, the one who is coming, for he has been enthroned with the one who is seated on the throne. The faithful witness and victor over death, the Christ of Revelation is the one in whom God reveals his victory over Satan.

6

The Revelatory Word

*T*he Gospel of John presents a story of Jesus that the Johannine epistles presuppose and reflect upon. Therefore, after we have investigated the narrative Christology of the Fourth Gospel, we will discuss how the Johannine epistles, especially 1 John, reflect upon this foundational narrative which underlies their community life.

THE GOSPEL OF JOHN

Although the Fourth Gospel belongs to the same literary genre as the Synoptic Gospels, it develops a markedly different Christology.[1] Indeed, one could argue that it is preeminently a work of Christology since Jesus is the focal point of its many signs and discourses.[2] The Gospel presents Jesus, and Jesus presents himself, as one who has come from heaven to reveal himself as the one sent by the Father. Having completed the work the Father entrusted to him, he returns to the one who sent him.

This Christology clearly goes beyond anything in the Synoptic Gospels. For, while each of the Synoptics develops a sophisticated Christology, none approaches the Christology of this work, which portrays Jesus as the incarnation of God's preexistent Word. Consequently, I have chosen to present the Christology of the Fourth Gospel apart from that of the Synoptics, even though the Gospels share a common genre.

Before I embark upon a study of the Fourth Gospel, it is important to make two points. First, there is a growing consensus that this Gospel has undergone several revisions during the course of which its Christology has grown and developed.[3] Because of these successive revisions, there are several christological strata in the Gospel; for example, there are traditional Christologies that present Jesus as the expected Messiah and more developed Christologies that present him as the Son of Man who has descended from heaven. Second, while all the writings of the New Testament have a tendency to reflect something of the community situations in and for which they were composed, this tendency is more pronounced in the Fourth Gospel.[4] Thus, stories such as the healing of the blind man in chapter 9 reveal as much about what was happening in the Johannine community as they do about Jesus.[5] Consequently, those who read the Gospel are reading two narratives: the story of Jesus and the story of the Johannine community in which this Christology was developed.

Generally speaking, these two points are more important for those investigating the growth and development of Johannine Christology than for those concerned with the Gospel's narrative Christology. Nonetheless, even those concerned with the Gospel's narrative Christology must be aware of the developments behind the text lest they approach it in a naïve and ahistorical manner.[6] The Christology of this Gospel was not spun out of whole cloth but developed in the bosom of a community that underwent several changes.

With this caution in mind, this chapter investigates the Gospel's Christology from a literary and narrative perspective. It begins with the premise that the prologue, which presents Jesus as the incarnation of the preexistent Word, should control the reading of the text and its Christology. Accordingly, titles found in the Synoptic tradition (Messiah, Son of God, Son of Man) take on a more profound meaning in the Fourth Gospel in light of the prologue.

The Word Incarnate (1:1–18)

In our study of the Gospel of Mark, I noted that its opening verses (Mark 1:1–13) present readers with privileged information about Jesus that is withheld from the characters of the narrative. Consequently, there is a discrepancy between what readers know and what the characters of the narrative must discover; namely, Jesus is the Son of God.

The Johannine prologue (1:1–18) functions in a similar manner.[7] At the outset of the Gospel, the narrator reveals the identity of Jesus; he is God's Word made flesh (1:14). Thus, even though the prologue was probably composed at a later stage in the Gospel's development, it now controls how readers understand the narrative, and they must interpret this narrative in light of the prologue.

There are, however, two differences between the Johannine prologue and the introduction to Mark's Gospel. First, in the Gospel of Mark, the narrator identifies Jesus with a title that reappears at key points in the rest of the narrative: the Son of God. In the Gospel of John, however, it is only in the prologue that the narrator identifies Jesus as the Word of God, and there is no climactic moment when the characters of the story confess that Jesus is the incarnate Word of God.

Second, while all narrators necessarily withhold information from their readers, telling the truth but not the whole truth, this process is more pronounced in the Gospel of Mark than in the Gospel of John. Thus, the Markan narrator discloses that Jesus is God's Son but does not reveal the nature of this sonship until midpoint in the narrative when he discloses that Jesus must suffer, die, and rise from the dead. While the passion, death, and resurrection of Jesus play an important role in John's Gospel, they are not revelatory moments to the extent they are in Mark's Gospel because the reader who knows that Jesus is the incarnate Word of God knows everything.

The Johannine prologue, then, functions more powerfully than the introductory verses to Mark's Gospel, for it is the Gospel in miniature. It tells the story of Jesus and the community that has come to believe in him. Moreover, if "revelation" is the overriding theme of the Fourth Gospel,[8] it is the prologue that most explicitly announces this theme.

The prologue orients readers in the following ways. First, its opening words ("In the beginning was the Word") set the Jesus story in eternity before the Word was made flesh. Before creation, the Word was already with God. The narrator explains that the Word was God,[9] all things were made through the Word, and the Word was life and light (1:1–5). At the outset of the prologue, then, readers already know the most profound secret of Jesus' identity and should not be surprised—as will be the characters of the narrative—by Jesus' bold claims that he reveals what he has heard and seen in God's presence. Nor will they be scandalized by his claim that he is life and light for the world.

Second, the prologue identifies John the Baptist as a witness to Jesus (1:6–8, 15), even before the narrator makes his climactic statement that the Word was made flesh (1:14). In addition to preparing for John's testimony in the opening episode of the Gospel (1:19–28), these verses foreshadow a theme that will be repeated throughout in the narrative: witness to Jesus should lead to faith that Jesus comes from God. Whereas the world condemns itself by not accepting this witness, those who believe are enlightened by Jesus, the light of the world.

Third, the prologue adumbrates the conflict between the Word and the world (1:9–13) that will occur throughout this Gospel. The world (*kosmos*) is the sphere of human beings who dwell in the darkness of sin and are unaware of the darkness in which they dwell. The Word comes into the world to enlighten it by testifying to what it has seen in God's presence. But even though the Word came to its own (the Jewish people), its own did not receive it. Those who accepted the Word, however, were given the power to become children of God. This part of the prologue is the story of Jesus' ministry, and it explains that even though Jesus revealed God's glory by many signs,[10] the world did not accept him (12:37–43). But his own disciples did, and, in his farewell discourse (13:1–17:26), Jesus prepared them for the time after his departure from the world.

Fourth, the climax of the prologue is the narrator's statement, "And the Word became flesh and lived among us, and we have seen his glory, the glory as of a father's only son, full of grace and truth" (1:14).[11] Here, the pronoun "we" suggests that the narrator speaks for the community of believers for whom he writes. This community believes in Jesus as the one who came from God and knows that he is the incarnation of God's Word, God's perfect revelation to the world. It has seen his glory in the signs and works he has done, a glory that identifies Jesus as the Father's only begotten (*monogenous para patros*). Thus the narrator clearly identifies the human one, Jesus, as the enfleshment of God's eternal Word, the only begotten of the Father.

Finally, in verses 15–18, the narrator compares Moses and Jesus Christ. Whereas the law was given through Moses, grace and truth came through Jesus Christ (1:17). The purpose of this statement is not to denigrate Moses or the law, for both witness to Jesus (5:46). But it clearly distinguishes the revelation that Jesus Christ brings from the law that was given to Moses. Jesus Christ is the only Son, God (*monogenēs theos;* 1:18),[12] who has made the Father known.

The christological content of the prologue can be summarized by the word "revelation." As the Word made flesh, Jesus is the perfect revelation of God. This is why the narrator identifies him as the Word, even though that concept will not appear again in the Gospel. By identifying Jesus as the Word, the prologue prepares readers for a narrative in which Jesus will present himself as revelation from God. The christological content of this prologue, however, is so dense that the prologue needs a narrative to illumine it. It is to this narrative that we turn.

Witness to the Word (1:19–51)

The story of the human one, Jesus, opens with the witness of John, as the prologue has already disclosed. His witness begins with a triple denial: he is not the Messiah, Elijah, or the Prophet (1:20–21). He is merely a voice crying in the wilderness who prepares the way for the Lord.

When Jesus makes his first appearance in the Gospel, John immediately identifies him as the Lamb of God who takes away the sin of the world (1:29). John then testifies that he saw the Spirit descend from heaven like a dove and remain on Jesus (1:32). Although John did not know who Jesus was at that time, the one who had sent him told him that the one on whom the Spirit descended and remained will baptize with the Holy Spirit. Having seen this one, John now testifies that Jesus is the Son of God (1:34).[13]

When Jesus appears the next day, John witnesses to two of his disciples (one of whom is Andrew) that Jesus is the Lamb of God (1:35–36). These two call Jesus "Rabbi" and accept his invitation to come and see where he lives.[14] John's witness leads to further witness, and Andrew testifies to his brother Simon (Peter) that they have found the Messiah (1:41).

On the next day, Jesus comes to Galilee and finds Philip, who finds Nathanael. Philip testifies, "We have found him about whom Moses in the law and also the prophets wrote, Jesus son of Joseph from Nazareth" (1:45). Nathanael then confesses that Jesus is the Son of God, the King of Israel (1:49). Jesus assures him that he will see "heaven opened and the angels of God ascending and descending upon the Son of Man" (1:51).

This is the most interesting section of the Gospel in terms of christological titles since it identifies Jesus as the "Lamb of God," "Son of God," "Messiah," "King of Israel," and "Son of Man" who is the point of communication between heaven and earth.[15] Furthermore, it describes Jesus as the one on whom the Spirit descends and remains, the one about whom Moses and the prophets wrote. It is difficult to find a comparable section of the New Testament that identifies Jesus in so many ways.

At an earlier stage of the Gospel's development, these titles were undoubtedly interpreted in traditional ways. For example, the King of Israel is the Messiah, the Son of God.[16] In light of the prologue, however, it is no longer sufficient to read them in such traditional ways, for the Messiah is the Lamb of God who takes away the sin of the world. He is the Son of Man who has descended from heaven and will be glorified at his death and ascend from whence he came. Most important, the one whom the community confesses as Messiah, the King of Israel, and the Son of God is the incarnate Word of God. This is why Nathanael will see the angels of heaven ascending and descending upon the Son of Man.

None of the characters within the narrative understand this when they confess that Jesus is Messiah, King of Israel, the Son of God. At this stage, they comprehend these titles in a traditional fashion. But the reader knows more than the characters of the narrative and realizes that, in light of the prologue, these titles have taken on new meaning.

The Word's Glory (2:1–4:54)

Jesus' ministry begins in Cana of Galilee, where "the first of his signs" (2:11) reveals his glory. From Galilee, he goes to Jerusalem for the feast of Passover, where he cleanses the Temple and performs still other signs (2:13–25). While Jesus is in Jerusalem, Nicodemus comes to him at night and, on the basis of Jesus' signs, acknowledges that Jesus has come from God (3:1–15). After this encounter, in which it becomes clear that Nicodemus does not grasp the significance of Jesus' identity, Jesus returns to Galilee by way of Samaria, where he meets the woman at the well (4:1–42). Upon returning to Galilee, he heals the son of a royal official (4:46–53), and the narrator comments, "Now this was the second sign that Jesus did after coming from Judea to Galilee" (4:54). Thus, this part of the narrative moves from Galilee to Galilee, where Jesus performs signs and reveals his glory.

Jesus' signs (*sēmeia*) point to him and reveal his glory.[17] For example, the sign at Cana manifests Jesus' glory as the one who ushers in the messianic age signified by the good wine that has been saved for last. Likewise, the healing of the official's son reveals Jesus' glory by pointing to him as the one who gives life, a theme that will be developed further as the narrative unfolds. While the characters of the story are amazed that Jesus can perform such signs, the reader knows that the one who does them is the enfleshment of God's Word (1:14). Consequently, the glory he reveals is God's glory.

Although Jesus finds an initially favorable reception in Galilee, there are intimations of opposition in Jerusalem. For example, even though the cleansing of the Temple points to Jesus as the new locus for true worship, the Jews ask, "What sign can you show us for doing this?" (2:18). And although Nicodemus acknowledges that Jesus comes from God, he does not understand what Jesus means by being born again (3:4). Nor does he comprehend what Jesus intends when he speaks of the Son of Man who has descended from heaven and must be "lifted up" (3:13–14).[18]

Jesus, however, finds a more favorable reception among the Samaritans, and the story of the Samaritan woman leads the reader through a series of questions and statements about Jesus' identity. It begins with the woman's asking if Jesus is greater than their ancestor Jacob (4:12).[19] Next, it moves to her declaration that Jesus is a prophet (4:19). Then Jesus speaks of worship in spirit and truth (4:23) and identifies himself as the Messiah (4:26). The woman tells others in the village about the one who told her everything she had ever done and wonders if Jesus is truly the Messiah (4:29). Her testimony leads to the climactic statement of the Samaritans that Jesus is the Savior of the world (4:42).

In this part of the story, several themes and titles identify Jesus. For example, Jesus is the one who reveals God's glory by ushering in the messianic age; he is the new locus of worship in spirit and truth; and he is the source of life. He is the Prophet, the Messiah, the Savior of the World. He is the Son of Man who descends from heaven and will return to God when he is lifted up (exalted) on the cross.

The controlling theme of this section, however, is found in two narrative comments that echo the prologue. The first occurs after Nicodemus's conversation with Jesus, when the narrator explains that God "gave" and "sent" his Son into the world as the light of the world, not to condemn but to save the world (3:16–21). The second occurs immediately before Jesus' encounter with the Samaritan woman and explains that Jesus testifies to what he has seen and heard because he comes from above (3:31–36). Like the prologue, these narrative comments enable the reader to understand the full significance of the titles and themes surrounding the person of Jesus. He is the one who testifies to what he has seen and heard in God's presence, the one whom God sent into the world.

Opposition to the Word (5:1–10:42)

Chapters 5–10 constitute the great central section of John's Gospel in which the christological debate between Jesus and the Jews comes to its climax. The focus of the debate is found in two verses.

> For this reason the Jews were seeking all the more to kill him, because he was not only breaking the sabbath, but was also calling God his own Father, thereby making himself *equal to God.* (5:18)

> The Jews answered, "It is not for a good work that we are going to stone you, but for blasphemy, because you, though only a human being, *are making yourself God.*" (10:33)

In these verses it becomes clear that the nature of Jesus' relationship to God is the central issue in the debate between him and the Jews.[20]

In chapter 5, we find Jesus in Jerusalem once more. Then in chapter 6, he is in Galilee again, where he feeds the crowd in the wilderness and then delivers a discourse in which he claims that he is the true bread that has come down from heaven.[21] From Galilee, Jesus goes to Jerusalem for the feast of Booths (7:10), where the crowds wonder if he is the Messiah, and he claims to be the light of the world (8:12). The healing of a man blind from birth shows that Jesus is truly the light of the world (9:1–41), and the man's expulsion from the synagogue leads to Jesus' further claim that he is the good shepherd who lays down his life for his sheep (10:11). While Jesus is still in Jerusalem for the feast of Dedication, the Jews confront him and demand that he tell them if he is the Messiah (10:22–39). He then leaves Jerusalem and goes to the place where John baptized earlier (10:40–42).

Equal to God

The first christological debate is occasioned by a Sabbath healing in Jerusalem (5:1–18), not unlike Jesus' Sabbath healings in the Synoptics. The healing is not explicitly called a sign, but it functions as one inasmuch as it points to Jesus as the Son whom the Father has sent with authority to give life and judge, as the ensuing discourse explains (5:19–29).

The debate begins when Jesus tells the Jews that he works on the Sabbath because "My Father is still working, and I also am working" (5:17). That is to say, since God does not cease from his work of caring for creation and judging, even on the Sabbath, neither does Jesus.[22] The narrator then comments that it was for this reason that the Jews were trying to kill Jesus, because he was calling God his own Father and so making himself equal to God (5:18).

From the point of view of the Johannine narrator, Jesus is equal to God because the Father has shown him all things and given him authority to do what God does: to grant life and to judge. Equal to God, however, does not mean independent from God, nor does the narrator present Jesus as a second God. For Jesus plainly says, "I can do nothing on my own. As I hear, I judge; and my judgment is just, because I seek to do not my own will but the will of him who sent me" (5:30). Jesus is equal to the Father because he is the one to whom the Father has shown all things (5:20). Therefore, to honor the Son whom the Father has sent into the world is to honor the Father (5:23). But, precisely because he is the Son, Jesus is not independent of the Father nor a second God alongside of God. The claim that he is equal to God derives from his relationship to God, a relationship clarified by the prologue, which presents him as the Word of God.

The One from Heaven

Jesus' discourse, in which he claims that he is the bread of life that has come down from heaven, is the climax of a section that begins with the feeding of the five thousand in the wilderness, where the crowd exclaims, "This is indeed the prophet who is to come into the world" (6:14), and concludes with Peter confessing, "Lord, to whom can we go? You have the words of eternal life. We have come to believe and know that you are the Holy One of God" (6:67–68).

The discourse is Jesus' exegesis of a text that the crowd proposes, when it says, "Our ancestors ate the manna in the wilderness; as it is written, 'He gave them bread from heaven to eat'" (6:31, quoting Ps. 78:24). The crowd interprets the text to mean that Moses gave their ancestors manna to eat in the wilderness, but Jesus explains it in reference to himself. What the text really means is that the Father gives Jesus as the true bread from heaven (6:32). He is the bread of life (6:35, 48), the one who comes down from heaven to do the will of the one who sent him (6:38). Thus, he is the bread that came down from heaven (6:41, 51). Whereas their ancestors ate manna in the wilderness and died, the one who eats the bread of life that the Father gives will not die (6:48–51). We can summarize the different interpretations of Jesus and the crowd in this way.

Ps. 78:24: "*He* gave them *bread* from heaven to eat."

Crowd's interpretation: Moses gave our ancestors *manna* in the wilderness.

Jesus' interpretation: God gives *Jesus* as the bread of life that comes down from heaven.

Although contemporary readers are inclined to attach a eucharistic interpretation to this chapter, its primary focus is christological.[23] Jesus, the Word incarnate, is the bread of life who has given his flesh for the life of the world (6:51). To eat this bread is to entrust oneself to him as the one whom the Father sent into the world. Because Peter and the disciples have already found life in Jesus' words, they do not leave him as some disciples do (6:66). They are not scandalized by Jesus' claim that he comes from God to bring life to the world. Or, in the language of the prologue, they are not scandalized that Jesus is the Word made flesh.

The Light of the World

Jesus' claim that he is the bread of life is followed by a further claim that he is the light of the world (8:12). This pronouncement does not come as a

NEW TESTAMENT CHRISTOLOGY

surprise to anyone who has read the prologue, which proclaims that the Word was the true light (1:9). But for the characters of the narrative, who are already questioning Jesus' origins, it is the occasion for further debate about his identity. At the end of this debate Jesus says, "Very truly, I tell you, before Abraham was, I am" (8:58).

The crowds in Jerusalem during the feast of Booths are sharply divided over Jesus. While some view him as a good man, others see him as one who deceives the people (7:12). The question of messiahship also comes to center stage. While some would disqualify Jesus from being the Messiah on the grounds of his lineage (7:27), others ask if the Messiah will do more signs than Jesus has already done (7:31).

On the last day of the festival, when Jesus says, "Let anyone who is thirsty come to me, and let the one who believes in me drink" (7:37–38), some exclaim, "This is really the prophet" (7:40), and others, "This is the Messiah" (7:41). But questions about Jesus' identity continue, since he comes from Galilee, whereas the Messiah should be a descendant of David and come from Bethlehem (7:41–42). In summary, the crowd is divided about Jesus. While some think that he is the Prophet or the Messiah, others disqualify him on the basis of his human origins.

Jesus, for his part, makes some statements about himself that clarify the nature of his identity for those who have read the prologue but only infuriate the characters of the story who are not privy to that privileged information. First, on two occasions he speaks about going where the Jews cannot come (7:33–34; 8:21). Second, he proclaims that he is the light of the world, and whoever follows him will never walk in darkness (8:12). Third, he tells the Jews that when they have lifted up the Son of Man, they will realize who he is and that he speaks only as the Father has instructed him (8:28).[24] Fourth, he asserts that he preexisted Abraham (8:58). Finally, he presents himself as the good shepherd who lays down his life for his sheep (10:11, 14–15).

To anyone ignorant of the prologue, Jesus' extravagant claims can only exacerbate a situation that is already contentious and divisive. Where is Jesus going that the Jews cannot follow? How can a human be the light of the world? What does Jesus mean when he says that the Son of Man will be lifted up? How can he, who is not yet fifty years old, preexist Abraham? How can he claim to lay down his life for others?

The answer to these questions is clear to those who know that Jesus is God's Word made flesh. Jesus is going to the Father from whom he came. He is the light of the world because, as the Word of God, he reveals the Father to the world. His death upon the cross will be his exaltation because it will be the moment he returns to the Father. Then all will know that Jesus truly was who he claimed to be. He preexists Abraham because in the beginning the Word was with God (1:1). He lays down his life for his sheep because he is the light of the world who has overcome the world's darkness (1:5).

Equal to God

Jesus' enigmatic claims during the feast of Booths do not satisfy the Jews. Therefore, at the feast of Dedication, they ask him directly, "If you are the Messiah, tell us plainly" (10:24). Jesus responds that he has already told them, but they do not believe because they are not his sheep (10:25–26). But when Jesus says, "The Father and I are one" (10:30), the Jews accuse him of blasphemy "because you, though only a human being, are making yourself God" (10:33).

This controversy between Jesus and the Jews (10:22–39) functions like the trial scene in the Markan passion narrative, where the high priest asks Jesus if he is the Messiah, the Son of the Blessed One. Although Jesus does not respond in the same way as in the passion narrative, the outcome is similar: Jesus is accused of blasphemy.[25]

The ultimate question, then, revolves around messiahship. But whereas the Jews continue to think in traditional terms, the reader of John's Gospel understands that the messianic question has been raised to a new level of which the story's characters are not aware. For the Fourth Evangelist, the Messiah is the preexistent Word of God, the Son whom the Father has sent into the world. This is why the Johannine Jesus can say, "The Father and I are one" (10:30), and, "the Father is in me and I am in the Father" (10:38). The Messiah need not be a descendant of David or come from Bethlehem, for the Messiah comes from God.

Reviewing this rather long section shows that the christological question has reached a high point that can only be understood in light of the prologue. The fundamental christological question is one of origins: where does Jesus come from? To those who are from below, he is merely a human being who comes from Galilee. But to those who have been born from above, he comes from God. He is the preexistent Son whom the Father sent into the world. Because the Father sent him into the world, he and the Father are one (10:30), the Father dwelling in him, he dwelling in the Father (10:38).

Rejection of the Word (11:1–12:50)

The world's rejection of the Word is ironic since it is occasioned by Jesus' last and greatest sign: the raising of Lazarus. This sign, more than any other, shows that Jesus is the source of life, as he claimed in the bread of life discourse. Moreover, Jesus himself tells Martha that he is the resurrection and the life (11:25), leading her to confess that he is "the Messiah, the Son of God, the one coming into the world" (11:27). But despite Jesus' last and greatest sign, the chief priests and Pharisees convene a council, and the high priest, Caiaphas, determines that it is better for one man to die for the people (*hyper tou laou*) than for the whole nation to be destroyed (11:50). From the point of view of the Johannine narrator, Caiaphas unwittingly prophesies that Jesus will not only die for the nation, he will gather into one the scattered children of God (11:51–52).

Aware of his impending death, Jesus interprets his anointing by Mary as an anointing for burial (12:7). He then enters Jerusalem at Passover time to cries that he is the King of Israel (12:13). When some Greeks ask to see him, he knows that the hour has come for the Son of Man to be glorified (12:23).[26] He then proclaims that if he is lifted up from the earth, he will draw all people to himself (12:32). This enigmatic statement leads the crowd to inquire who is this Son of Man. Since they have heard that the Messiah remains forever, they cannot understand how the Son of Man can be lifted up.[27]

This conversation about the Son of Man recalls Jesus' conversation with Nicodemus that the Son of Man must be lifted up (3:14), as well as Jesus' statement that, when the Son of Man is lifted up, people will realize that Jesus is who he says he is: that he truly comes from God (8:28). The crowd's question at the end of Jesus' public ministry, then, brings this discussion to a head. How can he say that the Son of Man must be lifted up? Who is he?

The answer is found in the ambiguous verb that lies behind "to lift up" (*hypsoō*). While it can mean to lift up someone or something physically, just as Jesus will be lifted up when he is crucified, it can also mean to exalt someone. But this is what the crowd does not comprehend. When Jesus is lifted up in crucifixion, he will be exalted because his death will be a triumphal return to the one from whom he came. The Son of Man is Jesus, the one who descended from heaven and is about to ascend from where he came. In light of the prologue, the Son of Man is the incarnate Word who has come from the Father.

The narrator's final verdict about the world is one of rejection. Although Jesus performed many signs, the world did not believe in him (12:37). Jesus himself adds his own testimony. He has come as light into the world. He has spoken not his own words but the words of the Father who sent him. Therefore, those who reject him judge themselves (12:44–50).

By the end of chapter 12, it is clear that the world has not accepted the revelation of God's Word, despite the many signs that Jesus performed. Nonetheless, there are some who have understood, and Jesus turns his attention to them.

The Word's Farewell (13:1–17:26)

In the second half of the narrative,[28] Jesus delivers a farewell discourse to his disciples who, unlike the world, have believed in him.[29] The purpose of this discourse is to prepare them for his departure and the time when they must live in the world without him. This last discourse, then, is the Word's farewell as he prepares to return from where he came.

The Word's farewell is also a profound christological meditation in which Jesus speaks of his origin and destiny. Thus, at the very beginning of the discourse, the narrator says, "Now before the festival of the Passover, Jesus knew that his hour had come to depart from this world and go to the Father" (13:1). In the rest of the discourse, Jesus will develop this theme of departure and return to the Father, thereby disclosing to the disciples the most profound secret of his identity. Moreover, by the end of the discourse, it will become clear that Jesus' death will not be a moment of humiliation and defeat but will be one of exaltation and glorification because it marks his return to the Father.

The content of the first part of the discourse (13:1–14:31) can be summarized in this way. Jesus, the Word made flesh, is about to return to the Father. His return will take place when he is lifted up on the cross, his exaltation and glorification. When he returns to the Father, Jesus will prepare a place for his disciples and will send them another advocate, the Spirit of truth, who will remind them of his words. This Spirit will be his presence to those who believe in him. Because Jesus came from and returns to the Father, there is a profound communion between him and the Father: he is in the Father, and the Father is in him. Thus, Jesus' claim that he and the Father are one (10:30) is confirmed and clarified in this discourse.

In this part of the discourse, Jesus also proposes a series of riddles as he did earlier, when speaking to the Jews (7:33–34; 8:21). For example, he says, "Little children, I am with you only a little longer. You will look for me; and as I said to the Jews so now I say to you, 'Where I am going, you cannot come'" (13:33). When Peter asks where Jesus is going, Jesus tells him that he cannot follow now, but he will follow later (13:36). When Thomas complains that the disciples do not know where Jesus is going (14:5), Jesus responds, "I am the way, and the truth, and the life" (14:6). Philip still does not comprehend and asks Jesus to show them the Father

(14:8), leading Jesus to reply that whoever has seen him has seen the Father (14:9).

A little later, Jesus proposes another riddle: "In a little while the world will no longer see me, but you will see me; because I live, you also will live" (14:19). When Judas (not Judas Iscariot) asks how is it that Jesus will reveal himself to the disciples but not to the world (14:22), it seems that the disciples have begun to grasp something of Jesus' riddles.

In the second part of his discourse (15:1–17:26), Jesus employs the image of the vinegrower, the vine, and its branches to explain the intimate relationship between himself, the Father, and the disciples (15:1–10). He is the vine, the disciples are the branches, and his Father is the vinegrower. Therefore, if they abide in him as he abides in them, they will produce much fruit, for the Father prunes every branch so that it will bear much fruit. The disciples have become Jesus' friends, and he has made known everything he has heard from the Father (15:15).

In 16:5, Jesus clearly says that he is going to the one who sent him. But the riddles are not over, for a few verses later he remarks, "A little while, and you will no longer see me, and again a little while, and you will see me" (16:16), leading the disciples to ask what Jesus means. Finally, he explains, "I came from the Father and have come into the world; again, I am leaving the world and am going to the Father" (16:28). The disciples exclaim that Jesus is speaking plainly and confess, "Now we know that you know all things, and do not need to have anyone question you; by this we believe that you came from God" (16:30).

While Jesus' farewell discourse contains several christological themes, none is more important than the theme of his departure and return to the Father who sent him into the world. To know where Jesus is going is to know where he came from. It is to understand that his death is a moment of return and exaltation rather than of humiliation and defeat. In this regard the farewell discourse is the perfect preparation for the Johannine passion narrative to which we now turn.

The Word's Departure (18:1–21:25)

There is no other section of the Johannine Gospel that so closely parallels the Synoptic tradition as the account of Jesus' passion and death. Nonetheless, there is an immense difference between these accounts. For, whereas the Synoptic Gospels present Jesus' death as a moment of humiliation and apparent defeat, in the Johannine passion narrative Jesus' death is the moment of his glorification. Consequently, there is no agony in the garden or cry of abandonment from the cross. Rather, Jesus is in full control of himself. When the arresting party comes to seize him, for example, he responds "I am he," and those who have come to arrest him fall to the ground; for they have encountered a divine and powerful figure (18:6). Likewise, Jesus' death is described as the completion of his work. Aware that he has finished the work God entrusted to him, he says, "It is finished" (19:30). He then bows his head and gives up his Spirit.[30] In a word, the Johannine passion narrative proclaims Jesus' victory and glorification, leading the thoughtful reader to muse if it is necessary to append any story of Jesus' resurrection.

The Johannine narrator relates the story of Jesus' death in light of the christological motifs he has developed in the rest of the narrative. For example, in the great trial scene before Pontius Pilate, Jesus tells Pilate that his kingdom is not of this world (18:36). He is a king, but he has come into the world to testify to the truth. When the Jews insist that Pilate should put Jesus to death "because he claimed to be the Son of God" (19:7), they reveal the true nature of the trial: it is about Jesus' identity, the point of contention throughout the Gospel. When Pilate hears this, he becomes afraid and asks the fundamental christological question of the Gospel, "Where are you from?" (19:9). The answer, of course, is that Jesus comes from the Father, for he is the one whom the Father has sent into the world.

Although the Johannine resurrection account is anticlimactic in light of this passion story, it contains two christological statements about Jesus' identity. First, when Thomas finally sees Jesus, he confesses that Jesus is his Lord and his God (20:28), the boldest christological confession of the Gospel, apart from the prologue. Then, at the close of chapter 20, the Johannine narrator explains why he has written, "so that you may come to believe that Jesus is the Messiah, the Son of God, and that through believing you may have life in his name" (20:31). From one point of view this is a rather traditional, almost disappointing, confessional statement with which to conclude this Gospel. For it is the kind of statement one would expect to find in the Synoptic Gospels. But in light of the story that the Gospel recounts, it should be apparent that Messiah and Son of God have taken on a more profound meaning than in the Synoptic Gospels. It is to explore this meaning that we turn.

Christology in John's Gospel

Like the Synoptics, the Gospel of John communicates its Christology by telling a story. Consequently, those who read or listen to the narrative are guided by a skillful narrator who presents them with a distinctive portrait of Jesus.[31] At the end of this process, however, readers and listeners will inevitably reflect upon what they have heard or read and raise questions about its narrative logic. I will deal with some of these questions as they pertain to the Christology of the Fourth Gospel.

Identifying Jesus

The Gospel of John identifies Jesus in a number of ways: the Word, the Lamb of God, the Messiah, the King of Israel, the Son of God, the Prophet who is coming into the world, the Savior of the world, the Holy One of God, the Son, the Son of Man, Lord, and God. But at two points, it is evident that "Messiah" and "Son of God" are the primary confessional titles of this narrative. First, when Jesus asks Martha if she believes that he is the resurrection and the life, she replies, "Yes, Lord, I believe that you are *the Messiah, the Son of God*, the one coming into the world" (11:27). Then, at the end of the Gospel, the Johannine narrator echoes Martha's confession when he explains, "But these things have been written so that you may come to believe that Jesus is *the Messiah, the Son of God*, and that through believing you may have life in his name" (20:31).

There is continuity, then, between the Christologies we have uncovered in the Synoptic Gospels and the Fourth Gospel inasmuch as "Messiah" and "Son of God" are the primary confessional titles of these writings. But, to the extent that each of the Gospels gives distinctive meanings to these titles, there is also discontinuity. Or, perhaps we should say, there is growth and development.

1. *Messiah.* There are a surprising number of references to the Messiah (*ho Christos*) in the Fourth Gospel.[32] At the beginning of the Gospel, for example, John denies that he is the Messiah, thereby confirming that Jesus is the Messiah (1:20; 3:28). Then Andrew claims to have found the Messiah in Jesus (1:41). Soon after, Jesus explicitly says that he is the Messiah (4:26), and the Samaritan woman asks if Jesus is truly the Messiah (4:29). The crowds at Jerusalem wonder if Jesus is the Messiah but question his qualification since they know that he comes from Galilee (7:26, 27, 41, 42). As for the religious leaders, they have decided to expel anyone from the synagogue who confesses that Jesus is the Messiah (9:22). Eventually, they demand that Jesus tell them plainly if he is the Messiah (10:24). Finally, Martha correctly confesses that Jesus is the Messiah (11:27).

There is little doubt, then, that the Gospel's final editor wished to emphasize that Jesus was the expected Messiah. But, as is the case with the Synoptics, the Fourth Gospel has profoundly redefined what it means to call Jesus the Messiah. In the Fourth Gospel, the Messiah is the one who comes from above, the one whom God sent into the world. Thus, although the crowd raises the correct question when it debates about Jesus' origin, it does not understand the full significance of its own question. The Messiah's origin is not a matter of Davidic lineage but of descent from above. Jesus is the Messiah because he is the one whom God sent into the world, the Son of Man who comes from above, God's Word made flesh.[33]

2. *Son of God.* Although there are fewer references to Jesus as the Son of God, this title plays a significant role in John's narrative.[34] For example, at the beginning of the Gospel, John testifies that Jesus is the Son of God, and Nathanael confesses, "Rabbi, you are the Son of God! You are the King of Israel!" (1:49). Although Nathanael employs Son of God in apposition to King of Israel, his confession is more profound than he realizes, as the rest of the narrative will show. Thus, in a comment that echoes the prologue, the narrator writes:

> Indeed, God did not send the Son into the world to condemn the world, but in order that the world might be saved through him. Those who believe in him are not condemned; but those who do not believe are condemned already, because they have not believed in the name of *the only Son of God.* (3:17–18)

Although references to "the Son" and "the Son of God" probably represent different strata of tradition, the Gospel account now reads them in light of each other.[35] Thus, whereas Nathanael identifies the Son of God as the king of Israel (the Messiah), the narrator identifies the Son of God as the Son whom the Father has sent into the world. In light of the prologue, it should be clear that the Son of God is the preexistent Son. That Nathanael is unaware of this deeper meaning is not surprising since, as a character of the narrative, he is not privy to the prologue.

In 5:25, "Son of God" appears in a section that otherwise refers to Jesus as "the Son" (5:19, 20, 21, 22, 23, 26). Speaking of the power that the Father has given to the Son, Jesus says, "Very truly, I tell you, the hour is coming, and is now here, when the dead will hear the voice of the Son of God, and those who hear will live" (5:25). These words find an immediate fulfillment in the raising of Lazarus from the dead (11:43), the story in which Martha confesses that Jesus is the Messiah, the Son of God who is coming into the world (11:27). They clearly indicate that Jesus is something more than the traditional Messiah, the King of Israel, for they identify him as the eschatological giver of life.

In the Fourth Gospel, the "trial" of Jesus takes place throughout his public ministry, as he reveals the glory of God to the world. But during the feast of Dedication, there is a scene in which this trial comes to a head. It begins when the Jews ask Jesus if he is the Messiah (10:24). When he says that he and the Father are one, they threaten to stone him for making himself God (10:30–33). Jesus responds, "can you say that the one whom the Father has sanctified and sent into the world is blaspheming because I said, 'I am God's Son?'" (10:36). Jesus then claims that the Father is in him, and he is in the Father (10:38).

Here, the Son of God is again related to the Gospel's Christology of the Son whom the Father has sent into the world. Thus, as the narrative progresses, Nathanael's confession takes on new and deeper meaning. It is not surprising then that the issue at Jesus' trial is the question of his sonship. For when it becomes apparent to the Jews that Pilate is not convinced of Jesus' guilt, they respond, "We have a law, and according to that law he ought to die because he has claimed to be *the Son of God*" (19:7). Although Pilate does not understand the full significance of this statement, he asks Jesus the correct question, "Where are you from?" (19:9). The answer, of course, is that Jesus comes from God and is returning to God.

When readers or listeners come to the narrator's comment that explains why he has written ("so that you may come to believe that Jesus is the Messiah, the Son of God," 20:31), they have received an entirely new understanding of what it means to call Jesus the Messiah, the Son of God. Jesus is Messiah and Son of God, as the Synoptics proclaim, but in a way that none of those authors dared to imagine.

3. *Son of Man.* Although "Son of Man" is not a confessional title in the Fourth Gospel, it is appropriate to consider it at this point. In our study of the Synoptics, we saw that, whereas "Son of God" and "Messiah" are confessional terms, "Son of Man" points to Jesus' destiny as the one who must suffer, die, rise from the dead, and return as God's eschatological agent. "Son of Man" is not a confessional title for the characters *in* the narrative, although it has become a title for the Evangelists and those for whom they wrote.

The situation is similar in the Fourth Gospel, inasmuch as "Son of Man" is not a confessional title for the characters of the story, though it probably has become one for the Evangelist and his community.[36] The situation is also similar inasmuch as Jesus refers to himself as the Son of Man when he speaks of his destiny to be exalted when lifted up on the cross. But the Fourth Gospel also goes its own way. Thus it employs "Son of Man" to clarify Jesus' origin and never refers to him as the Son of Man who will return on the clouds of heaven at the end of the ages.

Jesus refers to himself as the Son of Man for the first time in response to Nathanael's confession: "Very truly, I tell you, you will see heaven opened and the angels of God ascending and descending upon the Son of Man" (1:51). This text is an allusion to Jacob's dream of a ladder between heaven and earth on which the angels of God were ascending and descending (Gen. 28:12). The use of similar language here suggests that Jesus, like the ladder in Jacob's dream, is the means of communication between heaven and earth. Exactly how this occurs, however, is not yet clear.

Shortly after this, Jesus tells Nicodemus that no one has ascended into heaven except the one who descended from heaven, the Son of Man (3:13). Then, he makes the first of three statements that speak of the Son of Man being exalted when he is lifted up.[37]

And just as Moses lifted up the serpent in the wilderness, so must the Son of Man be *lifted up,* that whoever believes in him may have eternal life. (3:14–15)

When you have *lifted up* the Son of Man, then you will realize that I am he, and that I do nothing on my own, but I speak these things as the Father has instructed me. (8:28)

"And I, when I am *lifted up* from the earth, will draw all people to myself." He said this to indicate the kind of death he was to die. The crowd answered him, "We have heard from the law that the Messiah remains forever. How can you say that the Son of Man must be *lifted up?* Who is this Son of Man?" (12:32–34)

Two points are significant here. First the language of ascending and descending in 3:13 recalls Jesus' statement to Nathanael and clearly identifies Jesus as the one who descended from heaven. Second, the language of "lifting up" in 3:14; 8:28; 12:34 points to Jesus as the one who will be exalted when he is lifted up on the cross. Thus, when Jesus realizes that the hour for his death has come, he says that the hour has come for the Son of Man to be glorified (12:23). In referring to himself as the Son of Man, then, Jesus points to himself as the one who comes from God and, paradoxically, will be exalted, that is, glorified, when he is lifted up on the cross.

Son of Man does not refer to a messianic figure for whom people were waiting, since there is no point in the narrative when the crowd exclaims, "So then you are the Son of Man!" Indeed, the crowd is puzzled by this language and asks Jesus who this Son of Man is (12:34). Rather, Son of Man is the manner in which the Johannine Jesus speaks of his origin from God and his destiny to be glorified. Thus, when many of Jesus' followers are scandalized because he has presented himself as the bread of life to be eaten (6:53), he responds, "Then what if you were to see the Son of Man ascending to where he was before?" (6:62).

Although the Fourth Gospel does not employ Son of Man as another messianic title, Jesus' description of himself as the descending and ascending Son of Man who will be exalted by being lifted up on the cross enriches the Gospel's confession of him as Messiah and Son of God.

Jesus' Description of Himself

The claims that Jesus makes for himself constitute one of the most distinctive aspects of the Fourth Gospel when compared with the Synoptics. For, whereas the Synoptic Jesus points to the in-breaking kingdom of God, the Johannine Jesus points to himself. Among the claims he makes are the following:

> I am the bread of life. Whoever comes to me will never be hungry, and whoever believes in me will never be thirsty. (6:35, also 6:41, 48, 51)

> I am the light of the world. Whoever follows me will never walk in darkness but will have the light of life. (8:12)

> Very truly, I tell you, I am the gate for the sheep. . . . Whoever enters by me will be saved, and will come in and go out and find pasture. (10:7, 9)

> I am the good shepherd. The good shepherd lays down his life for the sheep. (10:11, 14)

> I am the resurrection and the life. (11:25)

> I am the way, and the truth, and the life. No one comes to the Father except through me. (14:6)

> I am the true vine, and my Father is the vinegrower. (15:1)

> I am the vine, you are the branches. (15:5)

These are, to say the least, extraordinary claims. We could even say that they tell us more about Jesus than the titles we have examined. Moreover, it is not difficult to grasp the immediate meaning of these claims since the Johannine narrator provides us with signs and discourses to clarify what he intends.

For example, Jesus claims to be the bread of life after he has fed the crowd in the wilderness at Passover time, a sign that leads the people to identify him as "the prophet who is to come into the world" (6:14). But when the crowd reminds Jesus that their ancestors ate manna in the wilderness (6:31), he explains that he is the true bread from heaven whom the Father has given. Later, when Peter exclaims that Jesus has the words of eternal life, it becomes clear that Jesus is the true bread from heaven because only he reveals the Father.

After Jesus claims to be the light of the world, he restores the sight of a man blind from birth. Likewise after claiming to be the resurrection and the life, he raises Lazarus from the dead. Each of these signs, however, points to a reality more profound than the restoration of sight or even life. Jesus is the light of the world because he reveals God to the world, "so that those who do not see may see" (9:39). His revelation is the life of the world. Therefore, even though Lazarus will suffer physical death again, he will not die forever if he believes in the one whom God has sent into the world.

This theme of life is present in Jesus' other claims. For example, Jesus is the gate, and those who enter by him will be saved because they will come to the Father. He is the good shepherd who lays down his life for the life of the sheep by his saving death. He is the way and the truth that leads to life because he goes to the Father. He is the vine without whom the branches cannot live because he reveals God to those who believe in him.

The life and light of which Jesus speaks in these metaphors is the revelation that he brings from God. Or, perhaps it would be more accurate to say, *the revelation that he is from God.* Thus, the central point of these sayings is to identify Jesus as God's life-giving revelation who enlightens the world of human beings who have alienated themselves from God. In doing so, these sayings clarify what it means to call Jesus Messiah and Son of God.

Jesus and the Father

The most significant aspect of Johannine Christology is what Jesus says about his relationship to God. To be sure, the most profound statement of that relationship is the Gospel's opening verse, "In the beginning was the Word, and the Word was with God, and the Word was God" (1:1). The reader who knows that the Word became flesh (1:14), and that Jesus Christ is the incarnation of this Word, knows the most profound secret of the Gospel. But the Gospel also explains the relationship between Jesus and God in other ways.

1. *The one sent into the world.* The Fourth Gospel identifies Jesus as the one whom God has sent into the world. In doing so, it makes use of two verbs, *apostellō* and *pempsō,* both of which mean "to send." The Evangelist, however, uses these verbs in different ways. He normally employs the

first (*apostellō*) in the simple past tense (the aorist) with "God," "Father," "that one," "living Father," or "you" as the subject, and "the Son," "whom," or "me" as the object. For example, in 3:17, he writes, "God did not *send* the Son into the world to condemn the world." And in 5:36, he says, "the Father has sent me." Although the subjects and objects may vary, the basic form remains the same: God (the Father) sent Jesus (the Son) into the world.

The Evangelist employs the second verb (*pempsō*) in a slightly different manner. In most instances, he uses it as a participial phrase that functions as an adjective describing God. Thus, the Greek phrase usually consists of an article, the aorist participle, and an accusative pronoun. Consequently, the phrase functions as an adjective that describes God as the one who sends Jesus. For example, in 4:34 Jesus speaks of "the will of him who sent me," or more literally, "the will of the one sending me." In 8:16 Jesus speaks of the "Father who sent me," or more literally, "the sending-me Father."

These two verbs clarify the relationship between Jesus (the Son) and God (the Father). The theology they develop may be summarized in this fashion. To be saved, the world must know the Father. Therefore, the Father has sent the Son into the world so that in seeing and hearing the Son, the world may see and hear the Father. Jesus' disciples are those who believe that he is the one the Father sent into the world. When Jesus returns to the Father who sent him, he will send his disciples into the world to announce what he has heard and seen in the Father's presence. Thus, the "work" that God requires is to believe in the one whom God has sent (6:29).

2. *Equal but not greater*. Like the Synoptics, the Fourth Gospel portrays the relationship between God and Jesus in terms of Father and Son. The claims of the Johannine Jesus, however, go beyond those of the Synoptic Jesus. For example, Jesus says that he and the Father are one (10:30) and describes this unity in terms of mutual in-dwelling, the Father in him, and he in the Father (10:38). By describing the relationship between God and Jesus in terms of a father and son, the Gospel finds a way to relate Jesus as closely as possible to God without making him another God over and against God.[38]

For example, in chapter 5 the Johannine narrator notes that the Jews were seeking to kill Jesus because he was calling God his own Father, "thereby making himself equal to God" (5:18). After this statement, Jesus describes his relationship to God in terms of a son who can do nothing on his own but only what his father does because his father has shown him everything (5:19–20). Thus, as the Father gives life, the Son gives life; and, if the Son judges, it is because the Father has given all judgment to him. Eventually, Jesus says, "I can do nothing on my own. As I hear, I judge; and my judgment is just, because I seek to do not my own will but the will of him who sent me" (5:30). In effect, this final statement qualifies the earlier statement of the Johannine narrator that Jesus was making himself equal to God. Jesus is equal to God because the Father has shown all things to him, but he cannot do anything apart from God.

The father-son relationship helps to resolve the tension between the narrator's comment in 5:18 that Jesus was making himself equal to God and Jesus' statement that "the Father is greater than I" (14:28). On the one hand, the Father is greater than the Son, as is any father who shows his son all things. But once a son has learned all things from his father, he becomes the father's equal. Thus, though the Johannine Jesus subordinates his will to the Father, he can claim unity, and even equality, with God because he does what the Father has shown him.

The Significance of Jesus

The central theme of the Johannine Gospel is revelation. But what does Jesus reveal? Is he, as some claim, a revealer without a revelation?[39] To be sure, the Johannine Jesus never states what he has seen and heard in the Father's presence. To that extent, he does not bring a new revelation about God. Rather, *the Johannine Jesus is the revelation of God.* To see and hear him is to hear and see the Father. Jesus is the way in which those who believe in him know God. Thus, "the Word" is the perfect concept for expressing the significance of Jesus. For, just as a word reveals the one who utters it, so Jesus reveals the Father who sent him. Put another way, Jesus is the revelatory word of God so that whatever he says and does is the perfect expression of the one who sent him.

THE JOHANNINE EPISTLES

The Johannine epistles provide the occasion for a comparative study in New Testament Christology inasmuch as there is a relationship between them and the Fourth Gospel. First John, for example, seems to presuppose that its audience is familiar with a story of Jesus similar to that narrated in the Gospel. In addressing its audience, however, 1 John brings certain aspects of that story to the foreground and leaves others in the background. But before I discuss this, it is important to say something about the genre, authorship, and dating of these writings.[40]

While 2 and 3 John are authentic letters, the literary genre of 1 John is problematic.[41] It begins with something akin to a prologue (1:1–4) rather than an epistolary greeting, and it concludes with something akin to an epilogue (5:13–21) rather than an epistolary farewell. Consequently, the author and those whom he addresses are never identified, and there is no consensus about the literary genre of this writing at present.[42] However, since the author explicitly focuses on questions of ethics and Christology in 1:5–5:12 in light of a schism within the community (2:18–19), it would appear that 1 John intends to warn and instruct its audience about issues that it views as central to the Christian life.

Although the author of 1 John does not identify himself, he is probably "the elder," the author of 2 and 3 John, since 2 John 7 presupposes a situation similar to that in 1 John: one group of believers seceding from another over questions of Christology and ethics.[43] The more disputed question is the relationship of the elder to the author or final editor of the Fourth Gospel. For, while the canonical titles of these writings give the impression that their author is "John," the complex literary history of the Fourth Gospel suggests otherwise.[44] Therefore, while the author of the epistles is thoroughly familiar with the Johannine tradition, he is not necessarily the author or final redactor of the Gospel, though he may have belonged to the circle of those who contributed to the preservation and growth of the tradition that lies behind it.

More important for the study of New Testament Christology is the literary relationship between the Gospel and epistles. If the epistles were written after or in light of the Gospel, as is usually thought, we can suppose that their author had the Gospel in view. But if the epistles were composed before the composition of the Gospel, or during the period of its composition, we cannot presuppose that their author knew the Gospel.

The Christology of the Johannine epistles plays a central role in the arguments of those who espouse an earlier dating for these writings. Pointing to texts that emphasize (1) Jesus' sacrificial and atoning death, (2) the importance of his flesh, and (3) his coming parousia, they argue that the epistles represent an earlier stage in Johannine Christology.[45] While acknowledging the presence of these traditional christological motifs, Raymond E. Brown and others argue that these texts are best explained as a reaction to a group of Christians which has seceded from the Johannine community. More specifically, the "secessionists," as Brown dubs them, so emphasized Jesus' divine origins that they no longer saw any role for his humanity in the work of salvation.

While it is always dangerous to interpret a document on the basis of a hypothetical situation derived from that document,[46] Brown makes an important point when he notes that the difference in the life situation of the epistles, when compared with that of the Gospel, suggests a later date for the Johannine letters. For, whereas the Gospel deals with external enemies and gives no impression that there are divisions within the community, the epistles focus on an internal dispute that has disrupted the community's life.[47]

Antichrists, False Prophets, and Deceivers

The Johannine epistles identify those who have disrupted the community's life as antichrists, false prophets, and deceivers. At one time, they belonged to the community, at least ostensibly (1 John 2:19; 2 John 7), but their withdrawal from the community proves that they never truly belonged to it. If they had truly belonged to the community, they would confess that Jesus Christ has come in the flesh (2 John 7). But now they have gone beyond the teaching of Christ (2 John 9), and they belong to the world (1 John 4:5). From the point of view of the elder, they deny that Jesus is the Christ. Consequently, they deny the Father and the Son, since any one who denies the Son cannot have the Father (1 John 2:22–23).

On first hearing, it may appear that the elder argues against a Christology from below since one of his major accusations is that those who have left the community deny that Jesus is the Christ and so deny the Father and the Son (1 John 2:22–23). This charge, however, must be read in light of the author's other statements that emphasize that Jesus Christ has come in the flesh (2 John 7), with blood as well as with water (1 John 5:6). Read in light of these texts, the emphasis falls on the denial by the secessionists that *Jesus* is the Christ. Thus, while they recognized Jesus' humanity, they "refused to acknowledge that his being in the flesh was essential to the picture of Jesus *as the Christ,* the Son of God."[48] Whereas the Gospel stresses that Jesus is the *Christ, the Son of God,* the epistles emphasize that *Jesus* is the Christ, the Son of God.[49] The following texts are the author's major statements about those who have left the community.

> Children, it is the last hour! As you have heard that antichrist is coming, so now many antichrists have come. From this we know that it is the last hour. They went out from us, but they did not belong to us; for if they had belonged to us, they would have remained with us. But by going out they made it plain that none of them belongs to us. (1 John 2:18–19)

239

Who is the liar but the one who denies that Jesus is the Christ? This is the antichrist, the one who denies the Father and the Son. (1 John 2:22)

I write these things to you concerning those who would deceive you. (1 John 2:26)

Beloved, do not believe every spirit, but test the spirits to see whether they are from God, for many false prophets have gone out into the world. (1 John 4:1)

and every spirit that does not confess Jesus is not from God. And this is the spirit of the antichrist, of which you have heard that it is coming; and now it is already in the world. (1 John 4:3)

They are from the world; therefore what they say is from the world, and the world listens to them. (1 John 4:5)

Many deceivers have gone out into the world, those who do not confess that Jesus Christ has come in the flesh; any such person is the deceiver and the antichrist! (2 John 7)

Everyone who does not abide in the teaching of Christ, but goes beyond it, does not have God. (2 John 9)

Christ, the Son of God Who Has Come in the Flesh

At the conclusion of the Fourth Gospel, the Evangelist writes, "But these are written so that you may come to believe that Jesus is the Messiah, the Son of God, and that through believing you may have life in his name" (John 20:31). In writing this, the Evangelist identifies "Messiah" and "Son of God" as the primary confessional titles of his Gospel. The Johannine epistles stand in this tradition inasmuch as "Son," "Son of God," and "Christ" remain the primary titles for identifying and confessing Jesus. Thus, "Son" or "Son of God" occur twenty times in 1 John and twice in 2 John, whereas "Christ" occurs eight times in 1 John and three times in 2 John.[50] Unlike the Gospel, however, the Johannine epistles make no reference to Jesus as the "Son of Man,"[51] nor is he identified as the "Word of God," the "Lamb of God," the "Prophet," or the "King of Israel," as he is in the Gospel. However, he is called the "advocate" (1 John 2:1; *parakleton*), the righteous one (1 John 2:1; also see 2:29; 3:7); the "Savior of the world" (1 John 4:14); the "one from the beginning" (1 John 2:13, 14; *ton ap' arches*), the "true God and eternal life" (1 John 5:20; *ho alethinos theos kai zoe aionios*). The primary confessional titles of 1 John, then, are "Son of God" and "Christ," as the following texts show.

240

Who is the liar but the one who denies that Jesus is the Christ? (2:22)

Everyone who confesses the Son has the Father also. (2:23)

every spirit that confesses that Jesus Christ has come in the flesh is from God. (4:2)

God abides in those who confess that Jesus is the Son of God, and they abide in God. (4:15)

Everyone who believes that Jesus is the Christ has been born of God. (5:1)

Who is it that conquers the world but the one who believes that Jesus is the Son of God? (5:5)

Those who believe in the Son of God have the testimony in their hearts. (5:10)

I write these things to you who believe in the name of the Son of God, so that you may know that you have eternal life. (5:13)

The author of the Johannine epistles, however, also adds a new dimension to this christological confession. Convinced that the antichrists have failed to appreciate the importance of Jesus' humanity in the work of salvation, he reminds his audience that Jesus Christ the Son of God has come in the flesh, and not only with water but with water and the blood (1 John 5:6). Thus, not only was the Son of God present in Jesus' baptism (the water), but he was also present in Jesus' death upon the cross (the blood). Consequently, the death of Jesus upon the cross was the death of the Son of God who came in the flesh; it was an atoning sacrifice (*hilasmos*) for sins, as the following texts from 1 John show.

and the blood of Jesus his Son cleanses us from all sin. (1:7)

and he is the *atoning sacrifice* for our sins, and not for ours only but also for the sins of the whole world. (2:2)

because your sins are forgiven on account of his name. (2:12)
You know that he was revealed to take away sins, and in him there is no sin. (3:5)

In this is love, not that we loved God but that he loved us and sent his Son to be the *atoning sacrifice* for our sins. (4:10)

This emphasis on the saving reality of Jesus' humanity, however, does not diminish the importance of his divine origins. For, even though there is no explicit statement of preexistence in the epistles, as there is in the

Gospel prologue, their author alludes to preexistence when he speaks of the Son being revealed, sent into the world, or coming. Thus, the author writes of "the eternal life that was with the Father and was revealed to us" (1 John 1:2). He notes, "The Son of God was revealed for this purpose, to destroy the works of the devil" (1 John 3:8). Likewise, he speaks of God sending his Son into the world (1 John 4:9, 10, 14) and of the Son coming in water and in blood (1 John 5:6), coming so that we may know him who is true (1 John 5:20). If the author writes in light of the Gospel, as many suggest, there is little question that these texts refer to preexistence.

A Story Retold

Even if the author of the Johannine epistles did not have the present form of the Fourth Gospel before him, the theological similarity between his writings and the Gospel suggests that he knew the Johannine story of Jesus in at least an incipient form. Thus, when he writes, "God sent his only Son into the world so that we might live through him" (1 John 4:9), and, "the Father has sent his Son as the Savior of the world" (1 John 4:14), one immediately recalls the central statement of the Gospel which summarizes its main plot: "For God so loved the world that he gave his only Son, so that everyone who believes in him may not perish but may have eternal life" (John 3:16), as well as the confession of the Samaritans, "we know that this is truly the Savior of the world" (John 4:42). Or, when 1 John notes, "We know love by this, that he laid down his life for us" (3:16), one immediately thinks of Jesus the good shepherd who lays down his life for the sheep (John 10:11).

In composing his writings, however, the author of the Johannine epistles has reflected on that story and applied it to a new situation. Aware that some have only focused on death as glorification and despised the flesh of God's Son, he reminds his readers that the Son of God has come in the flesh, by blood as well as by water, so that he might become an atoning sacrifice for the sins of the entire world.

7

The Diverse Unity
of New Testament Christology

*I*t should be clear from even a cursory reading of this book that
there are diverse Christologies in the New Testament. For example, Hebrews confidently presents Jesus Christ as the Son of
God, a high priest according to the order of Melchizedek. While
other writings of the New Testament would agree that Jesus Christ
is the Son of God, each presents Jesus in a distinctive manner.
None of them, however, speaks of Jesus as a high priest according
to the order of Melchizedek.

The diverse Christologies of the New Testament do not always complement each other. For example, it is difficult to reconcile the Synoptic presentation of the Son of Man who will
come at the end of the ages with the Johannine figure of the descending and ascending Son of Man who reveals what he has
seen and heard in the presence of the Father. Likewise, there are
differences between the Gospels of Matthew and Luke on the
one hand, which emphasize the Davidic origins of Jesus' messiahship, and the Gospels of Mark and John on the other, which
make little of his lineage. Beyond such differences and tensions,
however, there is a profound unity to the claims that the New
Testament makes about Jesus in the stories that it tells and presupposes. In what follows, I summarize these claims about (1)
Jesus' messiahship, (2) his significance for Israel and the
nations, (3) his relationship to the church and the world, (4) his
meaning for the human condition, and (5) his relationship to
God.

Jesus Christ, the Messiah of Israel

The most fundamental claim that the New Testament makes about Jesus concerns messiahship: he is the promised Messiah of Israel. Thus, when the New Testament identifies Jesus as Christ, Christ Jesus, or Jesus Christ, it implies that he is the Messiah.

The nature of Jesus' messiahship, however, presented the early church with a challenge: how could one who had been crucified as the king of the Jews be the glorious Messiah of Israel? While the early church eventually found confirmation for its claim in Israel's scriptures, its proof from prophecy tends to presuppose that one already believes that Jesus is the Messiah. Thus, in the Gospel of Luke, the risen Lord opens the minds of his disciples to understand what they could not previously comprehend in the scriptures: that the Messiah had to suffer and die before entering into his glory.

That the risen Lord must open the minds of his disciples to understand the fuller meaning of the scriptures suggests that there is something unique about Jesus' messiahship that goes beyond Israel's messianic expectations. As a result, the early church and the New Testament writers began a process of defining messiahship in terms of Jesus' life, death, and resurrection.

For example, whereas traditional messianic expectation looked forward to a restoration of Israel and its monarchy, the Synoptic Gospels proclaim that Jesus was God's Messiah because he announced and inaugurated the kingdom of God by his life, ministry, death, and resurrection. This, of course, is another way of saying that the Synoptics define messiahship in terms of Jesus, rather than Jesus in terms of traditional messianic expectation. For example, according to the Gospel of Mark, the Messiah is the Son of God who fulfills his destiny as the suffering and rejected Son of Man, who will return at the end of the ages as God's eschatological regent. The Gospels of Matthew and Luke build upon this portrait but develop it in new ways. Thus, for Matthew, Jesus is the Messiah because he is the obedient Son of God who relives the history of his people, Israel, and teaches a righteousness that surpasses that of the scribes and Pharisees. For Luke, Jesus is the Messiah because he suffered and died so as to enter into his glory. Having made his exodus through suffering and death, he is the enthroned Messiah who has become the Lord of all.

In the Pauline writings "Christ" has become, for all practical purposes, a proper name and is rarely used as a title. Nevertheless, there is little doubt that Paul, and those who wrote in his name, acknowledged Jesus as the promised Messiah of Israel. But, as with the Synoptics, it is the life and work of Jesus rather than traditional messianic expectations that define messiahship. The reason for defining messiahship in terms of Jesus, rather than Jesus in terms of messiahship, is especially clear when we come to Paul, whose call and conversion put into question his previous understanding of Israel's story.

Paul had viewed the crucified one as a blasphemer under the curse of God until God revealed that the crucified one was none other than his Son. Consequently, Paul begins the process of defining messiahship in terms of the crucified Christ. Paul can now say that the Messiah is the one God set forth to atone for sins (Romans); the Messiah is the one in whom God has inaugurated the general resurrection of the dead (1 Corinthians); the Messiah is the one in whom the promises to Abraham have been fulfilled (Galatians); the Messiah is the image of God on whose face shines the glory of God (2 Corinthians); the Messiah is the one whose shameful death upon the cross manifested God's wisdom and power (1 Corinthians). The Messiah is the one who will rescue believers from God's wrath (1 Thessalonians); the Messiah is the one who emptied himself and took the form of a slave (Philippians).

The deutero-Pauline letters adopt a similar approach but with new emphases. The Messiah is the Christ who is the head of the church and has overcome every power in heaven and on earth. The Messiah is the Savior God who has manifested himself in the flesh to save sinners and bring salvation to all people. Having appeared once, he will appear again.

Although 1 Peter makes the most extensive use of the suffering servant text of Isaiah 53, it never tries to prove that Jesus was the Messiah on the basis of that text. Rather it presupposes that the one who suffered in this way was God's Messiah. Likewise, instead of proving that Jesus was the Messiah, Hebrews and Revelation focus on his work and presuppose that the one who entered into the heavenly sanctuary by a perfect sacrifice of himself (Hebrews), and the one who shed his blood in witness to God (Revelation), was God's Messiah.

To summarize, although the New Testament claims that Jesus was the Messiah, it insists upon the uniqueness of his messiahship to the point of defining the Messiah in terms of him, rather than defining Jesus in terms of messiahship. Thus, it might be more appropriate to say that the Messiah is the one who does what Jesus did.

Jesus Christ, Israel, and the Nations

If the Messiah is Jesus, then Jesus has a distinctive relationship to Israel. The New Testament affirms this. Thus, the Gospels present Jesus as Israel's Messiah who proclaims the kingdom of God to his own people (the

Synoptics) and brings light (the Gospel of John). However, in each of the stories that the Gospels present, Jesus is rejected by his own people. Thus, the writers of the New Testament faced yet another difficulty. If Jesus was truly God's Messiah, how is it that the majority of Israel did not accept him? Furthermore, if Israel did not accept Jesus as its Messiah, what is Jesus' significance for Israel? The answers that the New Testament gives to these questions are intimately related to yet another issue: the significance of Israel's Messiah for the nations.

All of the Synoptic writers present Jesus in close relationship to the people of Israel. His ministry begins in Israel and is primarily directed to Israel. It is from this people that he chooses his first disciples and sends them on mission to Israel. While Jesus initially encounters a positive reception from Israel, he eventually finds himself in conflict with the very people to whom he proclaims the kingdom of God, especially its leadership. This conflict is essentially one of authority. Does Jesus have the God-given authority to teach, preach, and heal in the service of the kingdom of God, or has he usurped what properly belongs to God? Jesus' death upon the cross seems to belie his ministry, but by raising Jesus from the dead, God vindicates and confirms Jesus' God-given authority. Consequently, according to Acts, his disciples undertake a new mission to Israel that extends even to the nations.

On first hearing, it might seem that the church's Gentile mission was merely the result of Israel's failure to accept Jesus as its Messiah, and, in part, this is true. In the Matthean version of the parable of the vineyard, for example, Jesus says that the kingdom will be taken away from Israel and given to a people who will produce its fruit. And in Acts, Paul says that he will turn to the Gentiles when he is rejected in synagogue after synagogue.

The proclamation of the gospel to the nations, however, is not merely the result of Israel's failure to accept Jesus as the Messiah. All the Gospels seem to presuppose that the Gentile mission finds its ultimate origin in Jesus. Thus in the Gospel of Matthew, the risen Lord commands his disciples to teach all nations, and the Johannine Jesus knows that the hour has come for his glorification when even Gentiles seek to see him. Thus, all the Gospels proclaim the significance of Jesus for the nations as well as for Israel. The one who is Israel's Messiah in a new and unexpected manner is also the Messiah to the nations.

The significance of Jesus for the nations is more clearly apparent in the Pauline writings since Paul identifies himself as the apostle to the Gentiles. But, just as it was vital for Paul to rethink his previous understanding of the Messiah, it was necessary for him to reassess his understanding of the nations in light of Christ.

246

Before his call, Paul was a zealous defender of the law and its prescriptions, which identified Israel as the people of God. Indeed, he undoubtedly persecuted the church because its proclamation of a crucified Messiah contradicted the law. Moreover, Paul probably saw Jewish Christians, such as Stephen and the Hellenists, as breaking down the barriers the law had established between Gentiles and Jews. The essential issue that Paul needed to resolve after his call, then, was the relationship between Jesus and the law.

Prior to his call, he understood God's relationship to Israel and the nations in light of the law, but after his call he understood God's relationship to Israel and the law in light of what God had done in Christ. To put it boldly, Christ superseded the law for Paul. Christ, rather than the law, was the way in which Paul now understood God's plan for Israel and the nations.

As we have seen, Paul undertook a new reading of Israel's story in light of Christ. And now, in the light of Christ, he understood that the promises God made to Abraham were prior to the law in importance as well as in time. He understood that God had always intended to save the Gentiles by faith in Abraham's singular descendant who is Christ. Thus Paul does not envision his mission to the Gentiles as a fallback position because Israel did not accept Jesus as the Messiah. His mission to the Gentiles is an integral part of the gospel he preaches because God always intended to save the nations on the basis of faith in Jesus Christ. In terms of Christology, this means that Jesus has a salvific significance for Gentiles as well as Jews; he is the savior of the nations as well as of his own people. As Paul argues in Romans, Jesus Christ has universal significance for salvation because humanity finds itself in a common predicament: it is under the bondage of sin.

The deutero-Pauline letters tend to give more attention to the significance of Christ for the Gentiles since these writings come from a later period when the Gentile mission had grown and expanded. Ephesians, for example, presents Christ as the one who has broken down the barrier (the law) that separated Gentiles and Jews, creating in himself a new humanity. Christ, then, becomes the reconciler, not only between God and humanity but between Gentile and Jew. Colossians speaks of the circumcision of Christ by which Gentile believers are freed from their carnal body, and the Pastorals present Christ as a universal Savior.

In 1 Peter, Gentile believers are portrayed as God's priestly people and given the prerogatives of Israel. In Hebrews, the singular sacrifice of Christ has universal significance for the forgiveness of sins and makes the rites of the Levitical priesthood irrelevant. Finally, in the book of Revelation those who have endured the great struggle and followed the Lamb are from every tribe and race of humankind. It is not merely Israel that will be saved but all who persevere to the end.

The proclamation of the gospel to the nations, as well as to Israel, is significant for comprehending who Christ is. For, if the Gospel were limited to the people of Israel, Jesus would be a national messiah, and it would be difficult to understand how he is significant for others. Conversely, if the proclamation of the Gospel no longer includes Israel, it is necessary to raise the question of God's faithfulness to Israel, as Paul does in Romans 9–11, where he concludes that God has not rejected his people, and that all Israel will be saved. The witness of the New Testament, however, points to the universal significance of Jesus, who is Messiah to the nations as well as to Israel. In turn, the universal significance of Jesus suggests that he is a unique savior, the one savior who can redeem all from sin and transfer them to the new aeon because he is Israel's promised Messiah.

Jesus Christ, the Church, and the World

The relationship of Jesus Christ to Gentiles and Jews leads to a further issue: how the New Testament relates Christ to the community of believers and to the world in which they live. For, in relating Christ to the church and the world, the New Testament implicitly makes christological claims.

Although the Gospels recount stories of Jesus that occur prior to the time of the church, they reveal something of the church inasmuch as they are written from the perspective of, and for the benefit of, the church. Thus, a reading of these narratives suggests that the community of believers who heard them viewed Jesus as the risen Lord of the church, the one who is present to the church until the end of the ages because God has exalted him to his right hand. At present, the church waits for the return of Jesus in his capacity as the Son of Man, when the kingdom of God will be established in power. At that moment, the world will know beyond doubt that Jesus is God's Messiah and the Lord of all.

In relating its story of the church, the Acts of the Apostles discloses how the church is related to the risen Lord, who has been taken into heaven. Enthroned as Messiah, the risen Lord awaits the moment when he will come again to restore all things. But, in the meantime, he is still present to the church, revealing himself to Paul and even directing the Gentile mission. Thus, there is a keen sense that, even though Jesus has been enthroned in heaven, he is present to the community of believers as it struggles in the world.

In his letters, Paul portrays the church in its relationship to Christ and the world in several ways. For example, the church is the community of those who have been called and sanctified by what God has done in Christ. The church is the community of those who have been purchased at the price of Christ's blood. The church is one body in Christ since all eat of the one bread and drink of the one cup. Thus the church is a community of believers whom God has consecrated and called into being through the saving death and resurrection of Christ. Christ is the church's foundation, and the church exists in him. It is not surprising, then, that Paul uses phrases such as "in Christ," "through Christ," and "for Christ" with such regularity. The risen Lord now defines the boundaries of the church, just as the prescriptions of the law once defined the boundaries of Israel.

Because the church has been consecrated by God and sanctified in Christ, there is a distinction between it and the world. This is not to say that there is no hope for the world, or that the world has already been condemned. Romans is emphatic that the whole creation will be renewed when the final glory of the children of God has been revealed. But before that moment, the church must live between the times: between the old and new aeon. Therefore, it must preserve itself from any defilement that would prevent it from standing pure and blameless on the day of its Lord's parousia.

It is the deutero-Pauline writings, however, especially Colossians and Ephesians, that present the most profound reflection on Christ, the church, and the world. According to these writings, Christ is the cosmic victor who has overcome every power and authority, seen or unseen, on earth or in heaven. God has subjected all things to him, and believers are already raised up with him, seated at his right hand. Christ is the head of the body, which is the church, for which he died, and which he loves as his bride. Consequently, whereas Paul primarily focused on the church as a local community of believers baptized into Christ, and so forming one body in him, the authors of these letters speak of Christ and the church in cosmic terms. Christ's work of salvation and reconciliation has its impact on the entire cosmos, even affecting angelic beings. Nothing, then, escapes God's work in Christ, for in him God has restored and redeemed all things. It is not surprising, then, that the Pastorals identify Christ as a Savior, comparable to God, even though their ecclesiology does not approach that of Paul or his successors.

The book of Revelation portrays the risen Christ as the victor over death, the one who knows and is concerned for the sufferings of the church. Described as one like a son of man, the risen Lord instructs the church during its period of persecution, and he assures it that the final victory has already been won for those who persevere. As the slaughtered Lamb, the lion of the tribe of Judah, the risen Lord is worthy to open the seven-sealed scroll that holds the fate of the world. Thus, Revelation proclaims that the future of the world belongs to the victorious Christ. Because of his saving death and victory over Satan, the entire world will be redeemed, and there will be a new creation.

Although the Fourth Gospel portrays the world as hostile to Jesus, it also proclaims that God did not send his Son into the world to condemn the world but to save it. Moreover, even though Jesus' disciples are not of the world, he sends them into the world, as the Father sent him into the world, to bring the world to the saving knowledge that he is the one whom the Father sent into the world.

To summarize, the New Testament writings present Christ in relationship to the church and the world. In relationship to the church, he is its Lord, the risen One who remains present to it until the end of the ages, its cornerstone and foundation, the one in whom it lives, its head, the one who watches over and guides it. In relationship to the world, the Father has sent him into the world, and he comes into the world as its light to proclaim the kingdom of God. By his death he has saved, redeemed, and reconciled the world, even the cosmic powers that are hostile to God. Risen and alive, he will come again, for God has placed the world's destiny in his hands.

Jesus Christ and the Human Condition

The New Testament affirms that Jesus Christ has significance for Gentile and Jew, church and world, because humanity finds itself in a predicament from which it cannot extricate itself. Although Paul provides the most profound analysis of this situation, the need for salvation is presupposed in all the Christ stories we have uncovered.

For example, in the Synoptic Gospels, Jesus' proclamation that God's kingly rule is at hand presupposes that humanity has gone astray and fallen under Satan's rule. Consequently, Jesus comes to call Israel to repentance and announce the in-breaking rule of God. Through his ministry of preaching, teaching, and healing he inaugurates God's rule, and those who believe in the gospel already live in the sphere of this rule. But it is Jesus' death and resurrection that wins the decisive victory. Surrendering his life as a ransom for many, he is the one who has established a new covenant in his blood for the forgiveness of sins. Consequently, as the risen Lord he can commission disciples to preach the gospel of the kingdom for the forgiveness of sins to all the nations until he returns as the triumphant Son of Man to gather his elect. For the Synoptic Gospels, then, Jesus is the one who frees humanity from its bondage to Satan and sin by inaugurating God's kingly rule.

Although the Gospel of John does not present Jesus as the preacher of the kingdom, it is profoundly aware of humanity's need of salvation. According to its story, humanity dwells in the darkness of sin, unaware of its desperate plight. Therefore, God sends his Son into the world so that the Son can reveal what he has heard and seen in the Father's presence. This revelation brings life and light and frees those who believe in Jesus from the darkness and death that is sin.

Although the Johannine presentation of Jesus as the one who reveals the Father is strikingly different from that of Jesus the preacher of the kingdom of God, the stories of John and the Synoptics make a similar point: humanity is in desperate need of salvation. Under the power of Satan, it dwells in a darkness called sin of which it is not even aware. Therefore, it must be transferred to a realm of life and light, the kingdom of God. However, only one who comes from God can effect such salvation.

Paul was deeply aware of this, and, more than any other New Testament writer, he argued from solution to plight. There would have been no need for God to send his Son into the world if the Mosaic law could have brought humanity to righteousness and life. The fact that God sent his Son into the world, then, convinces Paul that humanity is in need of a salvation that the Mosaic law could not effect.

Paul employs a variety of images to describe what God has done in Christ. For example, he says that humanity has been justified, reconciled, redeemed, and sanctified through the death and resurrection of Christ, thereby implying that humanity was guilty, at enmity with God, in slavery to another power, deprived of God's holiness and glory. Therefore, Christ comes as the justifier, reconciler, redeemer, and sanctifier of the human condition.

Although Paul speaks of the kingdom of God, this concept does not play the major role in his writings that it enjoys in the Synoptic Gospels. Nonetheless, there is a conceptional relationship between the thought of Paul on the one hand, and the Synoptics and John on the other. Like John and the Synoptic authors, Paul is keenly aware that humanity must be transferred from one realm to another in order to be saved. For the Synoptic writers, humanity must be brought into the kingdom of God; for John it must be brought into the realm of light that comes from the Son's revelation. For Paul, humanity must be transferred from the realm of the old Adam, the sphere of sin, death, and the flesh, to the realm of Christ, the sphere of grace, life, and the Spirit. All have sinned, and all are in need of God's grace that has been freely bestowed upon those who believe in what God has done in Christ.

The deutero-Pauline writings continue this train of thought. Thus Colossians proclaims that believers have been transferred from the power of darkness into the kingdom of God's beloved Son, and 1 Timothy speaks of Christ Jesus giving himself as a ransom for all. But, as we have already noted, these writings (especially Colossians and Ephesians) also focus on the cosmic dimensions of Christ's work. Thus, they affirm that God reconciled all things in Christ, making peace through the blood of his cross. God has subjected every power in heaven and on earth under Christ, reconciling humanity to God, and humanity to itself.

Although most New Testament writings presuppose that Christ died for our sins, no writing of the New Testament deals more profoundly with the question of sin, and Christ's sacrifice for sins, than the letter to the Hebrews. Arguing that the death of God's Son has made the temple cult irrelevant, Hebrews presents Christ as a high priest according to the order of Melchizedek, who, after becoming perfected through suffering, offered a perfect sacrifice of himself to God, thereby entering the heavenly sanctuary where he ministers and makes intercession for believers. Like other writings of the New Testament, Hebrews presupposes a dreadful predicament of sin from which humanity could not free itself. And like Paul, it argues from solution to plight: God would not have sent his own Son as an offering for sin if the Levitical cult could have effected the forgiveness of sins. That Christ gave himself as an offering for sin, then, is a clear indication that humanity is in need of a redemption it could not procure for itself.

To summarize, there is a constant witness in the New Testament that God sent Christ to free, liberate, redeem, and save humanity from a predicament of sin and slavery to powers beyond its control. Thus, the New Testament establishes a direct relationship between Christ and the human predicament so that an analysis of the human predicament is determinative for Christology, just as Christology is determinative for an analysis of the human predicament. Put another way, there is only need for a savior if there is a predicament from which humanity cannot free itself. If there is such a predicament, as the New Testament affirms, it defines the kind of savior God has sent into the world.

Jesus Christ and God

Of Christ's many relationships—to Israel, the nations, the church, the world, the human condition—none is more determinative for Christology than his relationship to God. Moreover, how we define Christ's relationship to God determines how we view Christ's significance for Israel, the nations, the church, the world, and the human condition. Put most simply, the more closely Christ is related to God, the more significant he becomes for Israel, the nations, the church, the world, and the human condition.

In most instances, the stories of Christ that we have investigated relate him to God by identifying him as God's Son. Although the content of this title shifts from story to story, there is a constant affirmation that Jesus has a unique relationship to God, for he is the beloved Son of the Father, the one whom the Father has sent into the world. And, because he is God's beloved Son, his ministry and work have redemptive value.

In portraying Jesus as the Messiah, the Synoptic Gospels identify him as the Son of God so that "Messiah" and "Son of God" stand in apposition to each other. Thus, for the Synoptic authors the Messiah is God's Son. Exactly what these writings mean when they identify Jesus as the Son of God, however, can only be determined in light of the stories they tell.

The Gospel of Mark does not explain the nature of Jesus' sonship since it is primarily concerned with the destiny of God's messianic Son. For this Gospel, Jesus' sonship is intimately related to his destiny of suffering and death, as well as resurrection and parousia. Consequently, the Gospel wants to show that no one can confess that Jesus is the Son of God apart from confessing that he is the crucified Messiah. Thus, the Roman centurion is the only human character of the narrative to confess that Jesus was God's Son, and he does this only after Jesus has died.

In contrast to Mark, the Gospels of Matthew and Luke begin a process of reflecting on the nature of Jesus' sonship when, in their infancy narratives, they underscore his virginal conception through the power of God's Spirit rather than through the agency of a human father. Having made this point (independently of each other), they then follow the main lines of Mark's interpretation: namely, that the Son of God is the one who will suffer, die, rise from the dead, and return as the triumphal Son of Man. In following this Markan line, however, Matthew portrays Jesus as the obedient Son of God who relives the history of his people, Israel. Luke, for his part, focuses on Jesus as the Spirit-filled Son of God who proclaims good news to the disenfranchised.

The Synoptic answer to the nature of Jesus' sonship, therefore, is multifaceted. Jesus is God's Son because he is the Spirit-anointed Messiah who obediently follows the destiny of the Son of Man. While other human figures can be called sons of God, Jesus has a unique relationship to God, to the point of being conceived through the power of God's Spirit. It is not surprising, then, that he is the one who can inaugurate the kingdom of God, forgive sins, and call God his Father.

Although the "Son of God" title does not occur as frequently in the

Pauline writings as does "Christ" or "Lord," it underlies Paul's understanding of Jesus. In relationship to believers, Jesus is their Lord; in relationship to God, he is the Son. Thus when God called Paul to preach the gospel, he revealed that Jesus is his Son. From that moment on, Paul realized that the Son of God gave himself for the sins of humanity. In Galatians, therefore, Paul says that the Son of God loved him and gave himself for him. Aware of what the Son of God had already done for humanity by his saving death and resurrection, Paul is confident that God's Son will return at the end of the age to rescue believers from God's wrath.

Generally speaking, Paul's stories of Christ are primarily concerned with the death, resurrection, and parousia of God's Son. But on several occasions, Paul gives intimations of Christ's preexistence. In doing so, however, he never dwells on this concept, nor does he explain it. These intimations of preexistence, especially in Philippians, suggest that the Son of God enjoyed a relationship with God—not yet clearly defined—prior to human history.

In addition to the "Son of God" title, it is important to remember what Paul says of Christ as the "image of God." Jesus Christ is the *eikōn* of God because the glory of God shines on his face, transforming believers from glory to glory. One might even suppose that it was this glory that Paul beheld when God revealed his Son to him.

The deutero-Pauline letters make their own contribution to Paul's theology. For example, Colossians and Ephesians view Christ as filled with the fullness of God, and as the one in whom all things are brought together, whereas 1 and 2 Timothy and Titus focus on Christ as Savior. In identifying Christ as "Savior," however, the Pastorals apply a title to him which, like "Lord," is normally reserved to God. Thus Christ takes on a godly status, and it is not surprising that in the letter to Titus Christ is called "our great God and Savior."

In Hebrews and Revelation, Christology is taken to yet another level, since these writings relate Christ ever more closely to God. Thus Hebrews begins by presenting Christ as the reflection of God's glory and the exact imprint of his very being, through whom God created the world. Then in a series of scriptural quotations, God identifies Christ as the Son who is as far superior to the angels as is the name (Son of God) that he has inherited. In the book of Revelation, the "Son of God" title does not play a major role, though Jesus is clearly identified as God's Son. But it is this writing more than any other except the Fourth Gospel that pulls Christ into the orbit of God's being. Like God, he is the alpha and the omega, the beginning and the end. Only he is worthy to open the scroll, and, seated with God on the throne, he is worshiped by the heavenly court. Thus, at the end of Revelation, God and the Lamb are the temple of the holy city, leaving no doubt that Christ is divine.

The crowning achievement of the Christology in the New Testament, however, is the Gospel of John. With the appearance of this Gospel, there is no doubt that Christ is the preexistent Son of God, the Word of the Father made flesh. While other writings may intimate preexistence, the Fourth Gospel explicitly states it and identifies Jesus as God. More than in any other writing of the New Testament, Jesus calls himself the Son and is identified as the Son of God. Moreover, in identifying Jesus as the Son, the Fourth Gospel speaks of his intimate relationship to the Father: the Father dwells in him, and he dwells in the Father.

To be sure, the several writings of the New Testament do not present Jesus' relationship to God in the same way, even though most of them identify him as the Son of God. For example, if we only possessed the Synoptic Gospels, it would be difficult to argue that Jesus is the preexistent Son of God. But if we only possessed the Fourth Gospel, we might seriously question Jesus' humanity. Or, if we only possessed the Pauline writings, we would hardly appreciate the earthly life and ministry of Jesus. The genius of the New Testament canon is its ability to hold the diversity and unity of the New Testament in a creative tension that requires each generation to correct and deepen its understanding of Christ. Were we able to comprehend Christ once and for all, it would hardly be worth believing in such a savior. That no one writing can comprehend the fullness of his person testifies to the mystery of his being upon which we must reflect again and again.

Abbreviations

NCB	New Century Bible
NICNT	New International Commentary on the New Testament
NIGTC	New International Greek Testament Commentary
NIV	New International Version
NovTSup	Novum Testamentum Supplements
NRSV	New Revised Standard Version
NTS	*New Testament Studies*
NTT	New Testament Theology
PSB	*Princeton Seminary Bulletin*
RB	*Revue biblique*
REB	Revised English Bible
RNAB	Revised New American Bible
RSV	Revised Standard Version
RTP	*Revue de théologie et de philosophie*
SB	Sources Bibliques
SBLDS	Society of Biblical Literature Dissertation Series
SBLMS	Society of Biblical Literature Monograph Series
SBLSBS	SBL Sources for Biblical Study
SBT	Studies in Biblical Theology
SJT	*Scottish Journal of Theology*
SNTSMS	Society for New Testament Studies Monograph Series
SP	Sacra Pagina
StudNeot	Studia Neotestamentica
TDNT	*Theological Dictionary of the New Testament*
TJT	*Toronto Journal of Theology*
TS	*Theological Studies*
TU	Texte und Untersuchungen
TZ	*Theologische Zeitschrift*
WBC	Word Biblical Commentary
WMANT	Wissenschaftliche Monographien zum Alten und Neuen Testament
WUNT	Wissenschaftliche Untersuchungen zum Neuen Testament
ZNW	*Zeitschrift für die neutestamentliche Wissenschaft*

Notes

CHAPTER ONE

1. The earliest letter we have from Paul, 1 Thessalonians, was probably written at the end of the 40s or at the beginning of the 50s. Romans, which may be Paul's last letter, was written about A.D. 57–58. The Gospel of Mark was written about A.D. 70, and the Gospels of Matthew and Luke ten to fifteen years later.

2. Here, I am making a distinction between Christology from above and Christology from below. The Gospel of John exemplifies a Christology from above because its starting point is "from above," the eternal Word of God. In contrast to the Fourth Gospel, the Synoptics represent a Christology from below since their starting point is "from below," from the humanity of Jesus.

3. I presuppose the Two Source theory: Matthew and Luke made use of Mark, as well as a collection of Jesus' sayings and teachings (Q), in the composition of their Gospels.

4. Although there is a longer ending to Mark's Gospel (16:9–20) that includes resurrection appearances of the risen Lord, it is only found in later and less reliable manuscripts. The earliest ending of Mark's Gospel is the story of the empty tomb (16:1–8) with its enigmatic conclusion that the women did not say anything to anyone because they were afraid.

5. For a full explanation of the "plot of conflict" that underlies Mark's Gospel, see Jack Dean Kingsbury, *Conflict in Mark: Jesus, Authorities, Disciples* (Minneapolis: Fortress Press, 1991).

6. The term comes from William Wrede, *Das Messiasgeheimnis in den Evangelien,* 3d ed. (Göttingen: Vandenhoeck & Ruprecht, 1963). Contemporary scholarship understands the nature of this secret differently than did Wrede. See Christopher Tuckett, ed., *The Messianic Secret,* Issues in Religion and Theology 1 (Philadelphia: Fortress Press, 1983).

7. I am drawing on the insights of Meier Sternberg, *The Poetics of Biblical Narrative: Ideological Literature and the Drama of Reading* (Bloomington: Indiana University Press, 1987), especially chap. 7, "Between the Truth and the Whole Truth," 230–63.

8. This statement does not apply to the modern technique of the "unreliable narrator" who purposely leads readers astray. Biblical narrators tend to present themselves as omniscient and reliable, even though they do not tell the whole truth at the beginning of their narratives.

9. Although "prologue" may not be the best term, these verses clearly introduce the Gospel in a way that provides readers with the kind of privileged information that prologues provide.

10. The omniscient stance of the narrator is apparent from comments such as Mark 2:6, "Now some of the scribes were sitting there, questioning in their hearts, 'Why does this fellow speak in this way? It is blasphemy! Who can forgive sins but God alone?' "

11. Not all would agree with this interpretation. Many commentators see Mark 1:1 as a superscription and 1:2–3 as a separate sentence. In connecting v. 1 with vv. 2 and 3, I am following Robert Guelich, *Mark 1–8:26,* WBC 34A (Dallas: Word Books, 1989), 6–8.

12. It is possible to translate *tou euaggeliou Iēsou Christou* as the gospel *of* Jesus Christ; that is, the good news of the kingdom that Jesus preaches. But since Mark is narrating a story about Jesus, it is more likely that he means the good news about Jesus, which includes Jesus' own gospel.

13. On the relationship of the prologue to the good news proclaimed in Isaiah, see Joel Marcus, *The Way of the Lord: Christological Exegesis of the Old Testament in the Gospel of Mark* (Louisville, Ky.: Westminster/John Knox Press, 1992).

14. Although the "Son of God" title is not found in all manuscripts, it probably belongs to the original text of Mark.

15. On the significance of the "Nazarene" title, see Edwin K. Broadhead, "Jesus the Nazarene: Narrative Strategy and Christological Imagery in the Gospel of Mark," *JSNT* 52 (1993): 3–18.

16. By building up character, I mean the process whereby the narrator progressively reveals new information about a character so that readers can draw a full and rich picture of the character for themselves. See John A. Darr, *On Character Building: The Reader and the Rhetoric of Characterization in Luke-Acts,* Literary Currents in Biblical Interpretation (Louisville, Ky.: Westminster/John Knox Press, 1992). For a careful study of the manner in which Mark discloses the identity of Jesus, episode by episode, see Edwin K. Broadhead, *Teaching with Authority: Miracles and Christology in the Gospel of Mark,* JSNTSup 74 (Sheffield: JSOT Press, 1992).

17. Jack Dean Kingsbury (*The Christology of Mark* [Philadelphia: Fortress Press, 1983], 87–89) notes that Mark is developing a contrapuntal pattern here: demonic cry (1:24), question (1:27), demonic cries (1:34), question (2:7), demonic cries (3:11), question (4:41), demonic cry (5:7), question (6:3).

18. The term "Son of Man" will be discussed below.

19. On the significance of these journeys for the Gentiles, see Eric K. Wefald, "The Separate Gentile Mission in Mark: A Narrative Explanation of Markan Geography, The Two Feeding Accounts and Exorcisms," *JSNT* 60 (1995): 2–26.

20. On the use of irony in Mark, see Jerry Camery-Hoggatt, *Irony in Mark's Gospel: Text and Subtext,* SNTSMS 72 (Cambridge: Cambridge University Press, 1992).

21. However, there is an ironic truth hidden in these opinions. All of them suppose that Jesus is a figure from the past who *has been raised* from the dead. While Jesus is not a figure from the past, he *will be raised* from the dead.

22. The phrase "their hearts were hardened" will appear again (8:17). It suggests a lack

of understanding on the part of the disciples because of insufficient faith. Although the disciples believe in Jesus' initial proclamation of the kingdom, in subsequent episodes their faith fails.

23. Earlier, the woman with the hemorrhage was healed by touching Jesus, but now great numbers of people are healed by touching Jesus, and he does not object.

24. Matthew, in editing the account of Peter's confession, emphasizes that Peter's confession was the result of a gift from God (Matt. 16:17).

25. For a description of the royal Davidic Messiah, see *Psalms of Solomon,* no. 17. For a brief explanation of its background, see John J. Collins, *The Scepter and the Star: The Messiahs of the Dead Sea Scrolls and Other Ancient Literature,* ABRL (New York: Doubleday, 1995), 49–56.

26. Exactly where scripture says this, or what text the Markan Jesus has in mind, is not clear. The narrator may have the Psalms of Lament, which describe the fate of God's suffering righteous ones, in mind.

27. I am not counting Jesus' saying in 9:12 as a passion prediction. Thus the three passion predictions are 8:31; 9:31; 10:32–33.

28. I write "unwilling and unable" because the Markan narrator seems to be of two minds about the incomprehension of the disciples. On the one hand, there is an unwillingness on their part to accept Jesus' teaching about the Messiah. On the other, the disciples cannot fully understand who Jesus is until after his death and resurrection.

29. For William Wrede, this is the key text for understanding the messianic secret, as he conceived of it. Wrede argued that the church fabricated the secret of Jesus' messianic identity because Jesus' earthly life was *not* messianic. The church explained this nonmessianic life, according to Wrede, by saying that Jesus purposely kept his messiahship a secret.

30. This use of *Christos* is quite unusual since Jesus does not otherwise refer to himself as the Messiah/Christ. But in this instance, he identifies his disciples as those who belong to Christ. While the absence of the definite article suggests that Christ is a proper name, it is unlikely that its titular sense has been forgotten.

31. On the significance of Jesus as teacher, see Paul J. Achtemeier, "He Taught Them Many Things: Reflections on Marcan Christology," *CBQ* 42 (1980): 456–81.

32. This point will be developed further in the controversy about the Davidic descent of the Messiah (12:35–37).

33. During his Jerusalem ministry, Jesus never spends a night in the city before his arrest.

34. The quotation is from Isa. 56:7, and the reference to a den of robbers is an allusion to Jer. 7:11.

35. Jesus' exegesis of the psalm rests on the supposition of Davidic authorship of the psalms. In Ps. 110:1, the author (David) addresses the royal Messiah as his Lord. But since no father calls his son his Lord, Jesus concludes that the Messiah, David's Lord, is not David's son, as the scribes claim.

36. A similar subordinationalism is found in 1 Cor. 15:28.

37. On the centrality of this confession, see Philip G. Davis, "Mark's Christological Paradox," *JSNT* 35 (1989): 3–18. On the Christology in the passion narrative, see Edwin K. Broadhead, "Form and Function in the Passion Story: The Issue of Genre Reconsidered," *JSNT* 61 (1996): 3–28; and Donald Senior, *The Passion of Jesus in the Gospel of Mark* (Wilmington, Del.: Michael Glazier, 1984), esp. 139–48.

38. Although Mark and Matthew do not call this a new covenant, Luke does (Luke 22:20).

39. On Jesus and the Temple, see Donald Juel, *Messiah and Temple: The Trial of Jesus in the Gospel of Mark,* SBLDS 31 (Missoula, Mont.: Scholars Press, 1977).

40. Although there are longer endings to the Gospel that include resurrection appearances, the best manuscripts conclude the Gospel at 16:8.

41. For a comprehensive study of the narrative Christology, see Kingsbury, *Christology of Mark.*

42. Mark 1:1; 8:28; 9:41; 12:35; 14:61; 15:32.

43. On the background of this title, see James D. G. Dunn, *Christology in the Making: A New Testament Inquiry into the Origins of the Doctrine of the Incarnation* (Philadelphia: Westminster Press, 1980), 13–22.

44. For a detailed study of how Mark uses the term, see Douglas R. A. Hare, *The Son of Man Tradition* (Minneapolis: Fortress Press, 1990), 183–211.

45. In the book of Ezekiel, God frequently addresses the prophet as "son of man," which simply means mortal one. In the book of Daniel, however, the term takes on a more technical sense. "The one like a son of man" is contrasted with the beastlike figures that precede him (see Daniel 7). This "one like a son of man" probably refers to the holy ones of Israel who, after a period of persecution, are about to receive kingship and power from God. This may be the background for Mark's usage. After a period of suffering and persecution, Jesus will receive kingship and power, as did the one like a son of man in the book of Daniel.

46. Although Matthew uses "the kingdom of God," he most often employs "the kingdom of heaven." Both expressions, however, point to the same reality: the rule or kingship of God.

47. See Matthew 5–7; 10; 13; 18; 23; 24–25.

48. For a careful study of the titles Matthew applies to Jesus, see Jack Dean Kingsbury, *Matthew: Structure, Christology, Kingdom* (Philadelphia: Fortress Press, 1975).

49. Consequently, Matthew makes greater use of *kyrios* than does Mark.

50. On the plot of Matthew, see Richard A. Edwards, *Matthew's Story of Jesus* (Philadelphia: Fortress Press, 1985); Frank J. Matera, "The Plot of Matthew's Gospel," *CBQ* 49 (1987): 233–53; Jack Dean Kingsbury, *Matthew as Story,* 2d ed. (Philadelphia: Fortress Press, 1988); Mark Allan Powell, "The Plot and Subplots of Matthew's Gospel," *NTS* 38 (1992): 187–204; M. Eugene Boring, "The Gospel of Matthew: Introduction, Commentary, and Reflections," in *The New Interpreter's Bible: A Commentary in Twelve Volumes,* ed. Leander E. Keck (Nashville: Abingdon Press, 1995), vol. 8, 107–19, 288–94.

51. This point is made by Powell, "Plot and Subplots," and Boring, "Gospel of Matthew," esp. 288–94.

52. Ultimately, however, the disciples prove to be sons of the kingdom of heaven rather than sons of Satan.

53. For an interesting analysis of the genealogy, see Wim J. C. Weren, "The Five Women in Matthew's Genealogy," *CBQ* 59 (1997): 288–305.

54. It is disputed whether or not there is a Son of God theology in chap. 1. See J. Noland, "No Son-of-God Christology in Matthew 1.18–25," *JSNT* 62 (1996): 3–12. I am inclined to think that there is.

55. The word "worship" occurs frequently in this story (2:2, 8, 11). The Magi come to worship Jesus (2:2) and do (2:11). Herod says he wants to worship Jesus (2:8) but does not.

56. This expression occurs several times, and, according to Kingsbury (*Matthew: Structure,* 44–48), it is Matthew's way of reminding the reader of Jesus' divine sonship.

57. On this contrast, see David R. Bauer, "The Kingship of Jesus in the Matthean Infancy Narrative," *CBQ* 57 (1995): 306–23, on whom I am dependent here.

58. Note the quotation "my people, Israel," that is to say, God's people.

59. These are commonly called fulfillment quotations and also occur in the rest of the narrative. Matt. 2:6, however, is not technically a fulfillment quotation since it does not have the introductory formula, "This happened to fulfill . . ."

60. Matthew may have in mind Isa. 11:1 (the Messiah is called a branch [*nēser*] that will bloom from the root of Jesse), or Judg. 13:5, 7 (Samson, Israel's deliverer, is described as consecrated [*nāzîr*] to God). Matthew could have associated either word with Nazarene.

61. As in the case of Mark's Gospel, there is no account of Jesus baptizing with the Holy Spirit and fire in Matthew's story. Matthew and Mark presuppose that their intended audience knows of a Pentecost-like event.

62. "Withdraw" is a favorite Matthean word to describe how the meek and humble Messiah responds in periods of danger. Instead of responding with force or confrontation, he withdraws. See 4:12; 12:15; 14:13; 15:21.

63. Although Galilee was not an exclusively Gentile territory during the time of Jesus, Gentiles lived there.

64. There is no reference to the teaching of the disciples because they will not be empowered to teach until the end of the Gospel (28:20), when Jesus has suffered, died, and risen from the dead.

65. Similar summaries that emphasize Jesus' teaching, preaching, and healing are found in 9:35 and 11:1.

66. There is considerable debate about the nature of the Matthean beatitudes. Are they ethical imperatives or do they proclaim the blessings of the kingdom? While the Matthean beatitudes have an implicit ethical content, inviting disciples to adopt a particular ethical stance, they also announce eschatological blessings that only God's rule can effect. See Mark Allan Powell, "Matthew's Beatitudes: Reversals and Rewards of the Kingdom," *CBQ* 58 (1996): 460–79.

67. Jesus' ascent and descent from the mountain (5:1; 8:1) may recall Moses' ascent and descent from Sinai (Exodus 19 and 34), as Ulrich Luz urges (*The Theology of the Gospel of Matthew*, NTT [Cambridge: Cambridge University Press, 1993], 48), but Matthew has already indicated that Jesus is the Son of God (3:17), not a new Moses.

68. For example, the law forbids murder, Jesus forbids anger. The law forbids adultery, Jesus forbids lust. The law requires those divorcing their wives to give a written notice of divorce, Jesus forbids divorce except in cases of gross immorality. The law forbids false oaths, Jesus tells his disciples not to swear oaths. The law limits retaliation, Jesus forbids retaliation. The law calls one to love one's neighbor, Jesus calls disciples to love even their enemies. On this point, see W. D. Davies and Dale C. Allison, *The Gospel according to Matthew: A Critical and Exegetical Commentary,* ICC (Edinburgh: T. & T. Clark, 1988), vol. 1, 505–9.

69. The sign of Jonah will be Jesus' death and resurrection. As Jonah was in the belly of the whale, so will the Son of Man be in the heart of the earth. Although Jesus makes no explicit reference to his resurrection, it is implied, for as Jonah was rescued from the belly of the whale, the Son of Man will be rescued from death.

70. This statement is phrased in such a way that it recalls wisdom motifs, but I do not think that Matthew's purpose is to view Jesus as wisdom incarnate. His Christology focuses on Jesus as the Messiah, the Son of God, rather than on divine wisdom. See Frances Tay-

lor Gench, *Wisdom in the Christology of Matthew* (Lanham, Md.: University Press of America, 1997).

71. There is no essential difference between the kingdom of heaven and the kingdom of the Son of Man. Jesus does not have his own kingdom that is somehow different from God's rule. The kingdom of the Son of Man is yet another way of speaking of God's rule. The metaphor, however, does portray Jesus in a new role: God's eschatological regent.

72. See Matt. 16:27–28, where Jesus speaks of himself as the Son of Man who will return with his kingdom. This kingdom is not another kingdom over and against the kingdom of heaven. It is another way of speaking of God's rule.

73. Jesus also uses Son of Man to refer to his humble state (8:20) and his authority on earth (12:8), but in this section of the Gospel the emphasis clearly falls upon the suffering and future glory of the Son of Man.

74. There are references to the kingdom of the Son of Man in 13:41 and 16:28, but I take both of these expressions as alternate ways of speaking about God's eschatological rule.

75. Notice that Jesus' question in 16:13 is, "Who do people say the Son of Man is?" Peter's answer in 16:16 is, "You are the Messiah, the Son of the living God."

76. Note that this description is part of a section in which Jesus also reveals the intimate relationship between the Son and the Father (11:25–30).

77. For a description of just such a messiah, see *Psalms of Solomon* 17.

78. This point is made by Kingsbury, *Matthew: Structure,* 99–103.

79. There is a certain tension between this description of the Son of Man's parousia and that in 24:30–31, which makes no mention of judgment. This is probably due to Matthew's use of different traditions. The present form of the story, however, clearly indicates that the Son of Man will do much more than gather the elect; he will also judge the nations.

80. See John T. Carroll and Joel B. Green, eds., *The Death of Jesus in Early Christianity* (Peabody, Mass.: Hendrickson, 1995), 39–59, and Donald Senior, *The Passion of Jesus in the Gospel of Matthew* (Wilmington, Del.: Michael Glazier, 1985).

81. Note that the high priest's question (26:63) ironically echoes Peter's confession (16:16), and Jesus' Son of Man saying alludes to Ps. 110:1 and Dan. 7:13.

82. This point is made by Robert Guelich, *The Sermon on the Mount: A Foundation for Understanding* (Waco, Tex.: Word Books, 1982).

83. On this point, see Arland J. Hultgren, *Christ and His Benefits: Christology and Redemption in the New Testament* (Philadelphia: Fortress Press, 1987), 69–89.

84. On the Son of Man in Matthew, see Hare, *Son of Man Tradition,* 113–82.

85. See Matt. 24:30b and 26:64, both of which have parallels in Mark; Matt. 10:23; 12:40; 24:27, 37, 39, 44, which come from the Q tradition; and Matt. 10:23; 13:41; 16:27, 28; 19:28; 24:30a; 25:31, which are special to Matthew.

86. This point is made by Hultgren, *Christ and His Benefits,* and it is further developed by Rudolf Schnackenburg, *Jesus in the Gospels: A Biblical Christology* (Louisville, Ky.: Westminster John Knox Press, 1995), 74–130.

CHAPTER TWO

1. From the point of view of source criticism, Luke composed his Gospel in the following way. First, he employed five blocks of Markan material (Mark 1:1–15 = Luke 3:1–4:15; Mark 1:21–3:19 = Luke 4:31–6:19; Mark 4:1–9:40 = Luke 8:4–9:50; Mark 10:13–13:32 = Luke 18:15–21:33; Mark 14:1–16:8 = Luke 22:1–24:12). Second, he in-

serted two blocks of material from Q and other traditions available to him (L) into his Markan source. This material is called the small interpolation (Luke 6:20–8:3) and the large interpolation (9:51–18:14). Third, he introduced an infancy narrative that is peculiar to him (Luke 1–2), as well as additional stories regarding the risen Lord (Luke 24). Fourth, he omitted the following Markan material: Mark 6:45–8:26 (the great omission) and Mark 9:41–10:12 (the small omission).

2. On the Christology of Luke's Gospel, see the following: H. Douglas Buckwalter, *The Character and Purpose of Luke's Christology,* SNTSMS 89 (Cambridge: Cambridge University Press, 1996); Joseph A. Fitzmyer, *The Gospel according to Luke I–IX,* AB 28 (Garden City, N.Y.: Doubleday, 1981), 192–258; A. George, *Études sur l'oeuvre de Luc,* SB (Paris: Gabalda, 1987), 215–82; Joel B. Green, *The Theology of the Gospel of Luke,* NTT (Cambridge: Cambridge University Press, 1995); Jack Dean Kingsbury, *Conflict in Luke: Jesus, Authorities, Disciples* (Minneapolis: Fortress Press, 1991); Hultgren, *Christ and His Benefits,* 76–85; Schnackenburg, *Jesus in the Gospels,* 131–218. The first chapter of Buckwalter's volume provides a helpful review of research into Lukan Christology.

3. Matthew and Mark allude to the period after Jesus' death and resurrection when they speak of the parousia (Mark 13 and Matthew 24–25), but neither narrates the events that follow Jesus' resurrection, as Luke does in Acts.

4. See the classic volume of Henry J. Cadbury, *The Making of Luke-Acts* (London: SPCK, 1968, first published in 1927 by the Macmillan Co. of New York).

5. For a careful literary study of Luke-Acts that illustrates how Luke accomplishes this, see Robert C. Tannehill, *The Narrative Unity of Luke-Acts: A Literary Interpretation,* vol. 1: *The Gospel according to Luke;* vol. 2: *The Acts of the Apostles* (Minneapolis: Fortress Press, 1986, 1990).

6. This point is made by Jacob Jervell, *The Theology of the Acts of the Apostles,* NTT (Cambridge: Cambridge University Press, 1996).

7. "Deuteronomistic history" refers to the history of Israel contained in the books of Deuteronomy, Joshua, Judges, 1 and 2 Samuel, and 1 and 2 Kings. In 1943, Martin Noth proposed that these writings are the result of an earlier, hypothetical source that he called the Deuteronomistic History. He proposed that this source was written during the exile to explain why the exile occurred: Israel had not been faithful to the covenant as set forth in the Deuteronomistic law.

8. For a critical study of the prologue, see Loveday Alexander, *The Preface to Luke's Gospel: Literary Convention and Social Context in Luke 1.1–4 and Acts 1.1,* SNTSMS 78 (Cambridge: Cambridge University Press, 1993).

9. The majority opinion is that Luke was primarily writing to Gentiles. See Robert Maddox, *The Purpose of Luke-Acts,* Studies of the New Testament and Its World (Edinburgh: T. & T. Clark, 1982). But in a series of scholarly essays, Jacob Jervell has argued that Luke had a Jewish audience in view. See the concise and compelling statement of his position in *Theology of the Acts.* Hans Conzelmann did not even consider the infancy narrative in his classic work, *The Theology of St. Luke* (New York: Harper & Row, 1961, originally published by J. C. B. Mohr in 1953).

10. It is interesting to note that the Western text (D) of Simeon's canticle omits any references to the nations. Consequently, the canticle refers exclusively to the salvation of Israel.

11. I am of the opinion that Luke was writing for the type of believers described in the Acts of the Apostles: Jewish Christians, and Gentiles who had previously attached themselves to the synagogue ("God-fearers"). Thus Luke writes with a double audience in view:

Jews and Gentiles who believe that Jesus is the Messiah. He views his audience as the restored people of God rather than as a new Israel.

12. In this important text God promises David that his dynasty will last forever. "He shall build a house for my name, and I will establish the throne of his kingdom forever. I will be a father to him, and he shall be a son to me. . . . Your house and your kingdom shall be made sure forever before me; your throne shall be established forever" (2 Sam. 7:13–14, 16). These promises were revised as the fortunes of the Davidic monarchy changed. Compare Ps. 89:26–37 and Ps. 132:11–12 with this promise

13. The words of Zechariah in 1:77 suggest that this salvation is closely tied to the forgiveness of sins. Note that like Luke, Paul emphasizes the covenant with Abraham rather than the Mosaic covenant. On this point, see Galatians 3.

14. Like Matthew, Luke does not present Jesus as a physical descendant of David, for Joseph is not Jesus' biological father. Joseph, a descendant of David, has adopted Jesus into David's royal line.

15. But he will be designated as Savior in Acts. On Jesus as Savior, see George, *Études sur l'oeuvre de Luc,* 237–56.

16. Note how Isaiah, Jeremiah, and Ezekiel begin their prophecies by dating when the word of the Lord came to them.

17. Luke then omits the story of John's imprisonment that Matthew and Mark tell later in their narratives (Matt. 14:3–12; Mark 6:17–29).

18. This is part of Luke's strategy to show the superiority of Jesus to John. The same strategy also occurs in the infancy narrative where Luke narrates the announcement, birth, and circumcision of John and Jesus in a way that portrays Jesus as superior to his forerunner.

19. Luke consistently portrays Jesus at prayer before the important moments of his life. On the role prayer plays in Luke's christological portrait of Jesus, see George, *Études sur l'oeuvre de Luc,* 395–427, and Schnackenburg, *Jesus in the Gospels,* 210–18.

20. The Lukan genealogy differs from that found in Matthew's Gospel, which begins with Abraham and presents Jesus as the Messiah, the son of David, the son of Abraham. Luke's genealogy, which begins with Joseph, is more intent upon emphasizing that Jesus, the son of David, the son of Abraham, the son of Adam, is the Son of God.

21. The word "today" (*sēmeron*) plays an important role in Luke's Gospel. It stresses the present dimension of salvation the Messiah brings. See Luke 2:11; 19:9; 23:43.

22. This text is a mixed text from Isa. 61:1–2 and 58:6. This suggests that Luke, or the tradition he inherited, has carefully reflected upon it.

23. The citizens of Nazareth are unaware of the way in which Jesus was conceived and of the narrator's remark that Jesus was the son "as was thought" of Joseph (3:23).

24. Whereas the Markan Herod identifies Jesus as the Baptist raised from the dead (Mark 6:16), the Lukan Herod does not since Luke studiously avoids any suggestion that John and Jesus are equal.

25. On the composition and Christology of chap. 9, see Joseph A. Fitzmyer, "The Composition of Luke, Chapter 9," in *Perspectives on Luke-Acts,* ed. Charles H. Talbert (Danville, Va.: Association of Baptist Professors of Religion, 1978), 139–52.

26. Luke is the only Evangelist to explain what Jesus, Moses, and Elijah were discussing at the transfiguration: Jesus' exodus, which includes the events of Jesus' passion, death, resurrection, and return to the Father.

27. Luke does not develop the theme of the disciples' incomprehension in the way that Mark does. Moreover, Luke omits Peter's rebuke of Jesus, which occurs after the first pas-

sion prediction (Mark 8:32). For the Lukan narrator, the meaning of the passion and resurrection sayings are hidden from the disciples until after the resurrection (Luke 9:45; 24:25–27, 44–45).

28. This point is made by Jack Dean Kingsbury, "Jesus as the 'Prophetic Messiah' in Luke's Gospel," in *The Future of Christology: Essays in Honor of Leander E. Keck,* ed. Abraham J. Malherbe and Wayne Meeks (Minneapolis: Fortress Press, 1993), 29–42.

29. Luke's understanding of the relationship between the titles "Messiah" and "Son of God" is illuminated by an incident in which Jesus rebukes the demons for shouting that he is the *Son of God,* "because they knew that he was the *Messiah*" (4:41). For Luke the two titles are coterminous. The Messiah is God's Son.

30. The Gospel of Luke differs from the Gospels of Mark and Matthew in its presentation of the journey. First, the journey (rather than Peter's confession) is the turning point in Luke's narrative. Second, the journey consists of nearly ten chapters in Luke, whereas in Mark it consists of a single chapter (Mark 10), and in Matthew two chapters (19–20). Most of the material in the Lukan journey section is taken from Luke's special material (L) and the material he has in common with Matthew (Q). Beginning at 18:14, however, Luke rejoins his Markan source and makes use of Markan material. The precise meaning of the journey is greatly disputed. See Frank J. Matera, "Jesus' Journey to Jerusalem (9:51–19:46): A Conflict with Israel," *JSNT* 51 (1993): 57–77; and David P. Moessner, *Lord of the Banquet: The Literary and Theological Significance of the Lukan Travel Narrative* (Minneapolis: Fortress Press, 1989).

31. This remark refers primarily to the Lukan Jesus rather than the historical person Jesus. Whether or not the Jesus of history had such a messianic consciousness of his destiny is not the concern of this chapter.

32. Jesus is called teacher several times in this section (20:21, 28, 39; 21:7). Moreover, only Luke portrays him as "proclaiming the good news" during the period of his temple ministry (20:1).

33. Since the pronoun "them" (*autous*) in 20:41 refers to the scribes in 20:39, it would seem that this question is addressed to them. In Mark 12:35 the question is addressed to the crowds.

34. Unlike Mark's Gospel, in which Jesus delivers this discourse on the Mount of Olives (Mark 13:3), in Luke's Gospel Jesus delivers this final discourse in the Temple. Moreover, it now appears that the audience includes the people as well as the disciples (21:5). The instructions regarding the coming persecution, however, seem to be intended for disciples rather than the crowds in general (20:12–19).

35. Note that in Mark 13:11, it is the Holy Spirit who will speak through the disciples.

36. Joseph A. Fitzmyer (*The Gospel according to Luke 10–24,* vol. 28a [Garden City, N.Y.: Doubleday, 1985], 1347) interprets the times of the Gentiles as the time until the triumph of the Romans over the city of Jerusalem is complete.

37. This same conflict with the religious leaders will occur in the Acts of the Apostles when the apostles will teach in the Temple, thereby threatening Israel's religious leaders. In Luke's view, the apostles have become the eschatological rulers of the reestablished Israel. See Jacob Jervell, *Luke and the People of God: A New Look at Luke-Acts* (Minneapolis: Augsburg, 1972), esp. 41–112.

38. For helpful introductions to Luke's passion narrative, see Carroll and Green, *Death of Jesus in Early Christianity,* and Donald Senior, *The Passion of Jesus in the Gospel of Luke* (Wilmington, Del.: Michael Glazier, 1989).

39. The reader of Luke's narrative knows, on the basis of the story thus far, that both charges are false. Jesus has not claimed to be the Messiah; indeed, he has even questioned the nationalistic notion of the Messiah as the Son of David (20:41–44). Nor has he forbidden people to pay taxes to Caesar (20:20–26).

40. Most English translations render *dikaios* in 23:47 as "innocent," especially in light of Pilate's triple declaration that he finds no guilt in Jesus. But in my view, Luke sees a deeper significance to the term here. Jesus dies as the truly righteous Son of God since he (not his persecutors) stands in the proper relationship to God. In Acts, Jesus is called the Righteous One (3:14; 7:52; 22:14). See Frank J. Matera, "The Death of Jesus according to Luke: A Question of Sources," *CBQ* 47 (1987): 469–85.

41. John the Baptist also preached a baptism for the forgiveness of sins (3:3), but whereas John preached to Israel to prepare the way for the Messiah, the apostles will preach a forgiveness of sins in Jerusalem and beyond that has been effected by the Messiah.

42. Note that in 7:30 the Lukan narrator speaks of the plan of God (*tēn boulēn tou theou*) that the Pharisees rejected by refusing to be baptized by John. On this divine plan, see Green, *Theology of the Gospel of Luke*, 22–49.

43. Luke does make an important remark about the soteriological significance of Jesus' death in Acts 20:28. In my view, Luke assumes the soteriological significance of Jesus' death but does not develop it as do other New Testament writers.

44. Peter's comment at Pentecost that God has made Jesus Messiah and Lord (Acts 2:36) should be read in light of the angel's announcement to the shepherds that a savior has been born who is Messiah and Lord (Luke 2:11). Since the resurrection is the moment when God enthrones his Son, Israel should now know who Jesus *always* was.

45. On this point, see Jervell, *Theology of the Acts of the Apostles*, 61–75.

46. On the theme of the restored Israel, see Jacob Jervell, *Luke and the People of God: A New Look at Luke-Acts* (Minneapolis: Augsburg, 1972), esp. the essay, "The Divided People of God: The Restoration of Israel and Salvation for the Gentiles," 41–46.

47. The literature on the speeches of Acts is immense. For a helpful orientation to the literature, see the careful work of Marion L. Soards, *The Speeches in Acts: Their Content, Context, and Concerns* (Louisville, Ky.: Westminster John Knox Press, 1994). For an understanding of the speeches in their narrative context, see Tannehill, *Narrative Unity of Luke-Acts*, vol. 2. For a study of Luke's christological use of scripture in the speeches, see Darrell L. Bock, *Proclamation from Prophecy and Pattern: Lucan Old Testament Christology*, JSNTSup 12 (Sheffield: JSOT Press, 1987). For a discussion of how the speeches were intended to function, see the seminal essay of Martin Dibelius, "The Speeches of Acts and Ancient Historiography," in *Studies in the Acts of the Apostles* (London: SCM Press, 1956).

48. These speeches are delivered before the election of Judas's replacement (1:16–22); at Pentecost (2:14–40); in Solomon's Portico (3:12–26); before the Jewish authorities (4:8–12); before the Jewish authorities again (5:29–32); to the household of Cornelius (10:34–43); to the circumcision party (11:5–17); and at the apostolic conference (15:7–11).

49. This point is made by Tannehill, *Narrative Unity of Luke-Acts*, vol. 2, 20.

50. A similar story time is presupposed in Peter's speech to the household of Cornelius (10:34–43). But in that speech, the plotted time anticipates Jesus' return as judge (10:42).

51. Whereas "story time" or "the time of the story" is the actual time of the story (from the birth of Jesus to his ascension), the "plotted time" includes past and future events that are not part of the actual story but are referred to, or presupposed by, the story. For exam-

ple, in Luke-Acts the plotted time would include the history of Israel as well as Jesus' parousia. Thus the story of Jesus is part of a larger narrative, the story of Israel.

52. For a helpful discussion of the use of *kyrios* in Luke-Acts, see George, *Études sur l'oeuvre de Luc,* "Jésus, 'Seigneur,'" 237–55, esp. 240–42.

53. In 4:29, "Lord," in the prayer of the church, clearly has God in view. But in Stephen's prayer, the address "Lord" has Jesus in view (7:59–60).

54. Tannehill, *Narrative Unity of Luke-Acts,* vol. 2, 39.

55. This remark is not meant in a derogatory sense. It simply means that this Christology begins from below (with the humanity of Jesus) rather than from above (with Jesus' divinity).

56. For other references to the name in the first part of Acts, see 2:38; 3:6, 16; 4:7, 10, 12, 17, 18, 30; 5:28, 40, 41; 8:12, 16; 9:14, 15, 16, 21, 27, 28.

57. Soards, *Speeches in Acts,* 34.

58. One might have expected the narrator to write "in the name of Jesus of Nazareth" or "in the name of the Christ who is Lord." Instead, the narrator attaches "Christ" to the name of Jesus, whom he remembers as a human being, the Nazorean.

59. Soards, *Speeches in Acts,* 40.

60. This contrast between what human beings did at the passion of Jesus and what God did by the resurrection to reverse their actions is a constant theme of Peter's speeches.

61. Note that in the Gospel, Jesus heals a paralytic and forgives his sins (5:17–26). That incident foreshadows what happens in this episode.

62. Acts 3:21 is the only occurrence of *apokatastasis* ("restoration") in the New Testament. See the article of P. G. Müller, s.v. *apokathistēmi,* EDNT, vol. 1, 129–30.

63. J. A. Bühner, s.v. *pais,* EDNT, vol. 3, 6.

64. Ibid.

65. In John 6:69, Peter confesses that Jesus is the Holy One of God.

66. Luke is not simply saying that Jesus was innocent of the charges made against him; he affirms that Jesus was righteous in God's eyes; he was the suffering Righteous One.

67. See the article of P. G. Müller, s.v. *archēgos, TDNT,* vol. 1, 163–64. The word occurs only four times in the New Testament (Acts 3:15; 5:31; Heb. 2:10; 12:2).

68. I treat the prayer of the early church as a speech, as does Soards, *Speeches in Acts,* 47–50.

69. The expression "to hang on a tree" alludes to Deut. 21:22, and at the time of the New Testament it was a way of referring to crucifixion.

70. In the speeches before the Sanhedrin, there is no call for the religious leaders to repent as there is in Peter's speeches at Pentecost and in the Temple since the Lukan narrator sees little hope that the religious leaders will repent.

71. On these contacts, see Soards, *Speeches in Acts,* 77. Some of these points of contact are the baptism of John, the anointing of Jesus, Jesus' witnesses, the contrast formula, the description of crucifixion as hanging on a tree, and the forgiveness of sins in his name.

72. Bock (*Proclamation from Prophecy and Pattern*) sees this as the culmination of the Christology in Acts. It also explains why the Christology of Acts tends to be found in the first half of the book.

73. The use of *laon* here suggests that this is a word of encouragement for the people of Israel, as the sermon will confirm.

74. "God-fearers" refers to Gentiles who attached themselves to the Jewish synagogue but did not formally convert to Judaism by having themselves circumcised.

75. Note the similarity of this part of the speech with 1 Thess. 1:9–10, a text that suggests the content of Paul's preaching to Gentiles.

76. At the conclusion of his study of the speeches in Acts, Soards (*Speeches of Acts*) identifies "The Operation of God's Plan" as one of the major and consistent themes of the speeches. See pp. 187–89.

77. These "defense speeches" are delivered to the inhabitants of Jerusalem (22:3–21); the Jewish high council (22:30–23:10); Felix (24:10–21); Agrippa and Festus (26:2–23).

78. Whereas Paul tends to present his encounter with the risen Lord as a call in Galatians, Luke tends to present it as a conversion that has elements of a call.

79. Acts has already identified Jesus as the Righteous One in two other speeches (3:14; 7:52).

80. In the original quotation from Ex. 3:12, the place that Israel will worship God is the mountain of Horeb, but in Stephen's speech "this place" also refers to the Temple (6:14). Playing upon this phrase, Stephen seems to have the Temple in mind when he quotes from Ex. 3:12.

81. There are other parallels that I have chosen not to develop. Among them is the manner in which Joseph, Moses, and Jesus appear a second time to offer those who rejected them an opportunity to repent. Joseph appears a second time as the vice-regent of Egypt. God sends Moses to visit Israel for a second time. And Jesus appears after his resurrection to commission his disciples to preach repentance for the forgiveness of sins to Israel for a second time (the first time being his own ministry to Israel).

82. While I presuppose that Luke also had Jewish Christians in view, it seems to me that the majority of his intended audience was made up of Gentile believers, many of whom would have been former God-fearers.

83. George (*Études sur l'oeuvre de Luc,* 242) identifies thirteen instances in Acts where it is difficult to decide if "Lord" refers to Jesus or to God: 2:20, 47; 8:22, 24; 9:31; 10:33; 13:2; 14:3, 23; 15:40; 16:14, 15; 20:19.

CHAPTER THREE

1. See Stanley K. Stowers, *Letter Writing in Greco-Roman Antiquity,* Library of Early Christianity 6 (Philadelphia: Westminster Press, 1986).

2. See Leander E. Keck, *Paul and His Letters,* Proclamation Commentaries (Philadelphia: Fortress Press, 1979), 15–17.

3. J. Christiaan Beker, *Paul the Apostle: The Triumph of God in Life and Thought* (Philadelphia: Fortress Press, 1980), 23–36.

4. This is the approach of W. Kramer, *Christ, Lord, Son of God,* SBT (Naperville, Ill.: Alec R. Allenson, 1966).

5. This is the position of Hultgren, *Christ and His Benefits.*

6. These terms are explained by Joseph A. Fitzmyer, *Romans: A New Translation with Introduction and Commentary,* AB 33 (New York: Doubleday, 1993), 116–24. Also, see his essay, "The Christology of the Epistle to the Romans," in Malherbe and Meeks, *Future of Christology,* 81–90.

7. For example, Lucien Cerfaux, *Christ in the Theology of St. Paul* (New York: Herder & Herder, 1963). This work was originally published in 1951 as *Le Christ dans la Théologie du Saint Paul.*

8. See Richard B. Hays, *The Faith of Jesus Christ: An Investigation of the Narrative*

Substructure of Galatians 3:1–4:11, SBLDS 56 (Chico, Calif.: Scholars Press, 1983), and Ben Witherington III, *Paul's Narrative Thought World: The Tapestry of Tragedy and Triumph* (Louisville, Ky.: Westminster John Knox Press, 1994).

9. The closest he comes is Galatians 1–2, where he gives an extended autobiographical statement; Phil. 2:6–11, where he tells the Christ story in poetic or hymnic fashion; and Romans 9–11, where he deals with the question of Israel.

10. In speaking of the "grammar" of Paul's thought, I am using the vocabulary found in the stimulating article of Leander E. Keck, "Toward the Renewal of New Testament Christology," *NTS* 32 (1986): 362–77.

11. Although Paul tells his readers little about the events of Jesus' life, it is not unreasonable to assume that Paul and his readers knew more about Jesus than Paul indicates in his letters. Thus, if Paul told his converts even a rudimentary story of Christ when he preached to them, it would not be necessary for him to repeat that story when writing to them.

12. On the grammar of Christology, Keck ("Toward the Renewal of New Testament Christology," 363) writes: "the subject-matter of christology is really the syntax of relationships or correlations. In developed christology this subject of signification is expressed in relation to God (the *theo*logical correlation proper), the created order (cosmological correlation), and humanity (the anthropological correlation); each of these impinges on the others whether or not the impingement is made explicit. Consequently, from statements about God or world or humanity one can infer the appropriate christological correlates, and vice versa."

13. Peter Brooks, *Reading for Plot: Design and Intention in Narrative* (New York: Alfred A. Knopf, 1984), 5.

14. James D. G. Dunn ("Prolegomena to a Theology of Paul," *NTS* 40 [1994]: 407–32, 423) writes, "In enquiring after the theology of Paul, it is not realistic to attempt to confine ourselves to the theology of Paul's individual letters. At best that would give us the theology of Paul's controversies, rather than the theology of Paul. More important, however, the letters themselves, by their very character as one side of a dialogue, and by the very frequency of allusion which they contain, leave us no choice but to inquire after the fuller theology on which the particular letters draw, the fuller theology and context which surely inform the light and shade, the emphasis and lack of emphasis of the individual passages in the letters and thus enables us to build up a picture with both depth and focus and width of angle." This "fuller picture" of which Dunn speaks is akin to the story that underlies Paul's thought.

15. This is the approach of Witherington, *Paul's Narrative Thought World.*

16. For a description of this background, see David A. DeSilva, " 'Worthy of His Kingdom': Honor Discourse and Social Engineering in 1 Thessalonians," *JSNT* 64 (1996): 49–79.

17. This is the position of Karl P. Donfried, "The Theology of 2 Thessalonians," in *The Theology of the Shorter Pauline Letters,* Karl P. Donfried and I. Howard Marshall, NTT (Cambridge: Cambridge University Press, 1993), 83–89.

18. Jürgen Becker (*Paul: Apostle to the Gentiles* [Louisville, Ky.: Westminster/John Knox Press, 1993], writes: "Christology is found primarily as expectation of the coming of the Lord. Jesus' death (4:14; 5:10) and resurrection (1:10; 4:14) are seen this way. They do not have the independent meaning that they have later—for example, as early as 1 Corinthians."

19. Becker, ibid., 139, has a different point of view. "The God of the patriarchs becomes the God in Christ. Then the new understanding of history is significant: those addressed by

the gospel *are not inserted into a long history of salvation* [emphasis mine] but orient themselves toward the imminent judgment, the coming Lord, the Spirit of the end time."

20. On the theology of election in Paul's letters, see T. J. Deidun, *New Covenant Morality in Paul*, AnBib 89 (Rome: Biblical Institute Press, 1981). Although Paul does not explicitly speak of a new covenant here, in 1 Cor. 11:25 and 2 Cor. 3:6 he does so.

21. The Pauline authenticity of this text is disputed since many find its anti-Jewish tone incongruent with Paul's theology of Israel, especially as presented in Romans 9–11. But there is no external evidence that this text is a later interpolation, and it is not inconceivable that Paul could speak in such harsh tones about Jews who did not accept Christ.

22. The identity of the lawless one and the restrainer, or the restraining force, is much debated. For a discussion of this difficult text, see Earl J. Richard, *First and Second Thessalonians*, SP 11 (Collegeville, Minn.: Liturgical Press, 1995), 322–54.

23. The last expression is somewhat unusual and occurs in 1 Thess. 2:15, 19; 3:13; 4:1, 2.

24. Most commentators agree that Paul is quoting from an earlier tradition, but the precise extent of the tradition that he quotes is disputed. It may have comprised vv. 3b–7.

25. This point is made by Keck, *Paul and His Letters,* 44.

26. For an exposition of the role that wisdom played in Paul's Christology, see Ben Witherington III, *Jesus the Sage: The Pilgrimage of Wisdom* (Minneapolis: Fortress Press, 1994), esp. chaps. 6–7.

27. See Seyoon Kim, *The Origin of Paul's Gospel* (Grand Rapids: Wm. B. Eerdmans Publishing Co., 1981). For further discussion of Adam Christology in Paul, see Dunn, *Christology in the Making,* 98–128, and Morna D. Hooker, *From Adam to Christ: Essays on Paul* (Cambridge: Cambridge University Press, 1990).

28. See Beker, *Paul the Apostle,* 135–81.

29. On the theme of glory in Paul's Christology, see Carey C. Newman, *Paul's Glory-Christology: Tradition and Rhetoric,* NovTSup 69 (Leiden: E. J. Brill, 1992).

30. See the discussion of Richard B. Hays, *Echoes of Scripture in the Letters of Paul* (New Haven, Conn.: Yale University Press, 1989), 122–53. I am indebted to Hays for much of what follows.

31. Ibid., 131–49.

32. For background on the Galatian correspondence, see F. J. Matera, *Galatians,* SP (Collegeville, Minn.: Liturgical Press, 1992), 1–26.

33. See Hays, *Faith of Jesus Christ,* 85–137, for an analysis of the narrative structure of Galatians, and his "Christology and Ethics in Galatians," *CBQ* 49 (1987): 268–90.

34. Indeed, the only explicit reference to the resurrection in this letter is 1:1.

35. Here I am making an exegetical choice that Paul intends the subjective genitive, "the faith of Christ." This will be explained below.

36. Dunn (*Christology in the Making,* 40–44) strongly contests this.

37. This point is made by Brendan Byrne, "Christ's Pre-Existence in Pauline Soteriology," *TS* 58 (1997): 308–30, and Hultgren, *Christ and His Benefits,* 7–8.

38. On the faith of Jesus Christ, see Hays, *Faith of Jesus Christ,* 139–91; Morna D. Hooker, "Pistis Christou," *NTS* 35 (1989): 321–42; George Howard, "Notes and Observations on the 'Faith of Christ,'" *HTR* 60 (1967): 459–84; Matera, *Galatians,* 92–104. This faith is Christ's faithfulness to God, which is distinguished by his obedience to, and his trust in, God.

39. See Karl P. Donfried, *The Romans Debate: Revised and Expanded Edition* (Peabody, Mass.: Hendrickson, 1991).

40. These points are made by Fitzmyer, *Romans,* 79.

41. Ibid., 69.

42. On this point see Fitzmyer, ibid., 507–9.

43. Ibid., 416. The Vulgate reading, *in quo omnes* ("in whom all") suggests that all humanity sinned in the person of Adam.

44. See Fitzmyer, ibid., 116–24.

45. To clarify this point, the law made God's will known, thereby making it possible for human beings to violate his commandments in a specific manner. But from Paul's Christian perspective, the law could not empower humanity to do what is good; for the power of sin ruled over humanity and prevented it from doing the law's just requirements.

46. I suspect that preexistence is implied here, but Dunn (*Christology in the Making,* 44–45) disagrees.

47. See Morna Hooker, "Interchange in Christ," *JTS* n.s. 22 (1971): 349–61.

48. Two authors who argue for the concept of "the faith of Christ" in Romans are Leander E. Keck, "'Jesus' in Romans," *JBL* 108 (1989): 443–60, and Luke Timothy Johnson, "Romans 3:21–36 and the Faith of Jesus," *CBQ* 44 (1982): 77–90. Keck understands the faith of Christ in terms of the fidelity/obedience of Jesus (p. 458), whereas Johnson places greater emphasis upon the obedience of Jesus as the expression of his faith (pp. 87–90). The majority of commentators, however, still favor the traditional reading, "faith *in* Christ."

49. This point is made by Witherington (*Paul's Narrative Thought World,* 129–30): "If we ask why Adam and Abraham are writ large on Paul's thought but Moses comes in for lesser mention and David almost none at all, I suspect the answer lies in the fact that the Apostle to the Gentiles, whether consciously or unconsciously, is trying to ground his own telling of the drama of salvation in the more universal stories, stories that would be more congenial for Gentiles to appropriate, identify with, and in some respects model themselves on."

50. Romans 9:5 presents an important problem of punctuation that has significance for Christology; namely, does "God," in the concluding benediction of this verse, refer to Jesus or the Father? See the discussion of Raymond E. Brown (*An Introduction to New Testament Christology* [Mahwah, N.J.: Paulist Press, 1994], 182–83). He is swayed by the evidence that Paul attributes the title "God" to Jesus.

51. This point is made by Frank Thielman, *Paul and the Law: A Contextual Approach* (Downers Grove, Ill.: InterVarsity Press, 1994), 205–8.

52. See Stanley K. Stowers, "Friends and Enemies in the Politics of Heaven: Reading Theology in Philippians," in *Pauline Theology,* Vol. 1: *Thessalonians, Philippians, Galatians, Philemon,* ed. Jouette M. Bassler, 105–21 (Minneapolis: Fortress Press, 1991). Stowers argues that Philippians is a hortatory letter of friendship.

53. The place of Paul's imprisonment is disputed. I favor a Roman imprisonment rather than one in Ephesus or Caesarea. If this is correct, then Philippians comes after Romans, chronologically. But there is no certainty on the point of Paul's imprisonment, and if he wrote from Ephesus, Philippians precedes Romans, chronologically.

54. See the following passages in the LXX where the verb *gogguzein* is used in this context: Ex. 16:7; 17:3; Num. 11:1; 14:27, 29; 16:41; 17:5. This point is also made by Thielman (*Paul and the Law,* 156–58).

55. However, see the King James and the Douay Rheims, which translate this phrase as "the faith of Christ."

56. If the text in 3:9 is translated as an objective genitive, then the following phrase, "based on faith," seems redundant ("through faith in . . . based on faith"). But if the text is

construed as a subjective genitive, then Paul says that the righteousness based on faith is mediated *through* the faithful act of Christ for all who believe *in* Christ.

57. Hooker, "Pistis Christou," 332.

58. One can suppose that this Christ story formed the content of Paul's preaching at Philippi.

59. Paul seems to be speaking of believers here.

60. "Savior" is not a title in the undisputed Paulines, as it is in the Pastorals. And in this instance it is not used with a definite article. But Paul does use the verb "to save" in relation to Christ (Rom. 5:9–10), and so one can see the development from Paul to his successors.

61. For example, notice the similarity between Phil. 3:21 and Paul's discussion of the resurrection body in 1 Cor. 15:42–53. In both texts, it is clear that the lowly or earthly body will be changed and transformed according to the pattern of a glorious resurrection body. There is also a relationship between Phil. 3:21 and 2 Cor. 3:18, where Paul writes that believers are being transformed from one degree of glory to another, as well as with 1 Cor. 15:27, which speaks of God subjecting everything to the Son.

62. Although there is no certainty that this passage actually represents an early Christian hymn, I employ the terminology "Christ hymn" from time to time, without prejudice to the text's genre.

63. For a comprehensive review of the possible options, see N. T. Wright, *The Climax of the Covenant: Christ and the Law in Pauline Theology* (Minneapolis: Fortress Press, 1992), 56–98, esp. the helpful chart on 81.

64. For example, Dunn, *Christology in the Making,* 114–21, and Jerome Murphy-O'Connor, "Christological Anthropology in Phil. 2:6–11," *RB* 83 (1976): 25–50.

65. This is the position of Stephen E. Fowl, *The Story of Christ in the Ethics of Paul: An Analysis of the Function of the Hymnic Material in the Pauline Corpus,* JSNTSup 36 (Sheffield: JSOT Press, 1990), 49–101. I am indebted to him for many of the concepts presented in this section.

66. EDNT, ed. Horst Balz and Gerhard Schneider, 3 vols. (Grand Rapids: Wm. B. Eerdmans Publishing Co., 1990, 1991, 1993), vol. 2, 443.

67. Fowl (*Story of Christ,* 54) writes, "It seems most adequate, then, to take the *morphē* of God as a reference to the glory, radiance and splendor by which God's majesty is made visible. By locating Christ in this glory, it conveys the majesty and splendor of his pre-incarnate state." Dunn (*Christology in the Making,* 115) writes, "*morphē theou* probably refers to Adam having been made in the image (*eikōn*) of God and with a share of the glory (*doxa*) of God." If what Dunn says about *morphē theou* is so, it is odd that Paul chose *morphē* rather than *eikōn.*

68. For a summary of the patristic evidence, see J. B. Lightfoot, *Saint Paul's Epistle to the Philippians: A Revised Text with Introduction, Notes, and Dissertations* (London: Macmillan & Co., 1891), 133–42.

69. Dunn, *Christology in the Making,* 114–21.

70. C. A. Wanamaker, "Philippians 2.6–11: Son of God or Adamic Christology?" *NTS* 33 (1987): 183. Others who have criticized Dunn's position are Brendan Byrne, "Christ's Pre-Existence in Pauline Soteriology"; Wright, *Climax of the Covenant,* 56–98; Witherington, *Paul's Narrative Thought World,* 94–105; and Marshall, "Theology of Philippians," in Donfried and Marshall, *Theology of the Shorter Pauline Letters,* 127–37.

71. Cerfaux (*Christ in the Theology of St. Paul,* 384–85) writes, "The booty, then, is not

a *res rapta* not yet a *res rapienda*. Rather it is an object which is doubtlessly possessed justly, but which must not be used proudly or as if out of bravado."

72. This is the position taken by Wanamaker in "Son of God or Adamic Christology?"

73. For example, while Wright (*Climax of the Covenant,* 61) defends the preexistence of Christ in this passage, he writes, "Servant-christology and Adam-christology belong well together, and cannot be played off against each other. Both, in the last analysis, are *Israel-christologies.*"

74. The case for this is made by Wanamaker.

75. This point is made by Byrne ("Christ's Pre-Existence in Pauline Soteriology").

CHAPTER FOUR

1. For a discussion of the pseudonymous nature of these letters, see Raymond F. Collins, *Letters That Paul Did Not Write: The Epistle to the Hebrews and the Pauline Pseudepigrapha,* GNS 28 (Wilmington, Del.: Michael Glazier, 1988). Although I treated 2 Thessalonians in the previous chapter, most scholars classify it as deutero-Pauline.

2. For a brief discussion of how the deutero-Paulines develop Paul's thought, see J. Christiaan Beker, *Heirs of Paul: Paul's Legacy in the New Testament and in the Church Today* (Minneapolis: Fortress Press, 1991).

3. J. B. Lightfoot, *Saint Paul's Epistles to the Colossians and to Philemon* (London: Macmillan & Co., 1879), 122.

4. Ibid.

5. I employ the expression "hymnic passage" rather than "hymn," for though it is possible that an earlier hymn underlies 1:15–20, there is no way to establish the extent, original wording, or life setting of that hymn, despite the diligent work of many.

6. As regards these two passages, Witherington (*Paul's Narrative Thought World,* 107) notes that whereas Colossians is about Christ's cosmic victory, Philippians is about his personal vindication.

7. Many scholars argue that the early hymn is found in 1:15–18a (Christ's work in creation) and that the author of this letter added 1:18b–20 (Christ's redemptive work) to further explain the significance of Christ. For an introduction to these questions, see A. J. M. Wedderburn, "The Theology of Colossians," in Andrew T. Lincoln and A. J. M. Wedderburn, *The Theology of the Later Pauline Letters,* NTT (Cambridge: Cambridge University Press, 1993), 12–22. For a more detailed exegetical study, see Jean-Noël Aletti, *Colossiens 1,15–20: Genre et exégèse du texte. Fonction de la thématique sapientielle,* AnBib 91 (Rome: Biblical Institute Press, 1981).

8. The outline I propose is similar to that of Petr Pokorný, *Colossians: A Commentary* (Peabody, Mass.: Hendrickson, 1991), 23–26.

9. In this section, the author uses the first-person singular. Previous to this, he employed the first-person plural (1:3–14), the third-person singular (1:15–20), and the second-person plural (1:21–23). The key word *mystērion* ("mystery") occurs three times (1:26, 27; 2:2).

10. The nature of this "philosophy" is one of the most disputed questions of New Testament Studies. See Wedderburn ("Theology of Colossians," 3–12) for a brief introduction.

11. If Paul is the author of Colossians, we can suppose that the Christ story he has been developing throughout his ministry is in the background of his thought. But even if someone else writes in his name, it is likely that this person is familiar with Paul's writings and the Christ story they presuppose.

12. For the concept of a "spiritual" circumcision, see Phil. 3:3, where Paul writes, "For it is we who are the circumcision, who worship in the Spirit of God and boast in Christ Jesus and have no confidence in the flesh." Also, see Paul's comments on circumcision in Rom. 2:25–29, where he distinguishes between physical circumcision and circumcision of the heart.

13. For example, Colossians says that the life of believers is hidden above, where Christ is enthroned. When Christ appears, they will appear with him in glory (3:1–4). Thus, the temporal dimension is modified by a spatial dimension.

14. Aletti (*Colossiens*, 98–140) maintains that the passage emphasizes Christ as the sole mediator of creation and redemption.

15. Since Christ is the mystery, Col. 4:3 can speak of "the mystery of Christ" as well as "the mystery of God."

16. For a helpful exposition of the concept of "mystery" in Paul, see Cerfaux, *Christ in the Theology of St. Paul*, 402–38.

17. Although this is the only occurrence of the "Son of God" title in Colossians, it underlies what the author has to say about Christ in this letter. For example, note that this section (1:2–23) begins with Paul giving thanks to God who is the *Father* of our Lord Jesus Christ (1:3), thereby indicating that Jesus is God's Son. "Lord" occurs more frequently than "Son of God," because it expresses the relationship between the believer and Christ and is the way that believers address the risen Christ. But it is "Son" or "Son of God" that most adequately identifies Jesus' relationship to God and discloses his identity. On the Son of God in Pauline Christology, see Cerfaux, ibid., 439–60.

18. The other occurrences of the term in the New Testament are Luke 2:7; Rom. 8:29; Heb. 1:6; 11:28; 12:23; Rev. 1:5.

19. Dunn, *Christology in the Making,* 190; also see 187–94.

20. Although Paul's language is specific here, one should remember that it is metaphorical since one can hardly imagine what it means to say that God created the world in the sphere of Christ. On the use of these prepositions, see Fowl, *Story of Christ,* 107–12.

21. Here the preposition can be understood in terms of time or rank: The Son is temporally prior to all things; the Son is superior to all things in rank. Or, the phrase may combine both meanings: The Son who is prior to all things in time is superior to all things.

22. Whereas the earlier hymn viewed Christ as the head of the cosmos, the alleged gloss makes him the head of the church.

23. This point is also made by Cerfaux, *Christ in the Theology of St. Paul,* 420–24, and by N. T. Wright, "Poetry and Theology in Colossians 1.15–20," *NTS* 36 (1990): 444–68, 462.

24. For a summary of the issues, see Fred O. Francis and Wayne A. Meeks, eds., *Conflict at Colossae,* SBLSBS 4 (Cambridge, Mass.: Scholars Press, 1975), as well as the introductions to the commentaries of M. Barth, J. D. G. Dunn, F. F. Bruce, E. Lohse, R. P. Martin, P. T. O'Brien, P. Pokorný, and E. Schweizer.

25. In this regard, Hultgren (*Christ and His Benefits,* 91–143) is correct when he identifies the Christology of Colossians as redemption won by Christ, whereas he categorizes the Christology of the undisputed Pauline letters as redemption accomplished in Christ.

26. My comment on this enigmatic verse is purposely vague. The New Revised Standard Version translates the verse in a manner that suggests Christ's triumph over the authorities and powers: "He disarmed the rulers and authorities and made a public example of them, triumphing over them in it." However, Roy Yates ("Colossians 2.15: Christ Triumphant," *NTS* 37 [1991]: 573–91) argues for an alternate translation that does not view

the authorities and powers as enemies over which Christ triumphed: "Having stripped himself in death, He boldly made an open display of the angelic powers, leading them in triumphant (festal) procession on the cross" (591). This translation does not view the rulers and powers as enemies of Christ.

27. Most scholars who view Colossians and Ephesians as deutero-Pauline subscribe to the hypothesis that the author of Ephesians knew and made use of Colossians. However, the use of Colossians by Ephesians, or Ephesians by Colossians, are not the only possible solutions. Ernest Best ("Who Used Whom? The Relationship of Ephesians and Colossians," *NTS* 43 [1997]: 72–96) argues that the authors of Colossians and Ephesians were members of a Pauline school and discussed with each other the Pauline theology they inherited. Thus they produced similar writings, even though each wrote independently of the other.

28. Ernst Käsemann, "The Theological Problem Presented by the Motif of the 'Body of Christ,'" in *Perspectives on Paul* (Philadelphia: Fortress Press, 1971), 102–21, esp. 120–21.

29. Ernst Käsemann,"Ephesians and Acts," in *Studies in Luke-Acts,* Leander E. Keck and J. Louis Martyn, ed. (Philadelphia: Fortress Press, 1966), 288–97, esp. 288.

30. I agree with the remark of Brevard S. Childs (*The New Testament as Canon: An Introduction* [Philadelphia: Fortress Press, 1985], 327), that "the claim that ecclesiology has replaced christology in the letter to the Ephesians badly misconstrues the message of the book."

31. The words "in Ephesus" are absent from Papyrus 46, as well as the uncials, Sinaiticus, Vaticanus, 6, 424, and 1739.

32. The historical Paul warned the Gentile Christians at Rome not to boast of their newfound grace, as if God had forsaken Israel (Rom. 11:13–24). While Ephesians reminds its Gentile believers of their new relationship to the commonwealth of Israel, there is no indication that they have been boasting at Israel's expense. The problem seems to be one of forgetfulness and neglect.

33. Here, the author is most likely referring to the revelation of Jesus Christ associated with Paul's call. See Gal. 1:12, 15–17.

34. One would not expect the historical Paul to speak to the believers of Ephesus in this manner, which suggests that they have never seen him, since Paul spent three years in Ephesus, according to Acts. Thus, the tone of the letter is an indication that its author was not Paul. However, Child's (*New Testament as Canon,* 326) makes a shrewd remark about the canonical function of the text: "If Paul directs his letter to the Ephesian church which he once knew so well, the reader of the epistle would be led to infer that the purpose of his letter must be to address that new generation of Ephesians about whose faith he had only heard secondhand."

35. Colossians also refers to a hidden mystery, but whereas Ephesians speaks of the union of Jewish and Gentile believers as the mystery of Christ (Eph. 3:4–6), Colossians speaks of Christ as the mystery of God (Col. 2:2).

36. On the liturgical dimensions of Ephesians and its relationship to the Jewish *berakhah,* see J. C. Kirby, *Ephesians: Baptism and Pentecost: An Inquiry into the Structure and Purpose of the Epistle to the Ephesians* (London: SPCK, 1968).

37. Although the text speaks only of God's beloved, *en tōēgapēmenō* (1:6), there is little doubt that the author views the beloved as God's Son, for he calls God the *Father* of Jesus Christ and explicitly refers to Christ as God's Son in Eph. 4:13. Moreover, the use of

"the beloved Son" in Col. 1:13 suggests that "the beloved" in Ephesians should be interpreted as God's beloved Son. It is not surprising, then, that some manuscripts (D* F G) add the words "his Son."

38. For other places where God is described in similar terms, see 1:2, 17; 5:20; 6:23. When God is called Christ's Father, sonship is implied.

39. The notion of "mystery" occurs several times in Ephesians (1:9; 3:3, 4, 9; 5:32; 6:19), as it does in Colossians (1:26, 27; 2:2; 4:3). But whereas Colossians defines the mystery as Christ (2:2), Ephesians gives it an ecclesiological dimension (3:3–6). This notion of mystery has its immediate roots in the undisputed Pauline writings (Rom. 11:25; 1 Cor. 2.1, 7; 4:1; 15:51).

40. The preposition has been interpreted mythically, mystically, existentially, sacramentally, locally, historically, eschatologically, and ecclesially. Here, the basic issue is whether it should be taken in an instrumental or local sense. See the discussion in Markus Barth, *Ephesians: Introduction, Translation, and Commentary on Chapters 1–3,* AB 34 (Garden City, N.Y.: Doubleday, 1974), 69–71, and C. F. D. Moule, *The Origin of Christology* (Cambridge: Cambridge University Press, 1977), 54–69.

41. The manner in which Ephesians applies Psalm 68 to Christ and then interprets the psalm also suggests a notion of preexistence. See Eph. 4:8, "When it says, 'He ascended,' what does it mean but that he had also descended into the lower parts of the earth?"

42. References to the blood of Christ do not occur frequently in the Pauline writings. See Rom. 3:25; 5:9; 1 Cor. 10:16; 11:25, 27; Eph. 1:7; 2:13; Col. 1:20.

43. See the references to the blood of Christ (2:13) and the cross of Christ (2:16).

44. See the article by H. Merklein, s.v. *anakephalaioō,* EDNT, 1:82–83.

45. For a helpful discussion of this theme, see Martin Kitchen, *Ephesians,* New Testament Readings (London and New York: Routledge, 1994), 35–42.

46. There are places where Ephesians points to the future (1:14, 18, 21; 4:30; 5:5, 6; 6:13). But even when Ephesians retains apocalyptic language, there is no indication of a coming apocalyptic event such as one finds in the undisputed Pauline writings.

47. In contrast to Ephesians, Colossians still anticipates such an event. See Col. 3:4.

48. In Rom. 5:2, Paul writes, "we boast in our hope of sharing in the glory of God," and in Rom. 9:4, he lists "glory" as one of the prerogatives that belongs to Israel. See the extended section on the hope of future glory in Rom. 8:18–30.

49. Papyrus 46 does not contain the phrase "in the heavenly places."

50. There is a definite article before Christ in 1:20 (*en tō Christō*), which suggests that Christ is being used in a titular sense.

51. Moule, *Origin of Christology,* 70.

52. This is not to say that the functional dimension of the church is forgotten. See Eph. 4:7–13, where Ephesians lists the gifts (apostles, prophets, evangelists, pastors, teachers) that Christ bestows upon the church to equip it for ministry.

53. The Greek participle *plēroumenou* can be taken as a middle with an active sense, thus Christ is the one who is filling all things. Or it can be taken as a passive, Christ is being filled. For a helpful discussion, see Barth, *Ephesians,* 183–210.

54. Ibid., 159.

55. Most newer translations take this phrase (*tou plērōmatos tou Christou*) in an adjectival sense and render it "to the measure of the full stature of Christ" (NRSV).

56. On this chapter, especially 2:12–19, see Ralph P. Martin, *Reconciliation: A Study of Paul's Theology,* New Foundations Theological Library (Atlanta: John Knox Press,

1981), 157–98, and Peter Stuhlmacher, "'He Is Our Peace' (Eph. 2:14): On the Exegesis and Significance of Ephesians 2:14–18," in *Reconciliation, Law, Righteousness: Essays in Biblical Theology* (Philadelphia: Fortress Press, 1986), 182–200.

57. While Colossians also says that believers were raised with Christ, it does not claim that they have been seated with him. Raised with Christ, believers must seek what is above, where Christ is seated at God's right (Col. 3:1).

58. Hultgren, *Christ and His Benefits*, 91–143.

59. So, F. F. Bruce, *The Epistles to the Colossians, to Philemon, and to the Ephesians*, NICNT (Grand Rapids: Wm. B. Eerdmans Publishing Co., 1984), 343, and C. Leslie Mitton, *Ephesians*, NCB (Grand Rapids: Wm. B. Eerdmans Publishing Co., 1973), 147–48. But Dunn (*Christology in the Making*, 186–87) understands this as a descent to Hades.

60. For a survey of recent scholarship, see Andrew Y. Lau, *Manifest in Flesh: The Epiphany Christology of the Pastoral Epistles*, WUNT 86 (Tübingen: J. C. B. Mohr, 1996), 1–17. This monograph is the most comprehensive study of Christology in the Pastorals. Also helpful is the article by Jouette M. Bassler, "A Plethora of Epiphanies: Christology in the Pastoral Letters," *PSB* 17 (1996): 310–25.

61. Martin Dibelius and Hans Conzelmann, *The Pastoral Epistles: A Commentary on the Pastoral Epistles*, Hermeneia (Philadelphia: Fortress Press, 1972), 9.

62. A. T. Hanson, *The Pastoral Epistles*, NCB (Grand Rapids: Wm. B. Eerdmans Publishing Co., 1982), 38.

63. In addition to the works of Lau and Bassler cited above, see Lewis R. Donelson, *Pseudepigraphy and Ethical Argument in the Pastoral Epistles*, HUT 22 (Tübingen: J. C. B. Mohr, 1986), 129–54; Stephen E. Fowl, *The Story of Christ in the Ethics of Paul: An Analysis of the Function of the Hymnic Material in the Pauline Corpus*, JSNTSup 36 (Sheffield: JSOT Press, 1990), 155–74; Yann Redalié, *Paul après Paul: Le temps, le salut, la morale selon les épîtres à Timothée et à Tite*, Le Monde de la Bible 31 (Geneva: Labor et Fides, 1994), 157–256; Philip H. Towner, *The Goal of Our Instruction: The Structure of Theology and Ethics in the Pastoral Epistles*, JSNTSup 34 (Sheffield: JSOT Press, 1989), 51–56, 75–119; and Frances Young, *The Theology of the Pastoral Letters*, NTT (Cambridge: Cambridge University Press, 1994), 59–68. While these authors evaluate the Christology of the pastoral epistles differently, they agree that there is a unity to the Christology of these letters.

64. I am supposing that the same author composed all of these letters.

65. This sound teaching has been entrusted to Timothy by Paul. Timothy, in turn, must entrust it to reliable people who, in turn, will entrust it to a new generation. Thus the Pastorals establish a line of apostolic tradition.

66. For other examples of such sayings, see 1 Tim. 3:1; 4:9; 2 Tim. 2:11; Titus 3:8. These sayings, which are peculiar to the pastoral epistles, highlight the importance of certain material and are often associated with the theme of salvation.

67. There is, however, a soteriological dimension to these sayings. For example, Jesus comes into the world as its light (John 1:9; 3:19); for judgment (John 9:39); to testify to the truth (John 18:37).

68. I am not implying that the pastoral epistles are dependent on John or the Synoptics. But I am suggesting that the Pastor may have had access to traditions shared by these other writings.

69. *Christos* occurs thirty-two times in the pastoral epistles, fifteen times in 1 Timothy, thirteen times in 2 Timothy, and four times in Titus. In 1 Timothy the formula is always

"Christ Jesus," except for 5:11 (Christ) and 6:3, 14 (Jesus Christ). In 2 Timothy the formula is always "Christ Jesus," except for 2:8 (Jesus Christ). In Titus "Christ Jesus" occurs once and "Jesus Christ" three times. Of the thirty-two occurrences of Christ, then, twenty-five are "Christ Jesus," six "Jesus Christ," and one "Christ."

70. By this statement, I mean that the Pastor was aware of the scriptural background of this title: that it referred to Israel's anointed, the coming Messiah. This, however, does not imply that the Pastor understood Jesus' messiahship in traditional messianic categories. For the Pastor, as for Paul, Jesus was Christ in function of his saving death and resurrection. Thus, Paul and the Pastor understood messiahship in terms of what Jesus had done rather than in terms of specific messianic categories.

71. Commentators do not agree on the significance of this text for the question of Christ's preexistence. Dibelius and Conzelmann (*Pastoral Epistles*, 29) write that this expression "by no means contains the conception of preexistence." Hanson (*Pastoral Epistles*, 61) writes, "The phrase does seem to imply a doctrine of pre-existence . . . but this does not mean that the author of the Pastorals consciously held a doctrine of pre-existence." George W. Knight III (*Commentary on the Pastoral Epistles: A Commentary on the Greek Text*, NIGTC [Grand Rapids: Wm. B. Eerdmans Publishing Co., 1992], 101) writes that the saying "presumably carries the idea of coming from the Father into the world." The question of preexistence must be argued on the basis of the Pastor's entire exposition of Christ rather than upon a single text.

72. The Pastor refers to the story of Adam and Eve, but he does not employ it to explain the human predicament, as Paul does in Romans 5.

73. In saying that Christ Jesus gave himself as a ransom *for all* rather than *for many* (Mark 10:45), the Pastor (if he knew the Markan saying) is clarifying a Semitic expression that is inclusive rather than exclusive in intent.

74. This is the sole occurrence of mediator (*mesitēs*) in the Pastorals. The only other New Testament writing that applies this title to Jesus is the Letter to the Hebrews (8:6; 9:15; 12:24). Lau (*Manifest in Flesh*, 79) suggests that the use of mediator here includes the idea of covenant, even though specific covenant language is absent since the word is used in the context of the covenant in other New Testament texts. See Gal. 3:19 and Heb. 8:6; 9:15; 12:24.

75. A similar point is made by Joachim Gnilka, *Theologie des Neuen Testaments*, HTKNT Supplementband 5, Theologie des Neuen Testaments (Freiburg: Herder, 1994), 352–54.

76. On this passage, see Fowl, *Story of Christ*, 155–94; Robert J. Karris, *A Symphony of New Testament Hymns* (Collegeville, Minn.: Liturgical Press, 1996), 112–26; and Lau *Manifest in Flesh*, 91–114.

77. This is the position of Fowl, ibid.

78. Christ Jesus is not specifically named here, but he is clearly the subject of the hymn.

79. Lau, *Manifest in Flesh*, 96.

80. Ibid., 102.

81. Indeed, the very language of appearing suggests that the one who appeared previously existed but was not seen.

82. I am taking *ekērychthē* as an inceptive aorist and *ethnesin* as nations rather than merely Gentiles.

83. Notice how the passage moves from the earthly to the heavenly (stanza 1) and from the heavenly to the earthly (stanza 2), and concludes by moving from the earthly to the heavenly (stanza 3).

84. This is the only reference to Pilate in the Pauline writings, and one of the few places that his full name is used, aside from Luke 3:1 and Acts 4:27. The exact meaning of Jesus' confession before Pontius Pilate is not clear. Hanson (*Pastoral Epistles,* 111) takes it as "Christ's self-giving death," but Knight (*Pastoral Epistles,* 266) maintains that it "was his affirmative answer to Pilate's question, 'Are you the king of the Jews?'"

85. Thus Hultgren (*Christ and His Benefits,* 108) writes, "The redemptive christology of the Pastorals portrays Christ as a vigorous redeemer figure who comes to the rescue of humanity . . . . The redemptive christology is of the christopractic type, in which Christ performs the saving work on behalf of humanity."

86. Note the parallel with the life of Jesus, whose disciples deserted him at the moment of his trial.

87. These two men are mentioned in 1 Tim. 1:20, and this suggests that Timothy is in Ephesus.

88. The application of this title to Jesus is not surprising since Jesus is described as one who saves (1 Tim. 1:15; 2 Tim. 4:18). What is surprising is the application of the same title to God and Jesus. On the background of the "Savior" title, see Oscar Cullmann, *The Christology of the New Testament* (Philadelphia: Westminster Press, 1963 [originally published in German in 1957]), 238–45. While recognizing the Hellenistic background of this title, he believes that its Old Testament roots are more important for the New Testament.

89. See 1:16, 18; 2:7, 22, 24; 3:11; 4:8, 14, 17, 18, 22. Interestingly, the title "Lord" does not appear in the letter to Titus, where the title "Savior" dominates. See Young, *Theology of the Pastoral Letters,* 59–61.

90. Note that in 2 Tim. 1:18 "Lord" occurs twice: "May the *Lord* grant that he [Onesiphorus] will find mercy from the *Lord* on that day!" If Lord does not refer to the same person here, then it refers to both Christ and God, suggesting that Christ shares in the latter's divine status.

91. See 1 Tim. 6:14; 2 Tim. 4:1, 8.

92. Lau (*Manifest in Flesh,* 121) is much more direct. He writes, "This, therefore, clearly indicates the entrance of a pre-existent figure into the world to save, *viz.* the incarnation (personal manifestation) of Christ."

93. Ibid., 147.

94. See Karris, *Symphony of New Testament Hymns,* 158–72; Lau, *Manifest in Flesh,* 114–30; and Towner, *Goal of Our Instruction,* 100–107.

95. The manner in which the words "presbyter" and "bishop" are used interchangeably in 1:5, 7 suggests that the two roles are not yet distinct.

96. The remark of Donelson (*Pseudepigraphy and Ethical Argument,* 145) is apropos, but it also overstates the case since it does not give sufficient attention to the theme of redemption. He writes: "Christology for the author lives in ethics. The argument is clearly stated, Jesus appeared in order to teach his people how to live ethically. He has no real impact other than creating people who are zealous for good deeds and successful in pursuit of them."

97. Towner (*Goal of Our Instruction,* 111) writes: "Here the NT concept of salvation in Christ merges with the OT idea of a people cleansed and possessed by God (Ex. 19:5; Deut. 7:6; 14:2; Ezek. 37:23). From this emerges a picture of the Church as the true Israel of God, which Christ has bought and paid for."

98. For a full exegetical discussion that presents all the options, see Knight, *Pastoral Epistles,* 321–26.

99. C. F. D. Moule (*An Idiom-Book on New Testament Greek,* 2d ed. [Cambridge: Cambridge University Press], 109–10) believes that "our great God" probably refers to Jesus.

100. See Lau, *Manifest in Flesh,* 179–225.

CHAPTER FIVE

1. I include the Acts of the Apostles in the Synoptic tradition (Matthew, Mark, Luke) since Luke is its author. The Pauline tradition includes all the New Testament letters attributed to Paul, while the Johannine tradition comprises the Fourth Gospel and the Johannine letters.

2. D. A. Carson, Douglas J. Moo, and Leon Morris (*An Introduction to the New Testament* [Grand Rapids: Zondervan, 1992], 421–24) argue for Petrine authorship. The most recent and critical survey of the question can be found in Paul J. Achtemeier, *1 Peter: A Commentary on First Peter,* Hermeneia (Minneapolis: Augsburg, 1996), 1–42. On the nature of the Petrine circle, see John H. Elliott, *A Home for the Homeless: A Social-Scientific Criticism of 1 Peter, Its Situation and Strategy* (Minneapolis: Fortress Press, 1981), 267–88. For a popular summary of this material, see Ralph J. Martin, "1 Peter," in *The Theology of the Letters of James, Peter, and Jude,* Andrew Chester and Ralph P. Martin, NTT (Cambridge: Cambridge University Press, 1994), 87–133.

3. See Paul J. Achtemeier, "Newborn Babes and Living Stones: Literal and Figurative in 1 Peter," in *To Touch the Text: Biblical and Related Studies in Honor of Joseph A. Fitzmyer, S.J.,* ed. Maurya P. Hogan and Paul J. Kobelski (New York: Crossroad, 1989), 207–36, esp. 211.

4. For a discussion of the Christology of 1 Peter that focuses on the events in the career of Christ, see Earl Richard, "The Functional Christology of First Peter," in *Perspectives on First Peter,* ed. Charles H. Talbert, National Association of Baptist Professors of Religion Special Studies Series 9 (Macon, Ga.: Mercer University Press, 1986), 121–39.

5. For the sake of convenience, I refer to the author of this work as "Peter," even though the apostle Peter was probably not its author.

6. For a full discussion of this introductory section and its relationship to the rest of the letter, see David W. Kendall, "The Literary and Theological Function of 1 Peter 1:3–12," in Talbert, *Perspectives on First Peter,* 103–20.

7. I am following the outline of Achtemeier (*1 Peter,* 73–74). The main body of the letter is usually divided into three parts: 1:13–2:10; 2:11–4:11; 4:12–5:11.

8. While Achtemeier (*1 Peter,* 109–10) and Ernest Best (*1 Peter,* NCB [Grand Rapids: Wm. B. Eerdmans Publishing Co., 1971], 81) support a notion of preexistence in 1 Peter, Leonhard Goppelt (*A Commentary on 1 Peter* [Grand Rapids: Wm. B. Eerdmans Publishing Co., 1993; German original, 1977], 118–19) does not.

9. I am taking the participle *proegnōsmenou* as a divine passive. The one who knew Christ before the foundation of the world was God.

10. Because this letter consistently focuses on what God or Christ has done for its recipients, it often appears that the scope of salvation has been limited to only a few. This is due to the rhetorical purpose of the letter: to persuade its audience to adopt a particular form of behavior. Consequently, the letter emphasizes what God has done *for them.*

11. Once more, I take the participle *phanerōthentos* as a divine passive.

12. Best, *1 Peter,* 90; Goppelt, *1 Peter,* 116.

13. This point is effectively argued by Achtemeier, *1 Peter,* 128–30.

14. On the significance of this insight for the Christology of 1 Peter, especially the use of Isaiah 53, see Paul J. Achtemeier, "Suffering Servant and Suffering Christ in 1 Peter," in *Future of Christology,* 176–88.

15. Leonhard Goppelt (*The Theology of the New Testament,* vol. 2: *The Variety and Unity of the Apostolic Witness to Christ* [Grand Rapids: Wm. B. Eerdmans Publishing Co., 1982; the German original, 1976], 161–78) identifies the theme of 1 Peter as "Christian responsibility in society" (164).

16. The significance of these instructions to slaves and wives is debated. While some view them as examples of assimilation to the current ethos (David Balch), others do not (John H. Elliott). On this point, see the contrasting essays of Elliott and Balch in Talbert, *Perspectives on First Peter.*

17. Although this text functions as a christological justification for slaves to submit themselves to their masters, there are indications that the behavior 1 Peter urges here is intended for all believers. For example, in addressing *all* of the recipients of the letter, 1 Peter repeats the language of this passage: "Do not repay evil for evil or abuse for abuse; but on the contrary, repay with a blessing. It is for this that you were called" (3:9). Likewise, this passage is echoed in 3:17, where 1 Peter addresses everybody: "For it is better to suffer for doing good, if suffering should be God's will, than to suffer for doing evil." Thus, while the text is explicitly directed at slaves, this exhortation is for *all* the members of the community since all are "slaves of God" (2:16). Slaves "in this context have paradigmatic significance; they and their fate stand as exemplary both of the Christian's situation in the Roman Empire and of the Christlike reaction they must adopt to it." Achtemeier, *1 Peter,* 192.

18. At this point, some important manuscripts read "died," instead of "suffered." While "died" is the verb that one expects in a Pauline formula, "suffered" fits the theme of this letter since the author is trying to explain why his audience should endure suffering.

19. At this point some manuscripts read "we," which makes the text agree more closely with Isa. 53:5.

20. I am assuming that this passage is essentially the work of the author rather than an earlier christological tradition he inherited.

21. See Moule (*Origin of Christology,* 118), who lists the uses of *hyper* and *peri.* In the Pauline writings, *hyper* occurs in these significant passages: Rom. 5:6, 8; 8:32; 1 Cor. 11:24; 15:3; 2 Cor. 5:14, 21; Gal. 1:4; 2:20; Eph. 5:2, 25; 1 Tim. 2:6; Titus 2:14.

22. In 4:1 the author writes, "Since Christ suffered in the flesh, arm yourselves also with the same intention (for whoever has suffered in the flesh has finished with sin)." This verse might suggest that Christ sinned previous to his suffering. But the passage is not speaking of Christ's condition previous to his suffering; it is a moral exhortation to those who have suffered to put sin behind them.

23. I am taking the Greek word *psyche* in its broader sense: a person's life, whereas the NRSV and RNAB translate it in the more restricted sense of "soul."

24. Since this moral exhortation, addressed to *all* believers, is similar to the moral exhortation already given to slaves ("But if you endure when you do right and suffer for it, you have God's approval," 2:20), it should be evident that 1 Peter calls upon *all* believers, free as well as slave, to follow the pattern Christ set.

25. For other uses of *peri,* see Matt. 26:28; 1 Thess. 5:9.

26. For the occurrences of *hapax* in Hebrews, see 6:4; 9:7, 26, 27, 28; 10:2; 12:26, 27.

27. See Luke 23:47; Acts 3:14; 7:52, where this description has messianic connotations.

28. For other indications of Christ's sinlessness, see John 8:46; 2 Cor. 5:21; Heb. 4:15; 1 John 3:5.

29. See Achtemeier, *1 Peter*, 249–51.

30. For a thorough discussion of this text, see William Joseph Dalton, *Christ's Proclamation to the Spirits: A Study of 1 Peter 3:18–4:6*, AnBib 21 (Rome: Pontifical Biblical Institute Press, 1965). The commentators differ among themselves, as can be seen from the different interpretations espoused by three influential commentators. Achtemeier (*1 Peter*, 352–62) views them as rebellious angelic spirits and Christ's proclamation as one of judgment; Best (*1 Peter*, 139–40) views them as angelic spirits to whom Christ preached salvation; and Goppelt (*1 Peter*, 255–63) sees them as the people of Noah's generation to whom Christ preached salvation. For a popular presentation of this passage, see Karris, *Symphony of New Testament Hymns*, 142–57.

31. See Dalton, *Christ's Proclamation*, 15–41, for a history of the interpretation of this text. In addition to summarizing these positions, he categorizes the several variations of each.

32. Dalton, ibid., 115.

33. Rather 3:19 speaks of Christ having gone (*poreutheis*), the same verb used in 3:22 to describe his going to heaven. Thus there is no support for a *descent* to the dead, either in 3:19 or 4:6.

34. For a history of its interpretation, see Dalton, *Christ's Proclamation*, 42–57. Generally, four lines of interpretation have emerged. First, the text refers to Christ's preaching of salvation to all the dead who lived before him. Second, the text refers to Christ's preaching to the just of the Old Testament. Third, the text refers to the preaching of the apostles to those who were dead *spiritually*. Fourth, the text refers to Christians who heard the Gospel but had since died.

35. Hultgren (*Christ and His Benefits*, 112–16) describes the Christology of 1 Peter as "redemption won by Christ." While Christ plays an active role in redemption, I am not as confident as Hultgren that this is an adequate expression of how Christ functions in this letter.

36. I am indebted to Achtemeier (*1 Peter*, 68–69) for this insight.

37. Barnabas Lindars ("The Rhetorical Structure of Hebrews" NTS 35 [1989]: 382–406, 383 n2) takes both positions into account. He writes: "It is a letter, consisting of a homily, *sent* to the church of destination, because the author is not able to address the recipients in person, and the absence of a formal epistolary opening does not negate its essential character as a communication to specific persons from a distance."

38. For a fuller description of the situation underlying Hebrews, see Barnabas Lindars, *The Theology of the Letter to the Hebrews*, NTT (Cambridge: Cambridge University Press, 1991), 1–25. For a careful study of the background and thought of this letter, see L. D. Hurst, *The Epistle to the Hebrews: Its Background of Thought*, SNTSMS 65 (Cambridge: Cambridge University Press, 1990).

39. On the manner in which Hebrews employs moral exhortation, see Frank J. Matera, "Moral Exhortation: The Relation between Moral Exhortation and Doctrinal Exposition in the Letter to the Hebrews," *TJT* 10 (1994): 169–82.

40. While Albert Vanhoye (*La structure littéraire de L'épitre aux Hébreux*, StudNeot 1 [Paris: Desclée de Brouwer, 1963]) employs his careful structural analysis to argue for the primacy of doctrinal exposition, George H. Guthrie (*The Structure of Hebrews: A Text-Linguistic Analysis*, NovTSup 73 [Leiden: E. J. Brill, 1994]) uses text-linguistic analysis to advocate the priority of moral exhortation in Hebrews.

41. Although the NRSV begins a new sentence here by translating the relative pronoun *hos* as "he," the Greek text is a single sentence.

42. Although the NRSV begins a new sentence at this point, the Greek text does not.

43. The indefinite article ("a Son") does not imply that God had other sons. Rather, the author's purpose is to establish a contrast between speaking "by the prophets" and speaking "by a Son."

44. See Ernst Käsemann, *The Wandering People of God: An Investigation of the Letter to the Hebrews* (Minneapolis: Augsburg, 1984; this is a translation of the 2d German ed., 1957), 66–63. Nonetheless, promise and fulfillment do play a role in Hebrews. For example, in chap. 8, the author presents Christ as the mediator of a better covenant foretold by Jeremiah. But Hebrews does not employ a consistent pattern of promise and fulfillment.

45. See John Meier, "Structure and Theology in Heb. 1, 1–14," *Bib* 66 (1985): 168–89.

46. This outline raises questions that will be treated later. For example, how could the Son inherit the name "Son" if he was already the Son of God? How do we relate the pre-existent, the earthly, and the exalted Son?

47. See Harris Lachlan MacNeill, *The Christology of the Epistle to the Hebrews: Including Its Relationship to the Developing Christology of the Primitive Church* (Chicago: University of Chicago, 1914), 29–36.

48. Hebrews also speaks of Christ as "Son" in three Old Testament quotations (1:5 [twice] and 5:5), and then in five other instances (1:1, 8; 3:6; 5:8; 7:28). It speaks of Christ as high priest ten times (2:17; 3:1; 4:14, 15; 5:5, 10; 6:20; 7:26; 8:1; 9:11). For a full listing of the titles that Hebrews applies to Christ, see Hultgren, Christ and His Benefits, 117–18.

49. For example, there is probably a clearer statement of preexistence and incarnation in Phil. 2:5–11 than in Hebrews, and there certainly is a more explicit statement of both teachings in the prologue of John's Gospel.

50. Once one recognizes the rhetorical structure of Hebrews and the central role that exhortation plays, there is no need to suppose that the author argues against a christological error that makes Christ inferior to the angels.

51. For a thorough study of these quotations, see John P. Meier, "Symmetry and Theology in the Old Testament Citations of Heb. 1, 5–14," *Bib* 44 (1985): 504–33. Here, I am drawing upon his work.

52. Hebrews often employs scripture to relate dialogue between God and Christ. See 2:12–13 and 10:5–7, where Hebrews makes the words of scripture the words of Christ.

53. While it is possible to view these words as spoken by God in a timeless period before the creation of the world, the studies of Meier, noted above, convince me that the author is working with a pattern that begins with the Son's exaltation, moves back to the period before creation, and then moves forward until it reaches the exaltation once more. If Meier is correct, the author understands these quotations as the words God spoke to the Son on the day of the Son's exaltation.

54. The text (*ho thronos sou ho theos*) could also be translated, "God is your throne," but since the author is employing these citations christologically, he probably intends the *ho theos* to be read as a vocative, "Your throne, O God."

55. In its original setting, "Lord" referred to God, the creator of heaven and earth, but it is applied to the Son by God himself.

56. Although the term "Son" or "Son of God" does not occur in 2:1–18, there is no doubt that the author is still concerned with the theme of sonship, albeit in terms of the Son's earthly work since he speaks of Christ who was faithful as a son in the next section (3:1–6).

57. This is essentially the translation of the NRSV, except that I have changed the plurals of the inclusive NRSV to the singular so that the translation conforms more closely to the Greek.

58. Hebrews employs a rather striking phrase when it says that Jesus was made lower than the angels so that "he might taste death for everyone" (2:9).

59. On the similarities between the theology of Hebrews and Pauline thought, see Hurst, *Epistle to the Hebrews,* 107–24.

60. Perfection is a major theme in Hebrews and plays an important role in the Christology of this letter. See Albert Vanhoye, "La '*Teleiôsis*' du Christ: Point capital de la Christologie sacerdotale d'Hébreux," *NTS* 42 (1996): 321–38.

61. This is not to say that the sonship of Jesus and the sonship of humanity are the same. The preexistent Son of God is the "reflection of God's glory and the exact imprint of God's very being" (1:3) in a way that humanity is not. In theological terms, human beings are God's adopted sons and daughters, whereas Jesus is the only begotten Son of God.

62. It is clear from 4:15 and 7:26 that this did *not* include sin.

63. Hebrews implicitly introduced the theme of the Son's priesthood in 1:3, when it spoke of the Son having made purification for sins, but it does not explicitly identify the Son as high priest until 2:17.

64. Vanhoye (*Structure littéraire,* 114) identifies 3:1–6 as exposition, and 3:7–4:13 as exhortation. But in my view 3:1–6, as its introductory verse suggests, is exhortation rather than exposition. For a similar view, see Guthrie, *Structure of Hebrews,* 127–39.

65. Apostle, here, is to be taken in its root sense, one who has been sent. In this case, Jesus has been sent by God.

66. Although the author compares the faithfulness of Moses and Jesus to show the more excellent faithfulness of the latter, he does not denigrate the character of Moses. Moreover, while the author will show the superiority of the new to the old, there is no indication that he is anti-Jewish. On Moses in Hebrews, see Mary Rose D'Angelo, *Moses in the Letter to the Hebrews,* SBLDS 42 (Missoula, Mont.: Scholars Press, 1979).

67. See Dennis Hamm, "Faith in the Epistle to the Hebrews: The Jesus Factor," *CBQ* 52 (1990): 270–91.

68. Two other transition statements, both of which are related to this statement, are 8:1–2 and 10:19–25.

69. In 2:17, Hebrews said that the Son had to become like his brothers and sisters in every way so that he might be a merciful high priest; now Hebrews qualifies that statement by adding "without sin." In 7:26, Hebrews will describe this high priest as "holy, blameless, undefiled, separated from sinners." Other New Testament texts that witness to the sinlessness of Christ are John 8:46; 2 Cor. 5:21; 1 Peter 1:19; 2:22; 3:18; and 1 John 3:5. On the sinlessness of Jesus, see Oscar Cullmann, *The Christology of the New Testament* (Philadelphia: Westminster Press, 1963), 83–107.

70. This text is often viewed as an allusion to the Son's prayer and agony in the Garden of Gethsemane, but there is no need to identify it with this incident. Hebrews is more interested in the suffering that Jesus endured throughout his life rather than at a specific moment in his life.

71. Although Jesus has already been called a high priest, Hebrews identifies him as a high priest according to the order of Melchizedek for the first time in 5:10. Then 6:20 identifies him this way, before chap. 7 develops the theme at length.

72. The reference here is to the true sanctuary that is in heaven.

73. The Hebrew and Greek texts of Gen. 14:20 do not specify who gives tithes to whom, as does the text of Hebrews. In the Greek and Hebrew, the intended subject could be Melchizedek. For a study of how Hebrews employs this story, see Joseph A. Fitzmyer, "'Now This Melchizedek . . . '(Heb. 7:1)," in his *Essays on the Semitic Background of the New Testament,* SBLSBS 5 (Missoula, Mont.: Scholars Press, 1974), 221–43.

74. Hebrews adopts an exegetical technique that presumes that what is not mentioned in scripture does not exist. Consequently, if scripture does not mention Melchizedek's lineage or his death, one can conclude that he was eternal. At Qumran, there was speculation about Melchizedek, although it does not appear that our author is directly dependent on this speculation, but it may have been "in the air." See Joseph A. Fitzmyer, "Further Light on Melchizedek from Qumran Cave 11," in his *Essays on the Semitic Background,* 245–67, and Mikeal C. Parsons, "Son and High Priest: A Study in the Christology of Hebrews," *EvQ* 60 (1988): 195–216, esp. 210–14.

75. Vanhoye ("La 'Teleiôsis,' ") notes that the phrase "we have such a high priest" (8:1) should be read in conjunction with the preceding verse, "but the word of the oath . . . appoints a Son who has been made perfect forever" (7:28). The high priest of which Hebrews is speaking, then, is a Son who has been made perfect through suffering.

76. See 7:22, where the author has already written that Jesus has become the "guarantee of a better covenant" on the basis of the divine oath (Ps. 110:4) spoken to him.

77. Hebrews is relying upon the description of the wilderness tabernacle (Ex. 25:1–31:11; 36:1–40:38). For the Day of Atonement, see Lev. 16:1–34. Hebrews only mentions those elements of the ritual that are helpful for its purposes.

78. One might have expected Hebrews to say that the heavenly sanctuary Christ entered was the Holy of Holies, thereby maintaining the parallel with the high priest who entered the Holy of Holies on the Day of Atonement. Instead, Hebrews calls the heavenly sanctuary "the Holy Place" (9:12) since there is no need for a separate Holy of Holies in the heavenly sanctuary.

79. The author takes advantage of the Greek version of Psalm 40, which reads, "but a body you have prepared for me," whereas the Hebrew text reads, "but you have given me an open ear."

80. Vanhoye, "La *'Teleiôsis,'* " 335.

81. See ibid., 337.

82. On this point, and on the Son of God Christology of Hebrews, see Kenneth Schenck, "Keeping His Appointment: Creation and Enthronement in Hebrews," *JSNT* 66 (1997): 91–117.

83. On the genre of Revelation, see Richard Bauckham, *The Theology of the Book of Revelation,* NTT (Cambridge: Cambridge University Press, 1993), 1–17; Frederick David Mazzaferri, *The Genre of the Book of Revelation from a Source-Critical Perspective,* BZNW 54 (Berlin: Walter de Gruyter, 1989); and Elisabeth Schüssler Fiorenza, *The Book of Revelation: Justice and Judgment* (Philadelphia: Fortress Press, 1985), 35–67 and 133–56. While these authors recognize that there are elements of the apocalyptic and letter form in Revelation, they identify prophecy as its primary genre, as do I.

84. This point is made by J. Comblin, *Le Christ dans L'Apocalypse,* Bibliothèque de Théologie, Théologie Biblique, Série 3, vol. 6 (Paris: Desclée, 1965). He writes: "En premier lieu, nous verrons que le Christ y est en même temps l'auteur et l'objet. C'est lui qui donne la révélation, lui qui annonce la prophétie; c'est lui encore qui est le témoin. Et c'est aussi lui l'objet de la révélation, de la prophétie et du témoignage" (10).

85. Wilfrid J. Harrington (*Revelation,* SP 16 [Collegeville, Minn.: Liturgical Press,

1993] 14–17) discusses four basic approaches: Revelation is concerned with ideals and principles (nonhistorical interpretation); Revelation is a detailed prophecy of the future (world-historical interpretation); Revelation is only concerned with happenings at the end of the age (end-historical interpretation); Revelation is only concerned with the circumstances of John's day (contemporary-historical interpretation).

86. For the book of Revelation, the historical struggle was between the church and the Roman Empire.

87. This point is made by M. Eugene Boring, "Narrative Christology in the Apocalypse," *CBQ* 54 (1992): 702–23. In what follows, I am indebted to many of his insights.

88. On the theme of testimony or witness that pervades this narrative, see Allison A. Trites, *The New Testament Concept of Witness*, SNTSMS 31 (Cambridge: Cambridge University Press, 1977), 154–74.

89. The first six seals are the rider on the white horse who conquers, the rider on the red horse who takes peace from the earth, the rider on the black horse who brings famine, the rider on a pale horse who brings death, the lament of the souls of those who have been slain, and a great earthquake accompanied by cosmic signs.

90. The first six trumpets bring a variety of disasters: hail mixed with blood; a large burning mountain hurled into the sea; a large star fallen from the sky; a third of the sun, the moon, and the stars become dark; a great army of locusts; a cavalry assault of two hundred million.

91. The seven bowls are festering sores; the sea turning to blood; rivers and springs turning to blood; the sun burning people with fire; intense darkness; the kings of the east preparing for Armageddon; lightning, thunder, and a great earthquake.

92. A somewhat similar point is made by Fiorenza, *Book of Revelation,* 35–67, and by J. Lambrecht, "A Structuration of Revelation 4,1–22,5," in *L'Apocalypse johannique et l'Apocalyptique dans le Nouveau Testament,* ed. J. Lambrecht, BETL 53 (Louvain: Leuven University Press, 1980), 77–104. Each retelling, however, grows in intensity. For example, a quarter of the earth is killed by the opening of the seals, a third of the earth by the blowing of the trumpets, and then there is total devastation when the bowls are poured out.

93. Lambrecht ("Structuration," 103–4) makes this point when he writes, "Repetition itself functions as gradation. This is most evident both within each series of the plagues and within the three series as a whole. The trumpets are worse than the seals, the bowls are worse than the trumpets . . . . The last bowl is the end."

94. This theme, more than any other, is central to the work of Traugott Holtz, *Die Christologie der Apokalypse des Johannes,* TU 85 (Berlin: Akademie Verlag, 1962).

95. The most important studies on the Christology of Revelation are: Peter R. Carrell, *Jesus and the Angels: Angelology and the Christology of the Apocalypse of John,* SNTSMS 95 (Cambridge: Cambridge University Press, 1997); Comblin, *Le Christ dans L'Apocalypse;* and Holtz, *Die Christologie der Apokalypse des Johannes.* The following articles and chapters are also helpful: Bauckham, *Revelation,* 54–108; Boring, "Narrative Christology"; François Bovon, "Le Christ de L'Apocalypse," *Revue de Théologie et de Philosophie* 22 (1972): 65–80; Sara A. Edwards, "Christological Perspectives in the Book of Revelation," in *Christological Perspectives: Essays in Honor of Harvey K. McArthur,* ed. Robert F. Berkey and Sarah A. Edwards (New York: Pilgrim Press, 1982), 139–54; Hultgren, *Christ and His Benefits,* 128–35; Donald Guthrie, "The Christology of Revelation," in *Jesus of Nazareth: Essays on the Historical Jesus and New Testament Christology,* ed. Joel B. Green and Max Turner (Grand Rapids: Wm. B. Eerdmans Publishing Co., 1994), 397–409;

Mitchell G. Reddish, "Martyr Christology in the Apocalypse," *JSNT* 33 (1988): 85–95; and Edward Schillebeeckx, *Christ: The Experience of Jesus as Lord* (New York: Crossroad, 1981), 432–62.

96. Notice how John falls on his face when the risen Lord appears to him (1:17), just as Ezekiel did when God appeared to him (Ezek. 1:28).

97. Revelation never calls Christ "God" or "Father," and it reserves the title *pantokrator* for God (1:8; 4:8; 11:17; 15:3; 16:7, 14; 19:6, 15; 21:22). But it does bring Christ into the being of God. See Bauckham, *Revelation*, 58–65.

98. In 13:8, Revelation speaks of *en tō bibliō tēs zōēs tou arniou tou esphragmenou apo katabolēs kosmou*, which could be translated "in the book of life of the Lamb that was slaughtered from the foundation of the world," or "from the foundation of the world in the book of life of the Lamb that was slaughtered." The first translation, which is less likely, implies preexistence. But even if the translation is not accepted, it is significant that the Lamb is associated with the Book of Life that is from the foundation of the world.

99. The theme of the God's throne runs throughout Revelation but occurs especially frequently in chaps. 4–5, 7. See 4:2, 3, 4, 5, 6, 9, 10; 5:1, 6, 7, 11, 13; 7:9, 10, 11, 15, 17.

100. On the enthronement of the Lamb in chap. 5, see Holtz, *Die Christologie*, 27–54.

101. So Harrington, *Revelation*, 84–85.

102. In this regard, Revelation's messianic theology is similar to that of Mark's Gospel, which also defines messiahship in terms of one who must suffer and die before rising from the dead.

103. Comblin (*Le Christ dans L'Apocalypse*) argues that there is an important Son of Man theology in Revelation. I do not agree with his conclusions. In my view, Revelation is merely recalling the imagery of the figure in Daniel 7. Thus, it refers to Jesus as one like a son of man (1:13; 14:14), but without calling Jesus *the* Son of Man.

104. This point is made by G. R. Beasley-Murray, *Revelation*, NCB (Grand Rapids: Wm. B. Eerdmans Publishing Co., 1981), 67.

105. For a detailed study of the genre of these passages, see D. E. Aune, "Form and Function of the Proclamations to the Seven Churches (Revelation 2–3)," *NTS* 36 (1990): 183–204. He argues that the genre of these messages is akin to that of the ancient royal or imperial edict. They are seven proclamations issued by the King of kings, Jesus Christ, rather than seven letters.

106. God is also called the Father of Christ in 1:6.

107. Note how Revelation again relates Christ to God by speaking of the wrath of God *and* the Lamb.

108. On this point, see Trites, *New Testament Concept of Witness*, 164–70.

109. Again, note how Revelation relates Christ to God by speaking of the kingdom of God *and* his Messiah.

110. At this point there is a further interlude, the story of the woman and the dragon, and the account of the two beasts (chaps. 12–13), which I have described above.

111. The final defeat of the dragon does not take place until the next chapter, after Christ and his martyrs have reigned for a thousand years (20:1–10). This millennial rule functions as a prelude to Satan's final defeat.

112. So Harrington, *Revelation*, 193.

113. The Lamb's book of life plays an important role in Revelation. See 13:8; 17:8.

114. "Him" seems to refer to both God and the Lamb in the Greek text. If it does, we have another indication of how Revelation brings Christ into the being of God.

CHAPTER SIX

1. The following works provide surveys of research in Johannine Christology: Paul N. Anderson, *The Christology of the Fourth Gospel: Its Unity and Disunity in the Light of John 6* (Valley Forge, Pa.: Trinity Press International, 1996); Robert Kysar, *The Fourth Evangelist and His Gospel: An Examination of Contemporary Scholarship* (Minneapolis: Augsburg, 1975), and Maarten J. J. Menken, "The Christology of the Fourth Gospel: A Survey of Recent Research," in *From Jesus to John: Essays on Jesus and New Testament Christology in Honor of Marinus de Jonge*, ed. Martinus C. de Boer, JSNTSup 84 (Sheffield: JSOT Press, 1993), 292–320. The following works provide helpful discussions of Johannine Christology: John Ashton, *Understanding the Fourth Gospel* (Oxford: Clarendon Press, 1994), 238–373; M.-E. Boismard, *Moses or Jesus: An Essay in Johannine Christology* (Minneapolis: Fortress Press, 1993); Raymond E. Brown, *The Community of the Beloved Disciple: The Life, Loves, and Hates of an Individual Church in New Testament Times* (New York: Paulist Press, 1979); Rudolf Bultmann, *Theology of the New Testament,* 2 vols. (New York: Harper & Row, 1969), 2:3–92; Hans Conzelmann, *An Outline of the Theology of the New Testament* (New York: Harper & Row, 1969), 321–58; Hultgren, *Christ and His Benefits,* 145–60; Ernst Käsemann, *The Testament of Jesus: A Study of the Gospel of John in Light of Chapter 17* (Philadelphia: Fortress Press, 1968); W. R. G. Loader, "The Central Structure of Johannine Christology," *NTS* 30 (1984): 188–216; *The Christology of the Fourth Gospel: Structure and Issues,* BBET 23 (Frankfurt: Lang, 1989); D. L. Mealand, "The Christology of the Fourth Gospel," *SJT* 31 (1978): 449–72; Leon Morris, *Jesus Is the Christ: Studies in the Theology of John* (Grand Rapids: Wm. B. Eerdmans Publishing Co., 1989); Jerome Neyrey, *An Ideology of Revolt: John's Christology in Social Science Perspective* (Philadelphia: Fortress Press, 1988); Schillebeeckx, *Christ,* 305–432; Schnackenburg, *Jesus in the Gospels,* 219–94; Robin Scroggs, *Christology in Paul and John: The Reality and Revelation of God* (Philadelphia: Fortress Press, 1988); D. Moody Smith, *The Theology of the Gospel of John,* NTT (Cambridge: Cambridge University Press, 1995), 75–160; and M. M. Thompson, *The Humanity of Jesus in the Fourth Gospel* (Philadelphia: Fortress Press, 1988).

2. Conzelmann (*Theology,* 332) writes, "It could be said that the whole of Johannine theology is christology, though it could equally well be argued that it is soteriology (or anthropology)."

3. The introductions to most contemporary commentaries discuss the genesis of the Gospel. Excellent discussions are found in Raymond E. Brown, *The Gospel according to John,* 2 vols., AB 29, 29A (Garden City, N.Y.: Doubleday, 1966, 1970), and Barnabas Lindars, *The Gospel of John,* NCB (Grand Rapids: Wm. B. Eerdmans Publishing Co., 1972).

4. See Ashton, *Understanding the Fourth Gospel;* Brown, *Community of the Beloved Disciple;* J. Louis Martyn, *History and Theology in the Fourth Gospel,* rev. and enlarged (Nashville: Abingdon Press, 1979); and David Rensberger, *Johannine Faith and Liberating Community* (Philadelphia: Westminster Press, 1988).

5. Martyn shows this in his seminal study of John 9, *History and Theology.*

6. The seminal literary-critical study of the Fourth Gospel is the work of R. Alan Culpepper, *Anatomy of the Fourth Gospel: A Study in Literary Design,* Foundations and Facets (Philadelphia: Fortress Press, 1983). Recently, authors have called for a rapprochement between literary and historical studies of the Fourth Gospel. See M. C. De Boer, "Narrative Criticism, Historical Criticism, and the Gospel of John," *JSNT* 47 (1992): 35–48; Steve Motyer, "Method in Fourth Gospel Studies: A Way Out of the Impasse?" *JSNT* 66

(1997): 27–44; and Mark W. G. Stibbe, *John as Storyteller: Narrative Criticism and the Fourth Gospel*, SNTSMS 73 (Cambridge: Cambridge University Press, 1992).

7. See Morna D. Hooker, "John's Prologue and the Messianic Secret," *NTS* 21 (1974/75): 40–58.

8. This is the contention of Ashton (*Understanding the Fourth Gospel*, 381–553) and Bultmann (*Theology*, 2:49–69).

9. Although the prologue clearly identifies the Word as God (*kai ho logos ēn pros ton theon, kai theos ēn ho logos*), it does not call the Word *ho theos*, thereby preserving the distinction between God (*ho theos*) who is the Father and the Word who is the Son.

10. The signs that Jesus performs are changing water into wine (2:1–12); the healing of the official's son (4:43–54); the healing of the crippled man at Jerusalem (5:1–18); the feeding of the five thousand (6:1–15); his epiphany to the disciples on the sea (6:16–21); the healing of the man blind from birth (9:1–41); and the raising of Lazarus (11:1–44).

11. Whereas Bultmann (*Theology*) sees the first part of this verse as the key to the Gospel ("the Word became flesh"), his pupil, Ernst Käsemann (*Testament*), focuses on the second part of the verse ("and we have seen his glory"). Thompson (*Humanity of Jesus*) strikes a balance between these extreme positions.

12. The phrase could be translated in several ways: "the only begotten God," "the only begotten, God," "the only begotten [Son], God."

13. At this point, several manuscripts read "the chosen one of God," and a few, "the chosen Son of God." "The Son of God," however, seems to be the best reading.

14. The question, Where does Jesus dwell (*pou meneis*)? has a profound meaning that the disciples cannot comprehend; for, inasmuch as Jesus comes from God, he dwells with God. In his farewell discourse, Jesus will invite the disciples to dwell (*menein*) in his love, just as he dwells in his Father's love (15:9–10).

15. This point will become more apparent as the narrative develops and presents Jesus as the one who descended from heaven and will return from whence he came, once he has been glorified.

16. Although the Israelite king became God's adopted Son (Ps. 2:7; 2 Sam. 7:14) in virtue of his royal enthronement, he was not a divine figure. Rather, "son of God" identified him as one anointed and elected by God.

17. In the Synoptic Gospels, in contrast to the Fourth Gospel, Jesus' mighty deeds (his miracles) point to the in-breaking kingdom of God.

18. This is the first of three sayings about the lifting up of the Son of Man, the others being 8:28 and 12:32–34. These sayings are similar to, but not directly related to, the Synoptic passion predictions (Mark 8:31; 9:31; 10:33–34, and parallels) inasmuch as they point to Jesus' death.

19. The Jews ask a similar question in 8:53 in regard to Abraham, leading Jesus to proclaim that he existed before Abraham (8:58). The unexpressed answer to both questions is that Jesus is greater than Abraham and Jacob, as he is greater than Moses.

20. This debate between Jesus and the Jews is a reflection of the debate between the Johannine community and the Jewish community contemporaneous with it. See Wayne Meeks, "Equal to God," in Fortna and Gaventa, eds., *Conversation Continues*, 309–21.

21. The narrative logic of this section is complicated by the presence of chap. 6, which places Jesus in Galilee, whereas the rest of the narrative occurs in Jerusalem. Thus, many have suggested that this chapter is out of place and belongs before chap. 5, providing a sequence whereby, starting at 4:43, Jesus is in Galilee where he feeds the five thousand,

appears to the disciples on the sea, and then delivers the bread of life discourse (6:1–71). Then Jesus goes to Jerusalem for an unspecified Jewish feast, during which he heals a crippled man (5:1–47), returns to Galilee (7:1–10), and then attends the feast of Booths (7:11–10:21) and the feast of Dedication (7:22–42).

While this reconstruction makes better sense of the narrative sequence, our concern is with the present form of the text. According to the narrative logic of this sequence, Jesus returns to Jerusalem for a festival of the Jews soon after his return to Galilee (5:1). There, he cures a cripple on the Sabbath which leads to a christological debate about his claim that he works on the Sabbath because his Father never ceases to work (5:17).

22. For an explanation of the background to this passage, see C. H. Dodd, *The Interpretation of the Fourth Gospel* (Cambridge: Cambridge University Press, 1953), 318–28.

23. While the discourse of chap. 6 refers primarily to Jesus, vv. 53–58 seem to have strong eucharistic overtones, although not all would agree. For example, Thompson (*Humanity of Jesus*, 43) believes that these verses are "a metaphor for appropriating the benefits of Jesus' death by faith." Anderson (*Christology*, 110–36) follows a similar line.

24. Jesus says that when the Son of Man is lifted up, "then you will realize *egō eimi*" ("I am"). The *egō eimi* is not to be taken as the divine name but as an emphatic statement that Jesus is the one who he says that he is. See C. K. Barrett, "Christocentric or Theocentric? Observations on the Theological Method of the Fourth Gospel," in *Essays on John* (Philadelphia: Westminster Press, 1982), 1–18. He writes, "If a translation of *egō eimi* in these verses is sought I should be inclined to offer the colloquial English, 'I'm the one,' that is, 'It is me, to me, that you must look, it is I whom you must hear.' This corresponds with John's view of the person of Jesus, and harmonizes well with such passages as Isaiah 45.18–25" (13).

25. That is to say, Jesus does not respond with a saying about the coming enthronement of the Son of Man, as in the Synoptics (Matt. 26:64; Mark 14:62; Luke 22:6, 9), but his answer does evoke the accusation that he has blasphemed (John 10:33; Matt. 26:65; Mark 14:64).

26. Jesus knows that his hour has arrived because now even Gentiles ask to see him. The coming of the Gentiles is foreshadowed in the statement that Jesus' death will "gather into one the dispersed children of God" (11:52).

27. Note how the crowd equates the Messiah with the Son of Man of whom Jesus has been speaking.

28. The Gospel can be divided into a book of signs in which Jesus manifests his glory to the world by the signs he performs (1:19–12:5) and a book of glory in which he manifests his glory to his disciples by death, his return to the Father (13:1–20:31).

29. The present version of the farewell discourse was probably composed from at least two earlier versions. Note how 14:31 seems to conclude the discourse of 13:1–14:30. The material that follows (15:1–17:26) represents at least one other version of the farewell discourse.

30. Whether this verse means that Jesus dies, or that he gives up the promised Spirit, is not clear. The latter interpretation, however, is possible in light of 7:39.

31. In saying this, I am aware of the role that readers play in creating this portrait as they interact with the text.

32. *Christos* occurs with the article in 1:20, 25; 3:28; 4:24, 29; 7:26, 27, 31, 41, 42;

10:24; 11:27; 12:34; 20:31. It occurs without the article in 1:17; 9:22; 17:3. In 1:41, *ton Messiah* transcribes the Hebrew for "messiah."

33. Note the use of *Christos* as part of Jesus' name in 1:17 and 17:3, texts that also speak of Jesus' origin from above.

34. For references to "Son of God," see 1:49; 3:1, 8; 5:25; 10:36; 11:4, 27; 19:7; 20:31.

35. For references to "the Son," see 3:16, 17, 35, 36; 5:19, 20, 21, 22, 23, 26; 6:40; 8:36; 14:13; 17:1.

36. In my view, "Son of Man" is not a confessional title, even in 9:35–38. See Douglas R. A. Hare, *The Son of Man Tradition* (Minneapolis: Fortress Press, 1990), 104–6.

37. The underlying Greek verb, *hypsoō,* carries a double meaning: to lift something or someone up physically, to exalt or glorify someone.

38. The claims of the Gospel that the Word was God and that Jesus is God do not establish Jesus as another God vis à vis God. On the relationship of Jesus to God, see Barrett, " 'The Father Is Greater than I' John 14.28: Subordinationist Christology in the New Testament," in his *Essays on John,* 19–36.

39. Bultmann (*New Testament Theology,* 2:66) writes, "Thus, it turns out in the end that Jesus as the Revealer of God *reveals nothing but that he is the Revealer.* And that amounts to saying that it is he for whom the world is waiting, he who brings in his own person that for which all the longing of man yearns: life and truth as the reality out of which man can exit, light as the complete transparence of existence in which questions and riddles are at an end."

40. For a helpful introduction to the Johannine epistles, see Judith Lieu, *The Theology of the Johannine Epistles,* NTT (Cambridge: Cambridge University Press, 1991). For a brief overview of their Christology, see Hultgren, *Christ and His Benefits,* 156–60. For a thorough discussion of the situation that led to their Christology, see Brown, *Community of the Beloved Disciple,* 93–144, and *The Epistles of John,* AB 30 (Garden City, N.Y.: Doubleday, 1982), 47–115.

41. The author of 2 and 3 John identifies himself as "the elder." In 2 John he writes to a congregation that he calls "the elect lady" to warn of deceivers who do not confess that Jesus Christ has come in the flesh. In 3 John he writes to Gaius to commend Demetrius and complain of Diotrephes, who does not acknowledge his (the elder's) authority. There is no mention of Christ in this letter.

42. Brown (*Epistles,* 86–92) reviews the various proposals: universal religious tractate; circular epistle; homily; diatribe; informal tractate; pastoral encyclical. Brown himself views 1 John as a comment on the Fourth Gospel patterned on the structure of the Gospel.

43. On the question of authorship, see Brown, ibid., 14–35. While he argues that one author, the elder, is responsible for all the epistles, he does not think that the elder is the author of the Fourth Gospel.

44. The Fourth Gospel seems to have undergone several revisions over a period of nearly thirty years, and while we may speak of its author or final redactor, we must remember that many hands were probably involved in these revisions.

45. Kenneth Grayston (*The Johannine Epistle,* NCB [Grand Rapids: Wm. B. Eerdmans Publishing Co., 1984]) argues for the chronological priority of the epistles.

46. This is the criticism that Childs (*New Testament as Canon,* 482–85) makes of Brown's work.

47. Brown, *Epistles,* 34.

48. Ibid., 76.

49. Brown, *Community of the Beloved Disciple,* 111.

50. "Son of God" occurs seven times in 1 John (3:8; 4:15; 5:5, 10, 12, 13, 20), whereas "Son" occurs thirteen times in 1 John (1:3, 8; 2:22, 23, 24; 3:23; 4:9, 10, 14; 5:9, 10, 12, 20) and twice in 2 John (3:9). "Christ" occurs eight times in 1 John (1:3; 2:1, 22; 3:23; 4:2; 5:1, 6, 20) and once in a variant reading (4:15). In 2 John it occurs three times (3, 7, 9). In most instances "Christ" is part of Jesus' name, but in 1 John 2:22 and 5:1 it occurs with the article, "the Christ."

51. If the motif of the descending and ascending Son of Man contributed to the position of the secessionists that Jesus' humanity was not important for the work of salvation, then perhaps this explains the absence of the title from the epistles.

A Select Bibliography

Achtemeier, Paul J. "He Taught Them Many Things: Reflections on Marcan Christology." *CBQ* 42 (1980): 456–81.

Aletti, Jean-Noël. *Colossiens 1,15–20: Genre et exégèse du texte, Fonction de la thématique sapientielle.* AnBib 91. Rome: Biblical Institute Press, 1981.

Anderson, Paul N. *The Christology of the Fourth Gospel: Its Unity and Disunity in the Light of John 6.* Valley Forge, Pa.: Trinity Press International, 1996.

Ashton, John. *Understanding the Gospel of John.* Oxford: Clarendon Press, 1991.

Barrett, C. K. *Essays on John.* Philadelphia: Westminster Press, 1982.

Bassler, Jouette M. "A Plethora of Epiphanies: Christology in the Pastoral Letters." *PSB* 17 (1996): 310–25.

Bauckham, Richard. *The Theology of the Book of Revelation.* NTT. Cambridge: Cambridge University Press, 1993.

Bauer, David R. "The Kingship of Jesus in the Matthean Infancy Narrative: A Literary Analysis." *CBQ* 57 (1995): 306–23.

Berkey, Robert F., and Sarah A. Edwards, eds. *Christological Perspectives: Essays in Honor of Harvey K. McArthur.* New York: Pilgrim Press, 1982.

Bock, Darrell L. *Proclamation from Prophecy and Pattern: Lucan Old Testament Christology.* JSNTSup 12. Sheffield: JSOT Press, 1987.

Boismard, Marie-Émile. *Moses or Jesus: An Essay in Johannine Christology.* Minneapolis: Fortress Press, 1993.

Boring, M. Eugene. "The Language of Universal Salvation in Paul." *JBL* 105 (1986): 269–92.

———. "Narrative Christology in the Apocalypse." *CBQ* 54 (1992): 702–23.

Bousset, Wilhelm. *Kyrios Christos: A History of the Belief in Christ from the Beginning of Christology to Irenaeus.* Nashville: Abingdon Press, 1970.

Bovon, François. "Le Christ de L'Apocalypse." *RTP* 22 (1972): 65–80.

Breytenbach, C., and H. Paulsen, eds. *Anfänger der Christologie*. Göttingen: Vandenhoeck & Ruprecht, 1991.

Broadhead, Edwin K. *Teaching with Authority: Miracles and Christology in the Gospel of Mark*. JSNTSup 74. Sheffield: JSOT Press, 1992.

————. "Christology as Polemic and Apologetic: The Priestly Portrait of Jesus in the Gospel of Mark." *JSNT* 47 (1992): 21–34.

————. "Jesus the Nazarene: Narrative Strategy and Christological Imagery in the Gospel of Mark." *JSNT* 52 (1993): 3–18.

Brown, Raymond E. *The Community of the Beloved Disciple*. New York: Paulist Press, 1979.

————. *An Introduction to New Testament Christology*. Mahwah, N.J.: Paulist Press, 1994.

Buckwalter, H. Douglas. *The Character and Purpose of Luke's Christology*. SNTSMS 89. Cambridge: Cambridge University Press, 1996.

Bultmann, Rudolf. "The Christology of the New Testament." In *Faith and Understanding: Collected Essays*, 262–85. London: SCM Press, 1969.

————. *Theology of the New Testament*. 2 vols. London: SCM Press, 1952.

Byrne, Brendan. "Christ's Pre-Existence in Pauline Soteriology." *TS* 58 (1997): 308–30.

Carrell, Peter R. *Jesus and the Angels: Angelology and the Christology of the Apocalypse of John*. SNTSMS 95. Cambridge: Cambridge University Press, 1997.

Carroll, John T., and Joel B. Green, eds. *The Death of Jesus in Early Christianity*. Peabody, Mass.: Hendrickson, 1995.

Cerfaux, Lucien. *Christ in the Theology of St. Paul*. New York: Herder & Herder, 1963.

Chouinard, Larry. "Gospel Christology: A Study of Methodology." *JSNT* 30 (1987): 21–37.

Colleridge, Mark. *The Birth of the Lukan Narrative: Narrative as Christology in Luke 1–2*. JSNTSup 88. Sheffield: JSOT Press, 1993.

Collins, John J. *The Scepter and the Star: The Messiahs of the Dead Sea Scrolls and Other Ancient Literature*. ABRL. New York: Doubleday, 1995.

————. "The Son of Man in First-Century Judaism." *NTS* 38 (1992): 448–66.

Comblin, J. *Le Christ dans L'Apocalypse*. Bibliothèque de Théologie, Théologie Biblique, Série 3, vol. 6. Paris: Desclée, 1965.

Cullmann, Oscar. *The Christology of the New Testament*. Philadelphia: Westminster Press, 1963.

Dahl, Nils A. *The Crucified Messiah and Other Essays*. Minneapolis: Augsburg, 1974.

Dalton, William Joseph. *Christ's Proclamation to the Spirits: A Study of 1 Peter 3:18–4:6*. AnBib 23. Rome: Pontifical Biblical Institute Press, 1965.

Davis, Philip G. "Mark's Christological Paradox." *JSNT* 35 (1989): 3–18.

DeBoer, Martinus C., ed. *From Jesus to John: Essays on Jesus and New Testament Christology in Honour of Marinus de Jonge*. JSNTSup 84. Sheffield: JSOT Press, 1993.

de Jonge, Marinus. *Christology in Context: The Earliest Christian Response to Jesus*. Philadelphia: Westminster Press, 1988.

————. *Jesus, Stranger from Heaven and Son of God: Jesus Christ and the Christians in Johannine Perspective*. Missoula, Mont.: Scholars Press, 1977.

―――. *Jesus: The Servant-Messiah*. New Haven, Conn.: Yale University Press, 1991.

DiLella, Alexander A. "The One in Human Likeness and the Holy One of the Most High in Daniel 7." *CBQ* 39 (1977): 1–19.

Donahue, John R. "Recent Studies on the Origin of 'Son of Man' in the Gospels." *CBQ* 48 (1986): 484–98.

Dunn, James D. G. *The Christ and the Spirit: Collected Essays of J. D. G. Dunn*. Vol. 1: *Christology*. Grand Rapids: Wm. B. Eerdmans Publishing Co., 1998.

―――. *Christology in the Making: A New Testament Inquiry into the Origins of the Doctrine of the Incarnation*. Philadelphia: Westminster Press, 1980.

―――. *The Theology of Paul the Apostle*. Grand Rapids: Wm. B. Eerdmans Publishing Co., 1998.

―――. "Prolegomena to a Theology of Paul." *NTS* 40 (1994): 407–32.

Dupont, Jacques, ed. *Jesus aux origines de la Christologie*. BETL 40. Louvain: Leuven University Press, 1975.

Fitzmyer, Joseph A. *Scripture and Christology: A Statement of the Biblical Commission with Commentary*. New York: Paulist Press, 1986.

―――. *A Wandering Aramean: Collected Aramaic Essays*. SBLMS 25. Missoula, Mont.: Scholars Press, 1979.

―――. "4Q246: The 'Son of God' Document from Qumran." *Bib* 74 (1993): 153–74.

Fortna, Robert T., and Beverly R. Gaventa, eds. *The Conversation Continues: Studies in Paul and John: In Honor of J. Louis Martyn*. Nashville: Abingdon Press, 1990.

Fossum, Jarl. "Colossians 1.15–18a in the Light of Jewish Mysticism and Gnosticism." *NTS* 35 (1989): 183–201.

Fowl, Stephen E. *The Story of Christ in the Ethics of Paul: An Analysis of the Function of the Hymnic Material in the Pauline Corpus*. JSNTSup 36. Sheffield: JSOT Press, 1990.

Franklin, Eric. *Christ the Lord: A Study in the Purpose and Theology of Luke Acts*. Philadelphia: Westminster Press, 1975.

Fuller, Reginald H. *The Foundations of New Testament Christology*. New York: Charles Scribner's Sons, 1965.

Fuller, Reginald, and Pheme Perkins. *Who Is This Christ? Gospel Christology and Contemporary Faith?* Philadelphia: Fortress Press, 1983.

George, Augustine. *Études sur l'oeuvre de Luc*. SB. Paris: Gabalda, 1978.

Grayston, Kenneth. *Dying, We Live: A New Enquiry into the Death of Christ in the New Testament*. Oxford: Oxford University Press, 1990.

Green, Joel B., and Max Turner. *Jesus of Nazareth, Lord and Christ: Essays on the Historical Jesus and New Testament Christology*. Grand Rapids: Wm. B. Eerdmans Publishing Co., 1994.

Grob, F. *Faire L'Oeuvre de Dieu: Christologie et éthique dans l'Evangile de Jean*. EHPR 68. Paris: Presses Universitaires de France, 1986.

Hahn, Ferdinand. *The Titles of Jesus in Christology: Their History in Early Christianity*. London: Lutterworth Press, 1969.

Hamm, Dennis. "Faith in the Epistle to the Hebrews: The Jesus Factor." *CBQ* 52 (1990): 270–91.

Hare, Douglas R. A. *The Son of Man Tradition*. Minneapolis: Fortress Press, 1990.

Hasler, Victor. "Epiphanie und Christologie in den Pastoralbriefen." *TZ* 33 (1977): 193–209.

Hays, Richard B. *Echoes of Scripture in the Letters of Paul.* New Haven, Conn.: Yale University Press, 1989.

———. "Christology and Ethics in Galatians." *CBQ* 49 (1987): 268–90.

Heil, John Paul. "Jesus as the Unique High Priest in the Gospel of John." *CBQ* 57 (1995): 729–45.

Hengel, Martin. *The Atonement: The Origins of the Doctrine in the New Testament.* Philadelphia: Fortress Press, 1981.

———. *Between Jesus and Paul: Studies in the Earliest History of Christianity.* Philadelphia: Fortress Press, 1983.

———. *The Son of God.* Philadelphia: Fortress Press, 1975.

———. *Studies in Early Christology.* Edinburgh: T. & T. Clark, 1995.

Holtz, Traugott. *Die Christologie der Apokalypse des Johannes.* TU 85. Berlin: Akademie Verlag, 1962.

Hooker, Morna D. *The Son of Man in Mark.* London: SPCK, 1976.

———. "Pistis Christou." *NTS* 35 (1989): 321–42.

Howard, George. "Phil. 2:6–11 and the Human Christ." *CBQ* 40 (1978): 368–87.

Howell, David B. *Matthew's Inclusive Story: A Study in the Narrative Rhetoric of the First Gospel.* JSNTSup 42. Sheffield: JSOT Press, 1990.

Hultgren, Arland J. *Christ and His Benefits: Christology and Redemption in the New Testament.* Philadelphia: Fortress Press, 1987.

———. *New Testament Christology: A Critical Assessment and Annotated Bibliography.* New York: Greenwood Press, 1988.

Hurst, L. D., and N. T. Wright, eds. *The Glory of Christ in the New Testament: Studies in Christology in Memory of George Bradford Caird.* Oxford: Oxford University Press, 1987.

Jewett, Robert, ed. "Christology and Exegesis: New Approaches." *Semeia* 30 (1984).

Johnson, Earl S. "Is Mark 15:29 the Key to Mark's Christology?" *JSNT* 31 (1987): 3–22.

Johnson, Luke Timothy. "Romans 3:21–26 and the Faith of Jesus." *CBQ* 44 (1982): 77–90.

Jones, John Mark. "Subverting the Textuality of the Davidic Messianism: Matthew's Presentation of the Genealogy and the Davidic Title." *CBQ* 56 (1994): 256–72.

Karris, Robert J. *A Symphony of New Testament Hymns: Commentary on Philippians 2.5–11, Colossians 1:15–20, Ephesians 2:14–16, 1 Timothy 3:16, Titus 3:4–7, 1 Peter 3:18–22, and 2 Timothy 2:11–13.* Collegeville, Minn.: Liturgical Press, 1996.

Käsemann, Ernst. *The Testament of Jesus: A Study of the Gospel of John in Light of Chapter 17.* Philadelphia: Fortress Press, 1968.

Keck, Leander E. "Jesus in New Testament Christology." *AusBR* 28 (1980):1–20.

———." 'Jesus' in Romans." *JBL* 108 (1989): 443–60.

———"Toward the Renewal of New Testament Christology." *NTS* 32 (1986): 362–77.

Kim, Seyoon. *The Origin of Paul's Gospel.* Grand Rapids: Wm. B. Eerdmans Publishing Co., 1981.

———. *The Son of Man as the Son of God.* Grand Rapids: Wm. B. Eerdmans Publishing Co., 1985.

Kingsbury, Jack Dean. *The Christology of Mark.* Philadelphia: Fortress Press, 1983.

———. *Conflict in Luke: Jesus, Authorities, Disciples.* Minneapolis: Fortress Press, 1991.

————. *Conflict in Mark: Jesus, Authorities, Disciples.* Minneapolis: Fortress Press, 1991.

————. *Jesus Christ in Matthew, Mark, and Luke.* Philadelphia: Fortress Press, 1981.

————. *Matthew: Structure, Christology, Kingdom.* Philadelphia: Fortress Press, 1975.

Koester, Craig R. " 'The Savior of the World' (John 4:42)." *JBL* 109 (1990): 665–80.

Kramer, Werner. *Christ, Lord, Son.* Naperville, Ill.: Alec R. Allenson, 1966.

Kreitzer, L. Joseph. *Jesus and God in Paul's Eschatology.* JSNTSup 19. Sheffield: JSOT Press, 1987.

Kuschel, Karl-Josef. *Born before All Time? The Dispute over Christ's Origin.* New York: Crossroad, 1992.

Kynes, William L. *A Christology of Solidarity: Jesus as the Representative of His People in Matthew.* Lanham, Md.: University Press of America, 1991.

Lau, Andrew Y. *Manifest in Flesh: The Epiphany Christology of the Pastoral Epistles.* WUNT 86. Tübingen: J. C. B. Mohr, 1996.

Laub, Franz. *Bekenntnis und Auslegung: Die Paränetische Funktion der Christologie im Hebräerbrief.* Regensburg: Verlag Friedrich Pustet, 1980.

Lieu, Judith. *The Theology of the Johannine Epistles.* NTT. Cambridge: Cambridge University Press, 1991.

Lindars, Barnabas. *Jesus, Son of Man.* London: SPCK, 1983.

————. *The Theology of the Letter to the Hebrews.* NTT. Cambridge: Cambridge University Press, 1991.

Loader, William R. G. *The Christology of the Fourth Gospel: Structure and Issues.* BBET 23. Frankfurt: Peter Lang, 1989.

————. *Sohn und Hoherpriester: Eine traditionsgeschichtliche Untersuchung zur Christologie des Hebräerbriefes.* WMANT 53. Neukirchen-Vluyn: Neukirchener Verlag, 1981.

————. "The Central Structure of Johannine Christology." *NTS* 30 (1984): 188–216.

MacNeill, Harris Lachlan. *The Christology of the Epistle to the Hebrews: Including Its Relationship to the Developing Christology of the Primitive Church.* Chicago: University of Chicago, 1914.

Malherbe, Abraham, and Wayne A. Meeks, eds. *The Future of Christology: Essays in Honor of Leander E. Keck.* Minneapolis: Fortress Press, 1993.

Marshall, I. H. *The Origins of New Testament Christology.* Downers Grove, Ill.: InterVarsity Press, 1976; updated edition, 1990.

————. "The Divine Sonship of Jesus." *Int* 21 (1967): 87–103.

Martin, Ralph P. *Carmen Christi: Philippians 2:5–11 in Recent Interpretation and in the Setting of Early Christian Worship.* Grand Rapids: Wm. B. Eerdmans Publishing Co., 1983.

————. *Reconciliation: A Study of Paul's Theology.* New Foundations Theological Library. Atlanta: John Knox Press, 1981.

Mealand, D. L. "The Christology of the Fourth Gospel." *SJT* 31 (1978): 449–67.

Meeks, Wayne A. "The Man from Heaven in Johannine Sectarianism." *JBL* 91 (1972): 44–72.

Meier, John P. *The Vision of Matthew: Christ, Church, and Morality in the First Gospel.* New York: Crossroad, 1991; originally published by Michael Glazier, Wilmington, Del., 1979.

———. "Structure and Theology in Heb. 1, 1–14." *Bib* 66 (1985): 168–89.

———. "Symmetry and Theology in the Old Testament Citations of Heb. 1, 5–14." *Bib* 66 (1985): 504–33.

Mlakuzhyil, G. *The Christocentric Literary Structure of the Fourth Gospel.* AnBib 117. Rome: Pontificio Instituto Biblico, 1987.

Morris, Leon. *Jesus Is the Christ: Studies in the Theology of John.* Grand Rapids: Wm. B. Eerdmans Publishing Co., 1989.

Moule, C. F. D. *The Origin of Christology.* Cambridge· Cambridge University Press, 1977.

———. " 'The Son of Man': Some of the Facts." *NTS* 41 (1995): 277–79.

Newman, Carey C. *Paul's Glory-Christology: Tradition and Rhetoric.* NovTSup 69. Leiden: E. J. Brill, 1992.

Neyrey, Jerome H. *Christ Is Community: The Christologies of the New Testament.* Wilmington, Del.: Michael Glazier, 1985.

———. *An Ideology of Revolt: John's Christology in Social-Science Perspective.* Philadelphia: Fortress Press, 1988.

———. " 'Without Beginning of Days or End of Life' (Hebrews 7:3): Topos for a True Deity." *CBQ* 53 (1991): 439–55.

Noland, J. "No Son-of-God Christology in Matthew 1.18–25." *JSNT* 62 (1996): 3–12.

O'Collins, Gerald. *Christology: A Biblical, Historical, and Systematic Study of Jesus.* Oxford: Oxford University Press, 1995.

Parsons, Mikeal C. "Son and High Priest: A Study in the Christology of Hebrews," *EvQ* 60 (1988): 195–216.

Pollard, T. E. *Christology and the Early Church.* SNTSMS 13. Cambridge: Cambridge University Press, 1970.

Powell, Mark Allan. "The Plot and Subplots of Matthew's Gospel." *NTS* 38 (1992): 187–204.

Reddish, Mitchell G. "Martyr Christology in the Apocalypse." *JSNT* 33 (1988): 85–95.

Richard, Earl. *Jesus, One and Many: The Christological Concept of New Testament Authors.* Wilmington, Del.: Michael Glazier, 1988.

———. "The Functional Christology of First Peter." In *Perspectives on First Peter,* ed. Charles H. Talbert, 121–39. National Association of Baptist Professors of Religion Special Studies Series 9. Macon, Ga.: Mercer University Press, 1986.

Schenck, Kenneth. "Keeping His Appointment: Creation and Enthronement in Hebrews." *JSNT* 66 (1997): 91–117.

Schillebeeckx, Edward. *Christ: The Experience of Jesus as Lord.* New York: Crossroad, 1981.

Schnackenburg, Rudolf. *Jesus in the Gospels: A Biblical Christology.* Louisville, Ky.: Westminster John Knox Press, 1995.

Scroggs, Robin. *Christology in Paul and John.* Philadelphia: Fortress Press, 1988.

Senior, Donald. *The Passion of Jesus in the Gospel of John.* Collegeville, Minn.: Liturgical Press, 1991.

———. *The Passion of Jesus in the Gospel of Luke.* Collegeville, Minn.: Liturgical Press, 1990.

———. *The Passion of Jesus in the Gospel of Mark.* Wilmington, Del.: Michael Glazier, 1984.

————. *The Passion of Jesus in the Gospel of Matthew*. Wilmington, Del.: Michael Glazier, 1985.

Sim, D. C. "The 'Confession' of the Soldiers in Matthew 27.54." *HeyJ* 34 (1993): 401–24.

Sinclair, S. *Jesus Christ according to Paul: The Christology of Paul's Undisputed Epistles and the Christology of Paul*. Berkeley, Calif.: Bibal Press, 1988.

Slater, Thomas B. "One Like a Son of Man in First-Century C. E. Judaism." *NTS* 41 (1995): 183–98.

Smith, D. Moody. *The Theology of the Gospel of John*. NTT. Cambridge: Cambridge University Press, 1995.

Smith, Stephen H. "The Function of the Son of David Tradition in Mark's Gospel." *NTS* 42 (1996): 523–39.

Stibbe, Mark W. G. *John as Storyteller*. SNTSMS 73. Cambridge: Cambridge University Press, 1992.

Suggs, M. J. *Wisdom, Christology, and Law in Matthew's Gospel*. Cambridge, Mass.: Harvard University Press, 1970.

Talbert, Charles H. "The Myth of a Descending-Ascending Redeemer in Mediterranean Antiquity." *NTS* 22 (1975–76): 418–440.

Taylor, Vincent. *The Person of Christ: In New Testament Teaching*. London: Macmillan & Co., 1959.

Thielman, Frank. *Paul and the Law: A Contextual Approach*. Downers Grove, Ill.: InterVarsity Press, 1994.

Thompson, M. M. *The Humanity of Jesus in the Fourth Gospel*. Philadelphia: Fortress Press, 1988.

Tuckett, Christopher, ed. *The Messianic Secret*. Philadelphia: Fortress Press, 1983.

Vanhoye, Albert. "La *Teleiôsis* du Christ: Point capital de la Christologie sacerdotale d'Hébreux." *NTS* 42 (1996): 321–38.

Verelput, Donald J. "The Role and Meaning of the 'Son of God' Title in Matthew's Gospel." *NTS* 33 (1987): 532–56.

Walker, William O., Jr. "John 1.43–51 and 'The Son of Man' in the Fourth Gospel." *JSNT* 56 (1994): 31–42.

Wanamaker, C. A. "Philippians 2:6–11: Son of God or Adamic Christology?" *NTS* 33 (1987): 179–93.

Windisch, Hans. "Zur Christologie der Pastoralbriefe." *ZNW* 34 (1935): 213–38.

Witherington, Ben. *Paul's Narrative Thought World: The Tapestry of Tragedy and Triumph*. Louisville, Ky.: Westminster/John Knox Press, 1994.

Wright, N. T. *The Climax of the Covenant: Christ and the Law in Pauline Theology*. Minneapolis: Fortress Press, 1992.

Yates, Roy. "Colossians 2.15: Christ Triumphant." *NTS* 37 (1991): 573–91.

————. "Colossians and Gnosis." *JSNT* 27 (1986): 49–69.

Index of Subjects

5490903R0

Made in the USA
Lexington, KY
15 May 2010